MILL

IN SEARCH OF THE TRUE WEST

IN SEARCH OF THE TRUE WEST

CULTURE, ECONOMICS, AND PROBLEMS OF RUSSIAN DEVELOPMENT

ESTHER KINGSTON-MANN

PRINCETON UNIVERSITY PRESS

PRINCETON, NEW JERSEY

Copyright © 1999 by Princeton University Press
Published by Princeton University Press, 41 William Street,
Princeton, New Jersey 08540
In the United Kingdom: Princeton University Press,
Chichester, West Sussex

Library of Congress Cataloging-in-Publication Data

Kingston-Mann, Esther.
In search of the true West : culture, economics, and problems of Russian
development /Esther Kingston-Mann.
p. cm.
Includes bibliographical references (p.) and index.
ISBN 0-691-03187-8 (cloth : alk. paper)
1. Rural development—Russia. 2. Economics—Russia—History.
3. Russia—Civilization—Foreign influences. 4. Russia—Rural conditions. I. Title.
HN530.Z9C648 1999   307.1'412'0947—dc21   98-17379 CIP

This book has been composed in Sabon

Princeton University Press books are printed
on acid-free paper and meet the guidelines for
permanence and durability of the Committee on
Production Guidelines for Book Longevity
of the Council on Library Resources

http://pup.princeton.edu

Printed in the United States of America

10 9 8 7 6 5 4 3 2 1

. . . after eight weeks of induction into the elements of Political Economy, she [Sissy] had only yesterday been set right by a prattler three feet high, for returning to the quesion, 'What is the first principle of this science?' the absurd answer, 'To do unto others as I would that they should do unto me.'

Mr. Gradgrind observed, shaking his head, that all this was very bad; . . .

(*Charles Dickens*, Hard Times)

CONTENTS

E VER SINCE the eighteenth century, educated Russians have attempted to enter the Western cultural mainstream. As "outsiders," aware from the start that they were viewed by Europeans as cultural inferiors, they attempted to discover and appropriate Western solutions to the problem of economic backwardness. My own understanding of their efforts has been deepened and complicated by a contemporary conflict in U.S. higher education which has seen women and other historically marginalized groups challenge the traditional content of economics, history, psychology, and other fields of study. Like Russians in relation to the West, these U.S. "outsiders" have wanted above all to know if the cultural mainstream was homogeneous, its lessons truly universal, its character flexible and inclusive.

I do not stand apart from these struggles, or from the methodological issues they raise. Many of my most talented students at the University of Massachusetts–Boston (UMass-Boston) are outsiders to the cultural traditions and knowledge that I was taught to value. Predominantly non-elite students of diverse backgrounds, they are usually the first in their families to attend college. Perhaps because of my own non-elite social origins, their difficulties of entry did not suggest to me that my students were unintelligent, or "not college material." In my own experience, the effort to decode the academy's culture and to appropriate its version of the cultural mainstream was a painful and exciting process, which may yet even now be incomplete.

In contrast to urban commuter universities like UMass-Boston, the more competitive colleges and graduate schools that I attended included—as far as I knew—few students whose backgrounds resembled my own. Those of us who experienced doubts and misgivings did not pose a significant challenge to the intellectually stimulating but narrow conceptions of historical scholarship to which we were exposed. But the omissions were nonetheless troubling. Even as an undergraduate, I wanted to know more about the role of Ukrainians, Georgians, Armenians and other non-Russian ethnic groups in the history of Russia and the Soviet Union. Why, I wondered, was so little attention paid to the peasant majority?[1] Why was there no discussion of the female half of the population? Why did none of my professors raise these issues, and why were these topics absent from the books that they assigned?[2]

To the outsider, it is not always obvious which perspective and whose "story," approach, or economic strategy is most relevant and useful for understanding a particular issue. In attempting to make our way from margin to "center," we cannot always assume that we have understood the "core" values of Western, Russian, or any other culture. As a scholar and teacher, I have welcomed recent U.S. debates about issues of inclusion, exclusion, and the legitimate scope of modern scholarship, because they support and sustain (1) my effort to write and teach history in a manner that is more realistic than the one I experienced, and (2) my participation in wider initiatives for curriculum transformation.[3]

It should be emphasized that raising questions that fall outside the cultural norms of one's scholarly field is not a recipe for success within it. As I consider the Russianist scholars from whom I have learned the most, it is depressing to count the number whose dissertations were never published or who are no longer in the field. I think of Zack Deal, whose research documented the behavior of peasants as rational economic actors at a time when "the idiocy of rural life" was considered a more reasonable way to understand the peasantry.[4] Helma Repczuk's study of the Anglophile reformer Admiral Mordvinov contradicted prevailing scholarly notions of the Westernizer as an advocate of freedom and went unpublished,[5] as did Steven Grant's magnificent intellectual history of the peasant commune in Russian economic thought—a work which challenged the conventional wisdom that only anti-Western fanatics believed in the enduring power and complexity of the peasant commune.[6]

I have learned much from the dissertations (also unpublished) by Anthony Netting, Allison Blakeley, Janet Vaillant, and from the neglected work of Boris Ischboldin.[7] I am not personally acquainted with these scholars, and none of them are responsible for the use I have made of their research. Since I began work on this book, the field of Russian/Soviet history has become more inclusive. Many scholars are now writing about the role of women and non-Russian nationalities of the former Soviet Union, and a more balanced approach to the history of peasants has begun to make its way into the scholarly mainstream. However, critical approaches to Westernization remain uncommon.

I hope that my book will encourage a reexamination of the valuable scholarship produced by the authors I have cited above. But I should emphasize that these neglected studies are not of course any more "complete" than those which were successfully incorporated into the mainstream of historical scholarship on Imperial Russia; nor does this book claim to tell "the whole story" about Westernization in the Russian context.[8] For example, I do not emphasize the vast literature which documents positive aspects of Western economic influence, because I do not think that there is any danger that they will be forgotten. It is the heterogeneity, or what I have called "the light and shadow of the West," which in my view requires more study, and constitutes the focus of my research.

Conceptually, this study owes a great deal to the analytical insights of Patricia Hill Collins, a sociologist whose work on "outsider" perspectives helped me to better understand the dilemma of Russians as outsiders within Western culture.[9] For much of the nineteenth and twentieth centuries, educated Russians were aware that Western Europeans tended to view them not only as outsiders but as cultural inferiors. Hill Collins's emphasis on outsiders as a source of questions and insights not raised by those who are at home in the cultural mainstream, has deepened my understanding of why Russians came to value aspects of Western culture—German historical economics, for example, or Denmark's early twentieth century, peasant-led democracy—which are seldom the focus of modern-day U.S. histories of Western civilization.

As I see it, these Russian perspectives open the possibility for an engagement with the heterogeneity of Western culture which could contribute to a more complex and realistic view of the West. In this connection, it is useful to consider the contemporary research and insights of Japanese scholars of Russia and the Soviet Union, whose questions about rural development are informed by Japanese historical experience as well as by Western scholarship. Among others, I refer here to the historians Kimitaka Matsuzato, Shuichi Kojima, Yuzuru Taniuchi, and Hiroshi Okuda.[10]

The treatment of intersecting cultural terrains in the work of Cornel West and Edward Said,[11] and in particular the exploration of reciprocal links between Western and non-Western cultures, helped me to see more clearly that the connection between Russia and the West was not a one-way process—i.e., with knowledge transmitted only from the West to Russia. Neither in Russia nor in other developing countries were low levels of economic productivity linked with mediocre levels of intellectual or cultural achievement. Said's work was especially useful in sensitizing me to the significance of Western stereotypes about backward Russians as "Orientals" and "Asiatics," and led me to consider more carefully the reasons why educated Russians so eagerly applied the identical label to the peasants of their own society.

My treatment of Russian advocates of progress, whose claims to cultural, political, and economic domination crossed the ideological boundaries which traditionally divided capitalists from Marxists, has been much influenced by Peter Berger's study *Pyramids of Sacrifice* (1974). In arguments later developed by many other scholars, Berger contended that in the name of progress and development, both capitalist and communist-oriented regimes massively extended the coercive power of governments over their citizens (while insisting at the same time that the violence by which their policies were implemented was only "temporary").

In researching the uses of Western economic models, I have paid particular attention to those who—at different historical junctures between the eighteenth century and the outbreak of revolution in 1905—either advanced or deepened the debate on Russia's economic future. At each juncture, I have tried to present as many perspectives as are necessary to indicate major lines of development, some significant variations and occasionally the exceptional individual who proves the rule. As the story moves into the late nineteenth and early twentieth centuries and the field of Russian economics enlarges, my cast of characters inevitably becomes more selective.[12] My selection has been informed by reading much but by no means all of what was written by contributors to Russia's debate on development during these years. As the subsequent chapters indicate, I have been aided by a wide range of valuable secondary sources and by theoretical and empirical studies authored by scholars whose fields are quite distant from Russian history. The approach I have taken is designed to capture a central line of development in economic thinking about Russia and the West rather than the whole story of economics in the Russian context. Although the topic of industrialization is no less important than the issue of rural development, I have used Russian rural life—and peasants in particular—as the prism through which to examine the economics of Westernization.

ACKNOWLEDGMENTS

Over the years, Teodor Shanin has provided inspiration, bracing criticism, and support, and I am deeply grateful for the careful reading, invaluable suggestions, and tough-minded encouragement supplied by Heather Hogan, Rochelle Ruthchild, and Elvira Wilbur. In addition, the late Evsey Domar, Stanley Engermann, and Robert LeVine have read several chapters of the manuscript and provided insightful comments. From vantage points quite distant from the field of Russian history, my colleagues—the economist Lou Ferleger, and the political scientist Winston Langley—have introduced me to relevant scholarly literature that I would not otherwise have encountered.

I have also been inspired by the efforts of my students, who have shared with me not only their fears and self-doubts, but the sense of excitement sparked by the discovery that they might indeed be intelligent enough to view their experience in a widening historical perspective. As with my earlier books, my first and most sensitive reader and supporter has always been my husband, Jim Mann. One of my greatest recent joys is that in recent years he has been joined as an insightful critic by my daughter Larisa.

Some of the material contained in chapters 2 and 4 appeared in the article "In the Light and Shadow of the West: The Impact of Western Economics in Pre-Emancipation Russia" in *Comparative Studies in Society and History* 33, no. 1 (January 1991): 86–105. Chapter 7 includes some of the evidence and hypotheses that appeared in "In Search of the True West: Western Economic Models and Russian Rural Development," *Journal of Historical Sociology* 3, no. 1 (March 1990): 23–49.

IN SEARCH OF THE TRUE WEST

INTRODUCTION

> This Europe, will it become what it is in reality, i.e., a little cap
> of the Asiatic continent, or will this Europe remain rather what
> it seems, i.e., the priceless part of the whole earth, the pearl of
> the globe, the brain of a vast body?
> *(Paul Valery, "The Crisis of the Spirit," 1915)*

I N THE nineteenth and twentieth centuries, Russian economists, historians, revolutionaries, and reformers (and Western advisers) have
confidently provided explanations for Russia's persistent lack of economic success. Among the most frequently cited are the conflict between
a fragile "spirit of enterprise" and the power of a Leviathan state, the
apathy of a "peasant" or "peasantlike" populace, environmental obstacles, a scarcity of capital, and the difficulty of catching up with political
rivals already far advanced in industrial and agricultural development. To
this lengthy but incomplete set of explanations, I propose a consideration
of Russia's problematic relationship to a Western culture which includes
the social science of economics.[1]

My first book (*Lenin and the Problem of Marxist Peasant Revolution,*
1983) suggested that Lenin's emerging respect for the peasantry's political
"clout" coexisted with a denial—characteristic of many leading Western
progressives of the day—that peasants possessed values, institutions, or
a "way of life," i.e., a culture, to which they might feel some loyalty.
Given the human cost of the antipeasant policies of forced collectivization
which Stalin carried out in Lenin's name, it was both a tragedy and a
paradox that Lenin's extraordinarily flexible political stance coexisted
with an unwavering refusal to rethink the more peasantophobic economic, social, and cultural perspectives of the Marxist tradition. At the
turn of the century, Lenin made use of Marx's classic writings to frame a
vision of Western European history in which peasants appeared as mindless inhabitants of a prerational and prehistoric, natural economy. To
paraphrase Marx, peasants were for Lenin the "idiots" of rural life; they
entered into history only after they entered the era of capitalism.

Such views were not uniquely Marxist. Lenin's negative view of peasants and their communes was loudly seconded by state capitalist reformers of the tsarist regime. However hostile they may have been to socialism
and communism, progressive-minded officials were quite content with

the Marxist argument that peasants could only become productive and rational after they were liberated from the constraints imposed by backward village communities. In order to understand the similarities and convergences between tsarist and Marxist perspectives, I have put forward the following hypothesis: in nineteenth-and early-twentieth-century Russia, a "culture of modernization" emerged which crossed ideological boundaries and decisively shaped debates, strategies, and policies for rural development. Its proponents highlighted the parallels between Russia and the West, contending that (1) peasants were at best obsolete and at worst a "medieval" obstacle to progress, and (2) private-property rights constituted either the short-or long-term basis for modernization and development. On the eve of the Revolution of 1905, these narrowly productivist and property-oriented Western economic theories came to overshadow the more complex and pluralistic socioeconomic perspectives of Russia's leading professional economists.

In recent years, as historians of Russia began to consider the peasant majority of the population an appropriate subject of study, they—like scholars and thinkers who study non-Western societies—have discovered that peasant behavior could not easily be squeezed into capitalist or feudal categories derived from Western historical experience.[2] The view of peasants as hapless victims of gentry pressure or capitalist progress—or of both together—has been challenged by contemporary research indicating that peasants and their communities were in fact surprisingly resilient.[3] The abundant evidence of their survival has had to be integrated into traditional historical accounts which omitted these aspects of rural life. In economic terms, the dismal fate of tsarist and Soviet Russian development policies which demonized "obsolete" peasants and their "feudal" communes may have been linked to a modernizing mindset which ignored many significant features of the Russian countryside.

Learning from the West. From the outset, it was no secret to educated Russians that Western Europeans found them both culturally and economically backward. Russian responses to such judgments were complex and contradictory. Like their counterparts in areas colonized by the West, some came to admire Western ideals of freedom and democracy. Others attempted to acquire the material advantages and socioeconomic power which constituted the most visible attributes of a "Western" life-style. Initially, economics-minded Russians looked Westward to Prussia for techniques of surveillance and control which extended the power and reach of prevailing political elites and enhanced their ability to extract dues and services from a bound peasantry. I have elsewhere described Westernizers of the latter sort as proponents of a culture of "repressive modernization" which persisted—in various guises—well into the Soviet period.[4] The agents of this culture demanded a wide variety of changes intended to shore up and maintain existing forms of political domination.

In the nineteenth century, educated Russians did not agree on what was "typical" of Western history and culture. The sociologist Alfred Schutz's description of the outsider's dilemma is very apt: "To him the cultural patterns of the approached group do not have the authority of a tested system of recipes . . . because he does not partake in the vivid historical traditions by which it has been formed."[5] To Slavophiles, government officials, scholars, and dissidents, it was not self-evident, for example, that England's economic experience was more "Western" than the statist economic traditions of Germany or the cooperative-based economies of Denmark.

In the reform era that followed the peasant emancipation of 1861, the choices made by Russia's Westernizers continued to entangle them in the dilemmas that have always accompanied efforts at cultural borrowing. Profoundly influenced by a German school of economics that was eventually excluded from the Anglo-American cultural mainstream, most of Russia's leading economists and statisticians embraced comparative and historical approaches to economic issues and questioned the exclusive reliance on the universals of classical or neoclassical theory. However, historical economics was eventually relegated to the margins of Anglo-American economic thought. Westernized Russian scholars had—in Anglo-American terms—guessed wrong about where the center of mainstream economics would be located in the decades to come.

The Russian acceptance of German historical economics raises a number of important historical issues. On one level, it constitutes a case study in the process by which some traditions were established as the core values of Western culture, while others (German historical economics, for example) were ignored by later economists and historians of Western economic thought. On another level, the late-nineteenth-century "culture war" among Marxists, neoclassical, and historical economists clearly illuminates the continuing dilemma that faces would-be Russian Westernizers. It has turned out to be no easy task to borrow and apply Western categories, economic theories, and practices. In the later decades of the twentieth century, it is not yet clear how or whether to apply Western neoclassical economic theory to the Russian context.

The "True" West.   The rather too familiar dichotomies between "Western" and "anti-Western" Russians do not figure largely in this book. While the conflict between "Westernizing" progressives and anti-Western conservatives has framed the research of many intellectual historians of the nineteenth and twentieth centuries, I would argue that our definitions of "Westernization" and "progress" require far greater refinement if they are to help us to understand the realities of the Russian context. From the eighteenth century onward, there were very few educated Russians who were willing to say no to every component of Western culture. The number, balance, and size of these components shifted markedly in the nineteenth and twentieth centuries, as economic thinkers chose between Western models of repressive modernization and other, equally Western examples that linked economic transformation with fundamental changes in politics, society, and culture.

After 1861, German-oriented historical economists defended the cause of economic pluralism against Western-oriented government officials, and Marxists who believed that Russia was replicating the economic history of England as set out in the pages of *Capital*. On the eve of 1905, the demise of economic pluralism was engineered by the latter groups, who accused historical economists of being "anti-Western." Contending that Russia was no exception to the universal laws of history which governed Western European nations, Premier Witte and the Bolshevik Lenin were agreed that Russian peasants and their communes would suffer the same fate as all of the other backward and outmoded survivals of earlier, more "feudal" stages of human history.

Property Rights.   Because property rights—and the social choices about their configuration—are frequently considered to be at the core of the functioning of every economic system, this study highlights the issue of tenure as a central focus of Western economic thought, and as a prism through which to examine the history of Russian debates on development.[6] Ever since the reign of Catherine the Great, educated Russians were at great pains to discover whether the establishment of private tenure in place of the ubiquitous peasant commune was a precondition for modernization and development. To those accustomed to link privatization with struggles for freedom, it is worth noting that before the middle decades of the nineteenth century, private property advocates were usually admirers of autocracy and serfdom.

In the decades after Emancipation, both government officials and their critics were dismayed by the growing contrast between the power and wealth of Western empires governed by private property arrangements and the relative weakness of a Russian Empire whose peasant populace belonged to repartitional land communes. In the late nineteenth century, the fear that Russia might become an "India" if it did not somehow become an "England" generated a dichotomized image of the miraculous benefits of private property rights and the insuperable evils which flourished in its absence. Progressives routinely invoked the "sanctity" or "magic" of property as the only possible alternative to the utter irrationality of the peasantry's traditional communes.

However, in contrast to Westernizers of this sort, a number of Russia's leading economists of the late nineteenth century rejected such dichotomized strategies for economic development. Attempting to bridge the gap between an abstract—and to their minds, misleading—model of a wholly privatized West and a wholly collectivist, commune-dominated Russia, economists like A. I. Chuprov and A. S. Posnikov documented 1) the features of Western economic life which were not wholly governed by notions of individual and permanent tenure, and 2) the existence of private property rights within Russia's peasant commune. In Western Europe, they researched the achievement of English tenants, the success of German and Danish co-operatives, and the role of government economic initiatives. In Russia a wide range of economists and statisticians produced evidence which demonstrated that despite the commune's collectivism, communes did not command the labor of member households or appropriate the product of their labor; the dwellings and livestock of its members were privately owned.[7]

Political Economy. In contrast to the economic theories that came to prevail in England and the United States, Russian economic thought was always rooted in the assumption that domestic security concerns were inextricably linked with rational economic decision-making. From the time of Catherine the Great, officials, scholars, and social critics tended to judge economic policy first according to its role in fostering stability or disruption in society and the state, and only secondly according to its effectiveness in raising productivity rates. Until the middle decades of the nineteenth century, a predominantly German-born or German-trained coterie of advisers and officials relied on coercion as both an integral component of economic development strategy and as the fundamental guarantor of domestic peace.

On the eve of Emancipation, even the advocates of private-property rights came to support preservation of the peasant commune as a guarantee of social stability and domestic order. To further secure and pacify a free peasantry, the Emancipation of 1861 provided former serfs with allotments of land. In later years, the political component of Russian economic debate became more urgent and complex, as historical economists sought to discover whether a study of the West could teach Russians how to formulate government policies that minimized both the human costs and domestic unrest which elsewhere accompanied the process of economic development.

In the last years of his life, Karl Marx wrote letters to his Russian admirers suggesting that the survival of the peasant commune might enable Russia to follow a different economic path of development from Western Europe's. It is significant, however, that Marx's leading Russian disciples did not agree with him. Contending instead that Russia was following the "brutal yet progressive" capitalist path already marked out by the most advanced Western nations, they predicted that the contradictions of capitalist economic development would soon produce a desperate and revolutionary proletariat. However, when the Bolsheviks seized power in 1917, it is significant and revealing that they proved to be as devoted to questions of domestic security and order as their tsarist predecessors. In the early Soviet period, economic strategies to increase productivity rates were invariably subordinated to the political priority of preserving the Communist Party's monopoly on state power.

• • • • •

It may be that in their relationship to the West, progressive-minded Russians were not very different from marginalized groups or cultures in other times and places. Ever since the reign of Catherine the Great, they tried to understand Western economics and to influence it themselves. As outsiders, they were sometimes impressed by aspects of Western culture that did not become part of mainstream Western economic thought. As advocates of progress, they used their knowledge of the West to argue for repressive, liberal, or socialist economic strategies, and to make the case for either the retention or elimination of the repartitional land commune to which the peasant majority of the population belonged. On the eve of the Revolution of 1905, progressives were still at work to discover the "true," core values of the West, and the most appropriate economic model for Russia's future development. Their search for the key to Russian economic success in the social science and history of the West forms the major theme of this book.

Chapters 1 to 4 explore the Western economic traditions and practices from which educated Russians would borrow, as they attempted to appropriate key aspects of Western knowledge and experience between the eighteenth century and the Emancipation of 1861. Chapters 5 to 7 focus on the intersection of European and Russian economic ideas and on the debate on development which united "orthodox" Marxists and state capitalists in opposition to Russian historical economics in the decades preceding the outbreak of revolution in 1905. Chapter 8 considers the triumph of an anti-commune, modernizing mindset during the last years of the tsarist regime and the early years of Soviet power. The book's final chapter explores the impact of Russian traditions of dichotomized thinking upon the economic debates that erupted after the breakup of the Soviet Union in 1991.

Chapter One

THE TRUE WEST

ENGLAND, FRANCE, AND GERMANY

F OR MOST OF Western history, peasants were for educated Europeans a negligible phenomenon. Despite their ubiquitous presence in what was still a predominantly agrarian setting, peasants did not become a topic for intellectual debate and speculation until the eighteenth century. Responding to a rapidly changing socioeconomic landscape, European Romantics in search of an antidote to the evils of modernity constructed an idealized image of the peasant community as a haven for simple and peaceable folk, a living reproach to the soulless and vulgar calculations of the middle classes. In contrast, devotees of the Enlightenment imagined peasants and their communities as wretched survivors of a backward and medieval phase of human history.[1] In France and England, progressives came to rest their hopes for the future upon the triumph of a rational and productive "man of property" who was to replace the inefficient small producer. Enlightened Germans followed a quite different tack. Assuming that the common people were infinitely malleable, rather than hopelessly backward, German *Kulturträgers* set themselves to incorporate peasants into state-sponsored programs for economic development.

Inspired by a series of commercial, agricultural, and scientific revolutions, West European thinkers came to believe that human beings could by their own efforts infinitely multiply the fruits of the earth. A new kind of optimism (and perhaps an old-fashioned sort of *hubris*) came to dominate Western economic theory and practice. The astonishing array of Western achievements in science, technology, and money-making seemed a manifestation of Reason triumphant, a virtue whose transcendent power and force seemed to convey rights of domination over the nonhuman world of nature, and to justify the obliteration of "irrational" institutions and social elements. In the field of economics, progressives were inspired by a dream of unlimited growth, which was driven by the universal motive force of private-property rights and the rational choices of the private-property owner.

Although educated Europeans disagreed about the character and potential of peasants, they were in enthusiastic agreement about the universal benefits of private-property rights. In every time and place and for every social element, progressives described private ownership as the wellspring of virtues, which ranged from economic initiative to high moral character. In the history of European wars of conquest, the status of private-property rights was used as a way to distinguish between the "civilized" and the "uncivilized" peoples who needed and deserved to be defeated. Among the Irish or the American Indians of North America, the absence of clearly defined property rights was judged the mark of a "primitive," and served to justify the dispossession of those who failed to fence off their common lands. The Elizabethan poet Edmund Spenser described the Irish as brutes because they did not "Inclose" their lands. In centuries to come, English settlers claimed the right to drive Indians from the land of New England because—among their other deficiencies—Indians were considered unproductive farmers who left their common lands idle and unproductive. In Arthur Young's portrayals of the small producers of England and France, the "Goths and Vandals of open fields" seemed to embody every possible antediluvian evil. In general, Western European thinkers did not take empirical evidence to the contrary into account.[2] Although their judgments were neither dispassionate nor the product of careful study, they were quite consistent with the emerging dictates of eighteenth-century universal law and natural reason.[3]

Innovation and Communal Effort in European Village Life

Before the eighteenth century, European peasant communities were in no sense a community of equals. Differences in family size, farming ability, fertility of holdings, inheritance patterns, and the iniquities of patriarchal village power were among the many factors that contributed to wide disparities in village economic and social status. However, inequality and conflict were not the only significant features of peasant life. In the world peasants considered their own—apart from the systems of domination imposed upon them, and in addition to the burdens they imposed upon each other—peasants created a culture to defend themselves against the ever-present threat of environmental disaster and to keep their more or less importunate masters at bay.[4]

The farming strategies of West European peasants were neither inflexible nor unchanging. Even before the time of Charlemagne, peasants chose to replace traditional systems of walled square fields with a more productive and complex process of strip cultivation, which divided the plowland into strips scattered throughout the fields allotted to a particular village. Innovations of this sort were not cost-free. Strip cultivation required far more time, labor, and negotiating skill than the old system—peasants had not only to determine the size and location of strips allotted to each household but to obtain village-wide agreement to the new arrangements. In comparison with the old system, strip cultivation was far superior as a risk-spreading device. (Even within a single village, crop yields in various locations might vary enough to make it desirable for a family to hold a diversified number of scattered plots). Under strip cultivation, more land was open to farming, and it became more difficult for any household to monopolize all of the best land in a given area.[5]

Innovations in peasant farming practice continued in medieval times, as an increasing number of West European peasant communities adopted a three-field system of crop rotation, which slowed exhaustion of the soil by leaving a third of the land fallow each year and provided pasture for village livestock. Productivity rose, with economic innovation closely linked to village-wide, collective decision-making. In areas where serfdom was imposed, peasants retained the three-field system and extended strip cultivation to the *demesne* land of the lord. Peasants rather than masters or their appointed bailiffs were responsible for most day-to-day farming decisions.

Although the balance between private and communal effort in the peasantry's economic and noneconomic life varied widely, collective action was a quite ordinary village phenomenon. Sowing and harvesting usually began at the same time for all householders; nonconformists who gathered their crops later than their neighbors risked having their fields trampled after the general harvest, when the community's livestock was turned loose to pasture on the stubble of the plowlands.[6] In order to manage and oversee the sharing of common pastures or the farming of scattered strips of land, villages elected officers who established rules to set crop rotations, punish trespassers, and coordinate other farming and nonfarming activities. In contrast to many of the other political hierarchies of the day, village leaders worked side by side with those they governed and were themselves subject to the rules and regulations which they devised.

It should be emphasized that the communal behavior of European small producers was not due to any inherent "spirit of cooperation"; contemporary accounts document in detail the greed, violence, family feuds, and abuse of women endemic to traditional village life.[7] At the same time, as a variety of scholars have noted, peasants were not "blind, deaf and incapable of learning through experience and over time."[8] They constructed open-field systems differently from one locale to another, taking account of variations in geographic and historical circumstances.[9] To deal with agricultural activities for which there were efficiencies of scale—harvesting, fencing, and shepherding, for example—peasants devised rules and customs to prevent arbitrary and invasive behavior.[10]

Although it has been argued that common pasturing invariably led to over-grazing and the "tragic" ruin of the commons, much empirical evidence suggests that medieval villagers devised a variety of internal social controls to prevent this from happening.[11] Together with other traditions of interdependence and mutual obligation, the common rules and procedures which comprised eighteenth-century peasant culture reflected a quite plausible belief that without the community's protection and support, isolated individuals would be defenseless before the forces arrayed against them.

Eighteenth-century economic thinkers would describe communal practices as a "compulsory" constraint on individual freedom of action. Whether or not such judgments were accurate, it is significant that peasants were not asked for their view of the matter. In considering the drawbacks of traditional agriculture, economists accurately noted that (1) village communities discouraged private decision-making, and (2) threats of crop failure, famine, and starvation were omnipresent, and they set themselves to explore the possible links between these two features of rural economic life. At the very least, economists could demonstrate that communal practices coexisted historically with an inability to master and control the material environment. At most, they could argue that human beings the world over would remain forever enslaved by the forces of nature unless communal patterns of economic activity were eliminated.

England: The Romance of Property

> But who advances next, with cheerful grace
> Joy in her eye, and plenty on her face?
> A wheaten garland does her head adorn:
> O Property! O goddess, English-born
> *(Ambrose Philips, 1714)*

It was in England that the complex and resilient world of the European peasantry most dramatically and significantly gave way.[12] Over a period of 300 years, strip cultivation and three-field crop rotations were replaced by consolidated fields and a system of convertible husbandry that made use of all of the agricultural land each season; at the same time, great quantities of marsh and swamp were drained and transformed into plowland. Once it became possible to accumulate reserves against the possibility of crop failure, the scourge of famine (but not of poverty) was eliminated from the English countryside. It should be emphasized that the achievements of England's Agricultural Revolution were *not* a product of technological advance.[13] The unprecedented increase in agricultural productivity rates was primarily due to changes in field use; by 1800, convertible husbandry was widely (but unevenly) established throughout the English countryside.

THE AGENTS OF CHANGE

To England's leading economists, artists, theologians, and political reformers, the "improving landlord" was beyond question the hero of England's Agricultural Revolution. Small producers and their communities,
tenants, and agricultural laborers played no role in their modernizing scenarios, (except as obstacles to innovation and change). Amidst the celebrations of landlord achievement, the role of parliamentary legislation
and government subsidies receded as well.

However, in reality, risk-taking and innovation were not the monopoly
of any social group within English society. As early as the seventeenth
century, small farmers managed to introduce new crops into many common field routines despite their lack of schooling and the meagerness of
their resources to bear the costs and risks of change. In Oxfordshire, intelligent and farsighted individuals won the consent of their neighbors to
village-wide rural innovation, ensuring that the use of fodder crops spread
more rapidly on the open fields than on large-scale estates of the Thames
district.[14] According to G. E. Mingay, "The old picture of an extremely
conservative, rigid and inefficient system which persisted unchanged over
the centuries has had to be considerably modified."[15]

Some innovations were particularly well suited to open-field systems,
because the preparatory measures required beforehand were more easily
carried out on a community-wide basis.[16] Unlike private landowners, village communities could periodically reorganize their holdings to achieve
more compact or equitable distribution of the strips held by their members. In comparison with individual farmers, they could also increase the
number of fields in order to allow for more-complex crop rotations. As
Eric Kerridge has written, "the assumption that open fields were old-fashioned and enclosed ones new and improved is unhistorical [and] has little
bearing on the agricultural revolution . . ."[17]

Although supporters of open-field cultivation were frequently stereotyped as primitives and reactionaries, it is worth noting that the seventeenth-century "Diggers" advocated the introduction of new systems of
crop rotation on common land.[18] In the eighteenth century, the anti-enclosure radical Thomas Spence bitterly declared, "It is childish, therefore, to
expect ever to see small farmers appear again, or ever to see anything else
than the utmost screwing and grinding of the Poor, till you quite overturn
the present system of Landed Property." However, at the same time,
Spence called on agricultural laborers and small farmers to establish an
agriculturally innovative "People's Farm" which leased out allotments of
land for terms long enough to benefit the individual and allow for innovation, and in sufficient quantity to give the poor a chance at survival.[19] In

the outcry against his revolutionary efforts to organize collective action by the lower classes, the specifics of his economic program were drowned out. To the leading economic thinkers of the day, the combination of agricultural innovation, economic security, and opportunity for the poor was not a conceivable option.

The role of tenants in England's Agricultural Revolution was minimized as well. Although most historians agree that the changes in field use which lay at the heart of England's economic transformation were implemented by large-scale tenants rather than landowners, eighteenth-century economists tended to ignore data on tenant innovation and focused quite narrowly on the "man of property." It was argued that no farmer would invest in land improvements without secure guarantees of ownership. In the centuries to come, scholars failed to investigate the history of tenant efforts, or the specific connections between tenantry and high levels of economic initiative.[20]

Agricultural reformers like John Sinclair and Jethro Tull were particularly harsh in their complaints against unreliable farm laborers. Sinclair argued that a prime advantage of the threshing machine was that it could prevent the pilfering of corn by "labourers and other vermin." Tull confessed that he was driven to invent new tools by the "deceit and idleness" of his workers, whose nefarious behavior he sought to "disappoint" by devices which reduced his need for their labor.[21] While less misanthropic eighteenth-century improvers like George Boswell praised the gifted laborers who modified and adapted new tools and techniques for use in a particular context, most reformers had little positive to say about them. Among agricultural writers, few considered the possibility that successful innovation might in fact depend not only on the ideas and actions of the innovator, but on the talent for "user-modification" shown by the laborer whose job it was to put a particular innovation into practice.[22]

As eighteenth-century economic thinkers sought to identify the agents of innovation and change in the English countryside, their perspectives were quite narrow. Efforts by small proprietors, tenants, and laborers receded from view, as did the activist policies of a Parliament that imposed taxes to fund regional swamp-drainage projects and provided generous subsidies to landlords (who in turn charged their tenants a percentage of the cost of improvements). In place of the complex realities of economic change initiated by a variety of social elements and institutions, economists highlighted the heroic struggle between imaginative and hard-working landed magnates and ignorant country bumpkins, or bureaucratic government officials.[23]

England's "Agricultural Miracle" set off what has been called an age of "unprecedented intellectualizing about agriculture" by monarchs and statesmen, journalists and social critics.[24] Kings and princes debated the relative merits of dung as fertilizer; King George III established a model farm at Windsor Castle and contributed to *The Annals of Agriculture* under the *nom de plume* of Ralph Robinson. The younger William Pitt contributed an article on the storage of turnips, and Arthur Young, Voltaire, and Diderot reported to their readers on the agricultural wonders they discovered on the estates of men like Viscount "Turnip" Townshend and the Earl of Leicester.

In general, such celebrations of English achievement were not directed toward the general public; journals like *The Annals of Agriculture* specifically targeted the upper ranks of the landed gentry.[25] After 1750, agricultural societies, libraries, and journals sprang up in London, Berlin, Moscow, and Vienna. Writers like Arthur Young became world-renowned celebrities. Russia's Catherine the Great presented him with a golden snuffbox, while the Russian serfowner Ivan Petrovich-Belianin praised his English plowman, and asked Young to send him forty Arbuthnot plows and a farmer's cart "that does perform such a deal of work on your farm."[26]

THE ENCLOSURE MOVEMENT

Although the eighteenth-century English literature of agricultural improvement discussed such specialized topics as seed drills, fertilizer, and crop-rotation systems, its broader purpose was to explain and praise the logic of a process which was then transforming medieval manors into enterprises that resembled grain and meat factories. Yeoman farmers were being replaced by cotters, tenants, and farmhands—less rooted, or from an opposite point of view, less constrained—within the community of their forebears. By 1800 it was increasingly evident that the changes in field use advocated by Tull, Young, and Townshend were aspects of a fundamental revolution in English social life. The driving force behind this transformation was the enclosure of common lands traditionally used by peasants as a source of pasture, food, and fuel.

As early as the fifteenth century, English landlords had begun to convert the commons (and even cultivated holdings) into private sheep pastures. While some small farmers concluded voluntary enclosure agreements with the gentry, usually those who owned the most land beforehand received the greatest share of the territory enclosed.[27] Households traditionally protected by land claims based on labor or need lost out. According to the statistics of Gregory King, these cottagers and squatters comprised 30 to 35 percent of the agricultural population in 1688, and between 20 and 25 percent of the total population of England and Wales.[28] Proposals to provide land allotments of "three acres and a cow" to the dispossessed were rejected as obstacles to economic development.[29]

It may be, however, that the social group most immediately and nega-
tively affected by acts of enclosure were women. As the research of Jane
Humphries has indicated, the commons' value as a source of family income was largely derived from the labor of women (and children). They
were, after all, the primary exploiters of common rights within the peasant household—the gleaners, the cutters of wood and peat for fuel, who
scavenged the commons for the nuts, berries, mushrooms, and herbs that
supplemented the diet of their households. The elimination of the commons drastically limited their economic opportunities, increased their dependence on husbands and fathers and, in general, increased the
dependence of the household as a whole upon wage labor. (Arthur
Young frequently referred to the opponents of enclosure as "a few old
women.")[30]

Both the process and the impact of enclosure varied widely from region
to region. To some, a more privatized system represented a welcome
change from the morass of intricate and unproductive communal traditions and inspired hopes that the "magic of property" would eventually
bring prosperity to all.[31] Elsewhere, according to the medievalist Joan
Thirsk, the Midland peasant "saw rich farmers taking up more and more
land but giving less employment than ever before to the labourer. He
could have viewed the matter calmly had he lived in the Lincolnshire fens
or the Yorkshire dales."[32]

Resistance to enclosure did not erupt into large-scale rebellion, nor did
it focus on Parliament, which was popularly viewed as a partisan supporter of enclosures. Often, resistance took the form of what the political
scientist James Scott has described as "the weapons of the weak," which
ranged from foot-dragging, the theft of records of allotment decisions
from the house of the enclosure commissioner, to the spreading of false
rumors, not the writing of anti-enclosure songs and poems or threatening letters, and the destruction of fences.[33] The theft of fenceposts combined practical advantage with symbolic revenge against the enclosers. In
a fuel-scarce county, posts and rails were immediately taken home to be
burned.[34]

Among the middle and upper classes, both critics and supporters of
enclosure agreed that enclosed lands were more productively used. Although this belief went unquestioned in the centuries to come, modern
researchers have demonstrated beyond question that (1) the extinction
of common rights was not necessarily accompanied by improvement in
husbandry, and (2) common rights were not incompatible with economic
change.[35] According to G. E. Mingay, common-field villages that survived
enclosure introduced many innovations. In his words, "Fields were divided so as to allow more complex rotations and to reduce fallowing, and
holdings were consolidated by exchanges among the owners. New crops
were brought in and grass leys appeared within the common fields."[36]

Even enthusiasts like Arthur Young conceded that in some areas under open-field cultivation, crops were "inexplicably" good. According to Young, some open-field farmers were "sensible, intelligent men, for they agree among themselves to sow turnips instead of fallowing on many of their lands."[37] In his travels abroad, Young discovered what Russian advocates of enclosure would discover over a century later—many farmers "inexplicably" used the same outmoded techniques in open and enclosed fields. Young's insistence that enclosed fields were more productive was also at odds with the figures he himself compiled on the topic of grain yields. The economic historian Robert Allen has shown that "the data in his [Young's] tours show enclosure had little effect on yields"; enclosure did not necessarily foster economic innovation.[38]

But not even the evidence contained in his own data could divert Young from the increasingly seductive "romance of property." In his words, when common lands were fenced off and privatized, "The Goths and Vandals of open fields touch the civilization of enclosures. Men have been taught to think, and until that moment arrives, nothing can be done effectively."[39] Enclosure made the moors "smile with culture which before were dreary as night," as private ownership turned barren land into fertile and productive farm enterprises. In an even loftier rhetorical flight, Young declared the "magic of property" turned sand into gold. As Ambrose Philips had noted, property was truly a "goddess, English-born."[40]

In the eighteenth and nineteenth centuries, Parliamentary acts excluded the property claims of customary tenants who had earlier agreed to enclose at the expense of their poorer neighbors. Traditional claims to land use were replaced by short-term, even annual leases. As landowners complained about shiftless and destructive tenants who "scourged" the land shortly before the lease expired,[41] Parliament increasingly made good the landowner's claim to inalienable rights of dispossession. In general, English law-makers were sympathetic to the plight of the large-scale investor who felt hemmed in by the restrictions imposed by traditional land claims. They did not consider the economic disincentives created for the small producer whose successful agricultural experiments resulted in higher rents or eviction from the land.

In an increasingly privatized English rural scene, giant estates were managed by large-scale tenants who hired laborers to build barns, fence the moors, and drain marshes. These initiatives were rarely undertaken without substantial government support. Although some tenants were aided by their landlords, in general, they relied on Parliament to subsidize and organize the massive land-clearing efforts that transformed the English countryside. Understandably, the most prosperous landowners and the wealthiest tenants, rather than the hard-pressed yeomen or hired hands, were the most eager to claim that enclosure was the key to England's prosperity.

ADAM SMITH AND THE ENGLISH "MIRACLE"

The most powerful and influential celebration of England's economic transformation appeared in Adam Smith's *Wealth of Nations* (1776). Although he had relatively little to say about common rights, Smith eloquently linked private-property rights with the advance of Reason. Contrasting a medieval world where senseless restrictions thwarted private initiative with capitalism's more rational and productive property relationships, Smith contended that even "the lowest and most despised member of civilized [i.e., capitalist] society" was richer than the inhabitant of a traditional society.[42]

Gifted as both a myth-maker and economist, Smith helped to create a Western economic tradition that excluded a number of significant social, legal, and institutional factors from consideration. His ideal model ignored the substantial economic contributions made by leaseholders and hired laborers. Smith also downplayed the role of Parliament, which initiated, funded, and supervised vast projects for soil reclamation and supported gentry innovation by means of subsidies, advisory commissions, and enabling legislation. Smith's version of England's economic miracle emphasized the uniquely creative ability of private owners who each pursued their own interests and accumulated unprecedented wealth in a mysteriously harmonious fashion.

Although Smith praised individual effort, competition, specialization, and the division of labor, he also rather inconsistently argued that the free and unspecialized small producer was the most industrious of agricultural improvers. No eighteenth-century proponent of the "idiocy of rural life," Smith argued that farm labor was more complex and beneficial for an individual's mental development than the stultifying routine of specialized industrial work. In his words,

> The common ploughman, though generally regarded as the pattern of stupidity and ignorance, is seldom defective in his judgement and discretion. He is less accustomed, indeed, to social intercourse than the mechanic who lives in a town. His voice and language are more uncouth and more difficult to be understood by those who are not used to them. His understanding, however, is generally much superior to that of the other, whose whole attention from morning till night is commonly occupied in performing one or two very simple operations.[43]

Smith also valued the small proprietor, who knew his land better and took more pleasure in farming it than the owner of landed estates. It was significant for the future of economics as a discipline that Smith would never resolve the contradiction between his faith in division-of-labor principles on the one hand, and on the other, his sympathy for the ploughman and the small landowner. The latter concern generated only the feeble suggestion that great landlords might be encouraged to cultivate at least part of their own land.[44]

Smith contended that economic balance, equilibrium, or harmony could not be created by conscious or deliberate human effort; only an "invisible hand" could reconcile the conflicts between isolated individuals competing for private economic gain. When economic interests were in question, no Smithian individual could offer help to a neighbor without contravening what Smith defined as the rules of rational economic behavior. Believing that "combinations" by industrial workmen were doomed because of the superior resources and "steadiness" of masters and magistrates, Smith also denounced as obstacles to free competition the entrepreneurs who banded together to establish monopolies. As he saw it, neither the state, the community, the family, nor any other form of social organization could provide alternative frameworks either for the establishment of harmony or for the promotion of productive economic behavior.[45]

Although Smith's doubts and reservations reveal the extraordinary complexity and depth of his thinking, they did not greatly influence later generations of classical economists who admired his work. Seizing on his enthusiasm for the man of property, progressives read Smith as a brief for *laissez faire*, enclosure, and the elimination of the small producer. Conservative thinkers like Edmund Burke denounced government "interventions" which lowered food prices in time of poor harvests, arguing that it was not the government's task to "supply to the poor those necessaries which it has pleased the Divine Providence for a while to withhold from them."[46]

PRIVATE OWNERSHIP AND FREEDOM

In the eighteenth century, the cause of private-property rights was linked with the ideals of individual freedom and civilization. Adam Ferguson's best-selling *Essay on the History of Civil Society* (1767) contrasted civilized peoples to the barbarous nations, which paid "little attention to property, and have scarcely any beginnings of subordination or government . . . mankind in its rudest state, is not yet acquainted with property." Ferguson's book went through twelve printings by 1800, including a German edition published in 1768 and two French editions. William Russell's *History of Ancient Europe* (1793) was equally emphatic: "Personal Property in land, and the prospect of reaping exclusively the fruits of his labor, can alone give activity and perseverance to the labors of the husbandman, or fertility to the earth." Russell's *History* appeared in four editions between 1793 and 1801.[47]

As defined by the foremost legal and economic theorists of the day, freedom was particularly manifest in the individual owner's power to dominate and exclude the claims of others. According to the famous open-ing of book II of *Blackstone's Commentaries on the Laws of England* (a work that inspired the 1767 "Instruction" of Russia's Catherine the Great): "There is nothing which so strikes the imagination and engages the affections of mankind, as the right of property; or that sole and des-potic dominion which one man claims and exercises over the external things of the world, in total exclusion of the right of any other individual in the universe." According to Blackstone, the right to exclude others encouraged innovation as well. In his words, "who would be at the pains of tilling [the earth] if another might . . . seize upon and enjoy the product of his industry, art and labour?"[48]

Conflicting interpretations of freedom were very much at issue in the enclosure process. Enclosure advocates believed that the existence of the commons limited their freedom to draw on the laborer's wife and children as a seasonal labor force at hay-making and harvest times. But from the laborer's perspective, the common's woods and streams provided the la-borer's family with alternative sources of income, which (1) freed them—at least to some extent—from the beck and call of landowners, and (2) threatened the landlord's labor supply at key periods in the agricultural cycle.[49] In 1794, a Shropshire reporter to the Board of Agriculture com-plained that rights to common land encouraged among laborers "a sort of independence," which led them to reject the authority of their employers. As he saw it, once land was enclosed, hired laborers would "work every day in the year and their children will be put out to labor early," thus reinforcing "the subordination of the lower ranks of society which in pres-ent times is so much wanted."[50] The ploughman-poet John Clare turned the liberal argument upside down, declaring that enclosure operated as a constraint on the laborer's freedom. According to Clare, independence and liberty were indissolubly linked with rights to enjoy and make use of com-mon lands accessible to all. In his words, the new fences and signposts left "men and flocks imprisoned ill at ease. . . . Inclosure came and trampled on the grave / of labour's rights and left the poor a slave."[51]

Believing that small producers were at best the obedient instruments of the few who possessed the capital and intelligence to transform the com-mons into "smiling fields," Arthur Young contended that the disenfran-chisement of a backward majority was essential to a nation's prosperity. Traveling in France in 1789 after the outbreak of revolution, he wrote: "Under the new government which is established in France, I have great doubts whether any progress can be made in this great and leading step to all useful improvements in agriculture; as far as the present constitution can be understood, it is the will of the *people* that is to govern, and I know of no country where the will *of the people* is not against enclosures" (Young's emphasis).[52]

In fact, Young's fear that democratic governments would block the enclosure of common land would prove groundless. In the eighteenth and nineteenth centuries, progressives the world over came to accept enclosure not simply as a useful economic strategy, but as a universally beneficial economic reform. As Smith, Young, McCulloch, Hume, and other popularizers of the Agricultural Revolution declared England the embodiment of human reason, the economic theories of classical liberalism were indelibly linked with the universalist principles of the Enlightenment. The role of tenants and laborers, the innovative use of common land, and the human costs of enclosure were relegated to the margins of economic debate.

France: La Théorie Avant Le Pratique

> It is from the right of property, maintained in all its natural fullness, that all the institutions which make up the essential form of society *necessarily* flow; you can think of the right of property as a tree, and all the institutions are the branches which it shoots forth, which it nourishes and which perish when they are detached from it.
> *(Mercier de la Rivière, 1776)*

> The spirit of property doubles a man's strength—The possessor of property desires a wife to share his happiness, and children to assist in his labors. His wife and his children constitute his wealth. The estate of such a cultivator, under the hands of an active and willing family, may become 10 times more productive than it was before.
> *(Voltaire)*

Unlike England, where ideologies of progress and development emerged in the context of rapid economic change, French enthusiasm for a peasantless and privatized agriculture was largely imported from abroad. Before the Revolution of 1789, most of the rural population were subsistence cultivators of the land who owed seigneurial dues to their lords, made use of common lands, and employed a three-field system.[53] In general, the laws and customs of prerevolutionary France were "more tender to the interest of the landless" than the acts of enclosure by which English parliaments defined ownership rights over common lands.[54]

Inspired by England's example, eighteenth-century Frenchmen produced a flourishing literature of agricultural improvement. While only 130 French books on agronomy were published in the whole of the seventeenth century, 12,214 publications on this topic appeared in the eighteenth.[55] Visits to the estates of "Turnip" Townshend and Arthur Young became the fashion among French "moderns," who delighted in the achievements of "improving landlords" and returned home to establish agricultural societies and journals, which debated the latest English innovations. Voltaire wrote foolishly and eloquently of the prosperous and sturdy English peasant (who was then in a process of steady decline). French ministers like Maurepas and Turgot wrote admiringly about English agriculture; even Marie Antoinette did her part by starting an "English-style" garden.[56]

PROGRESS WITHOUT PEASANTS

In the eighteenth century, economics-minded French *philosophes* possessed inexhaustible reserves of contempt and disgust for the insuperable stupidity of the peasant "herd." Diderot described the multitude as capable of being right only "when it ceases to be itself, that is, when it finally sheds its unreason and prejudices (which are its essence) and adopts the views of a small number of sensible men."[57] Benevolent landlords like Voltaire described peasants as "ignorant wretches" whose mental deficiencies were exacerbated by a life of manual labor. As he wrote in 1769, "As to the people, they will always be stupid and barbarous. They are cattle and what is wanted for them is a yoke, a goad and fodder."[58] With a bit less callousness, Montesquieu wrote: "I like peasants because they are not wise enough to reason craftily,"[59] while Turgot observed that "Love itself is weak among our peasants, and often they will miss their cow more than their wife or son, because they can better calculate the price of the cow than the privations of the heart."[60] Baron Holbach was more ambivalent, describing peasants as economically valuable *gens du travail* who were unfortunately "scatterbrained, inconstant, imprudent, impetuous, and . . . the instruments of troublemakers."[61]

In negative images of this sort, the *philosophes* portrayed peasants as somehow both stupid and calculating, unfeeling yet filled with destructive passions, prone to violence but mired in stagnant tradition. At every essential point, they stood in contrast to the owner-investor, imbued with what Montesquieu described as a spirit of commerce, a spirit of "frugality, of economy, of moderation, of work, of wisdom, of tranquillity, of order and regularity."[62] Although the *philosophes* opposed serfdom, they did not believe that any component of the vulgar and degraded "*peuple*" were capable of rational action.

While Voltaire was sometimes compassionate toward peasant victims of feudal privilege, the Physiocrats were much more consistent and brutal in their outlook. Disciples of a harsh and unyielding economic code, Quesnay, Mercier de la Rivière, Roubaud, and the elder Mirabeau equated the triumph of Reason with the replacement of peasants and their communities by large-scale private proprietors. Insisting on both the "sanctity" and the material benefits of private-property rights, Physiocrats argued that economics was, like the science of physics, an expression of the will of God.[63] In keeping with England's example, Physiocrats proposed a capital-intensive development strategy directed by wealthy, large-scale rural entrepreneurs. To achieve this goal, they advocated the elimination of peasant communalism, the separation of peasants from the land, and the formation of a labor market.[64] Setting aside the joys of romantic love, victory in battle, and other activities that human beings are prone to celebrate, Mercier de la Rivière argued that the freedom to control one's property was "a supreme source of pleasure."[65]

Although they criticized feudal constraints as obstacles to competition and the rational investment of labor and capital, there was nothing either egalitarian or democratic about Physiocratic doctrine. Opposed to any lessening of status differences between the upper and the lower classes, they contended that economic development would increase rather than diminish social inequality. According to Quesnay, peasants freed from seigneurial obligations would work harder and increase their output without any dangerous equalization of wealth.[66] That the privileged would live in luxury while the rest remained poor was, in the words of Jacques Necker, "the inevitable effect of the laws of property." According to Necker, it was the task of religious instruction to teach peasants to accept their lowly economic status.[67] In many respects, the language of the Physiocrats resembled that of England's Edmund Burke, who declared that the masses "must learn to respect that property of which they cannot partake. They must labor to obtain what by labor can be obtained, and when they find, as they commonly do, the success disproportionate to the endeavor, they must be taught their consolation in the final proportions of eternal justice. Of this consolation, whoever deprives them, deadens their industry, and strikes at the root of all acquisition as of all conservation."[68]

To an economics which valued inequality, peasant traditions of sharing, cooperation, and communalism seemed to threaten both economic growth and the security of private property. According to Quesnay, French agriculture would never prosper unless the countryside was "cleared" of petty proprietors and their communal practices.[69] From the perspective of the Physiocrats, it was "not so much men as wealth which ought to be attracted to the countryside."[70] They therefore called for an "English-style" enclosure movement and a division of common lands in the interests of the largest landowners.

Contending that communal practices were both socially disruptive and economically backward, Physiocrats condemned the archaic practice of the *communion*—a patriarchal system that required family members to share the communal life of the family, right down to the use of the same fire and cooking pot, if they wished to inherit property from the head of the household. As they saw it, the customary gathering of all heirs under one roof was dangerously conducive to the murder of close relations. The very act of sharing was held to endanger the spirit of enterprise upon which economic progress was based.[71] To Physiocrats like Mercier, Quesnay, and Turgot, the dictates of pleasure, morality, and economics were identical. Communal practices deprived human beings of the "supreme pleasure" of property ownership; they were a source of primitive violence, and they hindered the productive use of agricultural land.

PEASANTS AND INNOVATION

Physiocratic ideas did not meet with widespread approval in eighteenth-century France. Members of the nobility were particularly fearful that fundamental economic change might destabilize rural life and encourage the rise of entrepreneurs from among the common people. The elder Mirabeau was briefly imprisoned for his writings, while Quesnay prudently undertook to reassure the nobility that Physiocratic doctrines did not threaten the interests of the nobility or the existing political order.[72] On the other hand, Physiocratic ideas were much appreciated by a small minority of gentry-improvers and by the upwardly mobile in the second half of the eighteenth century. In the *parlements* of provincial France, reformers cited Quesnay in support of proposals to eliminate peasant common rights. In the 1760s, a number of government measures promoted the enclosure of common lands; decrees were even issued to require that paths from one strip of land to another be included in enclosures, a measure that accelerated consolidation by making it impossible for peasants to reach their scattered parcels.

But in its response to enclosure, France was not like England. Before 1789, French peasants successfully resisted the enclosure of common lands; and in many regions, they implemented village-wide agricultural innovations.[73] In the province of Burgundy, when officials attempted to fence off "unused" common land, whole villages of men, women, and children, called out by the village *tocsin*, set off with staffs in hand to tear down the fences.[74] In the province of Picardy, peasant defenders of common rights incorporated more productive forms of field use into traditional commune practices by allowing for considerable innovation in cropping and in pasturing. Peasants of this region devised an intricate system intended to reconcile the retention of the commons with the requirements of agricultural productivity.[75] In the Walloon region of France guarantees of security were tied to economic innovation. Village communities in this area granted lifetime leases on the marshland commons *on condition* that families receiving land agreed to drain and plant their new holdings. The rents that communities received for these "household portions" were used to pay communal expenses and to sustain efforts by newly formed households or by outsiders who hoped for a household portion in the future.[76]

Although these peasant strategies did not prove that communities were more innovative than private owners—only that they were not uniformly indifferent to improvement—it is significant that communal efforts did not attract the attention of the Physiocrats.[77] Quesnay and Roubaud highlighted instead the irrationality and wasted labor that they viewed as typical of the peasantry's intricate social and economic arrangements. While the reasons for their focus on landlord innovation and peasant innovation are undoubtedly complex, the economic historian Robert Allen has suggested that their tendency to ignore evidence of open-field innovation was deliberate and carefully considered. According to Allen, "If it were known that respectable yields were reaped by . . . open-field peasant farmers in France, then the economic argument against enclosure and capitalist agriculture would have been much stronger."[78]

The historian Marc Bloch long ago suggested that eighteenth-century French advocates of progress were blinded by optimistic theories about property rights and by the prestige of English agriculture.[79] However, it should nevertheless be emphasized that there was no English-style agricultural miracle in the making in prerevolutionary France. According to the agronomist Duhamel du Monceau, the nobility opposed agricultural change either because they were apathetic, or afraid that a thoroughgoing, "English-style" enclosure movement might produce a revolutionary upheaval.[80] Even when Physiocrats became high government officials, fears that enclosure would produce domestic unrest blocked any thoroughgoing government commitment to its implementation. Educated and well-born Frenchmen may well have admired England's enclosure movement, but the prospect of a nationwide elimination of common lands posed political risks that few of them were willing to take. Even the most dogmatic of Physiocrats were reluctant to demand the systematic and immediate enactment of antipeasant and anticommunal projects.

Germany: Progress with Peasants

In the duchies and principalities of eighteenth-century Germany, peasant social status, organization, and agricultural practices varied far more dramatically than in France or England. To move from the Northeast to the Southwest was to leave a land of giant estates, bound peasants, and technological backwardness for a region where subsistence peasants managed communal resources, supervised the maintenance of paths and ditches, allocated grazing rights, and served as the guarantors of public order and morals. In contrast to East Prussia, peasant cultivators of the Rhineland district enjoyed a relatively high level of agricultural development as early as the sixteenth century, complete with eleven different types of field use and various forms of crop rotation.[81]

Before the seventeenth century, German village communities were usually production-oriented institutions whose members contributed their labor to the welfare of the household and to the *gemeinde*—a commune which functioned as an association of freemen with private-property rights based on military service and participation in the community's activities. In its agricultural operations, the *mark* (a geographic area shared out and appropriated by the community) was divided into three parts: (1) the common *mark*, which was jointly owned by the community, (2) the arable *mark* (*feldmark*) cut out of the common *mark* and apportioned in equal lots to all members, and (3) the *mark* of the township (*dorf*), which was also divided into equal lots and individually appropriated. Each household head was a joint proprietor of the common land and received land in the arable *mark*.[82]

As peasant autonomy declined in the wake of escalating attacks by a variety of German kings and princes, the *gemeinde* began to change from a production-to a consumption-oriented community, more dependent upon state authorities for the maintenance of order and less involved in organizing the labor of its members. Although estate-owners attempted to encroach upon village claims to autonomy, German rulers were the chief enemy of communal norms.[83] Intent on increasing their revenues and accumulating more subjects by settling new migrants on land jointly owned by peasant villages, German kings denounced the *gemeinde* as an obstacle to the expansion of state power and to economic progress. But the *gemeinde* survived nevertheless. Even in the strongholds of East Prussian Junker landlords, there were independent peasant communities "in which interference by either landlord or territorial lord in the jurisdiction and economic affairs of the village was very limited."[84]

CLASSICAL LIBERALISM IN THE GERMAN CONTEXT

Before the advent of Adam Smith, Germany's traditional economics was Cameralism, a scholarly discipline that linked economic interests with the interests of the state. In the eighteenth century, Cameralists were advocates of property rights, innovation by gentry entrepreneurs, and the accumulation of income for the state (with peasants as the prime source of revenue).[85] In their projects for reform, the enclosure of common lands was part of a broader plan to make government administration and estate management more efficient. The prestige and utility of Cameralism was such that in eighteenth-century Prussia, officials responsible for the management and development of the nation's resources were required to study cameralistic science, serve as apprentices on a royal farm, and pass entrance examinations on the subjects of economics, law, or public administration.[86]

Eager to draw on the economic wisdom of England and France, educated Germans led Europe in the translation of foreign texts in the second half of the eighteenth century. In the 1780s, a German Physiocrat proposed a general agricultural statute based upon the "unchangeable laws of nature," and at the court of Baden, Margrave Karl Friedrich wrote essays on Quesnay, appointed the Physiocrat Dupont de Nemours as his finance minister, and implemented a number of Physiocratic economic measures (with disastrous economic results).[87] Although French writings predominated in the field of economics, the work of Arthur Young outnumbered all of the rest.[88]

At the University of Halle, Ludwig von Jakob lectured to great acclaim on the evils of "feudal" restrictions on the property owner. According to Jakob, individuals would refuse to invest labor or capital in a farm unless they owned it and controlled the product of their investments.[89] The freedom to make economic decisions without regard for communal regulations symbolized for Jakob the triumph of natural law. At the University of Königsberg, Christian Kraus translated Arthur Young and rhapsodized over Adam Smith's *Wealth of Nations*: "since the time of the New Testament," wrote Kraus, "no writing has had more beneficial results than this will have when it becomes better known."[90] Kraus condemned both American slavery and Prussian systems of coerced labor as inefficient, unjust, and incompatible with Smith's teachings. In 1800, the views of Kraus attracted so much favorable attention that Baron von Schrotter, the Ober-präsident of East Prussia, decided that "no one would henceforth be permitted to enter the East Prussian administrative service without a certificate of having attended Kraus's lectures."[91]

The most influential German outpost of the Anglo-French Enlightenment was the University of Göttingen, where the work of Adam Smith, Ferguson's *Essay on the History of Civil Society*, and each volume of Diderot's *Encyclopedia* reached the university's library shelves within 18 to 24 months of publication in Paris, London, or Glasgow.[92] But Göttingen's Westward orientation was not uncritical. Although many Göttingen scholars advocated property rights and market reform, they considered English arguments for the universality of England's economic experience both unconvincing and self-serving. Eager to cite English and French economists to support the argument that private property endowed the individual with both a social identity and political rights, they uniformly rejected the arguments for *laissez faire* and/or limited government contained in the writings of Quesnay, Mercier de la Rivière, and Adam Smith. According to the political economist August von Schlözer, individual freedom and private ownership were important, but they were not *more* important than the state's obligation to protect and secure the welfare of its subjects.[93]

Adam Müller described Adam Smith as the "greatest political-economic writer of all time," but he did not view England's historical conditions as a model for any other nation. The celebrated agronomist Albrecht von Thaer rejected the notion of a "peasantless" Germany, arguing that "one can assume that a state can approximate its agriculture to [England's] only to the degree to which it is in a position to make the relationships of its agricultural classes comparable to those in England."[94] Relying on the state as chief arbiter of the nation's socioeconomic life, Thaer argued that it was the government's duty to create the conditions for the development of a freer market economy at some distant future date.[95]

The contrast between German and Anglo-French readings of Smith and Quesnay was striking. While in England and France, the teachings of Adam Smith reinforced the notion that small producers were obsolete survivors of an outworn and medieval past, in the states of Germany, economists drew on *The Wealth of Nations* to support the argument that small producers were as capable of rational economic action as members of other social groups. The Cameralist J. G. Justi agreed with the Physiocrat Quesnay that agriculture constituted the basis of a healthy Prussian economy, but ignored his arguments for *laissez faire*. According to Justi, the state was obliged to take the lead in eliminating obstacles to the free development of economic forces.[96]

In Justi's scenarios for economic development, private enterprise coexisted with unlimited state power. If these two goals conflicted, Justi's enthusiasm for productivity increase invariably gave way to the interests of the state. As an adviser to Frederick the Great, he recommended massive government projects for rural development, the abolition of serfdom, and the enclosure of common lands. Including private enterprise within a comprehensive system of government regulation and regimentation, Justi proposed that government officials decide both the size and location of peasant dwellings, and impose strict rules of family behavior conducive to hard work and obedience. Within this framework, he recommended the creation of a Christian educational system to preach the virtues of thrift and conscientious work habits among the lowliest of German cottagers.[97]

Joseph von Sonnenfels, a member of Joseph II's "brain trust" and the first professor of Cameralism at the University of Vienna, was equally convinced that the ruler's job was to manage the labor power of his people in order to maximize economic output. Sonnenfels urged the emperor (1) to sponsor an enclosure movement, (2) to require any proprietor too poor to cultivate his land properly to lease or sell it, and (3) to penalize anyone who took land out of productive use for three years or longer by requiring that they forfeit their property.[98] Although Cameralism has been described by the economist Joseph Schumpeter as *"laissez faire* with the nonsense left out,"[99] it is difficult to reconcile the intrusive and bureaucratic policies advocated by Sonnenfels and Justi with the freedoms envisioned by Adam Smith. The massive state interventions proposed by German Cameralists seem instead to prefigure a more or less totalitarian model for economic development, complete with minute and petty prescriptions for hierarchical controls over every aspect of the peasantry's social and economic life. In some cases, the Cameralist obsession with supervision and surveillance proliferated to the point that "the very routine of government operations threatened to swallow up the purpose for which it had been introduced."[100] As advocates of bureaucratic state controls to replace the "irrational" customs of the peasant community as the guarantor of domestic peace and prosperity,[101] Cameralists rejected Smith's "invisible hand." Instead, their ideal economic model centered on the activities of government bureaucracy and a *noblesse commercante* who was skilled in the art of economic and social control and supervision.

In contrast to the Physiocrats, Cameralists were able to convince many German rulers that their projects posed no threat to the stability of society or the state. Joseph II and Frederick II declared themselves both advocates of enlightenment and enclosure, but they clearly did not fear an eruption of independent private action or any challenge to traditional authority or privilege. When Frederick the Great settled thousands of colonists on newly cleared terrain and provided them with private allotments of land, he made sure that they would *not* become individualists who took sole responsibility for their successes and failures. On his orders, coercion was routinely used to enforce settler compliance with government orders. Settlers were encouraged, for example, to plant potatoes, fodder crops, and even mulberry trees for the raising of silkworms, but if settlers refused to grow one of the recommended crops they faced corporal punishment.[102]

THE INNOVATIVE AND OBEDIENT PEASANT

Progressive eighteenth-century Germans viewed peasants as an essential component of German economic development. In contrast to the gentry-oriented agricultural journals of England and France, enlightened German rulers provided small producers with access to knowledge of the new agriculture. In Prussia, Frederick the Great ordered 40,000 copies of a farm journal distributed to Silesian peasants free of charge, and generously subsidized efforts to teach peasants more productive agricultural behavior. After 1772, calendars, almanacs, and "agricultural" primers for peasant children began to circulate in the Prussian countryside, along with fictional success stories about "hard-working Hans," who found happiness and prosperity by manuring his fields and fencing off his property. The pedagogical treatises of Pestalozzi were filled with accounts of rural life which celebrated the virtues of sobriety and obedience, new systems of field use, and the delights of private ownership.[103]

The ideal German peasant appeared in 1761 in a book entitled *The Rural Socrates*, by a Swiss peasant named Kleinjogg.[104] To many progressives, Kleinjogg's maxims for a an obedient, conservative and hard-working small producer were a dream come true. He became an international celebrity, visited by Goethe and a variety of European kings and princes. His book was translated into French in 1762, and republished in 1764, 1768, and 1777, with a dedication to the elder Mirabeau; Arthur Young sponsored an English version in 1773. Even the Physiocrats—notoriously unsympathetic to peasants—were enthusiastic about Kleinjogg's ideas. In the words of Mirabeau, "Kleinjogg is my hero in all things." As a measure of his esteem for Kleinjogg, Arthur Young had *The Rural Socrates* bound together with his *Rural Oeconomics* and republished in English in 1773, 1776, and 1792.[105]

Although Kleinjogg was praised above all as a "simple peasant" who understood the virtues of enclosure, his popularity did not merely reflect the widespread eighteenth-century interest in farming. To well-born advocates of progress, Kleinjogg's reflections on religion, family life, and the joys of hard and uncomplaining effort to improve the land provided welcome reassurance that economic innovation by small producers need not threaten traditional social distinctions. Kleinjogg was living proof that agricultural improvement—including enclosure— would not destabilize the hierarchies of society and the state.

The belief that economically innovative peasants would be content with unequal economic, social, and political status may well explain why Germans of the upper class were more willing than their French counterparts to claim the peasant majority of the population as participants in the development process. While French progressives situated the peasant majority of the population at the periphery of their economic strategies, German reformers placed them much closer to the center.[106] Unlike *philosophes* who deplored the sufferings of primitive peasants, and Physiocrats who conceived of an agricultural economy without small producers, German reformers portrayed the peasant as an at least potentially rational and moral social element. According to Justi and Sonnenfels, small and medium-sized family farms were potentially both productive and efficient economic units. Sonnenfels even suggested that large holdings be broken so that family farms, which supported a larger population, could contribute to the increased productivity of the nation.[107]

According to eighteenth-century German reformers, agricultural revolution did not require fundamental change in any other sphere of political or social life. As they saw it, anticommunal measures could go forward while each social class remained fixed in its proper place. In keeping with their vision of modernization, a wealthy minority would remain in control of a peasant majority rendered more sensible, prosperous, and *politically passive* by education and technological progress. Neither Frederick the Great nor Germany's leading economists feared the emergence of a more highly educated, property-seeking lower class. The Cameralist Justi did not believe that schooling would lead peasants to question established authority; Sonnenfels was not afraid that the acquisition of capital would encourage a "rural Socrates" to challenge the power of Germany's traditional aristocracy. Eighteenth-century German scholars and officials argued that maintenance of the political and social status quo was perfectly compatible with fundamental economic change.

In contrast to their English and French counterparts, Germans placed a high priority on the schooling of the common people (Arthur Young's "Goths and Vandals"). Claiming that education—in the form of literacy campaigns or training projects to encourage new methods of field use— was a tool for *socializing* peasants rather than integrating them as equals within German society, Cameralists drew a clear distinction between changes in the production process and reforms which might threaten traditional power relationships within society and the state.[108] As they saw it, literate peasants who used modern agricultural techniques and practices would not become rebels or try to join the ranks of the gentry; they were instead likely to become conservative supporters of a benevolent state.

More than a century later, the Russian Bolshevik V. I. Lenin advanced the argument that the emergence of a capitalist economy—no matter how exploitative its social and economic features—did not guarantee the eventual outbreak of revolution. In his political tract *What Is To Be Done?* Lenin claimed that capitalists would devise fraudulent appeals and programs to fool the workers and ensure that even a sizable and impoverished urban proletariat would be reluctant to challenge the ruling elite. According to Lenin, the hegemonic power of capitalist ideology was so potent that unless workers were guided by a vanguard political party, they would humbly accept and even support inegalitarian social and economic systems.[109] In a sense, enlightened German scholars and officials of the eighteenth century might have understood Lenin very well. But for them it was not a challenge but a comfort to believe that transforming the agricultural economy—complete with the destruction of common lands and practices—posed no dangers to the survival of the traditional hierarchies of society and the state. In the eighteenth century, German proponents of economic development were confident that the sweeping changes they advocated would strengthen an authoritarian state and enrich a *noblesse commercante*.

Theories and Realities of Eighteenth-Century Rural Development

In general, German economists agreed with Anglo-French theorists that the controls traditionally exercised by peasant communities were incompatible with economic growth and development. But while Germans believed that a capitalist economic transformation required government leadership and guidance, English and French economists ignored or downplayed the government's substantial legal support for private economic initiatives. Classical liberalism's critique of peasants and their communities was not narrowly economic—it was argued that the disappearance of small producers and their brutish social ties enhanced the cause of individual liberty, creativity, cultural opportunity, and in the English case, the establishment of limited government. Liberal economic writings about England, Ireland, and the French countryside portrayed the peasant community as an obstacle to progress. In contrast, the "magnate-improver" was celebrated as a world-wide agent of civilization and economic progress whose achievements and contributions were impossible to overstate.

Romanticizing and exaggerating the very real achievements of the "man of property," liberal economists did less than justice to the evidence of complexity, flexibility, and initiative shown by English tenants, the peasants of Picardy, and the Walloon region of France. Although small producer claims to land on the basis of birthright, labor and community membership rather than deed and contract were denounced as conservative, such labels do not explain the small farmer's refusal to accept policies and principles whose immediate benefits accrued so disproportionately to other social groups. In the words of an anonymous letter written to the Duke of Buccleuch in 1792, "We are convinced that the Benefit, if any arising from Inclosure, will not be an Object worth of Your Grace's Notice to endeavor to increase Your Grace's Income at the expence of so many necessitated persons."

In Germany, support for enclosure and private enterprise coexisted with a positive view of the small producer. Viewing peasants as a social element capable of productive and profitable labor but wonderfully content to remain at the bottom of the social order,[110] economics-minded Germans praised the obedient and God-fearing, conscientious, and well-educated peasant as the ideal subject of a paternalistic state.

Both the Anglo-French models of unlimited freedom of choice and German strategies for unlimited state and seigneurial control were examples of utopian myth-making which obscured some of the complex realities of rural development in the eighteenth century.[111] However, as Georges Sorel so long ago observed, myths are not lies; they are ideas which inspire men and women with visions of the future and move them to collective actions to realize their visions.[112] The Anglo-French ideal of a peasantless world of powerful property owners acting on a large scale, unhampered by government restrictions or communal rights, shaped many European and US development strategies in the nineteenth and twentieth century.[113] The German approach exerted particular influence over the theory and practice of authoritarian modernizers elsewhere. Its leading proponents—most notably the economists Schlözer and Jakob—would pursue their professional careers in tsarist Russia, where they served with distinction as professors of economics, as officials in the Ministry of Finance, and as advisers to Russia's wealthiest serfowners.

Chapter Two

IN THE LIGHT AND SHADOW OF THE WEST

PROGRESS IN THE AGE OF ENLIGHTENMENT

T HE IDEA THAT Westernization is a process which produces only positive outcomes has dominated both Western and Soviet accounts of Russian intellectual and cultural history.[1] To describe someone as "pro-Western" has meant, by and large, that one believes in progress, rational economic behavior, political and religious tolerance, civilization, and human freedom. Although this rather uncritical approach to the study of Western influence has produced important research and analytical insights, the assumption that Western culture is homogeneous and without drawbacks is highly problematic. As we have seen, the economic histories of Germany, France, and England do not exemplify a single model or pattern.

This chapter tells an important part of the story of Westernizing economists, officials and, serfowners who sought to transform the Russian countryside during the reign of Catherine the Great. Because the educated Russians who looked Westward for ideals of freedom have already been carefully studied by other scholars,[2] I have chosen to pay particular attention to the more typical eighteenth-century Westernizer, whose motives for becoming "European" were far less idealistic. Long before the eighteenth century, members of Russia's elite sought to make use of Western culture in order to extend or to legitimize the power, privilege, and wealth that they already possessed. Their notions of progress may best be captured in the phrase "repressive modernization."

CONTEXTS FOR CHANGE

Peasant Farmers on the Russian Land

> Decrease and increase are under the authority of Almighty God.
> *(Archangel peasant, 1787)*

In the Russian context, the eighteenth-century Western faith in unlimited progress through the application of reason, technology, and the magic of property was not easily come by. In comparison with England, France, and the states of Germany, Russian farming was carried out against far heavier odds. The recurrence of agricultural catastrophe in different historical circumstances over the course of many centuries, suggests that the sense of powerlessness with which peasants and landlords traditionally faced the Russian land may have been neither ignorant nor unrealistic. Environment as well as culture conspired against the easy application of Western wisdom.

In the eighteenth century, Russia's population was concentrated in the forest zone north of the River Oka, a region covered by bogs and swamps where the heaviness and length of snowfall severely limited crop choice and provided far less time for fieldwork than in many Western nations. In the Moscow region, for example, most peasants cultivated grain but could not survive without the import of additional grain from other regions of the Empire. Although the newly acquired territory to the South was far more fertile, precipitation rates in this area were so erratic and produced such dramatic fluctuations in consumption and price levels that by the 1800s, the weather became increasingly important as a destabilizing factor in the national economy as a whole.[3] Both climatic and demographic challenges posed obstacles to the introduction of Western methods of field use. In comparison with England (where a temperate climate permitted livestock to live outdoors for eight months out of the year) Russians had to shelter their livestock indoors for six or seven months. This cut by roughly a third both the number of animals that could be fed by a season's forage crops and the amount of manure available as fertilizer. In the sparsely populated nonblack-earth region, the planting and harvesting of forage crops increased by a third the demand for labor at the two peak seasons if the same area were to be cultivated.[4]

Environmental constraints of this sort were neither occasional nor temporary. Centuries of struggle filled with foolish errors, unforeseeable setbacks, common sense, and ingenuity routinely produced disastrous results. In the Russian experience, human effort never succeeded in transforming either the thin gray soil of the frigid North or the drought-prone black-earth region of the Southwest into a reliable source of abundance. Although agricultural productivity rates seem to have risen in the course of the eighteenth century, there is no evidence that rural innovation was a contributing factor. As a result of Imperial Russia's successful wars of conquest, the cultivated land area increased by 250 percent; more grain was produced per capita in Russia than in any Western European country because a greater amount of land was devoted to grain production. In 1800, Russia's average grain yield per unit of arable land was the lowest in Europe.[5]

Far more than their masters or bailiffs, peasants were responsible for day-to-day agricultural decision-making.[6] In order to survive the Russian land and climate, they created for themselves a primitive but not irrational technology which included the *sokha*, an ancient hook plow made of wood except for its iron share, and in the late eighteenth century, the *plug*, a heavier, deep-digging plow. Manure was rarely used as fertilizer; its benefits were not unknown, but subsistence peasants could rarely afford to cultivate forage crops in sufficient quantity to support the number of cattle necessary for an adequate supply of dung. Like their West European counterparts, the peasants of European Russia typically employed open-field cultivation and three-field systems of crop rotation (except in the southern and eastern steppe zone, where farmers alternated periods of continuous cropping with periods of fallow). In some of the northern forest regions, a "slash-burn" method of cultivation sometimes produced even better yields than the three-field crop rotation.[7] However, as population increased and land in the Moscow heartland became more scarce in the course of the eighteenth century, peasants abandoned it for a three-field system. In the face of recurrent famine and a variety of other subsistence crises,[8] peasants' farming methods were neither stagnant nor unchanging.

PEASANT COMMUNALISM

The customs and practices associated with Western open-field cultivation were far more pronounced in the repartitional land communes to which the majority of Russia's population belonged. While scholars disagree over the commune's origin, the sparse and contradictory data available suggests that in ancient times, peasant communes managed common forests and pastures, divided state-imposed tax burdens among their members, and even enforced a system of collective responsibility for tax payment. The practice of periodic repartition was apparently a later phenomenon, encouraged and even initiated by seventeenth-century government officials and landlords in order to facilitate the collection of taxes and feudal dues.[9]

Communes were complex institutions that included a variety of private and collective property claims and practices. Member households possessed the right to farm an allotment comprised of scattered strips of land, and to use common pasture, meadow, and forests. Although allotments were periodically redistributed according to family size, the number of able-bodied workers per family, or some other collective social principle, each household cultivated an allotment with its own tools and livestock. At the same time, the commune's assembly and elected village elders (*skhod*) established rules to govern the frequency and methods of repartition, and various aspects of the crop cycle.

The actual process of repartition represented a powerful challenge to the skills, experience and diplomacy of village elders and the *skhod*. In order to divide commune fields into pieces of approximately equal size and productivity, they had to know the fertility, topography, accessibility, drainage, and all other significant features of commune land. Their job was to create a number of fields of roughly equal quality, subdivide each of them into smaller units, and divide each unit into strips of approximately the same size and shape. Each household was then allotted the number of strips appropriate to the number of "souls" or tax units living in the homestead. Even in the West and South of Russia, where repartitioning was rare and limited forms of hereditary (*podvornoe*) usage prevailed, village assemblies that included the head of each peasant household and one or more elected village elders carried out many of the same functions as their counterparts in repartitional communes. It was they who decided when crops were to be sown or harvested on the peasant allotments. Whether or not they practiced periodic repartition, peasant villages were held collectively responsible for the enforcement of gentry and government demands, and organized the labor of member households for the sowing, cultivation and harvesting of the master's *demesne* land.

The survival of the pre-Emancipation commune was not due to inertia or conservatism, but to the benefits it conferred upon a wide range of political and social groups within Imperial Russian society. Gentry and state authorities made use of it for the collection of taxes and feudal dues—once the total amount owed by a particular village was established, commune officials were required to determine the share of each peasant household and then to collect it. Villages with inadequate holdings might ask the government to grant them land used by another village with a surplus; in the interests of security and to ensure a stable flow of revenue for the gentry or the state, such requests were sometimes granted.

Egalitarian repartitions also served the interests of wealthier commune members, because redistribution applied only to household allotments and left untouched the inequalities in livestock and garden produce owned by individual households. When feudal dues were set according to the paying capacity of the village as a whole and collected according to a system of mutual guarantees, land equalizations freed richer peasants from financial responsibility for their poorer neighbors by enabling each household to meet its externally imposed burdens. Repartition also functioned to ensure that peasants equalized land among themselves instead of making land claims against the gentry.

It should be emphasized that peasant communes were in no sense havens of equality and harmony. Habits of acting in common were embedded in a system of patriarchal control by village elders and heads of households who fought with each other and freely inflicted violence upon the women and children subject to their authority. Community-based rituals of shaming and corporal punishment were routinely inflicted on the transgressors of village norms. It was not uncommon for votes by the village assembly to be decided according to the interests of wealthy families who supplied substantial amounts of liquor to the voters.[10] Nevertheless, as the Russian gentry noted with contempt and dismay, when times were hard, rich and poor banded together in collective actions that threatened the property, the wealth, or even the lives of their masters.

UNFREE LABOR

The symmetry of gentry and peasant interests became increasingly precarious in the course of the eighteenth century, because of the changes that took place in the condition of serfdom, which was Imperial Russia's other "peculiar institution." In important respects, the emergence of bondage highlights the difference between the historical trajectories of Western Europe and of Russia, where serfdom reached its height just as it was disappearing in the West. By 1800, bound peasants represented more than half of the adult male population of about 30 million. They paid their masters a portion of their crops (*obrok*), forced labor service (*barshchina*), or a combination of the two.[11] Particularly in the sparsely populated territory to the North and East, most peasants who did not live on gentry-owned land were bound to land belonging to the state. Required to pay *obrok* and taxes, and to render labor service (but far less than serfs), state peasants were not very closely supervised by government officials as long as they met their financial obligations. However, state peasants came increasingly under siege in the late eighteenth century, as ambitious serfowners sought to expand their estates and the size of their labor force by seizing state land and peasants.

Although it has been argued that peasants who owed labor obligations were far more closely supervised than those liable only for the payment of *obrok*, one study of eighteenth-century Novgorod province suggests that such distinctions may have been overdrawn. In Novgorod at least, serfowners apparently knew so little about farming and were so short of capital for improvements that even on *barshchina* estates, peasants were "on their own" when it came to farming the land.[12] In some areas, peasants were given the whole of the estate to cultivate, with the landlord collecting *obrok* once or twice a year. In *obrok* regions, landlords usually visited their estates during the summer months, and spent most of the year in government offices or filled the rolls of army regiments. Under the *barshchina* system, only a portion of the estate's land, and usually the smaller portion, was used by peasants to produce for their own needs.

On the bulk of the estate (the *demesne*) they were required to perform labor for a time period fixed by their masters. In general, intervention by serfowners into village life was seldom related to agricultural issues. Reports of peasant unrest,[13] a decline in *obrok* payments, or the opportunity to mobilize peasants as a private army for seizing land to which they possessed no legal claim were far more powerful as motivating factors.[14]

The high incidence of lawsuits, feuds, and pitched battles over territorial boundaries reflected the overwhelming gentry preference for expanding their estates rather than introducing new technology or field systems. As far as either productivity rates or modes of cultivation are concerned, it did not seem to matter whether the prevalent form of exploitation was *obrok*, *barshchina*, or a mixture of the two. It is equally difficult to find evidence that size counted as a factor; peasant farming methods did not significantly vary on large or small holdings. Even giant estates bore little resemblance to modern-day models of large-scale agriculture; most often, they were simply land units which contained a greater multiplicity of allotments and scattered strips than the smaller holdings.[15]

Although the gentry blamed low productivity rates on peasant stupidity and laziness, it should be noted that the institution of serfdom created powerful economic disincentives. Bound peasants were required to cultivate strips of land in the *demesne* before farming their own, with the profits of the master given first priority. Due to the master's overriding privileges, peasant households which—through luck, innovation, or hard work—were able to produce harvests on their own allotments that exceeded the harvest on the lord's *demesne* were forced to accept the product of the "worst" fields. In addition, it was customary for masters and bailiffs to impose fines upon peasants who failed to pay their rent or dues with the best grain they had (the lesser quality grain was to be used for sowing the strips cultivated by commune households).[16]

In the eighteenth century, serfs and state peasants alike would have been hard-pressed to recall any significant limitations on the degree of coercion that could be inflicted upon them by gentry or state authorities. Once the successors of Peter the Great hit upon the strategy of buying support for their dubious political claims by encouraging the gentry to rule as autocrats on their own estates, peasants were increasingly sold apart from their families and from the land (but together with horses and pigs on the same auction block). Although Russia's elite were in no sense uniquely or universally cruel, they were no more able to resist the temptations of absolute power than slaveowners in other parts of the world. Individuals, families, and whole villages were won and lost by the hundreds at card games, while good-looking peasant girls were transported by the shipload to St. Petersburg serf markets. A Russian serfowner could demand that a peasant's feet be held to the fire as punishment for drowning the puppies that his wife had been ordered to breast-feed. In 1753, the Russian Senate recognized that cutting off the hands of peasants as punishment for insubordination prevented them from performing useful work, and replaced this form of punishment by knouting or nose-slitting, which possessed the advantage of marking criminals for life even if they fled the estates of their masters.[17] In eighteenth-century Russia, Westernization emerged in the context of a dramatic expansion of gentry freedom of action and the degeneration of serfdom into a condition virtually indistinguishable from chattel slavery.

Early Perspectives on the West

That Western civilization might cast shadow as well as light upon the Russian scene was evident as early as the fifteenth century, when Russian churchmen looked Westward to the Spanish Inquisition for new strategies to deal with dissent and heresy. In 1490, the Archbishop of Novgorod wrote admiringly of Ferdinand of Spain: "Look at the firmness the Latins display ... the way in which the King of Spain cleansed [ochistil] his land." Russian inquisitions were subsequently launched to deal with the "Judaizer" heresy in the style of Western Europeans.[18]

The peasantry's early encounters with the West rarely inspired hopes for greater freedom or opportunity. In general, they responded with fear and hostility to Western military incursions, proselytizing efforts, and commercial dealings. Imperial Russia's rulers were more ambivalent; but even the most Orthodox and conservative of the tsars welcomed foreign military advisers and employed Western engineers to build armaments factories whose guns and cannons extended the repressive reach of the autocracy and tightened the bonds of serfdom.

As a Westernizer *par excellence*, Peter the Great increased government and gentry power over the peasantry even as he promoted Western science, industry, and education. His reign saw (1) the creation of a new and more wretched category of industrial serfs who were bound to mines and factories rather than land, (2) the increased use of the death penalty against those judged to be "insolent and dangerous," and (3) the imposition of flogging as a penalty for peasants who refused to use a "modern" scythe instead of a "backward" sickle. In many respects, Westernization widened the gap between Russia's ruling elite and the rest of the population. and further constrained the serf's freedom of action. In one of the more poignant fantasy images of retribution from below, an eighteenth-century cartoon portrayed the Westernizing Peter the Great as a cat being buried by a horde of mice.[19]

From the outset, Russia's Western orientation was overwhelmingly German, due to the Russian army's conquest of Baltic German territory, to Peter the Great's propensity for marrying his offspring to German rulers great and small,[20] and above all to the links between German Cameralism and the traditions of Russian statecraft. In the eighteenth century, Russians became a familiar sight at German universities in Strasbourg, Leipzig, and Göttingen. At the same time, the Russian government invited foreigners to settle in Russian cities and towns and to establish model agricultural colonies in the provinces. Hoping to making their fortune in service to the Russian "barbarians of the North," a host of scholars, merchants, bureaucrats, and soldiers from Germany and elsewhere in Europe poured into the country. In the forefront of this Eastward migration were an assortment of world-famous scholars like Ludwig von Euler and August von Schlözer, who left the University of Göttingen to found universities, advise government reformers, and mentor the numerous Baltic German and Russian students of law, history, and political economy who became government ministers and scholar-officials in the last decades of the eighteenth century.[21] At Moscow University, Germans constituted the majority of the faculty, lectured in Latin and, on occasion, outnumbered their students.[22]

In general, Russia's German *Kulturträgers* were Cameralists eager to bureaucratize the state and introduce manorial statutes, courts, and codes of behavior as the basis for enlightened estate management. Although whipping, forced military recruitment, and compulsory marriage came well recommended long before the introduction of "German" methods, émigré scholars encouraged Russian serfowners to believe that when exorbitant demands for labor or dues were made systematic and uniform, they could be justified as rational, Western-style economic management. In eighteenth-century German-Russian scenarios for reform, the ideals of reason and regimentation advanced in tandem.[23]

In many respects, the Cameralist mindset was quite familiar to reform-minded Russians. Like the German scholar Justi, the self-taught Ivan Pososhkov advised Peter the Great to regulate the size and location of peasant dwellings and establish peasant schools to foster "a fear of idleness" in addition to the elements of reading, writing, and ciphering.[24] Although Pososhkov also recommended aid to serfs mistreated by their masters, he was far more concerned to thwart the peasantry's "natural" propensity for dishonest and apathetic behavior. To encourage the use of more stringent compulsion and constant supervision, he proposed that landlords be held responsible for the prevention of carousing and excessive drinking by the peasants they owned.[25]

The use of heightened surveillance and control to increase productivity rates was very much to the mind of serfowners like A. P. Volynskii, who issued orders that the able-bodied poor in his villages be "handed over" to wealthier neighbors who would supply them with food and clothing in return for labor. To ensure the productive labor of each of his bound peasants, Volynskii demanded that one out of every ten men in each of his villages spy on the other nine by reporting on any "inappropriate" behavior. By providing incentives for spying rather than solidarity, Volynskii hoped to promote obedience, greater agricultural output, and an increase in his *obrok* payments.[26]

Far more humane in his outlook, the reformer V. N. Tatishchev argued that peasants deserved the right to make use of adequate-sized allotments, to have access to medical care, and to be free from arbitrary or excessive demands for *obrok* or *barshchina*. However, Tatishchev's benevolence was frequently overshadowed by his visceral hatred for peasant apathy and idleness. As he saw it, "laziness cannot be permitted; other than the few holidays when peasants are excused from work, they must not celebrate; whoever is lazy at work must go to jail and not be given food for 2–3 days."[27] Tatishchev proposed a comprehensive program for year-round peasant labor at sixteen hours a day, with lessons on appropriate moral and practical behavior provided for the peasantry's remaining time. Like Volynskii, he believed that the best way to teach peasants to avoid rebellious acts and thoughts, to fear idleness, and to use an improved plow, was to hand unfit laborers over to other commune households who would appropriate their land and support them until their behavior improved.[28]

Similar conceptions of order and progress pervaded the writings of the plebeian M. I. Lomonosov, Russia's leading scientist and all-around eighteenth-century "man of genius." As a Westernizer and a patriot, Lomonosov wanted Russians rather than Germans to take the lead as scholars and government advisers in initiatives for change. At the same time, in his approach to issues of rural economic development, Lomonosov's attitudes were quite "German." Adept at compiling lengthy lists of prohibitions on peasant idleness and "useless" holidays, Lomonosov translated a German study of estate management and wrote several essays on Baltic agriculture, which emphasized the need to replace arbitrary and "irrational" gentry demands with more systematic, comprehensive, and bureaucratic procedures, which defined peasant obligations to their masters.[29]

WESTERNIZATION IN THE REIGN OF CATHERINE THE GREAT

It was in this Cameralist-oriented context that the German-born Catherine came to power in 1762 through a coup which resulted in the murder of her husband, Tsar Peter III. With claims to rule even flimsier than the dubious eighteenth-century claimants to the Russian throne who preceded her, Catherine was at pains to placate a restive nobility. As she attempted to achieve this goal by promoting the expansion of the judicial and punitive powers of the serfowning gentry, she discovered that Western culture could also serve as a particularly effective legitimizing device.

Like Louis XIV, who devised elaborate social rituals to divert his nobles from engaging in politically subversive activities, Catherine quickly recognized the political advantage to be gained by promoting Westernization. In the early years of her reign, members of Russia's upper class who could afford it (and many who could not) were encouraged to develop an insatiable demand for the tutors, lackeys, and hairdressers who were to render them indistinguishable from the French nobility. The effort to become European knew no bounds. To the disgust and amazement of the remainder of the population, a tiny segment of Russia's upper class proclaimed themselves "Voltairean" in their contempt for the Russian church and for "medieval" peasant superstition. "Gallomania" spread to the provinces, and enterprising Swedes made their fortunes by hiring themselves out as tutors to gullible Russian serfowners who thought they were learning French![30] Aspiring "Westernizers" of this sort seldom traveled abroad, and read little foreign literature. Although they were eager to distinguish themselves from the "barbarism" of peasants by adopting European language, dress and manners, they showed little inclination to modify traditional Russian institutions or power relationships. Rejecting Western ideals of individual freedom, they considered the acquisition of a "Western" standard of elegance and luxury to be the true mark of a Russian "European."[31]

The Debate on Development Begins

> As I already had a certain understanding of economic societies in other countries . . . I almost jumped with joy . . . when I saw the same kind of thing had been set up in our country. . . . And my satisfaction grew even greater when I saw that, following foreign example, all nobles living in the provinces had been invited to communicate their economic observations to the Society, along with people of every rank. . . .
> *(A. T. Bolotov)*[32]

By the last decades of the eighteenth century, a familiarity with Western economic ideas became a further line of demarcation between the "Russian European" and less Westernized compatriots.[33] At the highest levels of society, Russians became Physiocrats and Liberals. D. A. Golitsyn, a disciple of the Physiocrats and Catherine's ambassador to Paris, authored a book entitled *The Spirit of the Economists*, and Count Jacob J. Sievers returned from many years' residence in England an admirer of Adam

Smith and an advocate of agricultural reform. Moscow University's S. T. Desnitskii and I. T. Tretiakov studied at the University of Edinburgh with Adam Smith, Adam Ferguson, and William Russell, who in turn attended Princess Dashkova's Edinburgh salon.[34] In the late eighteenth century, educated Russians from the lower ranks of the nobility discovered that by participating in debates over Western economic theory they could gain *entrée* into social circles which would otherwise have been closed to them. To agricultural experts like A. T. Bolotov, the opportunity to exchange ideas with enlightened Russian princes became a form of upward mobility.[35]

In 1765, Russia's entrance into eighteenth-century European economic debates was marked by the establishment of the Imperial Free Economic Society for the Encouragement of Agricultural and Household Management. Created by a handful of reform-minded German and Russian bureaucrats and academicians with the support of Catherine II, the Society appointed Western experts like Arthur Young and Jacques Necker as honorary members, promoted the translation of foreign scholarly works,[36] and published a variety of specialized journals as well as its own *Proceedings*. Like its Western counterparts, the Russian Society asked members to report on rural conditions and sponsored over 200 essay competitions dealing with questions of agricultural and economic development between 1765 and 1820. In the Society's first competition, it is significant that 129 of 160 entries were in German; only 5 were written in Russian.[37]

Neither peasant emancipation, systems of field use, technology, nor the scarcity of capital took center stage in the Society's early deliberations. Members were especially interested in questions of land tenure, and more specifically in the delicate issue of whether property rights should be extended to the bound peasants currently being bought and sold by the Society's founders and supporters. The Free Economic Society's first essay competition asked the question: "What is more beneficial to society . . . that the peasant should have land as property, or only movable property, and how far should the right to property be extended?"[38]

From the outset, defenders of private property encountered few critics. As a student of Adam Smith, the scholar Desnitskii argued that the more highly developed a nation, the more unwavering its defense of private ownership. Praising political systems which linked the franchise with property ownership, he contended that the insecurity of tenure was both a sign and a source of economic backwardness. As he reflected on the evils of serfdom, Desnitskii concluded that "worst of all, he [the serf] could not own even the smallest bit of property."[39] The Physiocrat Golitsyn cited Mercier de la Rivière's rather grandiose claim that private property "gives rise to security and spiritual peace; from this peace develops curiosity, and curiosity encourages all forms of knowledge of the arts, trade and the sciences."[40] Golitsyn argued as well that "culture and civilization prospered only in countries where peasants possessed rights of private ownership."

The Strasbourg-educated A. I. Polenov contended that by awakening in peasants the desire to acquire property, many of Russia's most pressing economic and noneconomic problems could be solved. Certain that the love of property constituted the chief incentive for productive human action, he argued that when peasants became landowners, they would become energetic, responsible, and filled with initiative. On the other hand, the peasantry's inability to own property caused the depression responsible for the high rate of peasant alcoholism. In the mind of Polenov, the "magic of property" was truly all-encompassing.

Beardé de L'Abbaye of Aachen University won the Free Economic Society's first competition with an essay which argued that private ownership was admirable precisely because it *reinforced* traditional power relationships. Beardé argued that peasants who owned land would become so intent on guarding it from trespassers and making it more profitable, that masters would no longer need to hire bailiffs and watchmen to keep serfs from running away. As he saw it, extending rights of landownership to peasants—and even freeing them—would bring peace and harmony to a gentry-dominated Russian countryside.

Even though Beardé's essay attempted to demonstrate that the introduction of private-property rights for peasants served the interests of the serfowner, it was only narrowly approved for publication. Influential critics like Count Sievers, the brothers Orlov and Prince M. M. Shcherbatov contended that the publication of writings which favored granting peasants the right to own landed property might encourage disobedience to seigneurial authority and encourage peasant claims on the property of their masters. Conservatives like Sumarokov declared that emancipation contradicted the dictates of common sense. In his words, "The canary bird would be better pleased to have no cage, and the dog would prefer to be without a chain. But the bird would fly away, and the dog would bite. One is therefore necessary for the peasant, the other for the noble."[41] It is revealing of the Society's fears that Beardé's essay and the other contest entries were circulated among the judges in a locked despatch case to which only they had the key.

Gentry discussions of emancipation usually focused on the liberation of serfs who belonged to others—church peasants, for example, or those belonging to the Imperial family. Arguing that freed peasants would be less sullen and more obedient, Prince Golitysn declared that Western experience had shown that freedom allayed the peasantry's "senseless hostility" to the nobility. Prince Gagarin suggested that masters ensure that only richer and more reliable peasants obtained their freedom by charging a hefty redemption payment of 250 rubles per head, to be paid in one lump sum. Beardé de L'Abbaye contended that if peasants were freed, "the rich, not being troubled by constant supervision, [would] receive their income punctually and in considerable amounts." Arguing that freedom would transform a serf prone to violence into a docile and grateful laborer, he asked, wouldn't any master prefer "an affectionate puppy" [a free peasant] to an "evil bear" [a serf]?[42]

In many respects, advocates of private-property rights attributed to property the role that Marx later ascribed to religion in the *Communist Manifesto*: Operating as an "opiate of the masses" rather than a source of Lockean-style aspirations toward liberty, property rights were to transform peasants into obedient servants of the gentry and the state. Like their German counterparts, members of the Free Economic Society argued that the economic theories of Quesnay and Adam Smith would serve to reinforce and strengthen traditional political and social power relationships. But they were notably unsuccessful in convincing either the empress or their gentry colleagues. And when Catherine invited the Physiocrat Mercier de la Rivière to Moscow, a single meeting with the famous Physiocrat convinced her to dismiss Mercier's theories as "dangerous nonsense" which could turn Russian society upside down.[43] In preparing her "Legislative Instruction" of 1767, Catherine did not draw on the wisdom of the Physiocrats. Instead, she ordered the English-trained Desnitskii to translate Blackstone's *Commentaries* and studied the Cameralist writings of Justi and Bielefeld.[44]

THE LEGISLATIVE "INSTRUCTION" AND ASSEMBLY OF 1767

To her European admirers, Catherine the Great's "Instruction" demonstrated that she was truly one of Europe's most Enlightened rulers. Voltaire, already in receipt of the financial subsidies which turned him into one of her most shameless publicity agents in Western Europe, proclaimed Catherine's "Instruction" "the finest monument of the century."[45] The German Romantic thinker Johann Herder, who was resident in Riga in 1767, welcomed the document as a sign that the German-born Catherine was destined to civilize her barbarian subjects (with the aid of educational treatises which Herder volunteered to write). According to Herder, Russia might bring Europe a second Renaissance, with the Ukraine serving as the West's new Greece.[46]

Whatever its virtues may have been, Catherine's 1767 "Instruction" contained a dizzying array of contradictory declarations and promises, which reflected not only the competing imperatives of classical liberalism and Cameralism, but also the cautious and fearful hand of the Russian nobles who censored it beforehand and deleted all references to peasant emancipation. At one point, the "Instruction" declared that the love of property would solve Russia's economic problems, and threatened the indolent with deprivation of the means of subsistence. At another, it recommended that all citizens be guaranteed "a certain support during life; such as wholesome food, proper clothing and a way of life not prejudicial to health in general." Between these two extremes, various articles suggested that both masters and serfs would benefit from a regularization of feudal dues and the granting of some property rights to the peasantry.[47]

While Catherine's "Instruction" did not become the basis for a new law code, it served as the prelude to the widely heralded "Legislative Assembly"" of 1767.[48] Convened with the unprecedented goal of encouraging public debate over Russia's future development, the Legislative Assembly included elements of the urban population and a number of state peasants, but was dominated by serfowners. Although it was probably as representative as many Western European parliaments of the day, Assembly delegates were in general far less Westernized, less well-born, and less receptive to change than the founders of the Free Economic Society. The "Instructions" and grievances they solicited from local inhabitants before the Assembly convened clearly demonstrate that in 1767, the gentry constituency for reform was extremely weak.[49]

Both the provincial "Instructions" and the Assembly debates were notably silent on the subject of agricultural change, innovation, property rights, or economic development. A study of the instructions from Tula province paints a gloomy picture of serfowners, unaware that there were more productive ways to make use of land and labor, and hostile to the slightest change in the status quo.[50] When the Assembly convened, a solitary delegate from Kostroma proposed a discussion of agricultural improvement, but the rarity of such comments highlighted what has been described as the general "obliviousness" to the fundamental issue of economic backwardness."[51]

Well aware of the conservatism of his colleagues, the economist Desnitskii declined to raise the issue of free labor as either a moral or an economic question.[52] A liberal-minded serfowner named Korobin who recommended the regulation of seigneurial demands and protection of peasant property from gentry encroachment was denounced as a "firebrand" and a "criminal agitator." Support for Korobin came from the twenty-nine-member peasant delegation, whose leaders courageously testified about gentry misdeeds before a predominantly gentry Assembly.[53] The state peasant Ivan Chuprov of Archangel asked serfowners to recognize their responsibility to protect and care for the poor. The peasant-soldier Ivan Zherebtsov of Nizhni Novgorod proposed that greedy and dishonest bailiffs be replaced by elders annually elected by the peasant communes.[54] But notions of this sort were summarily rejected by Assembly delegates.

Indifferent to questions of agricultural innovation or peasant welfare, delegates enthusiastically debated the best strategies to deal with peasant runaways, thieves, and brigands who, in the words of one delegate, "particularly kill the nobility." Merchant delegates—in flat contradiction to the Western image of the freedom-loving bourgeoisie—demanded that they as well as the gentry be granted rights of serfownership.[55] Terrified at reports of peasant unrest (apparently fueled by unfounded rumors that a statute limiting forced-labor service [*barshchina*] was in the offing), Assembly delegates demanded that villages be held collectively responsible for the wrongdoing of any one of their members. The use of torture was proposed both as a deterrent and as a strategy for obtaining speedy confessions. One delegate suggested that if a single peasant household "criminally" sheltered a suspect, the village as a whole should be required to pay aggrieved serfowners 300 rubles for each male and 150 for each female.[56]

Although progressive Europeans were quite aware of the convocation of Russia's first Legislative Assembly, it is unlikely that Russia's peasants knew very much about it. But an anonymous serf poet of Catherine's reign provided a devastating commentary on the Assembly's cruelty, viciousness and obsession with punishment. In his words, "They are changing the laws to their own advantage. They would give themselves the liberty to torture us to death."[57]

PROPERTY RIGHTS AND COERCION

In the reign of Catherine II, gentry projects for land reform consistently linked private ownership with the introduction of new constraints on peasant freedom of action. In a proposal by I. P. Elagin, communal property was to be replaced by hereditary allotments granted to the head of each peasant household, whose members were obliged to render absolute obedience to the head of the family, to a village leader appointed for life, and above all to a master who was to be regarded with "love and fear."[58] Economic initiative was to flourish on land that was privately owned, but could not be either bought or sold. According to Elagin's plan, innovative peasant proprietors would be guided and controlled by a new and more powerful set of authorities.

While Elagin's plan was never implemented, Count Jacob Sievers's reform proposals were put into effect with disastrous results. Sievers was a founder of the Imperial Free Economic Society, a fervent admirer of Adam Smith, and governor-general of Novgorod province between 1764 and

1781. Widely recognized for his commitment to agricultural innovation, Sievers's agricultural experiments in Novgorod transformed the economic and noneconomic lives of thousands of peasants who lived on Crown and state lands. Under his direction, peasants began to cultivate potatoes, communal tenure was eliminated, *barshchina* obligations were increased, and bailiffs were required to keep detailed, German-style inventories of peasant dues and obligations (*Wachenbücher*). While these innovations resulted in increased productivity rates, they also caused whole *volosts* to erupt in violent opposition. Peasants even risked the legal prohibition against petitioning the Crown in order to lodge complaints against Sievers to Catherine the Great. For his part, Sievers dismissed popular resistance as proof that peasants were far more backward than he had previously imagined.[59]

According to Russia's eighteenth-century Westernizers, the peasantry's character defects required constant regulation, control, and forcible correction. Like England's John Sinclair, who complained about the laziness and stupidity of "labourers and other vermin,"[60] the agronomist Bolotov complained that peasants were "stubborn, willful, petty-minded and vindictive"—too ignorant and apathetic to grasp the obvious superiority of private ownership to communal tenure.[61] On the other hand, the geographer P. I. Rychkov insisted that peasants were dangerous because they were too volatile—so easily aroused to acts of theft and murder that they required an extremely powerful hand to guide and punish them. As Beardé de l'Abbaye observed, "It was dangerous to let a bear free from its chain without first taming it."[62] In general, the gentry's strategy of choice for dealing with the twin evils of passivity and violence was to escalate the level of intervention (tutelage, or *popechitel'stvo*) into the peasantry's communal and private lives.

It should be emphasized that not all gentry interventions were to the peasantry's disadvantage. A number of eighteenth-century serfowners appealed to their colleagues to impose decent standards of hygiene, sanitation, and medical care. Bolotov maintained that "the reasonable proprietor will augment his revenues while trying to maintain in good shape and even to ameliorate [the condition] of the serfs, because they are the very source from which these revenues come." As Michael Confino has suggested, such gentry efforts reflected a certain recognition that the peasant was after all the "goose that laid the golden egg" and needed to be guaranteed a measure of protection and security.[63]

In practice, however, it was not always easy to distinguish between benevolence and unlimited intrusion. According to Bolotov, the "ideal bailiff" was to be everywhere, preventing waste, planting new crops, and getting as much work and revenue from the peasantry as possible. Attempting to keep home consumption down, he would make sure that any surplus was sold as expensively as market conditions would permit. Rychkov proposed to the Free Economic Society that peasant children be put to work at the age of ten in order to prevent them from becoming lazy. Timofei von Klingshtet, a founding member of the Society, recommended that estate stewards ensure that peasants went to church, married early, and made use of good midwives. While Prince Shcherbatov required his female peasants to marry at seventeen, P. A. Rumiantsev insisted the domestics not be permitted to marry "without his specific instructions." According to A. Rebken, "Girls of eighteen years of age ought to be married. Good farmers try to breed cattle and poultry and civilized men should care even more, with the help of God, for the breeding of the human race." Some masters imposed fines on peasants who remained single and ordered wholesale marriages for a particular age cohort.[64]

In general, enlightened serfowners preferred coercion and manipulation to the discipline of the market, the promotion of peasant education, or the assumption of individual responsibility for one's actions. Their strategies for surveillance and control were quite varied and imaginative. It was suggested, for example, that peasants be forcibly trained in new methods of crop rotation, set to teach their neighbors, and punished together with their pupils for any failure to learn. Klingshtet argued that freedom did more harm than good to peasants who didn't know how to make use of it. As an alternative, he recommended that deserving peasants be invited to dine with their masters, congratulated before the whole peasant community, singled out for special notice at religious ceremonies, and provided with special clothing to distinguish them from their neighbors. Although Klingshtet believed that positive reinforcements might well do the trick, other members of the Free Economic Society reported that they overcame peasant resistance to innovation by encouraging envy, conceit, and jealousy. According to Westernizers of this sort, the despicable character and attitudes of the peasantry left their masters with no option save the judicious use of force and deception. As Klingshtet observed, "One can always achieve success if one knows how to make use of human passions."[65]

Whether they advocated new systems of field use or private property rights, reformers like Bolotov assumed that the surest way to instill rational patterns of economic behavior into the recalcitrant minds of the peasantry was to impose "pitiless punishment." Although Bolotov was admired by his peers for his use of improved "English" and "German" systems of crop rotation, he was also known to his peasants as a master who taught them to behave more rationally by having them tied hands and feet, thrown into a bath of steaming water, fed salted fish without being permitted to drink, and then stripped, tarred, and feathered, and paraded through the streets of their villages.[66] Although there is no evidence that Bolotov questioned peasants about their practices and beliefs, he was nevertheless certain that they lacked useful knowledge of the land they cultivated. Dismissing peasants as a "vulgar" subject, Bolotov opted not to discuss them at all in the forty-two combined volumes of his *The Rural Inhabitant* and *Economic Workshop*.[67]

In general, gentry judgments about peasant economic behavior were based on their experience as serfowners, or on reports by other masters, bailiffs, or officials who highlighted peasant apathy, drunkenness, violence, and dishonesty. Although evidence of this kind is significant and revealing, it was—like much eighteenth-century data on the peasantry— quite one-sided. Neither serfowners, bailiffs, nor officials were neutral data-gatherers. While it is unlikely that the peasantry's rulers and supervisors simply invented anecdotes about peasant bad behavior, it would have been interesting to know how eighteenth-century peasant cultivators would have assessed the energy, honesty, intelligence, and farming skills of those who bought and sold them, punished them, and otherwise limited their freedom of action.[68] But this information is not available to us.

Russian reformers were not unique in their reliance on one-sided judgments and evidence. Eighteenth-century policy-makers in England and France were equally unlikely to ask the opinions of agricultural laborers or small-scale proprietors of land. In general, the improvement of rural life was considered the primary responsibility of those who owned or controlled a peasant labor force. Educated Russians who took a different tack were met with skepticism and hostility. When, for example, the Baltic reformer Pastor Eisen tried to involve peasant mothers as participants in his program to increase rates of smallpox inoculation, the local gentry advised him instead to undertake forcible inoculations "for the peasants' own good."[69]

Like the French *philosophes* they so admired, Russia's progressive reformers complained that peasant resistance to education constituted a major obstacle to agricultural improvement. Although available evidence is scanty, it casts a rather different light on peasant attitudes. Nineteenth- and twentieth-century researches indicate that in many cases, when peasants tried to obtain a measure of learning for their children, their masters refused to contribute funds to help them.[70] Reluctant to bear the costs of village schooling, they feared as well that literate peasants might forge passports, write petitions of complaint, or prepare seditious leaflets. The gentry reformer Rychkov contended that such dangers would be reduced if schooling was limited to more well-to-do peasants (and to no more than three percent in a given locale).[71] In an argument that resembled Edmund Burke's,[72] Prince M. M. Shcherbatov argued that it was both futile and dangerous to educate peasants. In his words, "If lowly people are educated, and compare their heavy taxes with the elegance of the rulers and the nobles, yet unaware both of the needs of the state and the uses of that elegance, will they not rebel at the taxes and finally rise in mutiny?"[73]

Among reformers who advocated peasant schools, much emphasis was placed upon the tranquillizing influence of education. Beardé de L'Abbaye recommended that the Russian government create a system of clergy-run schools to teach peasants that by their labor they served the tsar, the gentry, and all of society. Attempting to devise a quasi-religious mission for the peasantry, he contended that better-educated peasants were like soldiers asked to risk their lives in the service of a difficult but sacred calling, which required absolute loyalty and obedience to their superiors.[74]

While peasants were the preferred scapegoat for the ills that plagued Russia's agricultural economy, it is worth noting that serfowners were notoriously indifferent to their own need for schooling. Efforts to recruit them into the educational institutions established in the second half of the eighteenth century were quite unsuccessful. Between 1751 and 1765, only 80 of the 600 students at the Academy of Sciences Gymnasium were nobles (the rest were of plebian origin). Reformers like Bolotov complained that despite their superior resources and access to information, his friends and neighbors were strangely indifferent to appeals to their enlightened self-interest. In the words of Bolotov, "Are we to be like our peasants in our opposition to what is rational and progressive?"[75]

While some serfowners (particularly in the Baltic regions) were willing to make use of the full seigneurial arsenal of punitive measures to introduce German and English tools and field systems, few attempted reform and even fewer were successful. Indifference to agricultural change was widespread among the landed gentry. As A. N. Radishchev sarcastically noted, it was peculiar that in a society in which the only things that masters could *not* do was to free their villagers from state taxes, arrange marriages between relatives, and require them to eat meat during Lent, it was somehow impossible for serfowners to compel peasants to adopt more productive farming practices.[76]

Among the few eighteenth-century Russian Westernizers to question the primacy of coercion and surveillance in Russian rural life was the serfowner A. I. Polenov, whose essay for the Imperial Free Economic Society was awarded a silver medal in 1766. Citing the authority of John Locke, David Hume, and the Cameralist Justi, Polenov contended that Western experience had shown that a nation's prosperity depended on the establishment of rules of law to guarantee the security of persons and of property. While he did not advocate immediate emancipation, Polenov recommended that peasants be granted hereditary allotments in amounts adequate for sowing and for the pasturing of livestock. Denouncing Russian serfdom as a violation of natural law and an infringement on the fundamental right of individuals to own their own persons, he attributed peasant apathy to a lack of freedom. According to Polenov, the peasant would be transformed "only when his power was returned to him." Schools, doctors, and above all, freedom and property rights were in his view the best cure for the evils of Russian rural life. Polenov's essay created a sensation within the Free Economic Society. Although the judges awarded him second prize, they first decided that only a third of the text could be published, and then concluded that it would be better not to publish it at all.[77]

The Society was far happier with the invited comments of Voltaire, whose essay revealed that he was as ready to serve as an apologist for serfdom as he was to act as a publicity agent for Catherine the Great. Although Voltaire was a world-renowned critic of serfdom and of the "parasitic" French nobility, he argued against emancipation in the Russian context. As he saw it, Russia's peasants were so ignorant and brutal that there could be no possible justification for a "forcible" encroachment upon the Russian gentry's human property. It is significant that Voltaire's essay was duly published in its entirety by the Free Economic Society, but Polenov's critique did not appear in print until almost a century later.[78]

RADISHCHEV AND SHCHERBATOV: THE EXCEPTION AND THE RULE

In Russia's eighteenth-century debate on development, A. N. Radishchev was something of an anomaly. A well-born Westernizer who rejected the political caution of reformers like Polenov, Radishchev declared that the demands of justice, the laws of nature, and Russia's economic interests required an immediate emancipation of peasants with land. In his book *A Journey from St. Petersburg to Moscow*, Radishchev portrayed serfdom as a brutalizing relationship which destroyed whatever economic or non-economic potential that either masters of peasants might have possessed as individuals. Rejecting the conventional eighteenth-century century definitions of "society" which excluded the peasant majority of the population, Radishchev advanced the unheard-of suggestion that peasants might themselves possess the intelligence and ability to organize a productive agricultural economy. In a passage from *Journey from St. Petersburg to Moscow*, which probably contributed to the government's decision to place him in a mental hospital, Radishchev wrote:

> O! If the slaves weighted down with fetters, raging in their despair, would with the iron that bars their freedom crush our heads, the heads of their inhuman masters, and redden their fields with their blood! What would the state lose by that? At once from their midst great men would arise . . . to replace the

murdered generation; but they would be of another mind and without the right to oppress others. This is no dream, my vision penetrates the dense curtain of time that veils the future from our eyes. I look through the space of a whole century.[79]

In contrast to most Russian Westernizers of his day, Radishchev was peculiarly free of the reformer's predilection for tutelage, beatings, and psychological manipulation as strategies for change. As he saw it, nothing would so encourage a person to be productive and useful to society as individual freedom of action, the right to acquire property and to engage in unfettered economic activity.

Equally uncommon among Russian reformers was Radishchev's concern over the potentially negative socioeconomic impact of privatization. On the one hand, he admired the incentive-generating aspects of personal ownership; without property rights, it seemed to him impossible for economic initiative to flourish. Propertyless peasants were faced by insuperable constraints: "The fields are not theirs, nor do the fruits of their labor go to them. And so they work lazily and do not care whether the land will turn into wasteland . . ."[80] On the other hand, Radishchev was distressed at the economic inequality and insecurity that was characteristic of property-oriented Western societies. Perhaps, he suggested, the commune was somehow "bad" for agriculture but good for agricultural producers?[81]

Among eighteenth-century admirers of Adam Smith, Radishchev was among the few who shared Smith's belief in individual liberty as well as his misgivings about the negative impact of unfettered free-market competition. Certain that emancipation and political freedom were Russia's immediate priorities, Radishchev suggested that it was for those who came after him to "clarify the question of acquisition and preservation of property."[82] It was unfortunate for the future of Russia's debates on development that—like Adam Smith—Radischev failed to confront the problems which might arise once the constraints on individual freedom of action were eliminated.

In contrast to Elagin, Sievers, and Bolotov, Radishchev believed that economic progress was indissolubly linked to the struggle for fundamental political change. Autocratic rulers who deprived their subjects of civil liberties and personal freedom would in his view be unwilling to commit themselves to thoroughgoing economic reform. Even if the meager soil of the North were miraculously transformed into rich black earth, Radishchev maintained that "feudal Russia" would take no notice. Ignoring the economic achievements of Prussia and the other states of Germany, he rested his hopes for the future upon (1) Western-style liberal and democratic government, (2) civil liberties, and (3) the incentives associated with private-property rights and capitalism. In the writings of Radishchev, Russian reformers were posed with a stark and dichotomized "all or nothing" choice between the stagnation of authoritarian regimes and "English-style" progress.

The most profound critique of Radishchev's program for Western-style revolution came from Prince M. M. Shcherbatov—a conservative but quite Western-oriented proponent of economic change. Shcherbatov was an admirer of Peter the Great, a translator of Alexander Pope, Voltaire, and Montesquieu, and a fervent advocate of Western scientific and technological innovation. In many respects, he was a far more typical eighteenth-century Westernizer than Radishchev. Although Shcherbatov believed in "the laws of nature," he rejected John Locke's notion that human society evolved out of a free and anarchic state of nature.[83] As he saw it, the earth's first human beings lived in cohesive and highly structured tribal societies; only after centuries of heroic effort by gifted aristocrats had the first civilizations emerged out of the ruins of primitive and relatively egalitarian societies.

Arguing that it was both impossible and undesirable to return to a state of primitive backwardness, Shcherbatov called on Russia's upper class to recognize that society's inequities reflected the natural division between aristocrats and a peasantry devoid of intelligence or ability. Denouncing Radishchev and Polenov for their "criminal" efforts to preach equality to a horde of vicious, stupid and gullible peasant inferiors, Shcherbatov contended that peasants were incapable of becoming wise or constructive members of a productive and prosperous society. According to Shcherbatov, Westernizers who advocated peasant freedom and property rights represented a threat to the survival of the Russian Empire because they called into question the stratification upon which civilized achievements had always been built.[84]

In the writings of Shcherbatov, the coercive strategies of eighteenth-century reformers like Sievers and Bolotov were elevated to the level of a general principle. Arguing that it was only by compulsion that peasants could be induced to work more productively, he ridiculed the notion that Western-style freedom or property rights could somehow "unleash" the peasantry's potential. Sherbatov dismissed as well the argument that free peasants would provide greater revenues for their former owners. How, he asked, could a landlord hope to extract more from a free tenant than from a bound laborer? From both a political and an economic standpoint, it seemed obvious to Shcherbatov that if by some evil turn of events the peasantry were freed, they would not become docile and productive subjects. They would instead soon form a numerous, impoverished, and rebellious proletariat, eager to destroy both society and the state. (These were, of course, precisely the arguments later set out by Karl Marx, with the exception that Marx saw as progressive every aspect of the process that Shcherbatov decried.)[85]

In contrast to Radishchev, Shcherbatov insisted that serfdom was perfectly compatible with modern Western agricultural methods. Praising the Baltic German nobility for introducing comprehensive supervision and constraints on peasant labor, he argued that their efforts had transformed the poor soil of the Baltic seacoast into the most profitable land in the Empire. Shcherbatov called upon Russian nobles to imitate their Baltic counterparts by making full use of their seigneurial powers to transform and improve Russian agriculture. Linking Western-style progress with the material interests of his own social class, Shcherbatov proposed that all state land and state peasants be handed over to the nobility at reduced prices, so that "the nobility would enrich itself, agriculture and the domestic arts would spread . . . the peasantry would be better cared for and protected, arrears would disappear and the treasury would not only not lose by it but would receive a monetary increase."[86]

In the short run, Shcherbatov proposed that the gentry devise projects for the union of agriculture and industry so that peasants would have to work on a full-time rather than a seasonal basis. As he saw it, a gentry-imposed discipline that forced peasants to use modern Western farming methods, securely bound them to the land, and guaranteed them the use of adequate sized allotments, would lay the foundations for a "civilized" and orderly process of economic development. With a peasantry well protected and secure, Shcherbatov contended that the gentry and the state could wage a campaign against backwardness which mobilized all of the conventional weapons of war—in place of the feeble and unsettling process of law and education, he recommended gunpowder, exile, and the knout.

In contrast to Radishchev's hopes for a world of freedom and harmony whose contradictions were reconciled by an invisible Smithian hand, Shcherbatov's economic vision was tragic and brutal. Viewing Russia as a society of hereditary superiors and inferiors, he saw no alternative to coercion. According to Shcherbatov, the danger posed by a populace ignorant of its limitations and prone to disobedience was even greater in the modern age, because Westernized Russians incited their inferiors to rebel against the civilization that the gentry had so arduously striven to create. Shcherbatov's solution was for the government to place more resources and power in the hands of serfowners. As he saw it, Russia's hereditary elite needed more efficient techniques of coercion, Western science and technology, and more human capital in the form of serfs. They did not require free political, social, or economic institutions.

From Theory to Practice: Change and Continuity in the Russian Countryside

In the course of the eighteenth century, most Russian serfowners remained loyal to the traditions of their parents and grandparents. Instead of improving methods of cultivation or encouraging agricultural innovation, they encroached on the estates of their neighbors or the land cultivated by state peasants, and transferred an increasing number of peasants from *obrok* to the forced labor of the *barshchina* system. While a small coterie of educated Russians spoke more openly than ever before about private-property rights and freedom, peasants were silenced, immobilized, and enserfed in ever-increasing numbers, and communal institutions were introduced to millions of peasants who had not previously possessed them. The politics of domination shaped high-level economic debate and policy and, with few exceptions, even the most Western-oriented of progressives gave top priority to the maintenance of domestic order.

During the reign of Catherine the Great the opportunities of the serfowner expanded, even as the freedom of serfs, state peasants, and migrants became more precarious. In 1765, the gentry were permitted to exile serfs to Siberia without any reference to judicial process, and between 1768 and 1772, 20,515 serfs were banished to Tobolsk and Yeniseisk alone.[87] The power of the gentry as judge and jury over bound peasants was powerfully reinforced by provincial reforms, which shifted Russia's political center of gravity from Moscow to local serfowners. In keeping with the new legislation, landed magnates elected magistrates who proceeded (1) to make serfdom more oppressive, and (2) to legitimize gentry encroachment upon the land and labor of state peasants.[88]

In 1767, when Catherine issued her "Legislative Instruction" and eloquently praised the virtues of liberty, peasants of the Ukraine were introduced to the institution of serfdom. At the same time, the government dramatically escalated efforts to shield itself from peasant voices of complaint. After the receipt of 649 peasant petitions to the Crown in the summer of 1767, the Imperial Senate reminded the empress that the Law Code of 1649 prohibited serfs from making disclosures about "those to whom they belong." As a consequence, Catherine issued a decree declaring that henceforth "people and peasants" who dared to submit petitions concerning their landlords were to be knouted and sentenced for life to penal servitude in Nerchinsk.[89] In order to avoid arousing either gentry hostility or peasant disobedience, government officials attempted to ensure that any actions taken against estate owners found guilty of torturing their peasants be taken in secret.[90]

Although Catherine the Great proclaimed her support for private-property rights throughout much of her reign, neither she nor her Western-oriented advisers were willing to abandon traditional policies that protected peasants from the vagaries of the market. During her reign, officials maintained state granaries for the poor, transported grain from surplus to deficit areas like St. Petersburg, and intervened at the marketplace to fix prices at a level that permitted grain purchases by the needy.[91] In 1766, the Russian government prohibited all peasant land sales and ordered restitution without compensation of all land that state peasants had sold to non-peasants.[92]

The goverment's conflicted approach to property issues was clearly evident in its colonial and resettlement policies, which fostered rights to private ownership but surrounded its exercise with stringent constraints. Like Frederick the Great and other eighteenth-century monarchs who measured wealth and power according to the size of the population over which they ruled, the Empress Catherine invited new settlers to migrate to Russia and granted them "private" allotments of land. Between 1763 and 1775, 30,000 German "proprietors" were settled in the lower Volga region. However, foreign colonists were prohibited from selling, mortgaging, or dividing their allotments. Although they were praised as models of private initiative and productive labor, their land claims remained quite limited; if any peasant "landowners" decided to leave their designated colony, their holdings reverted to the community.[93]

At the same time, both the empress and her serfowning constituency continued to rely on the commune to promote stability and order, and to provide revenue and military recruits. In 1766, the government imposed communal tenure on all lands farmed by state peasants. In the 1770s and 1780s, government officials periodically descended upon particular villages to propagandize for equalization of allotments, and in 1782, Count I. I. Shuvalov instructed his bailiff to promote more egalitarian repartitions of land "so that one village will not have an excess of land while another has too little, in order that each will pay taxes on it without falling into arrears." According to the state peasant administration in Archangel in 1785, "the equalization of holdings is considered an inevitable necessity, as much for providing the means for peasants to pay their taxes as for the pacification of those who have not enough land." In the year after Catherine's death, the government set a norm for peasant allotments in the black earth region at 15 *desiatiny*. Those with less were to be brought up to this standard by communal repartitions.

In times of domestic peace, communes frequently served a conservative purpose, as village elders enforced the demands of serfowners and bailiffs, and informed against "troublemakers" (or against those who challenged the elder's own patriarchal authority).[94] But the symmetry of state, gentry, and commune interests was precarious. The authorities could seldom prevent village elders from "reinterpreting" or evading commands that they considered excessive or unjust. The reports of eighteenth-century bailiffs were filled with complaints about peasants' evasion, and magistrates bitterly denounced the lethargy with which peasants responded to their demands.[95] In general, peasants most quickly obeyed orders that were considered moderately acceptable, but if the demands of the authorities did not fall within what has been called "the zone of acquiescence," they were frequently ignored. During the reign of Catherine the Great, officials complained that peasant communities frequently waited "for the 3rd ukase"—the point at which the authorities might be expected to take punitive action.[96] Testing the resolve of masters and officials intent on controlling their behavior, they acted in accordance with a "moral economy" that accepted—but nevertheless attempted to limit or reshape—demands imposed from above.[97]

Neither government nor gentry strategies succeeded in maintaining peace and stability in the late-eighteenth-century countryside. In Moscow province alone, some 30 landlords were murdered between 1760 and 1769. According to reports on domestic unrest from officials, police agents, and estate managers, peasants tended to respond collectively when they set out to "punish" a hated master. In contrast to their slave counterparts in the United States, when Russian serfs resisted the demands of masters and bailiffs or rebelled against the authority of the government itself, they seldom acted in isolation.[98] With few exceptions, the peasant commune served as a framework for both small-and large-scale collective protest in the Russian countryside.

Although the criteria for defining what constituted a peasant uprising were not very consistent, it has been estimated that between 1762 and 1772, there were 40 major uprisings against the gentry in the provinces of Tver, Novgorod, Viatka, Kazan, and Smolensk. In 1773, three million Cossacks, Bashkirs, nomads, and peasants fought (unsuccessfully) for "land and liberty" under the leadership of the Cossack Emilian Pugachev. Reformers like Bolotov were terrified. In his words, "We were all convinced that the lower orders and the mob, and particularly all the slaves and our servants, were secretly in their hearts, . . . given to every wickedness . . . ready at the least spark to make fire and flame. The stupidity and extreme foolhardiness of our lower classes were too familiar . . . we could not rely even on the loyalty of our own servants, and still considered them our . . . most wicked enemies."[99]

The government responded by supporting gentry claims to expanded estates and *corvee* labor, and abandoning its own traditional rights to ownership of subsoil resources on seigneurial estates. In 1785, Catherine reinforced an earlier decree of Peter III by emancipating the gentry from the obligation to perform state service and abolishing the traditional imposition of corporal punishment and estate confiscation for members of the nobility who were convicted of crime.[100]

As we consider the eighteenth-century escalation of elite claims to human and landed property, and the eagerness of the authorities to rely upon the commune as fiscal agent, enforcer, informer, and pacifier of the rural populace, it becomes easier to understand why issues of coercion so dominated proposals for Westernization and economic reform.[101] With a few notable exceptions, the most enthusiastic advocates of Western economic ideas and agricultural methods were zealous defenders of surveillance and coercion as economic stimuli and as guarantors of domestic peace. Unwilling to reject the use of torture and beatings, Westernizing reformers like Bolotov and Count Sievers eventually transgressed even the extremely lenient eighteenth-century standards for the permissible treatment of serfs. The violence and cruelty they inflicted upon peasants under their control finally brought not only a reprimand from the empress, but an Imperial prohibition against the further use of corporal punishment on the estates they owned and supervised.[102]

However, prohibitions of this sort were quite rare. In general, repressive modernization remained an uncontested and characteristic feature of government policy and gentry behavior in the last decades of the eighteenth century. While there were some Westernizers who argued that property rights might in fact serve as a more powerful support for the status quo than the peasant commune, they would not win out until the Stolypin Reforms of 1906.

Chapter Three

THE LESSONS OF WESTERN ECONOMICS

SUPPORT OR CHALLENGE TO THE STATUS QUO?

> Some serf girls in the orchard there
> While picking berries, filled the air
> With choral song . . . as they'd been bidden
> (An edict that was meant, you see,
> To keep sly mouths from feeling free
> To eat the master's fruit when hidden
> By filling them with song instead—
> For rural cunning isn't dead)!
> *(Alexander Pushkin)*

THE CONSERVATIVE ECONOMICS OF WESTERNIZATION

IN 1801, WHEN Tsar Alexander I came to power through the murder of his father, he faced a landed gentry more powerful and privileged— and in Pushkin's sense, more cunning—than ever before. Efforts to regulate the master/serf relationship had failed disastrously in the reign of Tsar Paul I. Serfowners ignored Imperial decrees that limited forced labor (*barshchina*) to three days per week and prohibited the sale of Ukrainian peasants separate from the land. Bound peasants who sought freedom in the recently acquired Russian territory to the South were forcibly returned to their former masters; their more docile counterparts were transported by the tens of thousands to gentry estates then being established in the same region.

Liberal promises of change abounded during the early years of Alexander's reign. Unlike his father and grandmother, the new Tsar abandoned the practice of giving tens of thousands of serfs as gifts to his favorites and instead bestowed a short-lived emancipation upon the Livonian peasantry of the Baltic region. In 1803, Minister of Commerce Rumiantsev's decree "On Free Grain Cultivators" used the Smithian language of "enlightened self-interest" to encourage Russia's gentry to emancipate their bound peasants. Arguing that freedom would render peasants more productive and less rebellious, Rumiantsev proposed voluntary emancipation reforms which permitted the gentry to retain their traditional police and judicial powers, including the right to confiscate peasant allotments that were badly cultivated.

However, Rumiantsev's initiative fell flat. Between 1803 and 1824, only 161 serfowners took advantage of it. In some of the more notorious efforts to profit from the reforms, a Riazan estate owner agreed to free his peasants only after he was paid a total of 275,000 rubles over a ten-year period, plus another sum to the trustees of the estate (the owner having died by this time). Prince A. Golitsyn freed 13,000 of his serfs at prices ranging from 139 to 5,000 rubles, while the serfowner Shishkov of Vologda province promised to liberate 75 peasants if each paid him 3500 rubles annually for eight years. To peasants entangled in such exorbitant obligations to their former masters, freedom was rather a mixed blessing.[1]

Government educational initiatives produced equally contradictory results. More Russians than ever studied abroad, and new, predominantly German-staffed universities were established in St. Petersburg and Dorpat, which taught political economy and even—in the case of Dorpat—agricultural economics.[2] But in the 1800s, the appeal of education turned out to be no match for the fear generated by the prospect of a free exchange of ideas. In the early 1800s Russia's universities became the site of increasingly harsh government censorship of academic research and debate. Government officials were particularly troubled by empirical investigations of serfdom, and eventually "purged" many of the faculty whose work dealt with this topic.[3]

The Emergence of Russian Economics: Westernization in German Guise

The creation of economics as a Russian academic discipline was the work of German-born scholars like Christian von Schlözer, Gustav von Jakob, and Heinrich von Storch. The Göttingen-trained Schlözer, a professor at Moscow University between 1801 and 1826, authored the first Russian-language text on the subject of political economy. In his teaching and scholarship, he sought to demonstrate that there was no inherent conflict between capitalism, serfdom, and autocracy. According to Schlözer, it was the ruler's obligation to guide and subsidize the efforts of gentry entrepreneurs who were in turn completely free to organize serf labor as they saw fit. One wonders what Schlözer's Moscow University students made of his astonishing claim not only that Russia was capitalist but that their parents and friends were entrepreneurs who possessed—in addition to land, livestock and machinery—an ungrateful and unsatisfactory accumulation of human capital in the form of peasants.[4]

While no school of economic thought emerged to promote Schlözer's foolish assertion that Russia was already a capitalist nation, leading scholars—like the Hungarian-born and Vienna-trained Balugianskii of the University of St. Petersburg, the Polish Count Stroinovskii of Vilnius, the

Baltic German Kaiserov of Dorpat, and the Russian-born and German-educated Kachenovskii of Moscow—shared his faith in capitalism's benefits. Certain that Russia's gentry could prosper by imitating the behavior of "improving landlords" elsewhere, they attributed economic backwardness to the commune and to the peasantry's excessive leisure time.[5] According to Balugianskii, productivity rates were bound to rise if (with the government leading the way) the landed gentry took steps to eliminate the commune and to prohibit peasant celebration of the numerous local and religious holidays, which encouraged idleness and drinking.[6]

Ludwig von Jakob, who joined the University of Kharkov after Napoleon closed down the University of Halle in 1807, was equally certain that communes represented a major obstacle to economic improvement. According to Jakob, private-property rights and free labor served the interests of both government officials and the landed gentry. In his words, "The chief goal of my work is to demonstrate the practical possibility that Russian landowners might place peasants in such a position that they will eagerly and voluntarily occupy themselves with agriculture, and landowners will receive even larger incomes than from forced labor."[7]

However, although Jakob contended that neither freedom nor property rights endangered traditional social privileges, he paid far more attention to the the latter issue. After joining the Ministry of Finance in 1809, Jakob called for the transfer of all peasant-cultivated, commune lands into the hands of Russia's gentry. In this process, peasants would become "English-style" tenants who accumulated capital for investment in agriculture and were capable of paying higher rents than before.[8]

The defense of private-property rights was equally central to the work of the Baltic German economist Heinrich von Storch, whose research on Adam Smith brought him appointments to the Academy of Sciences in Paris, Naples, and Munich, the position of professor of political economy at the Imperial Academy of Sciences in St. Petersburg, and a brief appointment as tutor to the future Tsar Nicholas I. According to Storch, England's prosperity was rooted in a "sacred respect" for every form of private property; he agreed with Jakob that Russia's economic needs would be excellently served by an "English-style" enclosure movement. In a flight of fancy which would have astonished both the enclosure rioters and the Parliament which decreed their actions a capital crime, Storch described England's abolition of common rights as a wonderfully peaceful model of economic innovation which took place without "bloodshed or tears, or hatred of neighbors."[9]

In the aftermath of the French Revolution, Storch was as eager as Jakob to convince his readers that the abolition of peasant communes did not pose a political threat to the status quo. His *Cours d'économie* (1815) included the prudent reassurance that Adam Smith's ideas would not produce social or political upheaval, as well as the declaration that Smith's doctrine of natural liberty constituted "the single most important idea in modern political economy." Emphasizing that in the short term, peasant emancipation was a "chimerical hope,"[10] Storch cautiously suggested that productivity rates might well increase if (1) the collection of feudal dues were made less arbitrary, and (2) a measure of private property were allotted to serfs. It is significant that despite Storch's political prudence, the censor permitted his book to appear only in French, and prohibited any Russian translations.

Although Schlözer, Jakob, and Storch were all admirers of Adam Smith, they were extremely selective in their interpretations. Freely departing from both the spirit and substance of Smith's teachings, Schlözer celebrated the use of serfs as capital. In keeping with the teachings of Cameralism, Jakob portrayed free labor as a state of joyful submission rather than independence. For his part, Storch rejected Smith's assumption that division-of-labor principles applied to agriculture as well as industry (and disagreed with many of Schlözer's ideas about statistics and economics).[11] The only article of liberal economic faith upon which these "German-Russian" economists could agree was the sanctity of private-property rights.

In the early decades of the nineteenth century, most economics-minded scholars in Russia believed that the discipline of economics should focus above all upon the politically stabilizing, incentive-generating, and morally admirable institution of private tenure. Their priorities were shaped by a complex of foreign and domestic influences. Private tenure was promoted as a key principle of the classical economists they so admired; at the same time, it was an economic ideal that could be mobilized in support of ongoing efforts by landed magnates to encroach upon the vast reserves of state land occupied by commune peasants.[12] Presumably, the gentry were—as Storch and Jakob proposed—fostering economic development by taking land from "idle" commune peasants and transforming it into more productive private property. In many respects, the scholarship of Russia's German-Russian economists reinforced the notion that gentry land encroachments were not simply the seizure of peasant allotments but a contribution to Russia's modernizing efforts.

The Widening Economic Debate

> Property! A sacred right!
> The Soul of Society!
> The source of laws.
> Where you are respected, where you are inviolable
> That country is blessed, the citizen is tranquil and well off
> *(Ivan Pnin, 1804)*

In the 1800s, agricultural improvement became an increasingly popular topic of debate among well-born and Western-oriented Russians. In the

Proceedings of the Imperial Free Economic Society, The Economic Journal, and *Spirit of the Journals*, Prince E. Ia. Baratinskii reported on English systems of crop rotation, and Princess Dashkova published "An Opinion on the New and the Old Plow." In the tradition of eighteenth-century French pilgrimages to the English estate of "improving landlords" like the Earl of Leicester, enlightened Russian serfowners visited the estate of D. M. Poltoratskii in Kaluga province in order to view the successful implementation of Western-style agricultural methods.[13]

In an early nineteenth-century flurry of enthusiasm for Western economic theory, Minister of Finance Vasiliev ordered the translation of *The Wealth of Nations*, and Empress Maria Fyodorovna made Smith's book required reading for both her daughters and sons. A study of Smith by Göttingen's Georg Sartorius brought requests from as far away as Krasnoyarsk, Irkutsk, and Nerchinsk, and N. I. Turgenev (a student of Sartorius) published an influential book that summarized and discussed the fifth book of Adam Smith's *The Wealth of Nations*.[14] Count Kochubei, the English-trained Minister of the Interior, proclaimed himself a follower of Smith. Even Pushkin's Eugene Onegin, who found Latin too difficult,

> read, in compensation, Adam Smith
> and was a deep economist:
> that is, he could assess the way
> a state grows rich
> and what it lives upon, and why
> it needs not gold
> when it has got the simple product.
> His father could not understand him,
> and mortgaged his lands.[15]

Since Adam Smith was a leading proponent of individual freedom, the delight in his work expressed by Russians who measured wealth according to the number of individual "souls" they owned, requires some explanation. Manifesting an extraordinary talent for selective interpretation, Russian admirers of classical liberalism rejected the notion that principles of liberty applied to their primitive and insuperably backward dependents. Interpreting *laissez faire* to mean freedom from government intervention between master and serf, liberal Russian serfowners welcomed the argument that regulation of any kind constituted a "medieval" constraint on the functioning of their enlightened self-interest. In an equally self-serving interpretation of Smith, they demanded that all state land (together with its peasant cultivators) be taken from idle and inefficient state functionaries and transferred to gentry proprietors. According to the ideal scenario that emerged from the pages of the publication *Spirit of the Journals*, an aristocratic entrepreneur supplied with more land and freed from all state restrictions quickly became an energetic and innovative serfowning capitalist, committed to increased productivity and profit.[16]

The use of liberal economic doctrines to argue for expanding the master's freedom of action was not a uniquely Russian phenomenon. In the American South, slaveholders and proslavery economists argued that they were acting as classical liberals when they opposed government intrusion into the "natural" relationship between master and slave.[17] Proslavery liberals of this sort drew a sharp distinction between inequalities attributed to *natural* distinctions of talent, intelligence, race, and gender and those viewed as a product of *artificial* distinctions imposed by government institutions. Arguing that slaves were "naturally" inferior and thus a form of property, proslavery liberals insisted that the right to own a slave was as sacred as any other form of property ownership. According to one American scholar, the language of property rights and *laissez faire* "provided southern masters with a justification of slavery most compatible with liberal culture."[18] It is significant that when Africans demanded freedom in the Amistad Mutiny of 1839, the court arguments put forward both by their defenders and their prosecutors turned on the question of whether the Africans could be considered "stolen property."

Along similar lines, English factory owners of the early nineteenth century readily invoked liberal economic principles in defense of their freedom to hire, fire, or bargain at will with their laborers without having to suffer the "illegitimate" interference by public or governmental bodies. Using classical liberalism to oppose "medieval" government efforts to regulate relationships between master and serf or slave, or between factory owner and factory employee, English entrepreneurs and proslavery American economists interpreted the teachings of Adam Smith to justify the elimination of limits on the use of economic power against those who were without it.

In the Russian context, the link between freedom and the exercise of despotic power over others was forcefully set out by Admiral A. A. Mordvinov—a friend of Samuel Bentham and an Anglophile so fanatic that he imported the "best" English gravel to cover the roads of his estates. One of the most famous Westernizers of his day, Mordvinov served as president of the Imperial Free Economic Society from 1823 to 1840, founded an agricultural school modeled on the precepts of Arthur Young and administered by two Englishmen, and provided generous free loans to a Moscow factory that manufactured agricultural machinery. An innovative and extremely interventionist owner of 2.7 million acres of land, Mordvinov's contribution to Russia's debate on development was to purge the notion of private-property rights of any link to peasant freedom.[19]

On his own estates, Mordvinov was famous—or from the peasant perspective, infamous—for his zealous intervention into every aspect of the peasantry's economic and noneconomic lives. Unconstrained by any restrictions upon his own freedom of action, Mordvinov inundated the bailiffs and peasant elders on his estates with advice and demands. Inspired by a passion for reform, he threatened inhabitants of the villages he owned with dire consequences if they failed to consolidate allotments, delay periodic repartition, plant potatoes, vary their crops, or adopt new methods of swaddling their infants. In an ode to Mordvinov's agricultural achievements, his English-trained agronomist M. E. Livanov wrote: "Sterility and hunger banished by your hand / Flee from these fields. / On rich pastures, the sturdy ox grazes / And the peasant laughs among the yellow fields."[20]

At the same time, Mordvinov provided financial inducements to serfs who would "voluntarily" agree to leave their communities for his newly acquired estates in the fertile regions to the South.[21] In the hands of Mordvinov, progressive reform brought an escalation of surveillance and control. When Alexander I visited Mordvinov's estates in 1809, two thousand peasants lined the roads to complain of their master's intrusiveness and cruelty and to beg for mercy and relief.[22]

Although Mordvinov conceded that serfdom would inevitably die out at some future date, he argued that peasants were so lazy that without the pressures of bondage they would refuse to engage in swamp drainage, land clearing, or any other necessary economic tasks. According to Mordvinov, an "artificial" government-sponsored emancipation would simply abandon peasants to sloth and ignorance. Rejecting the liberal economist Turgenev's arguments for free labor, Mordvinov declared that Western history had proven that serfdom would disappear gradually and "naturally," once a higher stage of economic development had been achieved.[23]

Mordvinov's vision of private-property rights bore little resemblance to the ideal of property as the "bedrock of liberty" celebrated by European liberals ever since the time of John Locke. In his words, "On property are founded all present conditions and laws. It alone originally subdued the will of individuals and today strengthens societies and keeps them united and obedient. The right of private property and the right of supreme authority over others are in essence inseparable."[24] In his focus on property rights rather than peasant freedom, Mordvinov was probably a more typical Westernizer of the 1800s than his far more famous contemporary, M. M. Speranskii, who served as Alexander I's Minister of Finance.

Unlike Mordvinov, Speranskii was an abolitionist whose proposal for a Legislative Code reflected the combined influence of classical economics, the *Rechtstaat* doctrines of nineteenth-century Prussia, and old-fashioned Russian security concerns. Relying on France's Napoleonic Code, he recommended the establishment of a political system which guaranteed the rights of citizens on the basis of property ownership rather than hereditary status.[25] According to Speranskii, the introduction of peasant emancipation and voting rights for the wealthy could transform Russia into a prosperous nation. Rejecting the example of England's enclosure movement, he modeled his plan for peasant emancipation on Prussia's Stein-Hardenberg reforms. According to Speranskii, peasants should be freed with land, with the gentry permitted to establish rates of compensation for their former serfs. However, fearing that economic insecurity might endanger society and the state, Speranskii quite deliberately avoided the anti-communal aspects of the Prussian emancipation.[26]

Unfortunately for Speranskii, his challenge to serfdom and hereditary privilege came in 1812, just as Napoleon's Grande Armée was approaching the borders of the Russian Empire. Faced with imminent invasion, the autocracy sought common cause with its gentry constituency, sent Speranskii into exile, and rejected his Legislative Code. Russia's upper class, in no mood for plebian adaptations of the Napoleonic Code, celebrated Speranskii's fall as Russia's first "victory" over the French. Demanding an end to "faddish" imitations of the West which proposed to replace inherited privilege with legal rights based on property ownership, they denounced Speranskii as an atheistic commoner who was trying to destroy the sacred powers of the nobility. Once the war was over, the tsar rewarded the Baltic German landlords who defended the Empire against the French by rescinding the Livonian peasant emancipation of 1804.[27]

It is ironic, and revealing of the complexities of Westernization in the Russian context, that some of the staunchest defenders of "holy Russia" were patriots whose diatribes against the West were written in French, and deeply imbued with "Prussian-style" ideals of efficiency and order. The most consistent of the West's self-proclaimed enemies was Count A. N. Rostopchin, who feared that Russia might be fatally "infected" by the disease of European revolution. According to Rostopchin, the "criminal behavior" of Russians who "cringed" before Western expertise, power, and wealth weakened the nation and led to anarchy and rebellion.

Instead of "slavishly" following English and German agricultural manuals based upon Western European conditions, Rostopchin demanded that educated Russians pay attention to the specifics of the Russian context. It seemed to him ridiculous to imagine that England—a tiny, densely populated island nation located in a temperate climatic zone—could serve as Russia's model. According to Rostopchin, only a pack of zealots and fools could suppose that it was realistic to establish isolated and enclosed private farms on the vastness of the frigid steppe—clearly, peasants needed to cluster together in communal villages in order to survive on the

Russian land. In his anti-Western zeal, Rostopchin repudiated his earlier career as an "improving landlord" who employed a Scottish bailiff to manage his estates and made use of Western field systems. In his role as a patriot, he published a pamphlet intended to demonstrate that the ancient Russian plow (the *sokha*) was more appropriate to the soil of Russia than the various Western agricultural implements that were being imported at great cost from abroad.[28]

In an antiliberal tirade that prefigured the arguments put forward by Karl Marx in the "Communist Manifesto," Rostopchin contended that in England, employers heartlessly left their workers to die if they were sick, old, or disabled. Asserting that the principles of English "liberty" were only a facade to mask a callous indifference to the situation of the lower classes, Rostopchin declared that the laborers who wandered the streets of Leeds and Manchester were driven by an economic compulsion more cruel and inexorable than serfdom. In order for Russia to escape such horrors, he called upon the nobility to make use of their God-given powers and privileges to organize the life and labor of their peasant workforce.[29]

After 1812, tenderhearted Russian serfowners came forward to protest a capitalist division of labor that degraded the worker to a state in which his "mind becomes dull, his human nature debased." Denouncing England's labor violence, *Spirit of the Journals* quoted an 1820s proclamation by striking English workers, which declared that they lived "in the most inhuman oppression and slavery." In a particularly repellent analogy, the serfowner Pravdin described American free laborers as wild animals at the mercy of hunters who could at any moment drive them from their shelter or deprive them of food or of life itself. If a free laborer died due to unsafe working conditions, employers could simply hire another; they possessed no economic stake in the safety or well-being of their workers. In contrast, Pravdin compared the Russian serf to a cherished horse whose health and welfare served the interest of his or her master. If a horse (or a serf) should die of mistreatment, the owner had no choice but to invest in the purchase of a replacement.[30]

The self-serving character of such arguments did not mean that they were without foundation, either in the United States or in Imperial Russia. By many standards, the material life of free Western laborers had little to recommend it. In the 1820s and 1830s, US abolitionists who compared the living standards of English and Irish workmen to those of American slaves "gloomily admitted that the slaveholders had entirely too much truth for comfort on their side of the argument." According to Fanny Kemble, an abolitionist writer of the 1830s, the material life of enslaved African Americans was better than most Irish free peasants. Jakob Koepff, a German settler who came to live in Texas, observed : "Slavery belongs to the curses of the land and fills one with sorrow. Yet . . . I know for certain that 1/3 of the population in a German village is no better off than the Texas negro."[31] After a trip to Russia, the Englishman Thomas Raikes declared: "If a comparison were drawn between the respective situation of these classes in the two countries, I mean as to physical wants and gratification, how much would the scale leap toward the population of illiterate slaves? The Englishman may boast of his liberty, but will it procure him a dinner?"[32]

As Western classical liberals demanded freedom from government-imposed safety standards, working hours, and wages, their labor force sickened and died at a great rate. On the other hand, the Russian gentry's claim to be providing protection and guidance served to justify a massive increase in the levels of coercion and surveillance inflicted upon bound peasants.

Russian Military Colonies and US Labor Gangs

In 1810, Tsar Alexander I invited Admiral Mordvinov (our Anglophile *par excellence*) to draw up plans for the most far-reaching effort at repressive control of a labor force before the twentieth century. Identifying the advance of reason with increased regimentation, Mordvinov's statutes established a network of "military colonies" in the provinces of St. Petersburg, Novgorod, Mogilev, Ekaterinoslav, and Kherson. As administrator of the new colonies, the government appointed Count A. A. Arakcheev, a serfowning official whose orderly estates—with their identically shaped peasant cottages located at regular intervals along the sides of the road, and female inhabitants were ordered to produce at least one child per year—were a source of continuing delight to the tsar.

The official goal of the colonial experiment was to lower state military expenditures through a more efficient allocation of economic and military resources. To achieve this end, Mordvinov's plan guaranteed to each uniformed and clean-shaven male colonist under the age of forty-five an allotment of "private" property on condition that he cultivate it with conscientiousness and zeal. Colonists were to live in houses symmetrically arranged along a main road. At a given signal, all were to rise; peasant wives were to fire their stoves at the same time; and at the sound of another signal, all were to eat. They were then to farm the land with efficiency, stop work simultaneously, eat, and sleep for a designated time. Settlers were also obligated to make efficient use of the labor of unmarried soldiers quartered in their homes. Fines and corporal punishment were imposed for a failure to comply with any of the colony's rules.[33]

Such efforts at regimentation were not uniquely Russian. In the American South, plantation owners increased the productivity of slave labor through the regimentation of the infamous "labor gang" system. This strategy divided slaves into groups of five types of hands who followed one another in fixed order. Plowmen first ridged the unbroken soil, harrowers then broke the clods, drillers dug holes to receive the seeds, droppers planted seeds in the holes, and rakers covered them up. Drivers maintained the desired pace and intensity of labor by insulting, threatening, and whipping the laggards. To George Fitzhugh, one of the most thoughtful slaveholders of his day, coercion was desirable because: "Physical force, not moral suasion rules the world. The negro sees the driver's lash, becomes accustomed to obedient cheerful industry, and is not aware that the lash is the force that impels him."[34]

Although American slaveholders and Russian serfowners were equally wedded to the use of coercion, they used it to enforce quite different forms of labor organization. While Russian reformers accelerated old-fashioned work practices, US-style compulsion transferred assembly-line techniques to the plantation. Simplifying slave labor so that each worker became a cog in the mechanism of the labor gang, slaveowners focused narrowly on completing specialized agricultural tasks.[35] In contrast, Russia's military colonies took a more comprehensive approach to the task of raising productivity rates. Supplementing regimentation with compulsory education and guarantees of material security, they established schools for boys and girls, and supplied medical care, land, shelter, furniture, tools, and livestock on condition that inhabitants worked hard and obeyed orders.

The 750,000 inhabitants of Russia's military settlements achieved a striking measure of economic success. Between 1815 and 1825, Novgorod colonists increased the yield of rye per acre by 30 percent, and by 1825, the Kherson colony had doubled its agricultural output. But massive productivity increases did not reconcile peasant colonists to what they experienced as unbearable levels of constraint.[36] In one poignant encounter, a group of peasants pleaded with the Grand Duke Nicholas: "Increase our taxes, conscript for military services a son from every house, take from us everything and send us into the steppes; we should more gladly consent to this. We have arms, we will work and be happy there; but do not take our effects, the customs of our fathers, and do not turn us all into soldiers."[37] By the 1820s, violence had become endemic in the military colonies. In 1831, after a Novgorod uprising ended with 3,960 arrests, the government began to abandon its colonial experiment. However, leading government officials did not ever reject the progressive virtues of coercion, unlimited surveillance, and some variant of private-property rights. The failure of the colonies was attributed to peasant backwardness.

The fate of the US labor gang system and of Russia's military colonies illuminates some striking differences between the status and "political clout" of enslaved African-Americans and Russia's bound peasants. In the United States, the labor gang system was imposed upon a racially distinct, chattel slave minority. Its relatively peaceful implementation was a product of many decades of effort by slaveowners to fragment African American families, uproot them from their "home" communities, and weaken whatever collective or mutual support mechanisms they may have wished to create or sustain. Although these strategies were never completely successful, they made it difficult for slaves to rely on family, village, or community as a stable source of support or protection. In contrast, when a Russian peasant majority rooted in territorially based communities took to violence, the government retreated. Peasant "colonists" were able to make it too costly for the autocracy to maintain its military experiment, but the labor gang system persisted in the United States for many decades after the Civil War was over.

Tsar Nicholas I: Questions of Order, Progress, and Westernization

Alexander I died suddenly in December 1825. His successor, Tsar Nicholas I ascended the throne in the midst of a gentry-led "Decembrist" rebellion led by veterans of the Napoleonic Wars who had been stationed in the ill-fated military colonies. To the new tsar's horror and dismay, army officers of noble origin—the autocracy's most precious political constituency—were guilty of organizing a coup on behalf of representative government and peasant emancipation. Radicalized by their experience of Western European freedoms and by the repressive colonial policies, which impacted upon them as well as the peasantry, the Decembrists proposed to abandon their hereditary privileges. To later generations, their actions inspired the hope that the moral courage and social generosity of the upper class might transform a world dominated by serfdom and autocracy.[38]

Unfortunately for the Decembrist cause, gentry fear of the backwardness of the serfs whose freedom they championed almost equaled their hatred for the autocracy. Reluctant to invite peasants to participate in the struggle for peasant freedom, a number of Decembrist leaders recanted even as the rebellion began. In a matter of days, the uprising was suppressed. Its ringleaders were speedily executed—but not before the economics-minded Mordvinov presented an appeal for clemency, which argued that the talents of the Decembrists constituted part of Russia's scarce reservoir of human capital, and should be employed by the government in the economic development of Siberia.[39]

Confronted by violence and betrayal from his beloved officer corps, Tsar Nicholas I ruled from 1825 to 1855 as a demoralized and conflicted autocrat, obsessed with the fear of further betrayal, peasant unrest, and the "disease" of European revolution. Although the Decembrist uprising failed, it nevertheless indicated to the authorities that Western ideas of freedom might indeed threaten the political status quo. In the decades to come, government attitudes toward the West became increasingly tortuous and contradictory. While the tsar publicly recognized serfdom as a "flagrant evil" and established committees to discuss peasant emancipation, he kept their meetings secret, claiming that immediate abolition was an "evil more disastrous" than serfdom.[40] The government adopted the slogan of "Orthodoxy, Autocracy and Nationality," but eagerly made use of Western (primarily German) expertise in order to extend the reach of police and surveillance activities. Baltic German and Protestant officials who spoke German or French, but no Russian, accordingly took on the task of creating a Leviathan state that could crush its opponents just as Pushkin's *Bronze Horseman* had crushed the unfortunate Eugene.

After 1825, government economic policy was shaped above all by the German-born N. Kankrin, who served the tsar as Minister of Finance. A protégé of Arakcheev (the administrator of Tsar Alexander's military colonies), Kankrin was extremely pessimistic about Russia's economic prospects. Convinced that Russia could never compete with Western nations more generously endowed with fertile land, temperate climates, and easy access to lucrative foreign markets, he dismissed English, French, and German models for change. Liberal arguments for prosperity through the introduction of economic and political freedoms seemed to him little more than "utopian fantasy"; he even dismissed Cameralist-style projects for a state-sponsored economic development as unrealistic for a Russian nation so devoid of economic assets.[41]

Convinced that the social and economic insecurity produced by England's economic reforms simply incited the lower classes to violence and revolution, Kankrin argued that Russia did not need impoverished and violence-prone free laborers of the sort who walked the streets of Leeds and Manchester. Intent on holding the line against destabilizing Western influences, Kankrin extended both the size of the bureaucracy and its repressive powers.[42] In the 1820s and 1830s, the inspector generals who fanned out across the Russian countryside to delight the satirical eye of Nikolai Gogol came to symbolize for many the government's commitment to order without progress.

The preoccupation with security so characteristic of Russian policymakers was reflected even among Russia's first utopian socialists, who discovered in the theories of Cabet, St. Simon, and Fourier a new set of justifications for imposing constraints on peasant freedom of action. In the 1830s, a number of progressive-minded bureaucrats and middle-level army officers led by D. I. Petrashevskii called for the creation of giant,

Fourierist "phalansteries" to replace the wretched multiplicity of Russian peasant villages. To achieve socialist harmony and prosperity, Petrashevskii recommended stringent rules and regulations to "civilize" peasants, increase productivity rates, and raise living standards. To the young Alexander Herzen, always sensitive to the coercive aspects of gentry benevolence, the Fourierists were "Arakcheev socialists" whose phalansteries resembled the notorious military colonies of Tsar Alexander's reign. When Petrashevskii established a phalanstery on his own estate, peasants responded to life in Russia's first socialist enclave by putting it to the torch.[43] Like many earlier Russian reformers, the followers of Petrashevskii did not view peasant resistance as an indication that their own plans were flawed; as they saw it, opposition was due to the backwardness, ignorance, and conservatism of the common people.

THE KISELEV REFORMS

In 1833, in the wake of famine and a disastrous fall in agricultural prices, the tsar removed the administration of state lands and state peasants from Kankrin's Ministry of Finance and created a new Ministry of State Domains under the reform-minded Count P. D. Kiselev. Although Kiselev agreed with Kankrin about the peasantry's utter depravity and lawlessness, he was at the same time an optimist and an admirer of Jeremy Bentham and Adam Smith. Believing that peasants could be uplifted and transformed by government action, Kiselev established a network of officials (many of whom were followers of Petrashevskii) to take on the task of "civilizing" peasants and integrating them into the modern world.[44]

Kiselev's reform measures were unpopular from the start, especially when peasants realized that they—rather than the state or the gentry— were required to pay for new schools and seeds, as well as the requisite bribes to government officials.[45] In keeping with the traditions of repressive modernization, Kiselev's officials imposed stringent fines and corporal punishments for any peasant refusal to plant potatoes or adopt new field systems. As a rule, peasants were required to give up their best land for the planting of potatoes (in peasant parlance, "the devil's apples"). In the 1830s and 1840s, as their counterparts in Ireland approached the catastrophe of a "potato famine" which eventually cost one million lives, peasants in Viatka, Vladimir, the Northern Urals, and the lower-Volga regions destroyed the potatoes they had been ordered to plant.

The peasant experience of government reform was tellingly described by Alexander Herzen, who was exiled in Viatka province at the time. According to Herzen's account, government officials began by ordering peasants to bury their potatoes in special central pits for storage until after the harvest. In the following spring, peasants were required to dig up the frozen potatoes and to plant them. The only alternative to planting them was to pay a bribe of one ruble each to the appropriate official. In one district where peasants refused either to bribe or to plant, Cossacks were brought in to enforce submission by means of guns and cannons.[46] In general, peasants who fled rather than obey the orders issued by Kiselev's bureaucrats were pursued, brought to trial, knouted, and sent off to Siberia.[47]

From a very different perspective, Herzen's testimony was confirmed in 1842 by Count Benckendorff, head of the government's Third Section, who asked:

> Has their condition been improved by the establishment of new management over them? The peasants themselves answered this question. Disturbances arising among them last year in Olonets, Viatka, Perm, Kazan and Moscow province originated in two major causes: the oppression and extortion of the officials of the Ministry of State Domains and the desire to remain, as formerly, under the authority of the rural police. Although the police displayed no greater regard for the peasant welfare, at least they did not cost the peasant as much. Whereas previously the entire district supported a single police chief and two or three assessors, now officials by the dozens live at the peasants' expense.[48]

In the 1840s, some 500,000 peasants rose up in rebellion against the forcible introduction of potatoes as a crop, and a frustrated Kiselev denounced their resistance as both a sign and a symptom of their backwardness.[49]

In 1842, determined to continue his progressive mission, Kiselev proposed a new and more far-reaching set of reforms intended to apply to serfs as well as state peasants. Invoking the fears generated by the European revolutions of the 1830s, Kiselev argued that Russia had "to provide institutions and guarantees for these millions of people before they get the idea of demanding it themselves."[50] Using the language of Adam Smith, Kiselev argued that it was in the gentry's enlightened self-interest to promote domestic peace by permitting peasants (1) to acquire movable and immovable property, (2) to enter into contracts, and (3) to appeal for redress in courts of law. However, only three serfowners made use of the Kiselev reforms.[51] According to Prince Viazemskii, an old acquaintance of Kiselev, "many sensible and conscientious men are unable to explain them [the reforms] otherwise than being due to some secret influence, some occult conspiracy which acts perniciously on the state and has put it on a fatal course. Many men who occupy influential positions in the government will tell you that Kiselev is at the head of this conspiracy." To conservative nobles of this sort, Kiselev was fostering a dangerous departure from the traditions of serfdom which had for so long sustained Russian society and the state.

In general, when Kiselev's liberal economic goals conflicted with his duties as a government official, his liberalism gave way. Despite his belief in the virtues of private economic effort, Kiselev responded to the state treasury's escalating demands for revenue by ordering the forcible introduction of collective cultivation (*obshchestvennaia zapashka*) in villages where tax arrears were high. According to this system, peasants worked under the supervision of a government official who sold the grain they produced in order to meet the commune's tax obligations. In order to fulfill his political and fiscal responsibilities to the state, Kiselev employed the same coercive means that had served both reformers and traditionalists for centuries.

The peasant experience of change remained oppressive rather than liberating. As in the past, innovations were imposed by force. They entailed increased financial burdens, and were sustained by the addition of another notoriously corrupt layer of bureaucracy.[52] In equally traditional fashion, Kiselev relied on the peasant commune as a stabilizing political force in the countryside despite his belief in the economic superiority of private tenure.[53]

THE SLAVOPHILE/"WESTERNIZER" CHALLENGE[*]

In the 1830s and 1840s, Slavophiles and "Westernizers" posed the first concerted challenge to the traditions of repressive modernization. Although their differences have been much emphasized, they shared some important ideals and cultural values. Both groups publicly denounced serfdom as an abomination in any civilized society, and criticized the government's attempt to create a Prussian-style, bureaucratic police state. Equally united in their opposition to the slogan of "Official Nationality" which condemned all criticism of state policy as anti-Russian,[54] they refused as well to identify the advance of reason with Western strategies for surveillance, control, and manipulation.

Slavophiles shared with their adversaries a delight in Western culture.[55] The memoirist P. V. Annenkov described one encounter between members of both groups at an idyllic summer retreat at the Kireevskii estate in 1845, where "by tacit accord there was no talk about contemporary Russia. European affairs, ideas and discoveries formed the staples of daily conversation."[56] Convinced that Russia needed to look Westward for lessons and examples, Slavophiles differed most profoundly from the self-proclaimed "Westernizer" group in their refusal to believe that liberalism

---

[*]Because members of the self-proclaimed "Westernizer" group were by no means the only Russians who admired the West, I have used quotation marks to distinguish them from other Westernizers of the day.

represented the core value of Western experience. A. S. Khomiakov argued that the English Tories were as typically "Western" as the Whig supporters of Sir Robert Peel, and that the traditions of Prussian social and economic reform constituted a significant feature of Western historical experience.

Slavophiles as Westernizers

Slavophiles were above all enthusiastic admirers of German Romanticism.[57] Having shared a common experience of Napoleonic invasion, Slavophiles and German Romantics rejected the French claim that France was bringing universal principles of freedom and justice rather than political domination to the peoples of Germany and Russia.[58] Distrustful of the uses to which universal principles could be put, Russian students at the universities of Berlin and Vienna set themselves to understand the "organic" nationalist theories of Hegel and Schelling. Those who became Slavophiles were particularly sympathetic to the comparative and empirical approaches to the social sciences that German scholars devised as a defense against more universalistic Western doctrines of law, history, and economics.

Emulating the work of the brothers Grimm and Baron August von Haxthausen, the Russian brothers Kireevskii, V. Dal', and A. I. Afanasiev collected peasant folklore and proverbs, carried out ethnographic studies, and reflected on the institutions and values of the peasantry (the *narod*, or in German, the *Volk*). In a nineteenth-century world increasingly dominated by claims for the universal political, economic, and scientific achievements of England and France, Romantics emphasized the virtue of the nation, and of particular ethnic and social groups. Despite Western judgments to the contrary, Slavophiles argued that Russia possessed a history and culture which was worthy of respect.

In their effort to prove that Russia constituted something more than a receptacle for the riches of Anglo-French civilization, the Slavophiles emerged as the first group of educated Russians ever to claim that peasants possessed a culture and institutions that belonged to the present and future as well as to the past. Taking Tsar Nicholas I's slogan of "Orthodoxy, Autocracy and Nationality" far more seriously than it had ever been intended, they looked far into Russia's past and conjured up a world of free peasant communes—a place where the Orthodox Church did not function as a tool of bureaucratic authority, and the power of the Tsar was rooted in the spiritual bonds created by his patriarchal wisdom and guidance. As in other times and places, Romantic assertions of cultural legitimacy all too frequently led them to invent, exaggerate, or justify traditions that had little to recommend them.[59]

Extremely unlikely champions of the common people, the Slavophiles were serfowners who called for emancipation without imagining for a moment that peasants were—or could be—their social or political equals. It was inconceivable to aristocrats like Khomiakov and Iurii Samarin that a Russian society might come into being which did not accord them a leading role.[60] At the same time, when Slavophiles argued that the nation's true character did not reside in the nobility, the intelligentsia, or any other elite, but in the plebian communal institutions and Christian values of the peasantry, they unwittingly raised issues that transcended the limits of gentry self-interest. As creators of a national myth in which a wide range of Russians could take pride, Slavophiles represented far more than a landed gentry attempting to revitalize the religious and political traditions which sustained them in power. The Slavophile focus on popular tradition and practices inspired a generation of radical intellectuals to demand a peasant-oriented, revolutionary struggle for socialism.

The Romantic Slavophile vision of a Christian and communitarian *Volk* coexisted with a profound admiration for Western science and technology. Khomiakov frequently met with Slavophile estate-owners like A. I. Koshelev and I. V. Kireevskii to discuss the latest modern Western farm machinery, and he himself invented a steam engine christened "Moscow," which was eventually sent to the Great London Exhibition of 1851. According to Khomiakov, Russians were obliged "to borrow those Western inventions by which the law can be strengthened, businesses widened, social welfare improved. . . . We must now learn the difference between the achievements of our Western brothers which are universal human ones, and those of purely local, particular [application]."[61]

Attempting to discover the historical conditions that promoted the survival and enrichment of his aristocratic counterparts elsewhere, Khomiakov celebrated the English nobility's flexibility and receptiveness to change.[62] Like the Tory Edmund Burke, Khomiakov described progress as an organic process which preserved some aspects of the past. In Khomiakov's words: "One could hardly accuse England of remaining stationary, of turning her face away from new things. Only she does not cut century-old trees in order to plant feeble year-old seedlings. . . . She somehow guessed that only by preserving could she move forward, that true progress consists in what never repudiates its own origins."[63]

In general, Slavophiles rejected the dichotomized, "all or nothing" choices between the past and the present, or between the West and Russia that were characteristic of liberal models for change. Although Samarin agreed with liberal economic arguments for free labor and exchange, he insisted that other liberal doctrines were applicable primarily to the national cultures that had produced them. In his measured assessment of classical economics: "I remain convinced that this science (or more precisely this series of conclusions based on the history of the development of national economies in the West) deserves neither the disfavor with which respectable people have viewed it for some time, nor the great significance ascribed to it by those who see in society a company of stockholders, and in national life a trading venture." Agreeing with the Prussian reformer Lorentz von Stein that liberal capitalist economies were productive but "unbalanced" and biased toward the property owner, Samarin contended that revolutionary communist movements erupted in nineteenth-century Europe as a consequence of the "inordinate" concentration of property ownership in the hands of a few.[64]

Equally dismayed at what he described as the "savage power of property" in nineteenth-century England, the Slavophile Khomiakov condemned both the Whigs and the Tories for supporting policies that led to economic and social polarization.[65] According to the Slavophile Ivan Aksakov, England's enclosure movement permitted the gentry to dispossess the laborers who created their wealth, and placed landless peasants in a bitterly antagonistic relationship to capital. In an argument that might have come from Karl Marx, he contended that enclosure produced a forcible and "artificial" concentration of landed property in the hands of the upper classes: "In the absence of free soil, the impossibility of giving a definite bare minimum of land to the popular masses, all this in Europe gave birth to a class of landless agricultural laborers crushed by the despotism of capital which provided them with the work necessary for their subsistence."[66]

In search of a better Western model, Khomiakov looked to the French countryside, where small landed proprietors rather than giant estates were the norm. Hoping that the French agricultural economy would confirm the truth of Adam Smith's dictum that the best agriculture united owner and cultivator in the same person, Khomiakov discovered instead that French peasants were (1) relatively unproductive, and (2) in dire need of the tranquillizing presence of Smith's "invisible hand." According to Khomiakov, French small proprietors were obsessed with short-term economic gain. Delighting in the hope that they could profit from the ruin of their neighbors, French peasants pursued their farming and marketing activities in an explosive atmosphere of mutual antagonism and suspicion.[67]

Although classical liberal theorists claimed that productive and innovative economic behavior was rooted in private-property rights, Khomiakov observed that French small proprietors were far less innovative than England's large-scale tenants. Was it possible, Khomiakov asked, that liberal economists were wrong to assume that private property rights were a *sine qua non* for progress and innovation? If Russia's peasant communes repartitioned allotments less frequently, might it be possible to avoid both the evils of "English-style" proletarianization and the rapacity and short-sightedness of French peasant proprietors? Khomiakov proposed a careful study of the West in order to figure out how to introduce "initiative-generating" private allotments and other opportunities for private profit into the commune framework. If Russia were successful in such a venture, he argued that a modern Russian agriculture might prosper in a less violent and socially disruptive fashion than in England or France.[68]

In the writings of Khomiakov, economic progress was linked with freedom and material security but not with equality. Proposing that peasants be emancipated with allotments of land and as members of their traditional communes, he argued that without land, emancipation would produce little more than a horizontal shift from wretched serf to wretched proletarian; without the commune, freedom would simply establish "Western-style" isolation and conflict as the dominant feature of rural life. According to Khomiakov's ideal scenario for change, a commune peasantry secure in their claims to land would be encouraged to innovate by equally secure but far wealthier Slavophile estate owners.

In the peasant commune, Slavophiles discovered an alternative to the socially destructive egoism and greed which seemed to them typical of Western European economies governed by unrestricted private property rights arrangements. In the case of Khomiakov at least, Slavophile support for the commune was quite unsentimental. As he saw it, unlimited greed destroyed the social cohesion necessary for the survival of the nation; the communes functioned to protect society from such a danger. Although they were in no sense idyllic communities which prevented exploitation, violence, or the connivance of the strong against the weak, Khomiakov argued that anti-social behavior was inconsistent with commune principles and could be opposed by its members with some hope of success. In contrast, he asserted that inequitable power relationships were inherent and insuperable under private-property systems that encouraged individuals to triumph at the expense of their neighbors.[69]

Ivan Kireevskii denounced Western individualism as an ideal that encouraged isolation and alienation, by establishing each person "*within his rights*, a despotic, unlimited individual who is the law unto himself. The first step of every man in society is to surround himself with a fortress, from the depth of which he begins negotiation with other independent powers." Kireevskii insisted that the Russian peasant's repartitional land communes embodied social principles more profound and more just than the profit-seeking motives that inspired the proponents of bourgeois individualism. Rejecting the "narrowness" of Western ideals of respect for the individual, which ignored the individual's material needs, Kireevskii argued that in practice, liberals respected property more than its owner. He contrasted the Western habit of devaluing individuals who owned little or nothing with the Russian commune, whose respect for the individual was manifest in the guarantees it provided for the individual's material survival.[70] In many respects, the Slavophile ideal of the commune resembled the God of Russian peasant folktales, who granted prosperity to the undeserving, regardless of logical calculations of economic or noneconomic merit. In the generosity and "grace" of its promise of rights to livelihood for bad as well as good peasants, the commune embodied the Slavophile ideal of a Christian community.

Aside from their religious ideals, Slavophile enthusiasm for free peasants and communes was rooted above all in their political and economic interests as members of the landed gentry. As members of Russia's hereditary elite, they wanted to ensure that Russian peasants would not engage in a French-style revolution that destroyed the very principles of hereditary privilege. Fearing the vengeance of a free peasantry, Ivan Kireevskii abandoned the cause of emancipation in the 1840s, but held fast to his faith in the stabilizing influence of the peasant commune. The Slavophile Khomiakov made use of the commune to enforce his seigneurial demands and intended to profit handsomely from a peasant emancipation with land.[71] As Janet Vaillant has astutely noted, Slavophile admiration for the commune never led them to propose that they should themselves be placed in a position of dependence upon its rewards or subjection to communal limits upon their private ambitions or interests.[72]

The spectacle of serfowners proclaiming the "saintliness" of their peasant property aroused the contempt of unsympathetic observers. Ethnographic collections and books of peasant proverbs sometimes contained overwrought introductions and ridiculous claims for the noble simplicity of the *muzhik*, and works like I. P. Sakarov's *Legends of the Russian People,* sounded a distinctly xenophobic note. The Slavophile journal *Maiak* celebrated the immutable wisdom of the peasantry and denounced the teachings of an insuperably corrupt and immoral West. Slavophile love for the common people sometimes overflowed into sentimentality and foolishness. In one comedy of errors, Ivan Aksakov grew a beard, donned what he thought was a traditional kaftan, and set out in search of Christlike peasants, only to be mistaken by them for some kind of "Persian." The police, evidently operating on the same wavelength as Aksakov, ordered him to shave off the beard, which they considered to be a dangerous symbol of solidarity with the common people.[73]

The "Westernizers"

To members of Russia's first, self-proclaimed "Westernizer" group, Slavophile efforts to reinvent the brutal predecessors of Peter the Great as benevolent and patriarchal rulers seemed both ludicrous and contemptible. According to V. G. Belinskii and the young Alexander Herzen, the Russian people did not need a revitalized Romanov dynasty; they required instead precisely the kind of laws and constitutional guarantees that protected the citizens of Western European nations from the arbitrary cruelty to be found at every level of Russian society. In the context of censorship, political repression, and the brutal mistreatment of serfs, the Moscow University historian T. N. Granovskii contended that the "legalistic formalities" scorned by the Slavophiles were in fact the only reliable safeguard of individual freedom and dignity.[74] Above all, in contrast to Westernizers like Mordvinov, the "Westernizer" group of the 1840s were political dissidents who insisted that Western liberties could not be reconciled with the preservation of serfdom, autocracy, or hereditary privilege.

In comparison with the Slavophiles, "Westernizers" wrote very little on the subject of economics. They did not study Russian history and, as Anthony Netting has pointed out, they did not like what little they knew.[75] In the 1830s, Granovskii and Belinskii admired the audacity of eccentrics like Peter Chaadeev and Moscow University's M. T. Kachenovskii, who described Russia as a nation without culture or civilization, and dismissed Russia's past as "equal to zero." It is particularly revealing that Granovskii's famous Moscow University lectures on world history in the 1840s completely omitted Russia (along with other "nonhistorical" societies like China and India).[76] When these nations began to follow the Western European path of development, they would presumably enter into history; but for the time being, Granovskii did not consider them an appropriate topic in world history.

According to the "Westernizer," Russia's lack of history was directly linked to the character of its peasant population. Belinskii contended that the social relations of peasants were simple and brutal, their feelings monotonous, and their economic behavior irrational. In his words, one did not seek to discover the spirit of the Russian nation in "a homespun coat, bast slippers, cheap vodka or sour cabbage," but in "the social groups that emerged after the reforms of Peter the Great, and adopted a civilized way of life."[77] Viewing peasants as survivors of a primitive stage of human development in which all culture was absent, Belinskii ridiculed the Slavophiles as romantics who collected trivial information and proclaimed it "peasant wisdom."

"Westernizers" dismissed the peasant commune as a transitory social formation that corresponded to the needs of a primitive tribal people. Reflecting on the weakness of property rights among the peasantry, the young Alexander Herzen asked: "Is it surprising that among our peasants the right to property has not developed in the direction of individual tenure when we remember that his strip of land is not his own and even his wife, son and daughter do not belong to him?"[78] According to Granovskii, peasant communes were destined to be replaced by Western-style constitutional governments which guaranteed the rights of private ownership.[79]

Although Russia's "Westernizers" admired almost every aspect of Western society and culture, they were ambivalent about the virtues of the bourgeois property owner. V. Miliutin cited Sismondi's denunciations of the irresponsible Western entrepreneur, while Belinskii wrote in the language of an Old Testament prophet: "Woe to the state which is in the hands of the capitalist. . . . The huckster is a creature by nature vulgar, mean, base and despicable . . . more inexorable than death, he makes children work themselves to death for him." Nevertheless, however contemptuous he was of the "huckster," Belinskii feared that "states without a middle class [were] condemned to nothingness." Perhaps, he reasoned, it was the *petty* bourgeoisie who were responsible for the despicable cruelties of early-nineteenth-century capitalism. Or maybe the social and economic evils documented by Etienne Cabet and Pierre Proudhon were simply the survivals of feudalism—part of the Western effort "to free herself from the medieval social order and replace it by a system based on reason and human nature."[80]

In similar fashion, Miliutin denied the Slavophile claim that the poverty of French and English laborers represented a defect of Western civilization. In his words, "The terrible situation of the French working classes is the occasion for the most unfounded attacks on the West. Its present situation reveals only confusion and the clash of opinions and interests. But we are not prepared to realize that this clash of interests is a sign not of disintegration but of life, that it does not reveal the corruption of society but its maturity, its vitality, its energy."[81] In search of a social group capable of playing the role of historical agent of Russia's progress, "Westernizers" attempted to absolve the middle class of responsibility for the callousness of the huckster and the poverty of the proletarian.[82]

In contrast to their uncertainties about the middle class, "Westernizers" were confident in their judgment of the peasantry's character and potential. According to Anthony Netting's astute characterization of the "Westernizer" view of the peasantry, "the folk would become truly Russian only when they became human, human only as they acquired one by one enlightenment and the fruits of Western culture."[83] In stories written by the Westernizer D. V. Grigorovich, peasants were brutalized creatures, dehumanized by their isolation from the civilized, and by the oppressive bonds of serfdom. As Herzen wrote of the peasant, "His position is even worse than that of the proletarian. He is a thing, a mere tool to cultivate the fields, whose master can do everything except kill him. . . . Give him the legal right to self-defense. Only then will he be a man.[84]

Adopting the Western liberal view that peasants everywhere in the world were mired in some variant of the "Dark" or "Middle Ages" already traversed by Western Europeans, Russia's "Westernizers" labeled peasants and their defenders as "Eastern," "Oriental," and "Asiatic" in their backwardness and depravity. In the words of V. I. Miliutin, "the mind of the Russian people had not yet woken up," but remained sunk in "Oriental barbarism." According to Belinskii, their Slavophile defenders were hopelessly "Oriental." In their struggle to defend the West against the "folk-mania" of the Slavophiles, the "Westernizer" group were clearly far more afraid of being charged with sentimentality than than they were of the accusation that they were elitist and narrow-minded.

"Westernizers" vs. Slavophiles

Like the eighteenth-century *philosophes* they so fervently admired, Russia's "Westernizers" were eager to conceive of human progress as the differentiation of the best, the "thinking" elements—individuals not unlike themselves, perhaps—from a stagnant and featureless peasant mass. In Granovskii's words, "The process of history consists of the individuation of the masses by thought. Its goal is the morally enlightened individual, independent of determining conditions, and a society corresponding to the demands of such an individual."[85]

In the heartfelt response to Granovskii's Moscow University lectures of the 1840s, it is evident how important it was for educated Russians to prove to others (and to themselves) that they exemplified this individuation process. After one such lecture, Alexander Herzen recalled: "The applause, the shouting, the fury of approbation doubled, the students ranged themselves on each side of the stairs . . . Granovskii made his way, exhausted to the council-room; a few minutes later he left it, and again there was endless clapping; he turned, begging for mercy with a gesture and ready to drop with emotion, went into the office. There I flung myself on his neck and we wept in silence."[86] Responses of this sort do not simply demonstrate the passions of the Slavic temperament. By demonstrating that Russian scholars were as eloquent, gifted, and above all as *Europeanized* as any English subject or French citizen, Granovskii was proving to all and sundry that in its intellectual development, Russia had come of age as a civilized and European nation.

Believing that they were the hope of Russia's future, "Westernizers" like Granovskii, Belinskii, and Kavelin drew a sharp distinction between themselves and the backward peasant majority of the Russian population.

According to Granovskii, the masses were either "thoughtlessly cruel or thoughtlessly good-natured."[87] With rare exceptions, Belinskii agreed with Voltaire's judgments on the fanatic and bloodthirsty common people, who in Belinskii's words, delighted in "tortures and executions."[88] The "Westernizer" Kavelin described the peasantry as Russia's "60,000,000 half-wild and ignorant people."[89]

The courageous "Westernizer" demands for individual freedom, civil liberties, and the rule of law were strikingly at odds with the contempt and fear they expressed for the "backward." In contrast to Belinskii, the Slavophile Konstantin Aksakov challenged his fellow serfowners: "Give people a chance to do something by themselves . . . you are not dealing with cattle after all, but with people, who have a much better understanding of social matters than you, members of the honorable gentry assembly."[90]

The Slavophile Khomiakov contended that the "civilized" had no right to approach the common people as their superiors, in the manner of English colonials who claimed to love the Hottentots; it was important to treat ordinary peasants "with the respect of equals."[91] For his part, the "Westernizer" Belinskii contended that "the common people are always children, always immature," arguing that "Every educated man today, no matter how remote he stands in form and essence from the life of the people, well understands the *muzhik* without lowering himself to his level."[92]

To the Slavophiles, the "Westernizer" refusal to recognize that peasants were already human beings was both callous and dangerous. According to Ivan Aksakov, the denial of the peasantry's humanity could be used to justify efforts to assume total control over them—"to change the people into a *tabula rasa,* into such obedient material that Peter the Great hardly dared to dream of."[93] Progressives who considered peasants civilized only if they abandoned all things "Russian," were in his view likely to promote modernity by using coercion to obliterate "all-too-Russian" social elements or institutions.[94] Khomiakov pointed out that in centuries past, when Russia's landed gentry enslaved the peasantry and seized their land, they justified their actions by claiming that they were protecting peasants too helpless to survive on their own.[95] Fearing that Western liberal judgments about peasant backwardness could serve a similarly repressive purpose, Khomiakov predicted that a Westernizing elite might well emerge as "colonizers in their own country," who subjugated the peasantry for their own good and in the name of progress.[96] It is one of history's ironies that serfowning Slavophiles rather than commoners like Belinskii were more willing to recognize that peasants were neither tools nor, in Herzen's terms, "things," but human beings with a culture and with institutions which enabled them to endure the evils of serfdom that "Westernizers" so passionately denounced.

In general, Western and Soviet scholarly assessments of the "Westernizers" have contrasted their struggle for civil liberties with the patriarchal Orthodoxy of the Slavophiles and the economic interests that underlay the Slavophile "love" of the peasantry. But it may be that a particularly stringent and selective standard has been applied to the Slavophiles. Both Ivan Aksakov and Iurii Samarin were imprisoned in the Peter/Paul Fortress for writing on behalf of peasant emancipation. While the "Westernizer" Granovskii became the most popular lecturer at Moscow University and was eventually appointed dean of the faculty, Ivan Kireevskii, A. S. Khomiakov and K. T. Aksakov were forced to agree in writing not to publish anything without the prior approval of the government censorship office. In a letter to Herzen, Samarin observed that "If we were friends and allies of the Unforgettable (Tsar Nicholas I), you will agree that we concealed our friendship more skillfully than you people showed your hostility toward him."[97]

From a moral standpoint, Kireevskii's apologetics for the seventeenth-century Tsar Alexis and the Orthodox Church were not more (or less) reprehensible than (1) Belinskii's willingness to ignore Voltaire's support for Russian serfdom, (2) Kavelin's praise for the "progressive" virtues of Ivan the Terrible's *oprichinina*,[98] and (3) Granovskii's declaration that "What we need now is not only another Peter the Great, but also his stick, to teach the Russian ignoramuses reason."[99]

It took a measure of courage for the Slavophile gentry to argue that peasant welfare should be the standard by which Russian achievement should be measured. In later years, Minister of Education A. S. Norov described the political threat posed by Slavophiles in the following terms: "To present the lower orders as a pattern of all possible virtues and the upper classes as an example of all possible deficiencies and moral weakness is harmful and . . . likely to have fatal consequences."[100]

In the Slavophile/"Westernizer" controversy, admirers of Liberal notions of individual freedom enthusiastically consigned the landed gentry, the peasantry, and their communes to an obsolete and medieval past. In contrast, the aristocratic Slavophile proponents of Romanticism defended indigenous and traditional institutions, rejected notions of social equality, and were optimistic about the potential development of a national culture that included non-elite contributors. For their part, the self-proclaimed "Westernizer" group dismissed the claims of Russian history, tradition, and hereditary privilege, arguing that serfdom and autocracy were the worst of Russia's evils. Whatever their misgivings about the West, they could imagine nothing better than the replacement of "feudal" Russia with its peasant communes, autocratic rulers and serfowners, by a government of laws and free citizens whose middle classes were capable of doing battle with the survivals of a despicable past.

In contrast, Slavophiles insisted that the landed gentry, the monarch, the church, and the peasantry could all play a constructive role in Russia's economic and noneconomic future (with the gentry assuming a role similar to the Tory landowners of the English countryside). While "Westernizers" ridiculed the notion that there was any logic or rationality to peasant economic or social behavior, Slavophiles situated the peasantry within a complex network of—as they saw it—defensible and even admirable values and institutions created by peasants themselves. Far more empirically minded than their "Westernizer" counterparts, Slavophiles were the first folklorists and ethnographers of the Russian rural scene; it was only in the Slavophile journal *Maiak* that one could find the writings of peasants and laborers. As was the case for Romantics elsewhere, the investigations carried out by the Slavophiles were linked with the beginnings of social science.[101]

The Challenge of Empirical Data: August Haxthausen

In the context of a century of debate largely independent of any empirical grounding, Baron August von Haxthausen's study of the Russian countryside (entitled *The Russian Empire*) appeared to some as a revelation and to others as an unwelcome shock. The product of a 7,000-mile journey across European Russia undertaken in 1843 at the invitation of Count Kiselev, Haxthausen's book tended to support many of the contentions of the Slavophiles. In every region of the Empire, the Westphalian agricultural expert documented peasant customs of acting in common. In farming, in cottage industry, and even in prison, he discovered that peasants elected elders, defined their mutual obligations, and participated in activities based upon decisions they made in common. However, Haxthausen did not claim that such behavior was productive in economic terms. Periodic repartition and customs of buying and selling in common did not seem to foster increases in agricultural output, the quality of the crop harvested, or the profits of marketing. In many villages, the stronger, more intelligent, or more unscrupulous peasants took advantage of the weak. It seemed likely to Haxthausen that the growth of private interest and competition would eventually undermine traditions of communal behavior.[102]

However, while the technological backwardness and inefficiency of the commune came as no surprise, Haxthausen was astonished to discover a

flexibility and variation in communal economic practices, which contradicted prevailing liberal stereotypes about the commune's rigidity. Quite willing to modify methods or times of repartition as the occasion warranted, communes apparently did not mechanically or irrationally impose frequent repartitions upon member households. Although commune critics emphasized the disadvantages of insecure tenure, Haxthausen noted that many commune peasants expected to retain possession of their allotments for ten to fifteen years at a time. Like the Slavophile Khomiakov, who pointed out that long-term English tenants were more productive than small-scale French property-owners, Haxthausen suggested that if commune peasants could expect to reap what they had sown over an extended time period, they might well be willing to invest intelligence, labor, and capital into projects for agricultural improvement. As he saw it, communal patterns of interdependence and flexibility even possessed some advantages over private economic effort. For example, communes were more able than private individuals to organize community-wide efforts at land clearing or swamp drainage.[103] By the conclusion of his journey, Haxthausen had come to believe that that it might be possible for Russia's much-needed Agricultural Revolution to take place without the abolition of communal tenure.

It should be emphasized that there was nothing either democratic nor egalitarian about Haxthausen's analysis. Certain that it was for the well-born and well-educated social elements in Russian society to develop the peasantry's potential, he valued the commune above all for its stabilizing influence. At the same time, unlike Russia's "Westernizer" group, Haxthausen was considerably more willing to believe that peasants might be actors as well as victims in Russian rural life. Disagreeing with Belinskii's view of peasants who delighted in "tortures and executions" and Granovskii's description of the masses as either "thoughtlessly cruel or thoughtlessly good-natured," Haxthausen reported with benevolent enjoyment on the peasants of Saratov: "What handsome, vigorous-looking people! Their faces full of character, and with an expression of intelligence much above their cultivation but indicating what they may and will become, with time, opportunity and judicious guidance, if increasing earnestness and a better acquaintance with their national peculiarities be applied to their education."[104]

According to Count Benckendorff, head of the government's secret police, Haxthausen's views were "dangerously liberal." Moscow University's Ivan Vernadskii, Russia's leading economist in the 1850s, described Haxthausen as a representative of "the darkest reaction."[105] But to the erstwhile Westernizer Alexander Herzen, Haxthausen's work meant something very different. Haxhausen's study provided him with the empirical basis for a radical, peasant, and commune-oriented revolutionary ideology which dominated Russia's opposition politics, culture, and economics in the second half of the nineteenth century.

Alexander Herzen: Dilemmas of Progress

> It is painful and ugly to live in Russia, this is true; and it was all the more painful for us in that we thought that in other countries it was easy and agreeable to live. . . . Now we know that even there it is painful.
> (Alexander Herzen)

In the 1840s, Alexander Herzen began to distance himself from the "Westernizer" group. His change of heart was triggered by a deepening suspicion that at the core of Western liberalism there lay—alongside the unassailable ideal of individual rights and freedoms—a rigid denial that material poverty could undermine and destroy an individual's freedom of action. From a far more egalitarian perspective than the Slavophiles, Herzen suggested that liberalism bred arrogance and contempt for "the primitive" and a refusal to take seriously the values of any non-Western culture. As he saw it, these values coexisted with a wholly admirable Liberal commitment to reason and progress.

Exiled in Paris during the "June days" of 1848, Herzen looked on with horror as a democratically elected French National Assembly—with the *laissez faire* economist Frederic Bastiat solidly in the forefront—cheered General Cavaignac's massacre of the rebellious Paris poor and defended the rights of property. In the months to come, democratic parliaments went down to defeat in Paris, Vienna, and Frankfurt, with the help of a Russian government, which reclaimed its eighteenth-century role as counter-revolutionary "gendarme of Europe." The Russian liberal Boris Chicherin welcomed Russian military interventions and railed against the "democratic masses who rose up, without pretext and without reason, like an unbridled mob prepared to overthrow those very institutions that had been created for them."[106]

Herzen reacted very differently. As he saw it, the events of 1848 and 1849 had proven beyond question that without a substantial measure of social and economic democracy, politically democratic institutions could not resist the corrupting power of the wealthy. However free English and French laborers may have been, neither extensions of the suffrage, civil liberties, nor the guarantees provided by laws, courts, and constitutions empowered them to prevent the rich from transforming democracies into a tool for the perpetuation of economic inequality.[107] Disillusioned with what he considered the hypocrisy of Western liberal democracy, Herzen welcomed Haxthausen's evidence that within the humble peasant commune, illiterate serfs engaged in rudimentary but democratic decision-making about the organization of labor and land use. In his enthusiasm for Haxthausen's findings, Herzen proceeded to create a quite idealized image of the commune peasant who though "improvident and indolent by nature" was wonderfully honest in dealings with other peasants and averse to every form of private landed property.[108]

Although Herzen no longer viewed the West as a panacea for the evils that plagued Russian society and culture, he continued to admire many aspects of Western culture. According to Herzen, Western scientific achievements, "independent of political systems and nationality," were "ready to transform men's burdensome historical existence everywhere it encounters a suitable soil, understanding, strength and will."[109] Even as he argued that the peasant commune represented the "cornerstone" upon which Russia's future would be built, Herzen ridiculed any notion that "sharing the prejudices of the people meant being at one with them, or that it was a great act of humility to sacrifice their own reason instead of developing reason in the people."[110]

Herzen contended that the opportunity to take a *selective* stance toward the West represented one of the few advantages afforded latecomers on the path of modernization and development. Unlike England and France, the more backward nations could at least choose to adopt what was beneficial and reject what was inhumane or impractical. In Herzen's words,

> We have no reason to repeat the epic story of your emancipation, in the course of which your road has become so encumbered by the monuments of the past that you are hardly able to take a single step ahead. Your labors and your sufferings are our lessons. History is very unjust. The latecomers receive instead of the gnawed bones [the right] of precedence [at the table] of experience. All of the development of mankind is nothing else but [an expression of] that chronological ingratitude.[111]

Opposed to the notion that Russian had to drive peasants from the land in order to acquire "English" ideals of personal liberty or superior levels of scientific and technological advancement, Herzen contended that educated Russians could act as "apostles" of Western science and progress to peasants who already understood the realities of social cooperation.[112]

To his former "Westernizer" colleagues in Russia, Herzen's claim that peasant communal traditions were superior to Western guarantees of political and civil liberty seemed both reactionary and incomprehensible. Granovskii accused him of being out of touch with the dreary realities of a Russian political system that inflicted arbitrary censorship, imprisonment and exile upon its critics.[113] The novelist Ivan Turgenev warned that the long-suffering *muzhik* was no primitive socialist; in reality, Turgenev argued, peasants were potential capitalists—as greedy and calculating as they were competitive.[114] Herzen's response to Turgenev was revealing. Instead of defending the peasantry, he invited Turgenev to reflect upon the ease and confidence with which he and Turgenev—both men of high status within Russian society—passed judgment upon the peasantry's character and potential. Given the Russian elite's unearned social privilege and failure to undertake wide-ranging empirical investigations of peasant life, Herzen suggested that perhaps a measure of intellectual humility was warranted. Taking seriously his own alienated position, first as an educated Russian and secondly as a wealthy refugee in Western Europe, Herzen argued that the life experience of the upper classes did not automatically transform them into experts on the lives of ordinary people. In his words,

> We men of European urban civilization can, in general, live only a ready-made life. Town life accustoms us from early childhood to the fact that discordant forces are secretly balanced and kept in check behind the scenes. When we are by chance knocked off the rails on which this life installs us on the day of our birth and carefully moves us after that, we are as much at a loss as the impractical *savant*, accustomed to museums and . . . wild animals in cases, is at a loss when confronted with the traces of a geological cataclysm.

According to Herzen, there were intellectual drawbacks as well as stunning advantages to wisdom which was the fruit of privilege and alienation—there were limits as well as depth to the understanding possessed by a Western man of culture. Russian proponents of change had no right to approach the common people, about whom they knew so little, with demands that the peasants "give their blood" for any change, so long as it was designated as "Western." Herzen argued that it was high time that privileged Russians began "to toil for the benefit of the Russian people, which in its time has toiled enough for us!"[115]

In the middle decades of the nineteenth century, Herzen's perspective was quite unusual. At a time when Russia's "Westernizers" routinely complained of the "Oriental" backwardness of peasants and Slavophiles, and English thinkers like John Stuart Mill decried the "lifeless inertia of the oriental peoples" of China or Persia, Herzen questioned the implications of a worldview that dismissed the non-Western peoples of the world as insignificant and unworthy. Among educated Russians, he may have been alone in his observation that such liberal judgments were neither objective nor scientific. Noting the frequency with which liberals used words and phrases like "Asiatic cruelty," "Persian," or "Oriental" to express their contempt for "inferior" nations and peoples of the world, he rather mildly remarked: "In all fairness, I do not know, either, how it comes that China and Persia may be insulted with impunity."[116]

In the decades to come, Herzen's ideas were attacked by Slavophiles and "Westernizers" alike. According to Herzen, "In their eyes [the Slavophiles'] I am a man of the West and in the eyes of their enemies a man of the East." With a stunning lack of insight into the future course of Russia's relationship with the West, Herzen concluded, "This means that such one-sided labels have already become obsolete."[117]

Chapter Four

UNIVERSALISM AND ITS DISCONTENTS

THE LAWS OF HISTORY, ECONOMICS, AND HUMAN

PROGRESS

> England represents to other nations of the world the image of
> their future
>   *(Karl Marx)*

> Whoever knows the political economy of England, or even of
> Yorkshire, knows that of all nations, actual or possible.
>   *(John Stuart Mill)*

> Who in the world would dare to say that there is any form of
> order that would satisfy in an identical manner Iroquois and
> Irish, Arab and Magyar, Kaffir and Slav?
>   *(Alexander Herzen)*

The Romance of the Universal

RUSSIA'S INTELLECTUAL history during the second half of the
nineteenth century revealed how wrong Herzen was to predict
that polarized distinctions between "the universal perfections of
the West" and "the utter backwardness of the East" (including Russia)
would soon be a thing of the past. Instead, the notion that all human behavior could be understood according to principles derived by Western thinkers from the study of Western Europe took on the appearance of a scientific fact. As England acquired unprecedented power and wealth in the world of nations, it seemed equally logical to argue that English-style capitalism, property systems, and social classes embodied the universal truths of economic science. In a peculiar mid-nineteenth-century meeting of the minds, thinkers as different as John Stuart Mill, Karl Marx, and August Comte agreed that England represented to other nations the image of their future.

COMTEAN VISIONS OF ECONOMIC PROGRESS

It was August Comte—today the most neglected of the three, and the one least recognized for his economic insights—who may have contributed most to the belief that Western European economics was universally applicable. It is worth recalling that in the 1850s, Comte was viewed as one of the greatest thinkers of his day. In the middle decades of the nineteenth century, schools for the propagation of his ideas sprang up in Paris, London, and Berlin, where Comte's European admirers included Adolphe Quetelet, the "father of modern statistics," John Stuart Mill, and the German scientist Justus von Liebig. Elsewhere in the world, Comteans built temples of "Reason" in Rio de Janeiro, played a leading role in China's Taiping Uprising, published journals in Mexico and Colombia, and emblazoned the Comtean slogan of "Order and Progress" on the flag of Argentina (where it remains to this day).[1]

In Russia, *savants* from Herzen and Belinskii to the statistician Poroshin and the economist Balugianskii found something to admire in the vast outpouring of translations from Comte's work. Believing that the nation's future depended on Russia's capacity and will to replicate the steps taken by Western societies in their ascent from rags to riches, Moscow University's K. D. Kavelin declared that Comtean "laws of society" were as universal, scientific, orderly, and immutable as the laws of modern physics.[2] According to the Comtean scenario, as human history unfolded, backward and medieval peasant societies governed by priests and warriors everywhere gave way to a world dominated by experts charged with the task of creating a prosperous and scientific industrial paradise. To the followers of Comte, progress was a unilinear process along a path already marked out by the leading Western European nations.

In a world of constant evolution and change, it is significant that the institution of private property was Comte's one fixed point of reference. To the best-selling Comtean economist Frederic Bastiat, the desire to own property was the most natural and beneficial of human qualities. In his words, "man is born a proprietor . . . man lives and develops by the process of appropriation. . . . Appropriation is a natural, providential phenomenon . . ."[3] In primitive societies, Comte's disciples predicted that irrational and outmoded communal traditions would everywhere be replaced by gifted, profit-seeking, property-owners who would assume leadership and guarantee material abundance for all. In keeping with Comte's "science of society," scholars, technicians, industrialists, and financiers would gradually acquire the power and wealth that they so richly deserved. The masses—despite their lack of prudence, intelligence, and altruism—would come to enjoy both the prosperity and peace of mind provided for them by their betters.[4]

In the course of the ninteenth century, the "vanguard" orientation of Comte's "science of society" appealed to elites—or would-be elites—of every ideological orientation. Both conservatives and radicals warmed to Comte's "scientific" prediction that the intelligent were destined to triumph everywhere over the enemies of Reason. Political conservatives who feared that a revolution in the social sciences might lead to revolutions in contemporary political or social life were reassured by Comte's argument that modern social scientists were the most effective defenders of stability and order against the irrationality of the lower classes. In his *Du système sociale* (1848), the statistician Adolphe Quetelet proposed that monarchs make use of the new social science of statistics to "understand the factions that ordinarily divide a state, in order to judge the most appropriate means for combating and paralyzing them."[5] In some respects, Comte and his disciples performed an intellectual service which recalls the effort by an earlier generation of Cameralist thinkers who attempted to reconcile fundamental economic change with the preservation of traditional political authority.[6]

In December 1852 and April 1853, Comte addressed two obsequious letters to Tsar Nicholas I, inviting him to be the first of the world's rulers to implement a "System of Positive Politics." Praising Russia as a nation "innocent" of the corruption that plagued the West, he attempted to convince the tsar to adopt a "religion of humanity" that was neither democratic nor revolutionary. Comte predicted that, if Russia took such a "wise action," a gifted elite would soon emerge to create wealth, prosperity, and civilization for all in a painless and gradual process, which forever lifted the burden of political and economic decision-making from the shoulders of hapless commoners.[7]

Although there is no evidence that the tsar ever read Comte's letters, his message of "Order and Progress" attracted favorable notice in government journals and in publications like the *Economist, Russian Messenger,* and *Atheneum.* The legal scholar B. N. Chicherin argued that the Russian nobility was destined to take its place as a natural elite of *meliorés.* In a book entitled *The Aristocracy and the Interests of the Dvorianstvo* (1859), the economist and official V. P. Bezobrazov called upon the landed gentry to take their places within an emerging elite of talent capable of devising projects for the "betterment of humanity."[8]

IVAN VERNADSKII AND HIS SCHOOL: ENGLAND AS AN ECONOMIC MODEL

In the 1850s, Russia's leading professional economist was I. P. Vernadskii, a scholar whose contribution to Russia's Westernizing discourse has been curiously neglected by students of Russian intellectual history. A professor of economics and statistics first at Kiev and then at Moscow University, a delegate to the International Congress of Statisticians in Vienna (1857), London (1860), and Berlin (1863), an official of the Ministry of the Interior after 1856, and chair of the committee of political economy of the Imperial Free Economic Society, Vernadskii was also the publisher and leading contributor to the journal *The Economist*. A translator of Comte, Bastiat, and J. B. Say, and author of over a dozen monographs and textbooks, Vernadskii was widely recognized as the most enthusiastic and uncritical Westernizing economist of his day.[9]

Together with his wife, the political economist Maria Vernadskaia, Vernadskii edited a journal entitled *Economic Index*, which took a favorable view of every aspect of England's economic policies, theories, and practices. Ignoring the wage rates of factory workers in the first half of the nineteenth century, Vernadskaia declared that England's inhabitants enjoyed the highest level of material and moral well-being, intelligence, and talent in human history. Attributing this happy state to England's willingness to make use of division of labor principles and to secure the rights of property, Vernadskaia celebrated the benefits of the division of labor even among the plantation slaves of the West Indies. In her words, "the negro who gathers coffee beans works for the European, just as the European works for the negro by using his factories for the manufacture of the [negro's] multicolored clothing." Vernadskaia contended that any nation which ignored England's example was destined to stagnate. As she saw it, no other model existed for the triumph of humanity over the evils of backwardness, ignorance, vice, and poverty.[10]

In the aftermath of the Revolutions of 1848, liberal scholars at Moscow University and elsewhere constructed a liberal economic analysis that shield them from the attacks then being leveled at the more outspokenly abolitionist "Westernizers" and Slavophiles.[11] According to Ivan Vernadskii, the principles of English classical liberalism were profoundly conservative in their political and social implications. Assuring Russia's wary and skeptical upper class that Western culture posed no threat to the security of society and the state, he argued that it was wrong to associate the West with the subversive doctrines of Babeuf, Cabet, Weitling, and Karl Marx. According to M. N. Katkov, the essence of English society did not lie in communist tracts like Friedrich Engels' *The Condition of the English Working Class*. He urged his compatriots to look instead to the peaceful harmonies of the English system, which were "like Life or Nature in its development and creation."[12] Along similar lines, B. J. Utin praised the domestic tranquillity of mid-nineteenth-century England. Ignoring the contemporary activities of the Chartist movement, he assured Russian readers that no peasant uprising had taken place in England since 1381.[13]

According to Vernadskii, the West's true representatives were not radicals and revolutionaries, but economists like Adam Smith, Frederic Bastiat, and J. B. Say, whose work demonstrated the peaceful process of capitalist economic growth and development. Confident that the "best"

Western principles promoted order rather than social upheaval, Vernadskii argued against increased censorship or other repressive actions to block the spread of Western ideas. As he saw it, the government could best ensure domestic peace by eliminating the institutional laxness that permitted unsuitable students to enter Russia's higher educational institutions. Once universities were supplied with an "appropriate" student body, Vernadskii contended that government officials and scholars could devote themselves to the task of devising a rigorous and Western-oriented curriculum that promoted productive economic behavior.[14]

In the immensely popular economic tracts of Bastiat and Henry Carey, Russian liberal scholars of the 1850s discovered both the heroic mission of the entrepreneur and the harmony of interests that Providence had created between the captains of industry and their proletarian crew. Liberal journals like *The Economist, Economic Index, Atheneum,* and *Russian Herald* emphasized the laws of economic development, which were presumably everywhere at work to create a more peaceful, privatized, productive, and individualistic society. The St. Petersburg economist Gorlov defined liberal economics as the "natural laws" that shaped the economic life of nations and moved them in the direction of freedom and private enterprise; Sreznevskii of Kharkov described the "natural" process by which societies based on kinship and community gave way to more privatized and rational forms of social and economic organization.[15]

Although the Moscow University economists Linovskii and Kalinovskii continued to repeat Mordvinov's argument that serfdom should be permitted to disappear "naturally," without "artificial" government-imposed emancipation reform,[16] by the 1850s, most liberal economists were supporters of emancipation. At the University of Kazan, E. M. Maslov argued that Russia should imitate England's struggle to replace communal institutions with a free labor force and more productive forms of private tenure.[17] According to Nikolai Bunge, a rector and professor of economics at the University of Kiev (and later a Minister of Finance), the economists Henry Carey and Frederic Bastiat had proven beyond doubt both the advantages of free labor and the workings of harmonious and scientific economic laws that everywhere fostered the rights of property. In his words, Carey was "the pride of the United States," and Frederic Bastiat was "the pride of Europe."[18]

Ideas of this sort were not put forward as opinions or hypotheses; they were declared to be fundamental laws of scientific economics. According to Chicherin, a disciple of Bastiat and Comte, and Russia's most outspoken "Manchester liberal," the laws of history were pressing Russia steadily toward "the creation of markets which would eventually lead the government to grant constitutional elbow-room for the property accumulating individual and by bringing peasants under capitalism [these markets would] detribalize and only temporarily pauperize them.[19]

By 1856, when Tsar Alexander II came to power, liberal economic theories had become part of an emerging abolitionist culture. In the wake of Russia's devastating military defeat in the Crimean War, claims for the superior productivity rates of free labor became a regular feature of both liberal and Slavophile publications. The legal scholar Chicherin argued that the experience of the whole world demonstrated that "only free labor can permit the development of the industrial forces of the people," and the Slavophile Koshelev declared that in all times and places, the eagerness of free laborers was worth more than compulsion.[20] But Vernadskii and Chicherin were by no means at the forefront of the abolitionist movement. Moral and political arguments by scholars, journalists, poets, and novelists, played a far greater role in reinforcing fears of peasant unrest, and a growing belief that serfdom was an aspect of the backwardness responsible for the defeats of the Crimean War.[21]

It is significant and revealing of the priorities of Russian economists that some of the most heated polemics of the 1850s related not to abolition but to property rights and the peasant commune. Relying on Western economic theory rather than empirical evidence about Russia, the liberal economists Vernadskii, Terner, Strukov, and Sreznevskii blamed the commune for the retention of unproductive and outmoded field systems. In their writings, the commune *skhod* (assembly) was portrayed as a gathering of idiots—a place where ignorant and brutish majorities controlled the actions of the few who could recognize the benefits of improved crop rotations, plows, or fertilizer.

According to Strukov, communes were responsible for the fragmentation of allotments, the destruction of soil quality and, above all, for the lack of initiative characteristic of peasants from time immemorial. In the words of the economist A. I. Zablotskii-Desiatovskii, "without the confidence of the peasant in the continual ownership of those lands which he tills, there can never be any successes in agriculture, and all other efforts at improvement will be rendered impotent." Certain that private and hereditary systems of landownership constituted "the only means for improving the material and moral life of the rural populace," D. Strukov contended that Slavophiles supported the commune because they wanted to immobilize the peasantry as wage laborers on their estates.[22]

In *The Russian Herald*, Chicherin reported that patriarchal village elders imposed constraints, which kept commune members childlike and unable to develop adult qualities of self-reliance and personal responsibility.[23] His study, *Regional Institutions in the Seventeenth Century* (1856), argued that communes were a relatively recent and artificial phenomenon

in the Russian countryside. According to Chicherin, the practice of commune repartition was an eighteenth-century phenomenon. Relying on
government records, Chicherin argued that officials introduced repartition in order to facilitate tax collection and military recruitment. Certain
that peasants were utterly incapable of creating their own institutions, he
contended that Russian society and institutions were created from above
by a state that represented the only dynamic force in Russian history.[24]
Chicherin's conclusions were enthusiastically welcomed by Vernadskii
and Strukov. But his sources and his statistical analysis were challenged
by the Slavophile historian Ivan Beliaev, who argued that government
documents were not neutral on the subject of peasants, and were not the
best source of information about peasant traditions and practices.[25]

In the middle decades of the nineteenth century, the world of Russia's
liberal scholars constituted a rather strange spectacle. In a serf-ridden society ruled by an autocratic tsar, where most of the population lived in
communes, they celebrated a world without social bonds, where individuals were wholly free to pursue their private interests. The contrast between
liberal scenarios and Russian realities did not escape a number of contemporary observers. According to Count Kiselev, attacks on the commune
in the 1850s came neither from peasants nor their masters, but "from
scholars and those who consider themselves scholars in the name of so-
called science."[26] The legal scholar K. D. Kavelin observed that critics of
the commune were usually either professional economists or unrepentant
serfowners who found the commune an obstacle to their schemes for control or domination.[27] Attempting to discover a sort of "middle ground"
which balanced the competing claims of private initiative and economic
security, Kavelin argued that "individual property is the principle of
movement, progress and development, but it becomes the principle of
ruin and destruction . . . if it is not moderated and balanced by another
principle of landownership [i.e., the peasant commune].[28]

Challenges to Liberal Universalism

SLAVOPHILE PERSPECTIVES

In sharp contrast to Russia's liberal economists, Slavophiles of the 1850s
emphasized the need for historical, empirically based, investigations. Ivan
Aksakov demanded to know how the liberal historian Soloviev could
complete a magisterial study of Russia without mentioning the peasant
majority of the population. Koshelev observed that the liberal economist
Terner's dismissal of the peasant commune as hopelessly conservative was
based on abstract theory and assumptions about "common sense" rather
than systematic empirical study. Slavophile journals like *Agricultural Im-*

provement ridiculed Vernadskii's emphasis on England as a universal model. How, it was asked, could an English economy built upon capital investment rather than the employment of massive quantities of labor serve as a model for nations like China, which possessed little capital and a labor surplus, or more particularly for Russia, a country short of both labor and capital?[29]

The Slavophile Iurii Samarin argued that Russia's gentry would never agree to follow the "heartless" and socially disruptive example of Tory advocates of enclosure. In a book and several articles dealing with the Stein-Hardenberg reforms, he proposed a "Prussian" alternative, which freed peasants with land and avoided England's social upheaval. As Samarin saw it, Junker reforms, which retained traditional political authority while granting peasants freedom and a measure of security, represented a far better model for Russia.[30]

Throughout the 1850s, Slavophiles ridiculed "abstract" liberal scenarios which depicted the commune as a mechanical institution that forced individuals to await its orders before sleeping, eating their morning meals or commencing their daily labors. A.I. Koshelev pointed out that communes did not dictate or control every aspect of peasant life—for example, the village *skhod* did not command the labor or appropriate the harvests of its members. While collective agreements determined the farm calendar and the use of pasture and meadow lands, member households decided all other questions related to farming their own allotments. Not all property within the commune was communally owned; a variety of private and nonprivate property arrangements existed within its confines.[31] Although Slavophile contentions were in general quite accurate, in the polemical exchanges that took place on the eve of the Emancipation, liberal economists tended to ignore rather than challenge them.[32]

Claiming to be "true" conservatives, Slavophiles focused on the politics of emancipation and property rights. Insisting that both freedom and communal land guarantees were essential to the stability of the Russian countryside, they denounced the political shortsightedness of both the "feudal" conservatives who wanted a gradual abolition and the liberals who dreamed of a countryside without communes. Although Slavophiles were committed to peasant freedom, they viewed freedom above all as a measure that could eliminate the dangerous social tensions characteristic of any system of bondage. As certain as Karl Marx that rootless proletarians posed a threat to the preservation of order, they argued that no society could survive without providing a measure of economic security to its most numerous and impoverished elements.

However much they praised the commune, it should be emphasized that no Slavophile ever asked to join one. Slavophiles did not recommend that communal property systems be made mandatory for all, but argued instead that a healthy economy should permit more than one form of tenure. According to the Slavophiles, a countryside without gentry estates was no more desirable than one without peasant communes; both were essential to Russia's economic future. Sensitive to the political implications of serfdom and the absence of community, they faulted conservative serfowners and liberals alike for their refusal to recognize that both feudal oppression and economic insecurity could generate a Pugachev-style upheaval which destroyed Russian society from top to bottom.[33]

THE STATISTICAL FINDINGS OF LUDWIG TENGOBORSKII

In the 1850s, the empirical component of Russian debates on rural development was significantly expanded by the publication (in French) of the Polish-born Ludwig Tengoborskii's three-volume *Commentaries on the Productive Forces of Russia* (1852–53). The most comprehensive collection of statistical data yet published on the Russian economy, Tengoborskii's book challenged a number of prevailing assumptions about communes and serfdom. Although it was commonly argued, for example, that the commune perpetuated outdated three-field systems, Tengoborskii discovered that this mode of field use was equally common in the more privatized areas of the Russian Empire, and tended to prevail wherever land was abundant and labor scarce. In place of the popular denunciations of ignorant peasant conservatism, he cited peasant testimony indicating that where labor was in short supply, the three-field system was preferable to many-field crop rotations because it required less maintenance and less capital.[34]

In similar fashion, the familiar argument that communal tenure and serfdom bred indifference to farming was contradicted by evidence that commune peasants engaged in endless deliberations and disputes over allotment claims, plowing times and places, and harvesting procedures. On occasion, communes arranged repartitions in order to allow for soil variations within a particular village. Within and outside the commune, peasants apparently modified their economic behavior according to changing circumstances. Even under the pressures of serfdom, peasants in the provinces of Kiev and Simbirsk evidently tried to work the land as productively as they could, and introduced new crops into their field systems.[35] In general, Tengoborskii's statistical data revealed a peasantry which responded to constraints upon their behavior with economic actions that were flexible rather than rigid, occasionally innovative, but not very productive by West European standards.

Tengoborskii's relativist approach to the analysis of peasants and communes provided him as well with economic arguments in favor of preserving seigneurial power. Citing examples of land improvement carried out by bound peasants, Tengoborskii maintained that if gentry demands were moderate, a coerced labor force could be quite productive. In some respects, Tengoborskii's conclusions prefigured the twentieth-century debate among American economic historians over the economic benefits of slavery. Like the American scholars Robert Fogel and Stanley Engerman, Tengoborskii refrained from any defense of bondage on moral grounds. Focusing primarily on issues of agricultural improvement and productivity rates, he claimed that under certain circumstances, serfdom was compatible with economic growth.[36]

Tengoborskii's economic expectations for Russia were quite modest. As a former adviser to Kankrin, Tsar Nicholas I's pessimistic Minister of Finance, he believed that the Russian agricultural economy was backward for many reasons that were not amenable to change. Despite the efforts to build roads and schools and develop internal markets, Tengoborskii argued that Russia's devastating environmental constraints would continue to cause unpredictable and uncontrollable fluctuations in harvest yields and prices. As he saw it, new technology, field systems, and private enterprise might moderate, but could not nullify the disastrous power of the Russian soil and climate. In a thinly veiled reference to economists like Vernadskii, Tengoborskii suggested that those who imagined that by introducing modern Western techniques and destroying the commune Russia would be transformed into a green and prosperous England were laboring "under a strange illusion."[37]

Tengorborskii's two-volume study was translated into Russian by the liberal economist Vernadskii, who did not translate the sections of the book containing the data on peasant agriculture cited above, and made no mention of its existence. Instead, Vernadskii's introduction to Tengoborskii's works enthusiastically praised his research on industry and commerce. He ignored Tengoborskii's evidence about commune flexibility as well as his explicit rejection of England as an economic model for Russia.[38] The empirical evidence at odds with Vernadskii's theoretical framework thus became unavailable to Russian readers who did not also read French.

RADICAL SOCIALIST PERSPECTIVES:
THE EARLY WRITINGS OF N.G. CHERNYSHEVSKII

In the 1850s, the economic debate between Slavophiles and liberals was complicated by the harsher, more embittered and plebeian voices of radical socialists. The most significant newcomer was N. G. Chernyshevskii, the son of a village priest who—like others of his generation who overcame the heavy odds against becoming a university student in pre-

Emancipation Russia—became an advocate of Western-style revolution.[39] As a young man, Chernyshevskii saw the West as a beacon of light and liberty to progressives in the more backward regions of the world. Urging the appropriation of Western scientific, industrial, and revolutionary achievements, he denounced Russia's contemptible past. On the eve of the Revolution of 1848, Chernyshevskii described his general outlook as "admiration for the West and the conviction that we Russians count for nothing compared to them." Locating Russia at a lower level of human development than the West, he wrote: "They are men and we are children."[40]

However, the massacres and revolutionary defeats of 1848 shook Chernyshevskii's faith in Western political principles, and permanently destroyed his hope that liberals could be relied on to fight for either democracy or social justice. Indifferent to the relatively civil discourse of Vernadskii and his Slavophile adversaries, Chernyshevskii entered Russia's debate on development as an outsider, quite willing to argue that the views of Vernadskii and his colleagues reflected their complicity with the officials and serfowners who paid their salaries as university professors or government advisers.[41] Chernyshevskii's contempt for Russia's professional economists was more than evenly matched by Liberal disdain for Chernyshevskii and the other contributors to the radical journal *The Contemporary*. In his lack of civility, unwillingness to compromise, and indiscriminate hatred for every aspect of contemporary hierarchy and privilege, Chernyshevskii epitomized the kind of student that Vernadskii considered "unsuitable" for university life. At the same time, Chernyshevskii's character and the quality of his critique confirmed the fear of Slavophile landowners that social injustice might generate a particularly brutal Russian version of European communism.[42]

Rejecting the claim that liberal economics was a scientific doctrine, Chernyshevskii argued that liberals were inspired by a "superstitious faith" in "the magic of property." Instead of examining the virtues and defects of property rights in a comparative or historical context, he contended that they ignored evidence that property rights did not always guarantee economic growth and development. In England's much-celebrated Agricultural Revolution, Chernyshevskii observed that improvements were introduced by tenants rather than by the owners of large landed estates. In contemporary Spain, where rights of private ownership were well established, property arrangements were less important as economic factors than scarcity of capital, low levels of domestic and foreign demand, and virtually nonexistent transportation networks. According to Chernyshevskii, tenure considerations did not explain why small-scale proprietors in Spain were less productive than their Russian counterparts within the commune. As he saw it, the varying significance of private-property rights in different times and places required further empirical investigation. The advantages of private-property rights were for Chernyshevskii historical and specific rather than universal in character.[43]

In the 1850s, Chernyshevskii argued that the Slavophiles and Baron Haxthausen were more honest and intellectually serious than liberal economists. According to Chernyshevskii, liberals "fraudulently" claimed objectivity and refused to recognize their bias in favor of the private entrepreneur, while Khomiakov and Haxthausen admitted their class interest in an economic system guided by members of the landed gentry. Haxthausen carefully documented both the defects of the commune and its efforts at improvement. In contrast, liberals attacked the commune with "axioms" taken from Western economic theorists. Instead of gathering data, they trained their sights upon the politically defenseless and plebeian peasant commune.

Chernyshevskii argued that they found it safer to attack the commune than to criticize the power, inefficiency, and cruelty of the state and the serfowning gentry.[44] Ignoring the empirical evidence which demonstrated that *laissez faire* economies were arenas of class struggle rather than social harmony, they focused on the achievements and well-being of the entrepreneur and paid no attention to the wretched material situation of the European laborer. Slavophiles recognized that capitalist economies were extremely unstable and admitted that their own survival depended upon the labor of their peasant workforce. They did not—like Vernadskii and Strukov—try to outdo each other in expressions of contempt for the social group which produced their wealth.[45]

Chernyshevskii contended that low productivity rates were due neither to commune backwardness nor to peasant ignorance. Instead, peasants became apathetic because government and private authorities intervened at will in their lives, and undermined their economic initiatives within and outside the commune. According to Chernyshevskii, the province of Pskov could perish of hunger before it received a *chetvert* of grain from Little Russia, where peasants might desperately need to sell their surplus. He arged that although it was fashionable in certain circles to blame the commune for Russia's economic plight, the absence of roads between Pskov and Little Russia was not due to the commune peasant's lack of initiative. Communes were not responsible for the arbitrary and excessive financial burdens imposed upon them, or for the low priority placed upon the building of schools which might teach them about new agricultural methods.[46]

Contending that liberal economists did not even do justice to the Western economist they most admired, Chernyshevskii emphasized Adam Smith's assertion that productivity rates were likely to increase if owners were both managers and cultivators of their land. With unconcealed contempt, he suggested that if Vernadskii and Strukov "deigned" to engage in empirical research on the Russian countryside, they might discover that the commune more closely approximated the Smithian ideal than England's system of landlords, tenant and hired agricultural laborers. Chernyshevskii contended that if commune peasants gained equal rights within Russian society and if their economic and social burdens were lightened, liberal economists would be astonished at how quickly peasants within and outside the commune would develop a "European" desire to better the material conditions of their lives.[47]

Although Chernyshevskii defended the commune against its liberal critics, he was not particularly optimistic about its survival and never considered it the equal of any Western institution. In his carefully measured assessment, "it may be true that Russia has retained [in the peasant commune] a principle which corresponds to one of the solutions toward which progressives are aiming; it is nonetheless true that Western Europe is moving towards the realization of this principle quite independently of us."[48] In the decades to come, Chernyshevskii's hopes for the commune steadily diminished. But in 1859, he argued that despite its many defects, the communes alleviated the rootlessness and economic polarization that were the scourge of the Western laborer.[49]

Although both Chernyshevskii and Alexander Herzen valued the commune, the contrast in their approach to peasants, progress, and questions of economic development is instructive. In Herzen's writings, peasants appeared as noble savages, ignorant because they were deprived of schooling but superior in their egalitarian communal behavior to a corrupt, greedy, and callous Western bourgeoisie. Herzen was particularly sensitive to the cultural arrogance of Western Europeans toward "backward" Russia and of educated Russians toward "backward" peasants. In contrast, Chernyshevskii's peasants were uninformed, brutal, poorly armed small producers locked in struggle against a hostile material and social environment. Recalling his own childhood in provincial Saratov, Chernyshevskii found it ludicrous to suppose that peasants miraculously preserved some sort of elemental moral virtue amidst the wretched and degrading circumstances of their lives. Unlike Herzen, Chernyshevskii adopted many of the popular racial stereotypes of the day and routinely denounced the peasantry's "Asiatic" habit of cringing before the powerful.[50]

Refusing to claim, like the anarchist Bakunin, that the urge to destruction was a creative passion, Chernyshevskii argued instead that violence was an ugly but inevitable component of struggles for change carried out by peasants who routinely experienced "progress" in the form of military colonies, beatings, and increased dues and taxes. In 1860, arguing that oppression bred peasant brutality, Chernyshevskii declared, "I am not afraid of dirt, or of drunken peasants with sticks, or of massacres."[51] A commitment to the peasantry that conceded so much to the liberal view that peasants were "mindless barbarians" would have been inconceivable to Alexander Herzen—who was in other respects a far more imaginative thinker than Chernyshevskii.

While Chernyshevskii's understanding of peasant values and institutions was far more complex than Herzen's, he was utterly blind to the danger that radicals convinced of their cultural superiority to peasants might employ the same strategies of coercion, manipulation, and control used by other elites to "uplift" their inferiors. Quite willing to agree that barriers of class privilege might make it difficult for the well-born Herzen to communicate with a peasant, he never imagined that peasants might perceive little difference between the "guidance" of a revolutionary elite and the protective custody traditionally exercised by reforming serfowners and government bureaucrats. As confident as Lenin that the interests of revolutionaries and the masses could never diverge, Chernyshevskii wrote in 1861, "Assume that they [the people] need what you need, and you will not be mistaken."[52]

Toward Emancipation: Privatization in Theory and Practice

On the eve of the Emancipation of 1861, liberal economists like Vernadskii joined with the Slavophile Samarin to support both the peasantry's inalienable right to land and preservation of the repartitional land commune. Terrified by reports of peasant unrest and by the radicalism of Chernyshevskii and his supporters, they succumbed to Russia's first "Red Scare." In what Ivan Aksakov described as a Slavophile "victory," liberals precipitously abandoned the claim that unrestricted property rights would ensure domestic peace and prosperity. Repudiating the former editorial policy of his journal The Russian Herald, M. N. Katkov now discovered in the commune a "bulwark against communism which deserved the support of all educated Russians."[53] The peculiar (and temporary) reconciliation between Slavophiles and liberals reflected their heartfelt agreement that the preservation of domestic order far outweighed whatever benefits a more privatized economy might bring. As on many earlier occasions in Russian history, political priorities took precedence over economic profit.

As a participant in the Editorial Committees that prepared the emancipation statutes, the economist Nikolai Bunge explained that ignorance, backwardness, and the "imperfections of human nature" made it necessary to preserve the commune and peasant rights to inalienable land allotments. Once Russians became more civilized, Bunge argued, such guarantees of security would no longer be needed.[54] In 1860, Prince Cherkasskii apologized to a Belgian economist for the decision to preserve the peasant commune instead of encouraging the establishment of private-property rights in the Russian countryside. In his words, "Highly though the sound principles of science should be prized, all the same, in practical life, it is impossible not to make concessions to the temporary requirements of society."[55]

General Rostovtsev, who was sent by the government to observe the aftermath of Prussia's emancipation with land, put the political issue even more bluntly. In his words, "I don't want privileges for the peasants but I want to forestall revolt in Russia. I believe that by cutting off land from the peasantry, we shall set Russia afire." As he saw it, both peasant land allotments and communes were important as guarantees of domestic security. According to Rostovtsev, "the common people need a strong authority to replace the authority of the *pomeshchik*."[56]

On the eve of Emancipation, Russian reformers rejected the minority view of Prince Menshikov, whose conservatism led him to distrust the commune. According to Menshikov, it was politically wiser to divide the peasantry against each other instead of preserving the communal institutions which united them.[57] But the framers of the emancipation were in general unmoved by this argument. To the old-fashioned reliance on the commune and traditional guarantees of inalienable peasant rights to land, they added a new emphasis on the abolition of serfdom as a stabilizing factor. It was only after the Revolution of 1905 that Stolypin and his followers would succeed in making Menshikov's case that the commune constituted a disruptive force in the Russian countryside.

The Political Economy of Freedom: Russia, the United States, and Prussia

> There is something of the Negro in the nature of a Russian.
> (G. De Lagny, The Knout and the Russians, 1854)

Russia's "era of reform" began in 1861 with a series of Russian government initiatives, which included peasant emancipation, the creation of local organs of self-government (the *zemstva*), military intervention in Poland, and a wave of arrests directed at radicals like Chernyshevskii, who was eventually sentenced to twenty-five years of exile in Siberia. Although the story of serfdom's abolition has been extensively described elsewhere, a brief summary of its major features is in order: According to the terms of the emancipation statutes, 23 million peasants ceased to be the property of 104,000 members of the landed-gentry estate. Freed from personal bondage, they remained juridically isolated from the rest of society—without full civil rights or freedom of movement. Peasants were granted rights to use land allotments that were owned by repartitional land communes, and were held collectively responsible over a forty-nine-year period for the payment of redemption costs to their former masters. Minimum and maximum allotments were established by mutual consent; if the former serf agreed to relinquish three quarters of the statutory maximum, he was exempted from redemption payments.[58]

In many respects, the Russian emancipation followed the basic outlines of the Prussian model set out in the writings of the Slavophile Iurii Samarin in the 1850s. As in Prussia, the terms of peasant freedom were juridically complex, and the process by which peasants were freed and granted land—for which they paid dearly—was prolonged for almost a half century.[59] But in contrast to Prussia, Russia's government not only recognized the principle of land claims based upon labor and occupancy, but preserved the peasantry's communal institutions. As a consequence, the reform provided peasants with a substantial measure of direct access to the means of production and to the product of their labor.

The fear of radical social upheaval that led Russia's reforming liberals to abandon their economic principles highlights the contrast between the politics of emancipation in the United States and in the Russian Empire. In the United States, emancipation freed slaves who possessed far less political or economic leverage than their Russian serf counterparts. African Americans, as members of a racial minority held in a state of chattel slavery and deemed racially inferior, were far less able than the peasant majority of the Russian population to lay claim to the land they worked. It is interesting, however, that before 1861, many educated Russians referred to peasants as "dark people," supposedly incapable of rational behavior unless they were confronted by the threat of force. In the nineteenth and twentieth centuries, black was the color of any element of the lower class which engaged in behavior considered backward or threatening by educated people.[60]

The contrast between the socioeconomic position of bound peasants in Russia and of enslaved African Americans illuminates the important distinctions between slavery and serfdom. Russian serfs owned the animals and the tools with which they met their feudal obligations. On state and gentry land, they possessed communal institutions which organized farm work, although households were far more "on their own" in working on commune allotments than when they were collectively obliged to cultivate the master's *demesne* land. Although Westernizing landlords like Mordvinov could intervene at will in village life, Russian peasants were ordinarily able to make far more decisions both as individuals and collectively than were the slave communities of the American South.[61]

The terms of Russian peasant freedom reflected the profound respect of reformers for the peasantry's numerical strength and potential political power. Fearing—as their American counterparts did not—that a rejection of peasant claims to the land or communal guarantees of security would set off a firestorm of peasant violence,[62] Russian liberals set aside their intellectual commitment to a landless and anticommunal emancipation. In contrast, the United States enacted a landless emancipation, which freed slaves to compete as individuals for private economic gain. While African Americans in the United States gained far more control over their lives than they possessed as slaves, most modern experts agree that in general, the terms of their freedom failed to safeguard their rights either as citizens or as free laborers.[63] According to a number of American historians, the continued economic dependence experienced by former slaves in the aftermath of emancipation was due to landlessness and material insecurity.[64]

In the Russian context, the only consistency between the theoretical principles advanced by liberal economists in the 1850s and the reforms they came to support in 1861 lay in the procedures established for land allotment. In true *laissez faire* fashion, the size of allotments and redemption payments was determined by free and unmediated negotiation between former masters and former serfs. When landed magnates negotiated as equals with their former peasant property, they established redemption payments at an exorbitant 30 to 150 percent above market value (in order to compensate themselves for the loss of labor as well as land). As a consequence, peasants were freed with less land and higher financial obligations than before. Frequently, they lost access to common fields, forests, and water resources. (Peasants called the latter *otrezki*, or "cut-off" lands.) In addition, much heavier financial burdens replaced the exactions formerly required.[65]

Russia's emancipation statute was much influenced by Western models and examples. It has been estimated that over two thirds of the reference materials used by its framers came from abroad. However, in its final form, the terms of Russian freedom were in many respects less onerous than in the United States or Prussia. While Russian peasants lost out in negotiations with their former masters over the size and cost of their allotments, they were far less likely than their American counterparts to become a despised class of tenants or wage laborers. Russia's poorest peasants were not deprived by statute of rights to land use, but in Prussia, peasants too poor to "harness a team" lost all claims to land and were forbidden to use common pasture land for grazing. In East Prussia, for example, "free" cottagers were required to supply two to three members of their household to work six days a week from sunrise to sunset year round on the Junker estate in return for a small house, a half-acre garden, the right to graze some animals on the lord's meadow, the yield from several acres of the lord's crop land, and a small wage.[66]

Although the Russian Emancipation has been called Russia's version of an enclosure movement because it "cut off" lands traditionally cultivated by the peasantry and transferred them to the gentry,[67] in comparison with other enclosure movements, this judgment seems somewhat over-stated. "Domestic" and "factory" serfs certainly lost out in 1861, but commune peasants retained more of their traditional institutions and claims and incurred fewer obligations to their former masters than many of their counterparts elsewhere. It is difficult to imagine a seventeenth-century Digger or a Prussian family denied land because they could not harness a team, or an African American slave freed without land who would not have delighted in a Russian-style emancipation which recognized rights to land, a measure of personal liberty, and membership in a community governed by their elected peers. In the United States, freed slaves and Radical Republican members of Congress argued that a true emancipation should include "40 acres and a mule." As one freedman told a northern teacher: "Do, my missus, tell Linkum dat we wants land—dis very land dat is rich wid de sweat ob we face and de blood ob we back."[68] But African American demands were rejected. In contrast, an autocratic government permitted Russia's peasants to retain a substantial proportion of the land they had formerly cultivated.

That Russian peasants responded to the emancipation reforms with the claim that all land belonged to them, rumors of fraud, and outright violence, is a mark of the profound cultural difference between Russia and her Western neighbors. Decades earlier, Adolphe Périer, the French ambassador to St. Petersburg, lamented the attitudes of the Russian peasant as an aspect of "the moral grossness," or, at least, utter ignorance of the population.

> Almost everywhere the peasants think that, because they are serfs, they alone have a true right to own the land. Often an owner who wishes to move peasants from one department to the other meets that terrible force of inertia, backed up by the following words which constitute the Russian serf's entire code: "Our life belongs to you, you can take it. But you have no right to move us from the land which belongs to us." This dangerous prejudice is rooted in the souls of millions of people, nor can it be removed merely by laws. It will have to be the task of civilization, of moral improvement, and for this nothing has yet been done.[69]

In contrast, the Slavophile Ivan Aksakov argued that forcing peasants to pay for land which they, their parents, and grandparents had cultivated from time immemorial was like forcing "an oak to pay for the ground from which it grew."[70] Denouncing the reformers who criticized peasant refusal to accept the financial obligations imposed along with their newly granted freedom, Aksakov declared, "We should not expect any gratitude from them. What for? Because we order them in a sweet voice to irrigate our fields with their sweat? Thank God, there is no gratitude. . . . I believe, by the way, that the landowners are not badly off; the peasants are in a much worse position, not as compared with their former life, but as compared with their expectations and their lawful demands."[71]

Peasant assessments of the Emancipation are not easy to gauge, and few educated Russians of the 1850s and 1860s asked them for their opinion. Contemporary reports reflect wishful thinking, cynicism, dreams of justice, disillusionment, and anger. There were some who apparently expected that after 1861, the gentry would go off to live in the cities as the tsar's pensioners. In Kharkov province, peasants circulated a parody of the emancipation statutes which provided the gentry with an allotment of stony or swampy land to cultivate on their own. If the gentry could not manage a plow, their former serfs were required to show them how, "without laughing."[72]

Elsewhere, peasants refused to accept their diminished allotments, insisting that the "true Emancipation" issued by their beloved tsar had been hidden by a devious and greedy gentry. To enforce compliance, recalcitrant peasants were chained to plows and required to take symbolic possession of the land by pulling the plows along the boundaries of their new allotments. When the Emancipation settlement prohibited peasants from using the meadows, forests, and waters they had previously exploited, those who insisted on their traditional rights became criminals in the eyes of the law. As in the case of English farmers whose common lands were enclosed, Russian peasants discovered that "immemorial custom had become trespass and theft."[73]

The more violent aspects of peasant resistance did not persist for very long. But by all accounts, the belief that labor gave peasants rights to the land they cultivated remained strong. Although few educated Russians believed that backward peasants possessed a conception of justice, communes provided peasants with land on the basis of labor claims throughout the nineteenth and early twentieth century. In the post-Emancipation era, these claims influenced the projects of a new generation of historical economists and inspired the revolutionary hopes of Russia's radical socialist movement.

Chapter Five

INTERSECTIONS OF WESTERN AND

RUSSIAN CULTURE

RUSSIAN HISTORICAL ECONOMICS

> Before we could go forward, we needed to free ourselves from
> the influence of the Moscow Anglomaniacs.
> *(Dmitrii Pisarev)*

MODERN RUSSIAN economics came of age in the midst of a
European *methodenstreit* that called into question not only
the methods, but also the aims and goals of economics as a
discipline. In the 1860s and 1870s, educated Russians were both observers and participants in a high-stakes struggle whose outcome determined
whether historical economics or neoclassical liberalism would dominate
economics and economic policy-making in the modern world. Although
the "historians" were defeated, their failure was not a foregone conclusion. It was almost half a century before neoclassical and marginalist
theorists were able to establish a new consensus, that severely downplayed the use of historical and comparative perspectives on such topics
as property rights, the fate of the peasantry, and the meaning of economic
progress.[1]

After 1861, historical economics caught the imagination of a younger
generation of Russian radicals enraged at what they viewed as the hypocrisy of the Emancipation reforms. With some justice, dissident university
students like Pisarev, Chernyshevskii and Dobroliubov pointed out
that (1) the Emancipation saddled former serfs with higher fiscal obligations and smaller allotments than before, (2) an "Emancipator-Tsar"
sent Russian troops to suppress Poland's struggle for independence, and
(3) "freedom-loving" professors demanded the arrest of their dissident students. Convinced that government pronouncements in support of
libertarian ideals were a ploy to distract attention from its policies, radicals called for a "propaganda of the deed" and a historical, empirically
based economics committed to improving the material economic life of
the common people.[2] As we shall see, radical arguments exerted far more
influence upon historically minded scholars in Russia than in Western

Europe. Although leading Russian social scientists were unconditionally opposed to the use of political terror, many of them would attempt nevertheless to create precisely the kind of economics that their radical students demanded.

The European Context: The Challenge of Historical Economics

> Economics as understood by the classical economists of the nineteenth century was an a-historical subject, not to say an anti-historical one, while history was not conceived as being concerned with things economic.
> *(N. B. Harte, ed.,* The Study of Economic History, *1971)*

> the past was there to demonstrate the fallaciousness of past economic ideas and policy. Thereby it gave support to current political economy and what was presented as the unquestionable truths of a particular sort of economic theory and a particular set of policy recommendations.
> *(D. C. O'Brien,* J. R. McCulloch: A Study in Classical Economics, *1970)*

> Men had elevated landlord property and capitalist political economy to a fetish to be worshipped, and upon the altar of that fetish, Ireland perished.
> *(James Michael Connolly)*

In the middle decades of the nineteenth century, "the great liberal consensus" that had united English public opinion for at least half a century was irrevocably broken.[3] At the very mainstream of English intellectual life, old certainties were called into question, as famine and violence erupted in Ireland and India, and the urban poor—encouraged by the ideas of radical socialism—challenged and disrupted English social life. On the Continent, revolutions swept through France and Germany, and the growth of socialist ideas deepened and encouraged popular frustration and discontent.

The important changes to come were symbolized by John Stuart Mill's rejection of two centuries of argument (including his own) for private-property rights as the bedrock of liberty and prosperity in every time and place. Although Mill's *Principles of Modern Economy* (1848) was widely accepted as the classic statement of liberal economics, he declared in 1852 that the greatest enemy of English liberty was not government constraints on property owners, but the poverty which constricted the lives and opportunities of the lower classes. In order to correct what he viewed as "imbalances" in property ownership, Mill abandoned economic individualism and supported the formation of labor associations "collectively owning the capital with which they carry on their operations, and working under managers elected and removable by themselves."[4]

Responding to the famine tragedy of one million Irish dead, Anglo-Irish economists like T. E. Cliffe-Leslie and J. K. Ingram argued that liberal political economy focused too narrowly on England as a model for the economies of Ireland and other nations.[5] Denouncing as "arrogant" the liberal recommendation that England's economic arrangements be imposed upon post-famine Ireland, Cliffe-Leslie proposed that economists look elsewhere for models and examples. In England, Ingram, Thorold Rogers, and William Cunningham produced historical and statistical studies which argued that an important part of the social scientist's mission was to devise programs to diminish poverty and the propensity for violence among the lower classes.

According to Ingram, mainstream political economy had become increasingly suspect among the working class, "owing to the not unfounded belief that it has tended to justify too absolutely existing social arrangements, and that its study is often recommended with the real, though disguised, object of repressing popular aspirations after a better order of things."[6] In the 1870s, Mill and others who were skeptical about the benefits of unrestricted private ownership supported the formation of a Land Tenure Reform Association, which proposed that (1) the government place restrictions on the individual's right to control unlimited amounts of property, and (2) provide land allotments to small producers in England and Ireland.[7]

It should be emphasized that in nineteenth-century England, views of this sort were not rewarded either by scholarly approbation or professional advancement. Admirers of Mill's earlier liberal stance denounced his newfound collectivism as a betrayal of principle, which provided aid and comfort both to "feudalist" reactionaries and to the "communist" proponents of violent revolution.[8] In 1868, the historical economist Thorold Rogers lost his professorship in political economy at Oxford due to attacks upon his "radicalism" and incompetence as a scholar. According to his critics, Thorold Rogers paid disproportionate attention to "non-economic" issues like consumption and distribution. In a furious attack upon professional economists who emphasized the importance of empirical research, the economist J. E. Cairnes accused scholars who tried to "refute its [liberalism's] abstract principles by factual evidence" of being the "enemies of economics."[9] In later years, the eminent economist Alfred Marshall declared that if in fact liberal economics was on occasion "excessively abstract," this failing was chiefly due to the influence of David Ricardo, whose faults and virtues were not only "un-English," but "traceable to his Semitic origin."[10]

England's *methodenstreit* was ignited by a German-based revolution in the social sciences, which shifted the attention of economists the world over from London to Leipzig, Berlin, and Eisenach, and in particular to the work of Wilhelm Roscher of the University of Leipzig.[11] The new, historical economics drew heavily on the traditions of German Romanticism as well as the empirical and comparative strategies introduced by the legal scholar Savigny to the study of law, and by Ranke to the discipline of history. In contrast to the model-oriented economics of classical liberalism, Roscher's emphasis was historical, statistical, and institutional.[12]

Skeptical about the cultural assumptions which frequently underlay universalist claims, Roscher argued that liberal economists dismissed as inferior or backward any nation whose economic life was not organized according to liberal principles. Arguing that social scientists ought to take a less culturally arrogant and more objective view of the world, Roscher declared that, "The characteristic feature of the historical method is that it does away with the feeling of self-sufficiency, and the *bragadoccio* which causes most men to ridicule what they do not understand, and the higher to look down with contempt on the lower civilization.[13]"

Conceding the power, attractiveness, and utility of classical economics, Roscher argued nevertheless that it was perfectly rational for nations whose history differed from England's to pursue different economic strategies. In some historical contexts, it seemed to him undeniable that interventionist governments played an essential leadership role; in others, government hindered the increase of productivity and profit. Although Roscher believed that private property played a constructive role in most modern societies, he insisted as well that the degree of restriction surrounding its exercise should vary according to the specifics of the historical context. According to Roscher, it made no sense to assert that levels of government activism in economic affairs should remain minimal regardless of whether, for example, a nation was at war, wracked by social conflict or facing a natural disaster.[14]

Together with influential colleagues like Karl Knies of the University of Heidelberg and Bruno Hildebrand of Breslau, Roscher developed an economic analysis which argued that human economic behavior was shaped by historical situations that changed over time and deserved detailed empirical and historical study. Rejecting the image of human beings as "exchanging animals" with no economic interest apart from the accumulation of private property, Knies argued that the family was in fact a collective whose members survived or failed in common. As he saw it, private economic actions were powerfully shaped by collective loyalties to family, and to community, church, and nation.[15] According to Knies, liberal economists oversimplified by using Adam Smith's eighteenth-century economic model to explain the more complex realities of a modern industrial economy. By focusing on productivity rates to the exclusion of questions of consumption and distribution, Knies believed that they were treating "one aspect of the whole as if it were the whole."[16] To Hildebrand—whose massive statistical studies revealed the inequalities of income distribution in contemporary Germany—classical economists were peculiarly insensitive to the political danger that impoverished workers might take to revolution.[17]

In the 1870s, in the wake of an economic depression that confounded the optimistic expectations of Manchester liberals the world over, a younger generation of German economists attempted to make the case for economics as both an academic and an activist discipline. Led by the prolific scholar Gustav Schmöller of the University of Berlin,[18] they founded a *Verein fur Sozialpolitik* in 1872 in order to press for government action to check "excessive" concentrations of wealth and property in German society. Fearful that unrestricted free markets would destroy the sense of cohesion, solidarity, and common purpose essential to the survival of the nation, economists of the *Verein* demanded reforms that would permit "a continually increasing proportion of the population to acquire access to the highest material and cultural achievements of civilization."[19] In contrast to the classical economists, they insisted that all social elements—the peasantry, the gentry, the bourgeoisie, and the proletariat—should be mobilized as contributors to a more productive German economy.

Verein economists shared a belief in the importance of what they called "the social question," but they differed markedly in their proposed solutions.[20] Schmöller became an advisor to Bismarck and a supporter of his programs for empire-building and social reform. Adolf Wagner, who began his career as a professor of agricultural economics at the Imperial Russian University of Dorpat, later emerged as one of the University of Berlin's most outspoken advocates of government action to protect peasants—in Wagner's view the most "truly German" element of the population.[21] Lujo von Brentano's research on medieval guilds and modern cooperatives led him to support the formation of nonviolent labor organizations, while Roscher's student Karl Bücher investigated the economic basis for consensus between workers and employers, and recommended that progressives make common cause with the revisionist Marxist Eduard Bernstein.[22]

Historically oriented economists were far more concerned than liberals about the political dangers of economic inequality, but they seldom supported radical socialist movements. Although conventional, Anglo-American distinctions between Right and Left are not easy to apply to the German context, Roscher was easily one of the most antisocialist in his outlook. Contemptuously describing socialism as the "exaggerated idea of equality" that arose when the gap between rich and poor was too large, and the link between work and reward was less visible than the spectacle of unemployment and immense accumulations of wealth, Roscher looked instead to the ideally balanced society set out in the eighteenth-century writings of Rousseau. In his view, Germany needed a society in which there were no citizens so rich that they could buy another and none so poor that they had to sell themselves to someone else.[23]

Émile de Laveleye, one of the most widely respected historical economists of the day, described socialists as naive intellectuals who hated the present and sentimentalized about the future.[24] Like John Stuart Mill, he argued that unrestricted property rights fostered extremes of social inequality and class antagonism which profoundly threatened both the advance of political liberty and the stability of Western Europe. In Germany, Adolf Wagner and other economists who were labeled "academic socialists" (*kathedersozialisten*), demanded decisive government action to promote a more balanced distribution of wealth between rich and poor.[25] In general, historical economists like Roscher, Knies, Cliffe-Leslie, and Laveleye agreed that the only way to ensure that the course of economic development would remain peaceful and nonrevolutionary was to provide guarantees of security to the lower classes.[26]

CLASSICAL MARXISM AS AN ASPECT OF THE *METHODENSTREIT*

Far more than is usually recognized, the early writings of Karl Marx were embedded in Germany's challenge to classical liberalism.[27] It may even be argued that the Marx's vicious attacks on Romantics and the "amoral" relativists of the German Historical School were driven by a desire to conceal his substantial intellectual debt to the nonrevolutionary cultural traditions of his native land.[28] Long before the *Communist Manifesto*, German Romantics were arguing that liberal principles of free trade and property rights reinforced the disproportionate power and opportunities of the bourgeoisie. The economic writings of Roscher and Hildebrand were shaped by Hegel's notion of the dialectic; like Marx, they described contradictions within the modes of economic exchange in one stage of history as the source of transformation into the next.[29] The work of Knies and Schmöller was no less empirical, comparative, and institutional than Marx's own research. And whatever other claims may be made for it, it is difficult to deny that *Capital* was an example of historical economics, and a work of economic history.

Although Roscher and his school valued many aspects of classical economics, Marx's debt to liberalism was far greater. For most of his life, he was as confident as any liberal that capitalism represented the principal agent of humanity's advance from medievalism to the modern age. Choosing the world's most powerful capitalist nation as the subject of *Capital*, Marx claimed that England represented a universal model for the rest of the world. Like John Stuart Mill, who once described Yorkshire as a microcosm of human economic activity the world over,[30] Marx described industrial England as a nation that "showed to the less developed the image of its own future."[31]

In many respects, Marx's classic writings represent a synthesis of Romantic critique, historical method, and liberal economic analysis. While his debt to traditions he denounced does not diminish the revolutionary significance of Marxism, these elements of his thinking call into question the rigid dichotomies that are frequently drawn between Marxist and non-Marxist economic thought. In his major works, Marx used the familiar liberal scenario of peasants as victims of a brutal but progressive capitalist economic order. With a powerful mixture of pity and contempt, he argued that small property in land "creates a class of barbarians standing halfway outside of society, a class suffering all the tortures and all the miseries of civilized countries in addition to the crudeness of primitive forms of society."[32] Like August Comte and the early John Stuart Mill, Marx described the peasantry's tragic encounter with bourgeois civilization as a progressive process that drove them from the land to urban industrial centers, where they acquired higher knowledge and a measure of the culture they so woefully lacked.

Marx's generalizations about peasant agriculture and institutions were not rooted in the sort of systematic empirical study that he devoted to the analysis of capitalism. Knowing little about the agricultural sciences, Marx confidently—and ignorantly—denied the nitrogen-fixing properties of leguminous plants, dismissing reports by European agronomists on this topic as "fairytales of the English rural mind."[33] In similar fashion, he did not feel compelled to research peasant social relations in order to know that peasants entered the modern age as petty bourgeois individualists who knew little of cooperation. Based on cultural assumptions rather than any empirical study of peasant life, Marx asserted that "small peasants' property excluded by its very nature the development of the social powers of productivity of labor, the social forms of labor, the social concentration of capital, cattle-raising on a large scale, and a progressive application of science."[34]

Like other nineteenth-century advocates of progress, Marx dismissed claims for the small producer, the commons, or communes as idealizations of the "universal mediocrity" created by prehistoric small property relationships. According to Marx, this system "must be annihilated. Its annihilation, the transformation of individual and scattered means of production into socially concentrated ones, of the pygmy property of the many into the huge property of the few . . . this fearful and painful expropriation of the mass of the people forms the prelude to the history of capital."[35]

Although Marx repeatedly stressed the analytical importance of the social relations of production, he never researched the social relations of agricultural labor. In his writings, peasants possessed relationships to their masters but not to each other. As in the writings of Voltaire and Russian Westernizers like Belinskii, Marx's peasants were wretched or cunning brutes with no common interests or values, who lived in villages that resembled a "sack of potatoes" more than a community. In the middle decades of the nineteenth century, he discovered in the peasantry a phenomenon that no anthropologist since that time has ever been able to find—a social group with no discernible social relationships, institutions, or culture.

Despite his faith in the revolutionary power of the proletariat and his commitment to an all-encompassing program for social justice, it is significant that Marx never discovered anything positive in the social relations or culture of any exploited group. In his major works, the dispossessed of the world possessed nothing of value except their numbers, a willingness to fight their oppressors, and—all too rarely—the capacity to adopt the "best" elements of bourgeois culture. Along with family, household, and gender relations, he categorized peasant communities as prehistoric and "natural"; in no sense comparable to "class relations." According to Marx, the oppression of peasants could end only after they were incorporated into a system of wage labor and became revolutionary proletarians. As he saw it, only capitalism could create in peasants the potential for solidarity, rational economic behavior, or the development of revolutionary consciousness.

Marx's early writings suggest the possibility of a revolutionary alliance between landless proletarians and urban factory workers, but they do not dwell on this topic. His certainty about socialism's eventual triumph was rooted *not* in a respect for the institutions or values possessed by the exploited, but in the defects of capitalism and the massive size of the proletarian class it produced. It was left to those Marx labeled as "Romantics," or "amoral relativists of the historical school" to suggest that peasants might possess institutions and a culture that could serve as building blocks for change.

Russia and European Historical Economics

When the European *methodenstreit* began, many Western economists—particularly those of German origin—were already quite familiar with Russia's debate on development. The *Proceedings* of the Imperial Free Economic Society had been available in German translation ever since the early nineteenth century, and the *Landwirtschaftliches Centralblatt für Deutschland* regularly printed excerpts from the *Proceedings* in its own publications. Haxthausen's study of the peasant commune was first published in German, and the writings of Chicherin and Kavelin were also available in German translation. In one journalistic exchange in the German press, Chicherin denounced the Russian commune as a "social monstrosity" that destroyed all economic incentives for improvement, while Kavelin countered with an article that accused Chicherin of condemning as irrational any peasant action which failed to conform to liberalism's ideal of the "economic man."[36]

Roscher devoted a whole chapter of his *Nationaloekonomik des Ackerbaues* to what he described as the "German-Russian" school of economics. Citing data from German and Russian sources, he argued that the economic behavior of peasants and other social groups was shaped by loyalty to family and community and the impact of geography and climate, *as well as* by private interest. In the decades to come, he enthusiastically welcomed the relativist implications of research by the Baltic German economist Johannes von Keussler, whose empirical data suggested that no universal rules or laws could be said to govern tenure relations in every part of the Russian empire.[37]

Germany's challenge to liberalism's "economic man" was reinforced by Ludwig von Maurer, whose research into early German history indicated that peasants had once possessed an institution called the *mark*—a definite land area where a group of families owned, occupied, and cultivated land on the basis of equality, personal freedom, and communal property ownership. Contradicting the liberal notion that in every time and place "man is born a proprietor," Maurer suggested that communal tenure predated the emergence of private-property rights. Inspired by his research on the origins of German property systems, a younger generation of medievalists began to investigate the possibility that the *mark* existed in other areas inhabited by Germanic peoples.[38]

In one notable case, the economist Erwin Nasse of the University of Bonn documented the survival of "*mark*-like" common lands and open field systems in sixteenth-century England. According to Nasse, sixteenth-century English farming communities resembled those in Germany, but owing to the enclosure movement, England was now the only civilized country in the world in which the bulk of the land was not in the hands of small proprietors. Believing that "England represented the exception and not the rule for other nations," Nasse observed that in Germany, France, Italy, and Spain, agricultural economies were not dominated by large-scale tenants or hired laborers.[39]

Sir Henry Maine's *Ancient Law* (1861) and *Village Communities East and West* (1871) placed the *mark* in a broad comparative perspective, which included the communal property systems of Russia (the *mir*), India (the *panchayat*), and the English commons.[40] While Maine contended that communes died out because they were obsolete in the modern world,[41] Maurer insisted that the *mark*'s disappearance was due to persistent and violent attacks by a succession of German rulers in search of greater power and wealth. But both were agreed that communal tenure constituted a universal characteristic of human societies in earlier times.

THE PEASANT COMMUNE AS A MODEL FOR THE WEST:
THE WORK OF ÉMILE DE LAVELEYE

Nineteenth-century scholarly debate on the origins of property was not confined to the academic world. To historians, economists, and policy-makers, the findings of Maurer and Maine called into question over a century of liberal claims that private ownership and its unequal distribution throughout society constituted the only normal property arrangement in a civilized state. In this context, the case of Russia appeared particularly significant to Baron Émile de Laveleye, a professor of political economy at the University of Liège and one of the most prolific and widely read economists of his day. In his words: "the Russian commune stands so opposed to all of our economic principles and to the feeling developed in us by the custom of individual property that it is difficult for us to believe in its existence."[42] In his book *Property and Its Primitive Forms* (1871), Laveleye set out the lessons of the commune for European policy-makers. Citing Haxthausen, he contrasted the rigid polarities of West European ownership and nonownership with the complex and flexible rights to use and possession within Russia's peasant commune.[43] According to Laveleye, even the argument that communes were survivals of the past was contradicted by contemporary reports from Russia on the voluntary introduction of repartition in the Volga provinces of Saratov and Voronezh, and in the Siberian villages of Tobolsk.[44] If the Russian peasant commune constituted a viable mixed economy which permitted private as well as collective ownership, Laveleye suggested that the "Russian" system might well represent an alternative route to economic development which united the advantages of large and small-scale enterprise.

According to Laveleye, England's historical experience suggested that the connection between security of tenure and productivity increase was extremely complex. Like the German historical economists and the Russian radical Cheryshevskii, he began with Adam Smith's argument that the most productive forms of landholding vested ownership in the hands of the cultivator.[45] Praising Smith's ideal model, Laveleye pointed out that English capitalism had transformed owner/cultivators into propertyless laborers, tenants, and absentee landowners. If Smith was right, then economic incentive should have diminished among these social groups, who did not own or directly invest their labor in land. But in England's urban industrial centers, factory workers were productive even though they neither owned the factories where they worked nor possessed any rights to the fruit of their labor (either directly or by possession of a share in the common capital of the enterprise in which they worked).

Laveleye called for a rethinking of the relationship between permanent tenure and economic initiative. Rejecting the argument that commune peasants were perpetually insecure because they did not own land, he argued that peasants in the privatized economy of Ireland who succumbed to starvation as propertyless tenants at will were in fact far less secure than Russia's commune peasants.[46] Laveleye contended that a truer commitment to Smith's teachings might generate reforms which fostered a wider diffusion of property ownership among the primary producers of wealth in English society. (It is significant that John Stuart Mill, to whom Laveleye dedicated his book, enthusiastically agreed with Laveleye's argument.)[47] Although Laveleye praised the commune for providing a measure of much-needed security and opportunity for the lower classes, he advocated tenure reform as "a kind of rampart and safeguard for the holders of large estates." According to Laveleye, "peasant properties may, without exaggeration, be called the lightning conductor that averts from society the dangers which might otherwise lead to violent catastrophes."[48]

The Impact of Historical Economics

In Germany, historical economists became increasingly influential in public and academic life by the turn of the century. As members of the Reichstag, government officials, and advisors to labor associations, and as occupants of every important chair of economics in the country, they were criticized both by the Right and Left as "academic socialists," or *Kathedersozialisten*. The economist Karl Knies was accused of carrying out statistical research that legitimized radical Marxist critiques of German society. The *Verein fur Sozialpolitik* was denounced for advocating economic reforms that would "turn workers into parasites who worked no more than four to six hours a day, spending the rest of their time sleeping, drinking, and talking."[49] From the Left, the Marxist Karl Kautsky attacked historical economist Gustav Schmöller as an opportunist who proposed welfare legislation in a hypocritical "attempt to buy off union leaders."[50]

Outside of Germany, Roscher's *Die System der Volkswirtshaft* (1861) went through fourteen German editions, three American editions, and one French edition. His *Nationaloekonomik des Ackerbaues* was first published in 1865 and subsequently appeared in fifteen German editions, and a Russian translation was published in Moscow in 1869. Laveleye's *Property and Its Primitive Forms* went through five French printings; a Russian translation was published in 1875, four years before the German edition. His *Elements of Political Economy*, complete with copious references to Haxthausen, Chernyshevskii, Chicherin, Kavelin, Beliaev, and Keussler, went through nine French editions. It was published in English translation in 1884 and in three American editions between 1884 and 1889.[51] European historical economists helped to create a climate of opinion which supported (1) land reform, (2) laws on working hours and workplace safety, which placed limits on the unconditional right of owners to control their property, and (3) the abandonment of free trade.

Outside of Western Europe, historical economics was especially popular in the United States.[52] All of the founders of the American Economic Association were German-trained. In order to create an American version of the *Verein für Sozialpolitik*, they set themselves to oppose the abstract models of liberal economics, declaring "While we appreciate the work of former economists, we look not as much to speculations as to the historical and statistical study of actual conditions of economic life for the satisfactory accomplishment of that development."[53]

Among those who made their way to Leipzig and Berlin was the African American scholar W.E.B. Du Bois, who became an economic historian on Schmöller's recommendation. F. W. Taussig of Harvard, Richard Ely of Wisconsin, and Albion Small of the University of Chicago studied in Germany and passed on their knowledge of German scholarship to students like Thorstein Veblen and New Deal economists like Rexford Tugwell.[54] At the height of America's "historical" phase, Harvard University's Economics Department briefly offered courses on socialist and communist economics, the history and literature of economics, as well as a seminar entitled "The Labor Question in Europe and the United States: The Social and Economic Conditions of Workingmen." The economics textbooks of the historical economist Laveleye were required reading for Harvard economics undergraduates at the turn of the century.[55]

Russia

Unsurprisingly, the impact of German historical economics was more profound in Russia than anywhere else. In 1860, Roscher's student Ivan Babst replaced the Anglophile Vernadskii as professor of economics and statistics at Moscow University. As an editor, translator, and popularizer of Roscher's work, Babst was instrumental in convincing the government to issue a university statute in 1863 which made political economy a required subject for students of history.[56] In the ensuing decade, a younger generation of Roscher's students included I. I. Isaev, G. S. Sidorenko, I. I. Ianzhul, and A. I. Chuprov, who emerged as the leading Russian economist of the late nineteenth century.

In general, Russia's historical economists were more sympathetic to radical advocates of revolutionary socialism than their Western European counterparts. Faced with a repressive and autocratic government which condemned a wide range of dissidents to live out their lives in exile, in prison, or in mental hospitals, a number of them came to believe that radicalism was less dangerous than the status quo. For their part, radicals welcomed *Capital's* historical analysis of the destruction of England's small producers, Thorold Rogers's economic history of English agricultural development, and Cliffe-Leslie's critical account of liberal economic policies in England and Ireland. At the same time, they argued that Russia did not need to acquire from the West a rapacious bourgeoisie, a destitute proletariat, or a paternalistic German state.[57] From his place of Siberian exile, the radical A. P. Shchapov investigated the voluntary establishment of communes by Buryat peasants on the shores of Lake Baikal, and acknowledged his intellectual debt to Sir Henry Maine.[58]

Faced with competing Western traditions, G. E. Eliseev rejected both the universalism of classical liberals and the moral relativism of Roscher and his school.[59] As he saw it, Russia was not irrevocably destined to re-create each of the economic stages through which Western Europe had passed. In the words of M. I. Mikhailov: "We have already sufficiently aped the French and Germans. Do we really still have to ape the English?" Shelgunov contended that agricultural and industrial advance could be manifest in either more or less destructive forms; it was therefore necessary for radicals to devise alternative strategies for a democratic and socialist economic development.[60] Responding to the opposition by Proudhon and Michelet to equal rights for women, Mikhailov even advanced the audacious suggestion that on some topics, Western thinkers were as much in need of enlightenment as Russians.[61]

In the 1860s, undaunted by his confinement to a mental hospital as punishment for political dissidence, N. Bervi borrowed the title of Friedrich Engels's Marxist classic for his book *The Condition of the Russian Working Class* (1869). Writing as a historical economist, Bervi argued that the social context within which economic achievements took place was all-important. According to Bervi, the increase in England's productivity rates was due to the "despotic power" exercised by Whig property owners over a desperately poor English and Irish workforce. Drawing on research by Engels, Cliffe-Leslie, Laveleye, Nasse, and Proudhon, Bervi contended that the typical Englishman was not "the man of property." The laborer whose life was constrained by hunger was in his view more typical of the English social scene.[62]

According to Bervi, most people in Western Europe and Russia lived out their lives within an economic system that placed them at the mercy of masters and employers whose aim was to extract the maximum labor in return for the smallest possible reward. With a gift for eloquent and impassioned research that won the admiration of Lev Tolstoi and Karl Marx, he documented the efforts by peasants and workers to survive, prosper, and change, and detailed the abuses of human dignity inflicted upon Russian peasants by their supposed "betters."[63]

The radicalism of Bervi went well beyond the demand that more attention be paid to the plight of the working classes. A century before social theorists like Peter Berger, Thomas Luckman, and Denis Goulet,[64] he raised questions about the intellectual's attraction to missionary approaches to economic development. According to Bervi, the self-described enemies of backwardness were all too prone to argue that any means were justified in the struggle for progress. In Bervi's day, this was an unusual issue for a scholar to raise. Nineteenth-century Russian intellectuals were as reluctant as their counterparts elsewhere to question the "progressive's" right to unlimited power over the objects of their concern—above all, over a peasantry believed to lack useful knowledge or the capacity for reason.[65]

The uncompromisingly elitist ideas of August Comte encouraged educated Russians of every ideological bent to take on the role of missionary to the backward. In the 1860s and 1870s, enthusiastic and idealistic students eagerly purchased Comtean journals, enrolled in schools established by the "Society of Lovers of Humanity" to teach the ideas of Comte, and read Russian translations of G. H. Lewes' *Comte and the Philosophy of Science* and John Stuart Mill's *August Comte and Positivism*. Comte's appeal was neither faddish nor superficial. In setting out a "scientific" theory of social development that explained the past, present, and future, Comte supplied educated Russians with a much-needed reason to hope that however dismal the present might appear, they were nevertheless part of an international vanguard of progressives advancing the cause of humanity. As the extraordinary young mathematician Sofia Kovalevskaia wrote, "We were all so exalted by these new ideas, so convinced that the present state of society could not last long, that a glorious time of liberty and general knowledge was quite certain."[66] To idealists of this sort, it seemed obvious that they were destined to lead the struggle to uplift a mindless multitude.

Radicals were rather more ambivalent toward the masses they sought to transform. Shchapov's generous commitment to serve the peasantry coexisted with old-fashioned claims to power, guidance, and control. Certain that the abysmal backwardness of the *narod* required an educated minority to establish "guardianship," he recommended a "moral dictatorship" over the people in the people's own interest. Like the followers of Lenin in later decades, Shchapov was dedicated to a common people he judged so lacking in initiative, intelligence, and energy that they required large quantities of control by a revolutionary elite.[67] Due to the ignorance and apathy of the masses, dissidents ranging from the amoral Sergei Nechaev to the Jacobin Peter Tkachev considered themselves obliged to assume dictatorial authority (on however temporary a basis).

While Shchapov feared that ignorant peasants might not understand what was best for them, radicals like Vera Figner and Peter Kropotkin feared the consequences of intellectual arrogance. G. E. Eliseev pointed to the intellectual insecurity of Russian scholars of the 1850s who in his view were so afraid to jeopardize their status as Westernized "men of science" that they uncritically accepted every aspect of classical liberalism and contemplated English agricultural models instead of researching the Russian countryside.[68] To the young N. K. Mikhailovskii, the nineteenth-century intellectual's quasi-religious faith in science could turn out to be a mixed blessing. Once the authority of science was invoked, he contended that "experts" could make use of it not only to justify the liberation of human beings from arduous labor, but also—in the style of Western adherents of "scientific" Social Darwinism—to justify policies that assumed the biological inferiority of women, Africans, or Indians.[69]

In his *Alphabet of the Social Sciences* (1871),[70] Bervi suggested that men of science could easily dismiss protests against the suffering inflicted by their policies as a sign that the masses were incapable of appreciating progress. Citing the example of nineteenth-century Egyptian reformer Mehemet Ali, he observed that progressives were quite capable of claiming that the coercive policies which drove peasants from the land epitomized the triumph of Reason and Science over backwardness.[71] In contrast to Comte (and Shchapov), Bervi contended that the common people were quite capable of understanding their own interests and prospects. If provided with freer access to technology, education, and land, he believed, they could themselves play a leading role in the transformation of Russian agriculture.[72]* While systematic empirical evidence on the commune's internal operations was as yet quite scanty, Bervi contended that it was unlikely the commune was either an all-powerful proprietor that con-

---

A Note on Populism: Despite the frequency with which the term "populism" has been applied to Russians sympathetic to peasants and communes, I have decided not to use it in the discussion which follows. It seems inappropriate to describe socialists like Bervi in terms which (1) they did not use to describe themselves, and (2) were intended to denigrate their efforts. It may also be the case that the term "populist" carries so much emotion-laden baggage, i.e., to be populist is to be "sentimental, reactionary, irrational, anti-Western," etc.—that it serves as a barrier rather than an aid to understanding. My own research strongly supports Richard Pipes's judgment that the word "populist" was first introduced and popularized by Marxists in the 1890s, who lumped various socialists together, linked them to the Slavophiles, and contrasted them to Westernizers and Marxists. However, for a perspective sympathetic to Lenin's view that "populists" were anti-Western reactionaries, see the work of Andrzej Walicki. Pipes's view is set out in his "Russian Marxism and Its Populist Background: The late Nineteenth Century," *The Russian Review* 19, no. 4 (October 1960): 316–77, and *Struve: Liberal on the Left* (Cambridge, Mass.: Harvard University Press, 1970), p. 85; Walicki's is contained in *The Controversy over Capitalism: Studies in the Social Philosophy of the Russian Populists* (Notre Dame, Ind.: University of Notre Dame Press, 1989), pp. 2–3.

trolled the property or the allotments of its members, *or* an insuperably irrational and obsolete survival of feudalism.

With a remarkable sense of restraint, given his hopes for the commune, Bervi refused to claim that the commune was a panacea for Russia's ills. As he saw it, the discovery of communal institutions in India and Germany did not guarantee that the Russian commune would turn out to be a viable economic institution. Insisting that the positive features of the commune could not easily be detached from its local context, Bervi warned against the danger that intellectuals would raise the commune to the level of an abstract and ahistorical ideal. According to Bervi, intellectuals possessed the defects of their virtues. Tending to delight in abstractions, they were quite capable of (1) abandoning their certainty that communes were obsolete for a belief that they were perfect, and (2) demanding that communes should therefore be made mandatory for all. If progressives were to play a constructive role in Russia's future development, Bervi suggested, they must first acquire a measure of humility, and a better understanding of their own biases and special interests.[73]

Whatever outcomes Russian intellectuals might prefer, Bervi argued that the commune's future would nevertheless be decided by the specifics of the Russian context. As he saw it, scholars were in dire need of more concrete empirical data about rural economic life. "Taking the peasant's side" in epistemological as well as sentimental terms,[74] Bervi called for systematic empirical research based on direct peasant testimony rather than the more customary reports by landlords, bailiffs, police, and government officials.

Although Bervi was inspired by a romantic faith in communitarian peasant values and a delight in the innate good sense of the peasantry, it is worth noting that romanticism was not the monopoly of peasant sympathizers. Liberal economists like the government official V. P. Bezobrazov were far from dispassionate about the achievements of England's "improving landlord." Viewing the desire to acquire property as a law of nature and the embodiment of Reason, they claimed that property rights were "sacred," and appealed to the "sanctity of property." At the other end of the ideological spectrum, the radical Eliseev described the impulse to re-establish the commune as a "sacred" impulse, rooted in the peasantry's innate and natural virtues. In practice, radicals and classical economists were each prone to romanticize different social elements, while describing their own idealizations as both realistic and morally enlightened.

THE BEGINNING OF RUSSIA'S *METHODENSTREIT*

Within the Imperial Free Economic Society, the debates of the 1860s and 1870s reflected both the impact of radical activism and the influence of historical economics. The steadfast Vernadskii reasserted his earlier faith in Western liberal models, declaring in 1865: "It is foolish to think that one must not imitate Europe, but continually work out in everything one's own independent principles, including the exchange of private for communal ownership, just as if someone began believing it unnecessary to walk on two feet as the Europeans do and for the sake of working out national principles, one should walk on all fours.[75]

But others looked to the Russian countryside and posed a virtually unprecedented complaint—in the words of I. I. Kudritskii: "I have heard nothing here from peasants because they are not present. What kind of farmers are they? What do they themselves understand as their task?"[76] Within the Society's Statistics Division, members debated the link between tenure and productivity rates. Like the Belgian economist Laveleye, they considered the wealth of English tenants and the productive capacities of propertyless factory workers. V. A. Panaev (who wrote for the radical journal *The Contemporary*) pointed out that in Russia there was as yet no systematic empirical evidence to demonstrate that the peasantry's economic incentive declined because their communal allotment holdings were temporary.[77]

In the 1870s, the contemporary findings of the French *Enquête Agricole* and the British Royal Commission inspired the Russian government to fund a new series of empirical studies of the Russian countryside. However, the Valuev Commission established for this purpose in 1873 did not deal with the concerns of Kudritskii or Panaev. Relying instead on the testimony of provincial officials and representatives of the landed gentry, it reached the predetermined conclusions set out by Valuev, the Minister of State Properties and a commune critic. Although most of the Commission's data did not refer to the commune, its report concluded nevertheless that communal tenure constituted the primary obstacle to rural progress. According to foreign commentators like Laveleye, Paul Leroy-Beaulieu, the German scholar Christian Walcher, and the British journalist Donald Mackenzie Wallace, the Valuev Commission's report was seriously flawed by the arbitrariness of its conclusions and by its failure to invite direct peasant testimony.[78]

In the post-Emancipation debate on development, both sides relied on Western economic authorities. For some, the West was best represented in the writings of Karl Marx. For others, the best way to learn from the West was to study Ricardo, Schmöller, or Émile de Laveleye. Because neither side could draw on a wide range of empirical evidence on the Russian agricultural economy, the clash of *cultural* assumptions about peasants and progress remained paramount.

Among Russia's professional economists, the careers of Alexander Chuprov and Nikolai Ziber epitomized the initial struggle to decide which models, which evidence, and which social elements should guide Russia's future development. Chuprov was a student of Wilhelm Roscher, whose long career as a political economist at Moscow University began in the midst of a "movement to go to the people" (the "*khozhdenie v narod*"), which brought together radical students intent on bridging the gulf that divided them from the peasants whose lives and communal institutions they wished to defend.[79] As they went out to the countryside in 1873 and 1874, and were arrested and imprisoned by the hundreds, a sympathetic Chuprov lectured his Moscow University students on the reasons why the social sciences needed to be brought closer to life, which had "suffered so much from the separation." Insisting that without empirical research, the science of economics could degenerate into a sterile intellectual exercise,[80] Chuprov organized Russia's first student seminar on the subject of statistics and introduced into Russian academic life the first university courses in applied political economy. His lectures were mimeographed by devoted students, and became the standard introduction to economics for undergraduates in the second half of the nineteenth century. Together with students like A. S. Posnikov and N. A. Kablukov, Chuprov attempted to emulate the work of his counterparts within the German *Verein fur Sozialpolitik*. His deliberate intention was to link scholarly research with policy proposals intended to improve the material conditions of the Russian people, and of the peasant majority in particular.[81]

Chuprov agreed with Bervi that in the 1870s, economists knew relatively little about Russian rural life. It was essential, he argued, that wide-ranging and systematic empirical study be carried out in order to demonstrate 1) whether peasants and their communities were rigid, conservative, and historically obsolete, or 2) whether private owners were in fact more productive. In the last third of the nineteenth century, Chuprov became widely recognized as "the heart and soul" of the *zemstvo* statistical investigations, whose researchers interviewed 4.5 million peasant households by the turn of the century. In this process, *zemstvo* statisticians—many the recipients of jail terms imposed for their participation in the events of 1873–74—created the world's largest data base on a peasant population. In some respects, these investigations may have represented the most successful and influential component of the "movement to go to the people."[82]

From the outset, Chuprov's conception of the West included German as well as Anglo-French contributions. Convinced that contemporary conflicts in economics were not battles between good and evil, Chuprov argued that both liberal and socialist perspectives were essential to the education of a modern economist. As he saw it, Russians needed to learn from the "Manchesterite" emphasis on the innovative individual free of political or social constraints, and from socialists who focused on the destructive impact of economic inequality and insecurity. Contending that individualism, equality, and security were all profoundly significant as economic factors, he refused to elevate any of them to the level of a supra-historical value to be imposed at the expense of the others in every time and place.[83]

At the opposite pole from Chuprov was the economist Nikolai Ziber of the University of St. Vladimir. Ziber has been described by several generations of Soviet scholars as the foremost Russian economist of his day,[84] and his work was studied and praised by a wide range of late nineteenth century Russian Marxists, liberals, and conservative government reformers. Primarily a theoretician, and an expert on the writings of David Ricardo, Ziber did not carry out any studies of the Russian economy. He taught only briefly in Russia, and spent most of his professional life in exile, where he came to know and respect the work of Karl Marx.

Like an earlier generation of Russian liberal economists, Ziber was a supporter of autocracy as well as classical liberalism. But in the 1860s and 1870s, he was drawn to the laws of historical economics set out in the writings of Karl Marx and August Comte, and to a notion of progress as a process that obliterated all survivals of the past (except, presumably, the Russian autocracy). In the first volume of *Capital*, Ziber discovered an "iron law" of economic development as intellectually satisfying as Ricardo's "iron law" of wages. Admiring Karl Marx above all other living economists, Ziber declared him a worthy heir of the English liberal economist David Ricardo. According to Ziber, *Capital* demonstrated beyond question that the emergence of capitalism in England prefigured the development of all other nations the world over.[85]

In the 1870s, when Russian liberals like Chicherin, V. I. Guerrier, and Iu. Zhukovskii accused Marx of being "narrowly" concerned for proletarians and indifferent to the far more significant "psychic labor" of the entrepreneur, Ziber came to Marx's defense. Downplaying Marx's commitment to revolution, he argued that Marx was a brilliant economic theorist of world-wide significance,[86] whose research demonstrated that primitive communal property systems invariably gave way to more productive and profitable forms of private tenure.[87] Ziber discounted Marx's belief that capitalism would eventually be replaced by socialism. As he saw it, the significance of Marx's work lay not in his misguided socialist "dreams and fantasies" but in his depiction of capitalism's inevitable forward march. To Ziber, it was Marx's genius to have recognized that nowhere was capitalism's permanent triumph more instructive than in nineteenth-century England. In Ziber's interpretation of Marx, the liberal assumptions that the latter shared with Ricardo took center stage and Marx's critique of capitalism became insignificant.[88] As the following chapter indicates, the struggle to define the "true" character of Marxism became a central point of contention in Russia's *methodenstreit*.

Chapter Six

CAPTURING THE "ESSENCE" OF MARX

THE EMERGENCE OF ORTHODOX MARXISM

> England shows to the less developed nations of the world the image of their future.
> *(Karl Marx,* Capital, *1859)*

> The English system is completely incapable of fulfilling the conditions on which the development of Russia's agriculture depends.
> *(Karl Marx, 1883)*

IN THE MIDDLE decades of the nineteenth century, educated Russians discovered in the classic writings of Marx an explosive mixture of historically oriented economics, a Eurocentric conception of progress, a revolutionary demand for social justice, and a class-based critique of capitalism. In the last years of Marx's life, the balance among these elements dramatically shifted. The questions raised for him by contemporary European research on property and by the case of "peasant Russia" led Marx to rethink some of the central features of his earlier work. For the first time in his career as a revolutionary political economist, Marx confronted the issue of cultural difference. Retreating a bit from a liberal notion of progress which situated the West at the top of Civilization's ladder, he examined the possibility that social groups and "natives" previously dismissed as backward might contribute to human progress. By the 1880s, Marx was far less comfortable with the conventional Liberal distinctions between the West and "lower" societies.

His growing skepticism about the West as a universal model was reflected in voluminous notes and correspondence, but not in any published books or essays. Marx's relative silence as a writer during the last fifteen years of his life may well have reflected how difficult it was for him to integrate less Eurocentric ideas and research into his earlier theoretical framework. But whatever the reasons may have been for his silence, the absence of published work which incorporated his changing views meant that the "essence" of Marxism for future generations would be determined by the outcome of a bitter struggle among his Russian admirers during the last decades of the nineteenth century.

Questions of Progress

The most striking casualty of Marx's later reconsiderations was his conception of progress. Until the 1870s, there was little to distinguish Marx from the eighteenth-century *philosophes* who viewed culture, reason, and civilization as the unique creation of a bourgeoisie whose historical task it was to demolish barbaric and irrational peasant societies. In most of his writings, the bourgeoisie appeared both as agents of an exploitative capitalist system and as representatives of a distinctly higher level of civilization. In contrast, peasants were portrayed as a social element with neither a past nor a future; either as wretched survivors of "medievalism" or as small producers engaged in a futile quest for bourgeois status, their future was bleak. According to Marx, the fate of peasant institutions was equally dubious. In the 1860s, Marx considered the peasant commune an institution "compatible with Russian barbarism, but not with bourgeois civilization."[1] In a letter to Engels written in 1868, Marx expressed delight that the development of capitalism in Russia was at last bringing "all that trash" to an end.[2]

Although Marx ridiculed the notion that liberals were objective in their assessment of capitalism, he did not question their objectivity on the peasant question. Because he himself was quite convinced of the "idiocy of rural life," Marx saw no bias in the liberal assumption that peasants lacked a culture, values, or institutions to which they might legitimately feel some loyalty. Viewing peasant communities as reactionary and conservative in both the medieval and capitalist stages of socioeconomic development, he argued in the first volume of *Capital* that the low degree of division of labor within medieval villages reinforced an oppressive, backward, and "Asiatic" feudal order.[3] Later, in volume three, he argued that under capitalism, associations of peasant producers fostered illusory hopes of prosperity and thus reinforced existing systems of bourgeois exploitation. According to Marx, strong peasant communities served either to anchor and fortify a feudal order or to promote the short-sighted goals of petty capitalism. In both cases, they were obstacles to progress. Until the last years of his life, Marx was as eager as any of his liberal counterparts to dismiss those who rejected such judgments as romantics, reactionaries, and "enemies of science."[4]

Outside of Western Europe, Marx's assessment of communal peasant institutions was equally negative. In the 1850s, his opposition to colonialism did not extend to the anticommunal policies implemented by British colonial administrators. Viewing their policies as progressive though brutal, Marx found it hard to reconcile what he called "the natural repugnance as fellow creatures to the sufferings of Orientals while their society is being violently transformed, with the historical necessity of these transformations." In keeping with his view that communes formed part of the "medieval" stage of human history, Marx argued that the disappearance of the *panchayat* was a tragic but inevitable feature of India's transformation into a modern capitalist society in which class struggle between wage laborers and entrepreneurs would eventually produce a productive socialist order. Warning against the evils of Romanticism, Marx wrote, "we must not forget that these idyllic village communities, inoffensive though they may appear, had always been the solid foundation of Oriental despotism, that they restrained the human mind within the smallest possible compass, making it the unresisting tool of superstition, enslaving it beneath the traditional rules, depriving it of all grandeur and historical energies."[5]

It was only after he began to study nineteenth-century European and Russian research on the origins of property that Marx began to question some of his earlier cultural certainties. In Maurer's investigations of the German *mark*, he was impressed by the evidence that medieval German kings and princes used the accusation of economic backwardness to justify destruction of the *mark*'s relative autonomy and the imposition of new forms of political domination. After reading Maurer, Marx was notably less willing to believe that communes disappeared naturally, as a result of their obsoleteness in the modern world.[6] In 1873, he deleted earlier attacks on commune advocates like Alexander Herzen and Baron Haxthausen from the second edition of *Capital*, and began to train his critical sights upon the failings of liberals who defended the "sanctity" of private-property rights.[7]

Citing the work of the Russian scholar Maxim Kovalevskii on the Indian *panchayat*, Marx ridiculed the "poetic" language that British colonial officials in India used to describe the commune's disappearance. According to Marx, "saccharine" laments over the stubborn backwardness of the *panchayat* permitted the British to avoid responsibility for the poverty and suffering caused by their own, anticommunal policies. In his words: "British officials in India, as well as critics like Sir Henry Maine who rely on them, describe the dissolution of communal ownership of land in the Punjab as if it took place as the inevitable consequence of *economic progress* despite the affectionate attitude of the British towards this archaic form. The truth is rather that the British themselves are the *principal* (and active) offenders responsible for this dissolution—to their own danger."[8]

In North Africa, where Britain's French counterparts rehearsed similar laments over the backwardness of indigenous peoples, Marx argued that expressions of sympathy were invariably followed by the use of coercion to accelerate the demise of communal institutions. Although French imperial authorities claimed to be serving the cause of economic development when they forcibly introduced private tenure, Marx argued that they were in fact pursuing the political aim of destroying the basis of Algerian society. As he saw it, idealized notions of the civilizing impact of private-property rights simply disguised French efforts to subjugate the Algerian countryside. Marx went on to denounce the "disgusting *poetry of landownership* (*Grundeigentumspoesie*) that exceeded in its *depersonalization of human relationships* even the poetry of Capital (*Kapitalpoesie*)."[9]

In Marx's later writings, *Capital*'s analysis of a modernizing world dominated by "a cash nexus," which created ever simpler and more polarized social and economic relations, gave way. In place of an economic model that established capitalism triumphant over all of the contradictions of "medievalism," we find Marx's growing recognition that in the course of human history, socioeconomic development became increasingly complicated rather than simpler. Challenging *Capital*'s image of a backward peasant world crumbling before the insuperable onslaught of capitalism, he raised the question of whether peasant and nonpeasant societies might in fact coexist—like consecutive geological strata in the earth's surface.[10]

Marx's Later Writings: The Russia Factor

The initial interest of Marx and Engels in Russia was sparked by their hope that the exploits of the terrorist People's Will (*Narodnaia Volia*) would ignite a revolutionary upheaval in Western Europe.[11] But they were also intrigued by Russian scholarship and welcomed enthusiasm of Russians for their work. (According to Marx, *Capital* was more popular in Russia than anywhere else.)[12] Like many other European thinkers of the 1870s and 1880s, Marx and Engels recognized that important intellectual currents in nineteenth-century European thought proceeded from Russia to the West as well as in the more widely recognized opposite direction. Citing Chuprov and other Russian social scientists, Engels observed that the Russian historical school of economics was far superior to the German because it was less subservient to the authoritarian policy concerns of government officials.[13] For his part, Marx praised Chernyshevskii's "masterful" analysis of the economics of John Stuart Mill, and described N. Bervi's *The Condition of the Russian Working Class* as the most important work of economic history since Engels's study of the English factory workers (with the characteristic, vitriolic *caveat* that it contained a certain amount of "well-meaning twaddle," which was suited "to the stage of development reached by the people for whom the book is intended").[14]

In the 1870s and early 1880s, Marx's leading Russian advocate was N. F. Daniel'son, an economist who coauthored the first Russian translation of *Capital*. Daniel'son supplied Marx with many of the over two hundred books on Russia that he counted on his shelves by 1883, and encouraged Marx to immerse himself in Russian literature, history, and economics. Marx accumulated some 30,000 pages of notes on the Russian peasant question during the ten years before he died, and according to his wife, he studied Russia in the 1870s, as if "it was a matter of life or death."[15] To Daniel'son's delight, Marx reported in 1872 that he planned to devote a whole section of the forthcoming volume three of *Capital* to the topic of Russian forms of landed property.

Viewing Russian scholarship as an integral part of Western European debates on the origins of property, Marx observed to Daniel'son that "Berlin professors" cited the work of Chicherin to prove that communal tenure was "artificially" created by Russian rulers in order to facilitate the collection of seigneurial and state revenues. How could this be true, Marx asked, when so many European scholars had already discovered that "in all other countries it [communal property systems] appeared as a necessary phase of development?" Daniel'son responded by sending Marx the writings of Chicherin and Beliaev, some of the more recent *zemstvo* statistical investigations, and a lengthy review article on the peasant commune by K. D. Kavelin.[16]

Daniel'son's choice of Kavelin as a source of information for Marx was particularly significant. Kavelin was a legal scholar, a member of the "Westernizer" group of the 1840s, and after 1861, the president of the Imperial Free Economic Society. His writings on economics and law were available in German translation, and the historical economist Wilhelm Roscher described Kavelin as a leading representative of the "German-Russian" school of economics. In contrast to the economist Ziber, who praised Marx as a Ricardian liberal, Kavelin admired Marx above all as a historical economist. However, he agreed with Ziber that the first volume of *Capital* was an *anti-revolutionary* work of German scholarship that documented the long-term and politically nonviolent process by which English small producers gave way to the social classes essential to the building of an advanced industrial society. In Kavelin's words, "These [Marx's] words alone should suffice for those who can take heed; but there are very few such people."[17]

Positioning himself as a moderate in Russia's increasingly bitter debates over the peasant commune, Kavelin warned against oversimplified analogies between Russia and the West. According to Kavelin, those who were distressed at the backwardness of Russia's commune-based agriculture were all too eager to draw the facile conclusion that if communes were abolished, Russia's agricultural economy would automatically advance. In Kavelin's words, "God knows where such simple analogies lead us!" Equally critical of idealizations of the commune by conservatives and radicals, Kavelin argued that the commune was neither an immutable guarantor of order and stability nor an embryonic form of Russian socialism.[18]

According to Kavelin, the virtues of the commune were real but limited, and primarily of a political nature. At best, communes might prevent the dangerous levels of social and economic polarization that prevailed in Western Europe, where the claims of private property owners were considered sacrosanct and permitted to escalate without restraint. Kavelin insisted that the social tensions endemic to Western society were not a product of private tenure. As he saw it, private tenure generated social and economic disruption only when—as in the West—it was granted *monopoly* status as the only legitimate form of ownership. According to Kavelin, the excessive inequality that developed in the absence of a mixed economy was politically dangerous. As he saw it, "unbalanced" Western capitalist economies were likely to produce revolutions that would eventually engulf even the legitimate and productive owners of property.[19] Welcoming the new research by economists and ethnographers like Posnikov, Keussler, and E. I. Iakushkin, Kavelin expressed the hope that systematic and empirically based scholarship on the Russian peasant commune might lay the foundations for more balanced and scientific judgments about the relationship between communal and noncommunal tenure in the Russian countryside.

Marx's writings of the 1880s reflect the impact of Kavelin's essay. He took seriously the data indicating that communes were flexible rather than static in their economic behavior, and considered more carefully than ever before the complexities of communal ownership. Evidence of the distinctions between various forms of movable and immovable property within the commune framework, and the different rules that governed the use of household allotments, "private" garden plots, "privately" owned livestock, and "common" pasture land, served to reinforce Marx's growing skepticism about the stages of economic development set out in his earlier writings.

Considering the possibility that the commune might provide a basis both for social security and economic development, Marx observed: "on the one hand, communal property and all the social relations which derive

from it give it a solid base, whereas the private house, the parcelled cultivation and the private appropriation of the fruits of labor allow a development of individualism which would have been incompatible with the conditions obtaining in more primitive communities."[20] By the late 1870s,
Marx no longer argued that the commune's fate was linked with "Russian
barbarism" or predetermined by general laws of economic development.
Placing himself explicitly in opposition to the deterministic notions of
progress associated with the theories of August Comte, Marx responded
to an 1877 letter from the Russian radical N. K. Mikhailovskii with a
denial that his writings were ever intended to be a "historico-philosophi-
cal theory of the general path fatally imposed upon all peoples, whatever
their historical circumstances." According to Marx, "history offered Russia" a chance to avoid capitalism if the latter's relentless advance were
somehow checked.[21]

N. F. DANIEL'SON: MARXISM ACCORDING TO MARX'S WRITINGS ON RUSSIA

Daniel'son was delighted by the direction of Marx's thinking, and repeatedly urged him to publish an authoritative study of Russian economic
development.[22] Although Marx refused, he encouraged Daniel'son to take
on this task. In a multi-volume study of the post-Emancipation economy
entitled *Outlines of the Post-Reform Economy* (1885), Daniel'son investigated the process of primary accumulation and the transition to commodity production which Marx had traced out in *Capital*. Focusing on Russia's economic relationship to the West and the peculiar role of Russia's
nascent bourgeoisie, Daniel'son contended that the economic prospects
of Russia and the West were markedly different.

    According to Daniel'son, a Russia confronted by the expansionist colo-
nial ambitions of the nineteenth-century West could not afford to emulate
either the tempo or the policies characteristic of England's economic experience. Neither England's relatively slow-paced, three-hundred-year process of economic development and capital accumulation nor the introduction of the free markets and private-property rights that had so
dramatically and successfully transformed the English economy were in
his view useful models for Russia. Emphasizing that contemporary Russian development initiatives were occurring in the face of powerful external threats to the nation's survival as a great power, he noted that a fearful
Russian government relied on foreign grain sales as a source of capital,
and used the army to extract "surplus" grain from subsistence small producers. Certain that such Draconian government measures were doomed
to failure, Daniel'son declared that Russia was no match for Western nations using rails and steam instead of carts and barges for the transport

of grain. Like other capital-poor nations, Russia was destined for defeat by predatory and far more economically advanced Western adversaries. As he saw it, peasant sacrifices at the altar of primitive accumulation would not achieve their goal.[23]

On the domestic scene, Daniel'son found little evidence that Russia's bourgeoisie were prepared to emulate either their French or their English counterparts. In a scenario which prefigured the 1990s machinations of the Yeltsin era, Daniel'son noted that industrialists formerly dependent on state subsidies eagerly proclaimed themselves capitalists, and appealed for lucrative government contracts. Outside of this government "market," he predicted that such state-supported "entrepreneurs" would be reluctant to assume the risks of manufacturing the inexpensive clothing, tools, or shelter necessary for a mass market. Daniel'son contended that state capitalists concerned with the rapid acquisition of substantial profits would prefer to satisfy demands by the wealthy for an ever greater quantity of luxury goods. According to his class analysis, the bourgeoisie would avoid the risks and costs of developing a peasant market and peasant living standards would plummet.

Daniel'son himself took the position that it was *morally* irresponsible for Russian progressives to welcome the material disaster for peasants and workers that unrestricted capitalism brought in its wake—a disaster which, he emphasized, would be unredeemed by economic success either at home or abroad. According to Daniel'son, capitalism could never bring prosperity to Russia or any other nation short of capital and unable to compete effectively in the export of industrial goods. He did not, however, deny that capitalism might develop. As he saw it, progressives could not in good conscience justify the acceptance of capitalism's brutal inequalities on the grounds that popular suffering would eventually produce a socialist society which brought justice for all.

Daniel'son insisted instead that economists and social critics were obliged to devise humane and rational strategies for development which drew upon the commune's potential and the requirements of Russian industrial growth.[24] Citing Marx's 1877 letter to Mikhailovskii, Daniel'son argued, "We do not have to wait until all the peasants are deprived of their land, and are replaced by a capitalist agriculture. . . . We must graft scientific agriculture and modern large-scale industry onto the commune, and at the same time give the commune a form that will make it an effective tool for the organization of a large-scale industry and the transformation of that industry from a capitalist to a public one."[25]

In the decades to come, Daniel'son was accused of advancing a sentimental, "populist" argument that Russia's unique history and traditions made it "impossible" for capitalism to develop. Although this charge became extremely popular, it was unfounded. Among professional economists and other social scientists who researched communal property systems in Russia and the West, one searches in vain for a denial that capitalism, complete with bourgeois entrepreneurs and proletarians, existed in the cities and in the countryside.

When the first volume of Daniel'son's study was published in 1880, Marx praised its originality and encouraged him to continue working along similar lines.[26] But many Russian admirers of Marx reacted very differently. How, they asked, could a class analysis that included peasants, communes, and proposals for a state-sponsored "socialization" of agricultural and industrial production, be squared with the classic teachings of *Capital*? According to M. A. Silvin, "It was an 'evil day' " for Russia's Marxists when Daniel'son's book appeared.[27] Fearing Daniel'son's authority as a translator and personal acquaintance of Marx who used Marxist terminology to analyze a wealth of empirical data, Silvin (and the others who established Russia's first Marxist political organization) argued that Daniel'son's work represented not a contribution but a *disservice* to the cause of socialism.

THE EMANCIPATION OF LABOR GROUP: MARXISM ACCORDING TO CAPITAL

In 1881, a Russian radical and former terrorist named Vera Zasulich wrote to Marx, requesting his advice to radical socialists in a backward peasant society. What, she asked, were the lessons of *Capital*? In a country where proletarians were few, were radicals simply to live for the future, calculating all the while how many decades needed to pass until the bourgeoisie had triumphed, and how many "centuries, perhaps" before Russia's economic and social development made it appropriate to organize a proletarian struggle for socialism?[28] Marx did not find Zasulich's question easy to answer, and after two years of drafts, redrafts, and revisions, he finally wrote to advise Zasulich and her comrades not to give up either on peasants or their communes. According to Marx, "the special research into this subject which I conducted, the materials for which I obtained from original sources, has convinced me that this community is the mainspring of Russia's social generation, but in order that it might function as such one would first have to eliminate the deleterious influences which assail it from every quarter and then to ensure the conditions normal for spontaneous development." In a manner that has been described as "aussi peu 'Marxiste' que possible," Marx suggested that in Russia, "thanks to an extraordinary concatenation of circumstances, the peasant commune, still existing on a national scale, can gradually shake off its primitive qualities and develop directly as an element of collective production on a national scale. Precisely because it is a coeval of capitalist production, it is in a position to assimilate its positive achievements without going through all its horrors."[29]

This was not the response that Zasulich either expected or wanted. By the time Marx's letter arrived, she and her comrades had already decided to turn their attention from the peasantry to Russia's urban proletariat. Fresh from participation in a "movement to go to the people" which failed to incite a commune-based peasantry to revolution, they were not interested in Marx's newly acquired hopes for the Russian commune. Zasulich, G. V. Plekhanov, and P. B. Aksel'rod preferred to discover in Marxism a "scientific" justification for the difficulties they had experienced in the Russian countryside. How indeed could Russian radicals have been expected to succeed with a social element described by Marx in *Capital* as "a class of barbarians standing halfway outside society, a class suffering all the tortures and all the miseries of civilized countries in addition to the crudeness of primitive forms of society"?[30]

Plekhanov seized on the evidence of economic polarization contained in V. I. Orlov's 1879 study of Moscow province to argue that universal laws of historical development were creating in Russia an economic situation which replicated the era of Western Europe's transition to capitalism.[31] Orlov's economic data, combined with a "Marxist" explanation that focused upon the obsoleteness of peasants and peasant institutions, reinforced the impulse to turn away from the majority of the population. Repudiating what Plekhanov described as an "ungrateful and unreceptive" peasantry, Plekhanov, Zasulich, and Aksel'rod shifted their allegiance to a small but presumably far more deserving class of urban proletarians.[32]

In the 1883 manifesto of Russia's first Marxist organization, the Emancipation of Labor group, Marxism was defined as an urban and proletarian-centered revolutionary movement. Throughout the document, it was assumed that all human societies moved inevitably from medieval backwardness to more rational and productive stages of industrial capitalist development, and then on to socialism. Constructing a Marxist orthodoxy that excluded Marx's later views, the group declined to publish Marx's 1877 letter to Mikhailovskii,[33] and denied the existence of his letter to Zasulich. Zasulich herself declared "no such letter had been received." (The letter was not discovered until 1924, when the scholar B. I. Nikolaevskii found it in the papers of Akselrod, and published it for the first time.)[34]

The Marxism advocated by Plekhanov and his colleagues was rooted not only in a denial of Marx's comments on Russia, but in a deep-seated revulsion against the peasantry, who had so disappointed them. In the 1880s and 1890s, peasants appeared in Plekhanov's writings as increasingly sinister and repellent figures—"barbarian-tillers of the soil" or brutalized primitives whose lives were bereft of "solidarity, broad social interests, or ideas."[35] Although Plekhanov conceded that Russian peasants showed no eagerness to become individual proprietors, he attributed their reluctance to ignorance and backwardness.[36]

According to Plekhanov, "scientific Marxism" had demonstrated beyond question that Russia and Western Europe would follow similar historical trajectories.[37] Although in 1879 Plekhanov argued that Russia had not yet entered upon the capitalist "path," by 1881, he declared: "The matter is settled. . . . All other paths, conceivable, perhaps, for some other countries, are closed to her."[38] In his book *Our Differences* (1885), all those who disagreed were described as un-Marxist, subjectivist, and "populist"; in his later publication *The Monist Conception of History*, all references to Marx's writings on the Russian peasant commune were completely excluded. Despite many obstacles to progress, Plekhanov insisted that nevertheless, "capitalism goes on its way, dislodging the independent producers from their unstable conditions and creating an army of workers in Russia, by the same tried and true method" set out in the pages of *Capital*. Far less dialectical than Marx in his treatment of capitalism, Plekhanov emphasized above all the historical service which capitalism performed as a precursor of socialism, and welcomed the evidence that Russia had at last entered onto the capitalist path which had already transformed the West.

In the writings of P. B. Struve, who authored the first manifesto of the Russian Social Democratic Party in 1898, the basic doctrines of Marxism and classical liberalism became virtually indistinguishable. Struve did not long remain a Marxist. Soon abandoning revolutionary activity in order to align himself with the Legal Marxist movement, he later abandoned the cause of socialism for a long-term commitment to liberal capitalism. But even before he left the Marxist fold, Struve portrayed capitalism as a magnificent stage in human progress toward a distant socialist paradise. In Struve's words, "On the side of capitalism stood and stands almost everything, namely that which counts the most: *economic progress.*" In his review of a book by the German economist Friedrich List, Struve praised List's "victory hymn of triumphant commodity production, proclaiming to all its cultural historical power and its relentless advance." Throughout the 1880s and 1890s, Struve contrasted the individual freedom, civil liberty, cultural achievement, and rational economic activity typical of capitalism with the communal barbarism of the peasant village. In his words, "the cultural-historical link connecting economic progress with the institution of private property . . . is all too often forgotten. Only by ignoring this link is it possible to expect that an economically and culturally immature society can attain economic progress."[39]

Struve's equation of all culture and progress with capitalism struck many of his critics as a peculiar attitude for a revolutionary Marxist advocate of the working class to assume.[40] As the economist A. A. Manuilov caustically noted, "If Mr. Struve thinks that every factory smokestack necessarily signifies social progress, let him say so openly, rather than sowing confusion among his Russian readers."[41] Even in his Marxist phase, Struve was far more repelled by peasant backwardness than by the exploitative features of capitalism.[42] In the aftermath of the famine of 1891, as peasants were dying of starvation, Struve rather callously described the famine year as a "regrettable episode" on Russia's road to economic progress.[43] In a brilliantly insightful observation made long after 1917, Struve himself observed that in late nineteenth-century Russia Marxists played the role that liberals had earlier played in Western European history. Their most powerful critiques were directed *not* against capitalism but against the backward system of "natural economy" in all of its peasant and communal manifestations. Placing great faith in the civilizing mission of capitalism in Russia, they denounced as "reactionaries" those who defended "medieval" social elements and institutions.[44]

During his brief career as a Marxist, Struve rejected the predictions of capitalist-generated poverty set out in the writings of Daniel'son as far too gloomy, and ridiculed the "sentimentality" of the economist Vorontsov, whose statistical research documented economic innovation within the peasant commune. Both Daniel'son's pessimistic view of capitalism and Vorontsov's hopes for the commune seemed to Struve a symptom of the Russian "disease" of populism. He accused Daniel'son (inaccurately) of denying the link between capitalism and increased productivity, and charged Vorontsov (inaccurately) with ignoring peasant poverty within the peasant commune.[45] At the turn of the century, Struve succeeded in establishing populism for a century to come as a synonym for xenophobic, reactionary, and antiscientific opposition to progress and industrial development. His arguments became very popular among Marxists and capitalist-minded government officials, and his books eventually found their way onto the desk of Finance Minister Witte himself.

Mikhailovskii, Daniel'son, and Vorontsov, who were the chief targets of Struve's attack, strongly rejected Struve's usage of the term "populist." In the words of Daniel'son, "Under this label, which he treats as a pejorative one, [Struve] includes persons holding the most diverse views. . . . It is, of course, self-evident that a considerable majority of the authors whom he cites share with Populism only the desire to uncover the causes of the deterioration in the peasantry's condition, and to indicate those remedies which, in the opinion of each, can change it for the better."[46]

In contrast to Struve, the young Lenin was far more dialectical in his analysis of the brutalities of capitalist progress. But he agreed with Struve that capitalism's progressive historical function was to obliterate the "Asiatic" survivals of feudal backwardness in the Russian countryside. Like Plekhanov and Struve, Lenin employed many of the racist stereotypes which then prevailed in nineteenth-century intellectual circles. Adopting the view that every noncapitalist region of the world was mired in conditions of "feudal" backwardness that were analogous to—but far worse than—the feudal era of medieval Western history, Lenin denounced the scourge of "Orientalism" in Russian rural life.

Among Russia's new Marxists, "Asia" became a sort of codeword for cultural, political, and economic stagnation and for any form of backwardness, cruelty, servility, and unreason. Plekhanov described Russia's commune peasants as "Asiatic" in their indifference to the outside world; no better than the Chinese, the Russian peasant was like "a beast of burden whose life provided no opportunity for the luxury of thought." Extending the racist stereotype to include the peasantry's sympathizers, Plekhanov described advocates of the commune as "Easterners."[47] Struve demanded that Russia exorcise the legacy of "Orientalism" which was the nation's curse, while Lenin repeatedly denounced populists for ignoring the "Asiatic" abuse of human dignity which prevailed in the Russian countryside.[48]

The Triumph of "Orthodox" Marxism

Although Marx devoted himself to the study of Russia during the last decade of his life, the Russia question both enthralled him and reduced him to silence. When he died in 1883, the task of pronouncing the last word on Russia was left to Friedrich Engels. Although Russian radicals were eager for Engels to intervene in their increasingly bitter ideological disputes, he was initially reluctant to take sides. Still hopeful that Russia's revolutionary terrorists might set off a massive social upheaval against the tsarist regime of Alexander III, he did not want to weaken the hand of the peasant-oriented radicals of the *Narodnaia Volia* who had succeeded in assassinating Tsar Alexander II in 1881. As a consequence, Engels responded to Plekhanov's vitriolic attacks on Daniel'son in 1885 with the curt suggestion that Plekhanov would do better to attempt "serious research work" on the agrarian question instead of "polemical articles."[49]

For his part, Daniel'son attempted to re-create with Engels the supportive relationship that he previously enjoyed with Marx. He sent Engels numerous statistical studies and economic analyses, arguing that "in Russia the most crazily different facts exist side by side"—hired laborers and market development coexisted with the establishment of new communes by peasants in Siberia.[50] But Engels remained unconvinced. Certain that Russia was destined to follow the same path of historical development as the rest of the world, Engels argued that Russia was would soon "undergo an agricultural revolution that will bankrupt both lord and peasant."[51]

There was something poignant in Daniel'son's repeated efforts to convince Engels of the merit of his arguments and evidence. In 1885, as he impatiently awaited the publication of volume two of *Capital*, Daniel'son wrote Engels to ask if Marx had included any material on Russian economic life. "As you know," Daniel'son wrote, "he considered it an important question."[52] Years later, after he had already translated volumes two and three of *Capital* into Russian, Daniel'son wrote Engels to express his regret that Marx had not included Russia in his discussion of rent. Reminding Engels that Marx had planned to use Russia as a case study, Daniel'son asked, "Are there any notes left behind that would give an idea of what he had planned to do?"[53] Engels replied in the negative.[54]

Engels's growing hostility to Daniel'son was probably more due to events in Germany than to any particular concern about the Russian economy. By the 1890s, it was evident that Daniel'son's arguments against the annihilation of the peasantry closely resembled contemporary demands by German "revisionists" for a Marxist economic strategy that promoted peasant welfare.[55] Dismissing this goal as part and parcel of the Revisionist Eduard Bernstein's retreat from revolutionary class struggle, Engels sided with Plekhanov and against Daniel'son. Faced by the German Revisionist challenge to his version of "Orthodox" Marxism, Engels insisted that the annihilation of the peasantry by capitalism constituted a painful, essential, and revolutionary step forward. In 1895, Engels refused even to publicly criticize Struve's "celebrations" of capitalist development. Making no reference to Marx's reflections on Russia, he refrained as well from protesting either the refusal of the Emancipation of Labor Group to publish Marx's letter to Zasulich or the conspiracy of silence that surrounded it.[56] In 1894, Engels agreed with Plekhanov that arguments against the inevitability of further capitalist development in Russia were not only "untrue" but "very dangerous."[57]

Even as Daniel'son continued his efforts to communicate with Engels, Engels was writing to Plekhanov:

> It is quite impossible to debate with that generation of Russians to which Daniel'son belongs, a generation which continues to believe in the elemental communistic mission allegedly distinguishing Russia, the real Holy Russia, from the other, infidel nations. . . . In any case, in a country like yours, in which industry is still linked to the commune and intellectual life is so isolated, it is no wonder that such monstrous ideas evolve. It is a stage the country must pass through. As cities expand, the isolation of talented minds will cease as you have the opportunity to communicate with one another.[58]

In this meeting of the minds between Engels and Plekhanov, the future direction of Russian Marxism had taken on its final form.

From this time forward, the self-described "true" followers of Marx and Engels would label any suggestion that Russia might fail to replicate the economic history of the West as proof that the speaker was an enemy of Marxism, a reactionary, and/or a populist. An urban-centered, unilinear process of economic development was defined once and for all as the essence of Marxism.[59] From this economic perspective, the peasant's best hope was to disappear as quickly as possible.

By the 1890s, to be a Russian Marxist was to believe that the communal institutions to which the peasant majority laid claim lacked any economic or political significance. In later years, neither "legal Marxists," Bolsheviks, nor Mensheviks called into question this interpretation of Marxism. Ignoring Marx's comments on Russia, they refused as well to admit that their analysis of the Russian countryside was based upon the exclusion of massive quantities of evidence indicating that the commune was not dying out.[60] However bitterly they differed on a wide range of political and economic issues, those who came to lead the Russian Marxist movement in the twentieth-century had arrived at a fundamental agreement about the urban, antipeasant and anticommunal direction of Russia's economic development.

Chapter Seven

IN SEARCH OF THE TRUE WEST

ENGLAND, DENMARK, AND GERMANY

> "All the possible relations to labor have been studied and
> defined," he said. "What is left of barbarism, the primitive
> commune with its mutual guarantees, is disintegrating by itself.
> Serfdom has been abolished, and there is nothing left but free
> labor. The agricultural laborers, the hired man, the farmer—
> you can't get away from that."
>
> "But Europe is dissatisfied with this system," said Levin.
>
> "Dissatisfied and is looking for new methods. And, no
> doubt, will find them."
>
> "That's exactly my point," replied Levin. "Why shouldn't
> we look for them ourselves?"
>
> "Because it would be just the same as inventing again the
> way of constructing a railway. It's been invented; it's ready."
>
> "But what if it doesn't suit us?" said Levin. "What if it is
> stupid?"
>
> *(L. N. Tolstoi,* Anna Karenina, *1870)*

> As a matter of historical record, Russia did not follow the capi-
> talist path, it did not emulate Britain, but, short-circuiting capi-
> talism, evolved a type of state socialism not unlike that envi-
> sioned by radical opponents of capitalism in the nineteenth
> century. Those who held this view turned out to have been
> much closer to the truth than the Social Democrats who abused
> them as "utopians" and insisted that Russia had no choice but
> to emulate the West.
>
> *(Richard Pipes,* Struve: Liberal on the Left, *1970)*

I N THE LATE nineteenth century, communal tenure seemed to many
educated Russians both an indicator of and an explanation for the
growing disparity between peasant Russia and and a privatized, powerful, and expansionist West. Communes came to symbolize the obstacles
that prevented Russia from entering into the modern world. The progressive-minded, empowered by the prestige of science and by a romantic
faith in capitalism's civilizing mission, denounced the social scientists

who dissented from this view as populist advocates of a uniquely Russian path to the future. However, as the historian Richard Pipes long ago observed, these charges were unfounded. In his words, "No prominent economist or even publicist of this era was so naive as to believe that Russia was immune to capitalism, for signs of its penetration were visible everywhere. . . . The prevailing view held that Russia had a mixed economy in which two systems—'capitalism' and 'popular production'—were locked in mortal combat. The outcome of the battle depended on the government."[1]

Relying on massive *zemstvo* statistical investigations, which documented rural innovation as well as poverty and subsistence cultivation, a number of leading economists suggested that dire predictions about the demise of peasants or communes were at best premature. At the turn of the century, five out of seven professors of political economy and statistics at the University of St. Petersburg and four of Moscow University's economists were convinced that the peasant commune was not dying out.[2]

Influenced by the historical traditions of German scholarship, a number of gifted scholars focused on the medieval era as a period when common rights and communal institutions still prevailed in Western Europe. Believing that research on this topic would provide data and insights of practical use to the Russian people and to peasants in particular, they rejected the notion that socially committed scholarship lacked objectivity.[3] According to the legal historian Paul Vinogradov: "I don't know anyone who would at present declare that the study of the formation and disintegration of the rural commune in the West has no significance for the policies and conceptions which interest the modern life of the rural communes in the East."[4] Along similar lines, the research carried out by Moscow University economists A. S. Posnikov and N. A. Kablukov was intended to contribute to both academic and nonacademic knowledge. They hoped that the investigation of Western economic experience would generate realistic and humane strategies for Russian rural development.

The Origins of Property: Russians as Economic Historians of the West

Neither in the West nor in Russia did scholarly debate over the origins of private and communal tenure remain within the confines of the academy. In the 1870s and 1880s, the historians Fustel de Coulanges, F. W. Maitland, and Frederick Seebohm attacked the work of Maurer and Maine, defended *laissez faire*, and opposed contemporary initiatives for land reform as encroachments on historically sanctioned rights of property ownership. Like the Russian scholar Chicherin, who argued that the commune was created by rulers rather than peasants, Seebohm contended that common rights were introduced by kings and nobles as a fiscal device. In an immensely popular book, *The English Village Community*, he maintained that private landownership prevailed in England and on the continent long before the medieval era, with common lands and communal practices operating—like serfdom—as a "feudal" constraint upon individual freedom of action. Convinced that the establishment of private property represented the highest achievement of the English spirit, Seebohm argued that the commons disappeared because it was incompatible with the productive and rational economic behavior characteristic of the modern age.[5]

While a number of Western scholars disagreed with these claims, some of the most insightful critiques came from an extraordinary group of Russian medievalist scholars who participated in the late-nineteenth-century European debates over the origins of property. Westernizers all, Ivan Luchitskii, N. Kareev, Maxim Kovalevskii, D. M. Petrushevskii, and Paul Vinogradov believed that English civil and political liberties were quite rightly the envy of the world,[6] and helped to organize Russia's fledgling struggle for constitutional government. Convinced that research into the socioeconomic origins of the liberal political order they so admired would serve both their scholarly and political interests, they looked above all to the teachings of Maurer on the German *mark*.[7] The investigations of Luchitskii and Kareev indicated that communes were not created by kings and princes, but were destroyed by them. The data they gathered on medieval Spain, France, and England was strikingly at odds with the claims of Seebohm and Fustel for the historical primacy of private property, the repressive character of the medieval commune, and the historical link between personal freedom and rights of private ownership.[8]

By far the most influential rejoinder to Seebohm's assertions came from Paul Vinogradov. With a command of the sources and a judicious style of exposition and argument which won him the respect even of his critics, Vinogradov demonstrated that the English commune (1) predated the advent of serfdom, (2) neither introduced nor exacerbated the system of constraints associated with the feudal era, and (3) was destroyed by kings and princes bent on plunder and conquest. Although neither individual freedom nor economic innovation were encouraged by prefeudal village communities, the documentary record indicated that they permitted individuals to dispose of their own labor, leave the community, and attempt private cultivation if they possessed the means to do so. According to Vinogradov, peasant freedom of movement was not restricted by village communities, but by feudal lords who feared a loss of dues and services if peasants were free to act independently.[9]

Emphasizing the importance of historical context in shaping individual behavior, Vinogradov demonstrated that English common rights coexisted with both free and servile institutions. The positive or negative role played by village communities seemed to depend on the specifics of a particular agrarian situation, the existing levels of culture, and the other prevailing economic and social arrangements.[10] Condemning Seebohm for ignoring a wide range of relevant evidence, Vinogradov accused him as well of manipulating data to advance a *laissez faire* political and economic agenda on the contemporary political scene. Seebohm did not admit to the latter charge. But he conceded that Vinogradov's research was so massive and so carefully organized and presented that it carried the weight of a "judicial decision," and did not launch a counterattack.[11] Vinogradov's contributions to Western scholarship eventually won him an appointment as professor of jurisprudence at Oxford University (as successor to Henry Maine). But Seebohm's work remained far more popular among English scholars, policy-makers, and the general reading public.

In comparison with Vinogradov, the work of Maxim Kovalevskii exerted a far wider—though more contradictory—influence in Russia and elsewhere. The author of over forty books dealing with comparative law, economics, and sociology, Kovalevskii considered himself a disciple of August Comte, Henry Maine, and Karl Marx.[12] In the late nineteenth century, he was quoted by tsarist officials to prove that the commune was doomed, and by Karl Marx to demonstrate that it was not. These contradictory interpretations reflect Kovalevskii's own ambivalence about the commune and its modern fate.

For those who read only the introductions and conclusions to his many books, Kovalevskii's message was clear and unambiguous: universal laws of history, which replaced backward peasant communities the world over, would eventually raise Russia and other nations to England's level of economic and political achievement. According to Kovalevskii, historically obsolete village communities the world over invariably experienced a process of internal decay, which led to the emergence of more productive, "English-style" private enterprise and parliamentary government. As he saw it, there were no exceptions to this general rule. Both in the past and in the present, "Everywhere the change-over from common to private property is brought about by the same phenomenon one encounters the world over—the conflict of interests."[13]

However, the body of research contained in Kovalevskii's many publications was frequently at odds with such generalizations. His data indicated that in regions of the world colonized by Western nations, the commune's demise was decisively affected by external pressures, and resulted in short-term economic decline rather than prosperity. In India, for example, Kovalevskii described the break-up of the Indian *panchayat* as a prime goal of British colonial administrators, followed soon afterward by (1) the concentration of ownership in the hands of a few, (2) the decline of competition, and (3) the disappearance of mutual aid practices among the peasantry. As the masses became landless rural proletarians, they "quite legitimately"—in Kovalevskii's opinion—opposed the destruction of their livelihood.[14] Worst of all, from an economic point of view, his data indicated that elimination of the commune failed to generate any significant improvements in field use or productivity rates.

As a fervent admirer of Marx, Kovalevskii agreed that the horrors of primary accumulation and the separation of small producers from the land in Western Europe produced economic polarization, class hatred, and violent revolutionary outbreaks on the part of desperate and despairing proletarians. But Kovalevskii was not a revolutionary. In contrast to Marx, he hoped that a more liberal-oriented Russian government would implement sweeping reforms to avert the violent upheaval likely to result from the imposition of an English-style enclosure movement.[15] In many respects, Kovalevskii's vision of Russia as a nation whose liberation depended on the triumph of Western-style property rights and freedom contradicted both his historical research on the violence with which private-property rights were introduced into the non-Western world, and his fear that if the Russian government imitated England's example, violent revolution would break out.

According to Moscow University economist A. S. Posnikov, the English model was not so much inappropriate as misleading. Posnikov was a student of Chuprov, a participant in contemporary *zemstvo* investigations of the Russian countryside, and a founder of the liberal Kadet (Constitutional Democratic) Party, best known for his economic studies of communal landownership in Russia and the West. In his research on England, Posnikov challenged prevailing assumptions about the risk-taking and innovative "improving landlord,"[16] by demonstrating that eighteenth-and nineteenth-century English landowners not only passed on the costs of improvement to their tenants, but demanded and received generous Parliamentary support for initiation of a variety of swamp drainage and irrigation projects.[17]

Posnikov found that large-scale tenants were far more entrepreneurial in their behavior than estate-owners. Seven-year rental contracts did not seem to diminish their economic incentive. As England's commercial opportunities expanded, tenants actively improved farming methods on land to which they did not hold title—they did not scale down their investments of time or money simply because their land claims were temporary. Unaware that the Slavophiles and the radical Chernyshevskii had already raised these issues,[18] Posnikov concluded that tenure was less important than other economic, political, social, and environmental factors for the analysis of either productivity rates or agricultural innovation.

The statistician-economist N. A. Kablukov was equally skeptical about the virtues of the "man of property." Kablukov was also a student of

Chuprov and an advocate of liberal political reform, whose research focused on the impact of the late-nineteenth-century agricultural crisis upon English agriculture. His data indicated that, despite the prevalence of private tenure in England, levels of innovation and productivity were currently in a state of decline. Rural entrepreneurs abandoned cultivated fields to "rough grazing," and drastically curtailed their agricultural investments instead of attempting to check the general deterioration in land use. However private and free their economic efforts may have been, Kablukov observed that large landowners did *not* transform their methods, vary their crops, or their systems of land use. Their response to short-term market fluctuations was to work harder and exhaust the soil, to give up intensive cultivation for cheaper and more primitive modes of cultivation or to abandon agriculture altogether as a source of livelihood.[19]

The evidence that England's rural entrepreneurs were going bankrupt or leaving the agricultural sector for more lucrative opportunities elsewhere led Kablukov to surprising conclusions. To a nineteenth-century audience dazzled by England's power and prosperity, Kablukov suggested that the reluctance of landowners to commit themselves to agriculture if easier profits beckoned elsewhere—when combined with the problems created by an "unbalanced," industry-centered economy—would eventually undermine and destroy England's position as a great power.[20] At a time when many progressives viewed English power and prosperity as permanent and unassailable, Kablukov pointed out that England's share of world trade had steadily declined between 1867 and 1904.

Moscow University's A. A. Manuilov was more optimistic than Kablukov about England's economic future (though not about free trade or *laissez faire*). Praising the British Parliament's flexibility and good sense, he reported on the passage of Small Holdings Acts, which granted low-interest loans for land purchases by cottagers, and Parliamentary adoption of a system of protective tariffs to defend English agriculture from foreign competition. According to Manuilov, English MPs possessed a level of political and economic wisdom sadly lacking among Russian policy-makers. They recognized—as the Russian autocracy did not—that the real threat to domestic peace and prosperity lay in rural poverty and the depopulation of the nation's agricultural districts.

Convinced that Russian policy-makers could not do better than to imitate Parliament, he praised the recent decision to incorporate Ulster traditions of "tenant right" into British law. By requiring incoming tenants to compensate the previous renter for any long-term agricultural improvements, the new legislation encouraged innovation by individuals whose land tenure was temporary. In Russia, where commune peasants were uncertain if they could bequeath the fruits of their labor to their children,

Manuilov suggested that a variation of tenant right might encourage private initiative without eliminating traditional guarantees of security.[21] (He was apparently unaware that Russian peasants had in fact already devised for themselves a variety of intricate reward systems to compensate innovators within the commune framework.

Late-nineteenth-century *zemstvo* statistical researches revealed that in widely diverse regions of the Russian empire, peasants who fertilized their communal allotments either received special monetary payments at the time of repartition, or a similar plot, or the right to retain their original allotments.)[22] Research of this sort suggested to K. K. Arseniev that there were reasons for optimism about Russia's future path of development. Writing in 1882, he pointed out that in England at the time of the enclosure movement, "there existed none of the literature of historical knowledge that we have now, and no one could explain, or understand themselves, what the people lost and what dangers were entered into with the development of private ownership. But we are now in a happier position: we have the experience of many nations; we have a literature and various indications on this question. Aided by all this, we can reach completely different foundations."[23]

England as the World's Economic Model

Educated Russians who considered England the prototype of a modern nation did not ignore the achievements of other Western states, but they accepted Marx's claim that England—a nation peasantless and virtually devoid of communal institutions—provided to less developed nations of the world "the image of their future." According to the economist Ziber, at a certain point in history, peasant communal institutions became a "fetter" or obstacle to further development, with capitalism the only appropriate mechanism for the efficient organization of labor and productive investment of surplus.[24] I. I. Tsitovich of Kharkov University contrasted Comte's "scientific" claims for the universal benefits of "English-style" property rights with the greed, callousness, apathy, and lack of incentive reported by gifted observers of the commune like Skaldin (F. P. Elenev) and G. I. Uspenskii.[25] In the 1870s, D. A. Stolypin, a prominent agriculturist and chairman of the Moscow Agricultural Society, wrote a booklength study on the lessons of Comte for Russian peasant agriculture. As he saw it, positivist science, the laws of history, and the medieval stagnation of the peasant commune required the introduction of "English'" forms of private enterprise.[26]

Along similar lines, the Marxist Plekhanov cited Orlov's statistical data and the conclusions of Kovalevskii to support the argument that "the same tried and true methods which had created modern English society" were at work in the Russian countryside.[27] The "Legal Marxist" M. I. Tugan-Baranovskii contended that England's economic development demonstrated a process which took place "in all civilized nations of our time; Russia does not constitute an exception."[28] Lenin marveled at "how far the main features of this general process in Western Europe and in Russia are identical, notwithstanding the tremendous peculiarities of the latter, in both the economic and non-economic spheres."[29]

The tsarist Minister of Agriculture Ermolov praised Karl Kautsky's "realistic" recognition that capitalist development was inevitable. As he saw it, "We must also follow the usual, well-trodden path of our West European neighbors." However different their long-term goals may have been, Russian Marxists and reform-minded government ministers were agreed that peasant property owners constituted the basis for all future progress and development. In the 1880s, Minister of Finance Bunge was fond of quoting the famous statement that John Stuart Mill had borrowed from Arthur Young: "If you guarantee to a man the rights of property in the desert, he will turn it into a smiling garden, but if you lease the garden to the same man for nine years, he will turn it into a howling desert."[30] Although by the 1860s, Mill had become a supporter of labor cooperatives, his Russian admirers were either unaware of, or indifferent to, Mill's changing views. As proponents of state capitalism, they were eager to align themselves with the views of a prestigious British thinker who had once championed the economic virtues of private-property rights.[31]

In general, the government officials most enthusiastic about private-property rights were also opponents of liberal and democratic reform. Konstantin Pobedonostsev, an architect of Tsar Alexander II's Russification policy, viewed the commune as an inherently backward institution, which stunted the intellectual development of its members. As he saw it, individuals who reached a level of "adult" self-consciousness would eagerly renounce both collective responsibility and collective labor.[32] Count Vorontsov-Dashkov, Minister of the Imperial Court and a powerful member of the State Council, advocated the extension of private tenure as a way to *limit* rather than extend peasant freedom of action. Like the eighteenth-century enclosure advocates who complained that rights to common land were dangerous because they provided laborers with "a sort of independence," Vorontsov-Dashkov denounced peasant communes for being "excessively democratic." By encouraging peasants to imagine "that by living in the commune they became invulnerable to individual punishment," they undermined the civilized respect for authority that flourished wherever individuals were secure in their ownership of property.[33] Vorontsov-Dashkov would undoubtedly have agreed with his English predecessors that the destruction of the commune served to reinforce "the subordination of the lower ranks of society which at present times is so much wanted."[34]

Minister of Agriculture Ermolov contended that the peasant propensity for deliberating in common over social and economic tasks and passing the time together was a sign of backwardness. Viewing such "herdlike" behavior as a survival of earlier times when individuals were forced to huddle together for protection against bandits, wild beasts, or Tatar nomads, he argued that communes perpetuated primitive fears and practices. According to Ermolov, Russia's peasants had not yet reached the stage of human development that would enable them to enjoy the civilized pleasures of privacy and private economic effort. As they became more rational and intelligent, he believed that they would be eager to establish their own homesteads, zealously guard their boundaries against the incursions of others, respect the property and individuality of fellow peasants, and act decisively to check any threats to their own property or to the property of others.[35]

The Marxist Plekhanov expressed a quite different but equally positive view of the urban "man of property." Although there was no evidence that merchant-industrialists of the 1880s were promoting bourgeois-democratic revolution, Plekhanov insisted that they were destined to play the same role as their Western counterparts. In 1883, Plekhanov declared that it would not be long before Russia's middle class emerged to champion the "Rights of Man" just as the French had done in 1789. In a rather peculiar argument for an advocate of class struggle, Plekhanov criticized Russia's fledgling proletariat for their "inappropriate" hostility to the bourgeoisie. According to Plekhanov, Russia's bourgeoisie could not "speak with the authorities in language worthy of a citizen" because workers stubbornly refused to support liberal and constitutional struggles.[36] To reforming tsarist officials and Marxist revolutionaries, property owners constituted the best hope for Russia's immediate future. While the autocracy hoped that property owners would support an authoritarian government which protected private tenure, Marxists contended that they would lead a bourgeois-democratic revolution, which would prepare the way for socialism.

Along similar lines, Russia's Anglophiles celebrated the English hired hand, or proletarian. A. I. Skvortsov, a devoutly Orthodox and monarchist economist at the Novaia Alexandriia University in Russian Poland, praised English agricultural laborers as hardy and prosperous individuals who carefully negotiated binding but limited contracts and took responsibility for their financial successes and failures.[37] For his part, the Marxist Plekhanov argued that wage-earners who could strike for higher wages or go elsewhere if they were dissatisfied, were far better off than commune peasants mired in local ties and habits of dependence.[38] Although the Legal Marxist P. B. Struve conceded that the use of improved technology was no more prevalent on privately owned large estates, he insisted nevertheless that private estates were *inherently* more progressive because they made use of wage labor.[39]

Such references to the happy state of the English farmhand reflect the extraordinary appeal of idealized views of England among educated Russians during the late nineteenth century. For whatever the joys of working as a hired hand in Hereford or Suffolk may have been in earlier times, in the 1880s, the living standard of England's hired agricultural laborers was in a state of rapid decline.[40] Russia's Anglophiles ignored this phenomenon, but viewed the elimination of peasants and their communities from the English scene as both a progressive phenomenon and a necessary step forward. Brutal imagery became commonplace: the Legal Marxist Struve matter of factly asserted, "a certain portion of the peasant economy was doomed to liquidation."[41] For his part, the economist Ziber suggested that like the English small farmers of the sixteenth and seventeenth centuries, Russia's small producers would soon be "cooked up in the industrial boiler," from which they would presumably emerge as proletarians.[42]

According to Plekhanov, Russian peasants were like the English small producers described in *Capital*—incapable of the specialization and efficient use of technology required for the introduction of modern production methods—but far more isolated and ignorant. Commune peasants were so primitive that they could not grasp the advantages of private ownership even when explanations were repeated to them "ten times over in ten different ways." Himself incapable of imagining that the peasants' refusal to be convinced could be due to anything except "medieval ignorance, " Plekhanov nevertheless took on the thankless task of advising commune peasants to become petty capitalist entrepreneurs.

Im many respects, Marxist reproaches to the peasantry resembled the complaints of Western colonial administrators who—like Plekhanov—complained about the primitive inertia which gave "such pain to educated people in any backward agricultural society."[43] In Southeast Asia, French empire builders lamented peasant failure to understand why their traditional holdings and common lands should be replaced by a plantation system.[44] In Africa, Britons in Kenya, Ghana, and Uganda were no less impatient with the static life of the natives, who could not and would not grasp the English notions of deed and contract.[45]

However, in the late nineteenth century, most leading tsarist officials continued to believe that domestic order could only be maintained through guarantees of security to peasants and their communes. In the 1880s, government decrees prohibited the confiscation or sale of any movable property judged to be necessary for the maintenance of a peasant family and livelihood, and declared illegal the use of allotments to secure a loan. At the same time, against the background of continued government protection for the commune, an orientation quite similar to Plekhanov's began to emerge within Russia's "economic" ministries of finance, agriculture, and commerce.

The advent of Sergei Witte as Minister of Finance symbolized a growing impatience with the commune as an economic institution. Appointed in the wake of the famine of 1891, Witte distinguished himself from the outset as an enthusiastic supporter of private enterprise in the urban sector. But in 1891, he did not advocate privatization in the Russian countryside. In his "pro-commune" phase, Witte cited contemporary data on commune peasants who built roads, drained swamps, and cleared forests. In a striking analogy, he compared private enterprise to a glove, which permitted each finger to move freely and separately, and the peasant commune to a mitten, which kept the hand warmer because all of the fingers were held close together. At the height of his enthusiasm for the commune, Witte observed: "as individualists, we are accustomed to be chilly and to have full rights to maintain our own habits; but the peasants are accustomed to warm each other in their communally organized life and we have no basis for encouraging a colder mode of existence." To bolster this argument, Witte even quoted Bismarck's statement that the whole strength of Russia lay in her communal society.[46]

However, by 1896, Witte began to abandon such notions. In a memorandum to the Council of Ministers, he argued that peasants throughout the Russian Empire were desperate to establish themselves as independent farmers on private land. As he became a more consistent advocate of both urban and rural capitalism, Witte no longer consulted economists who took the commune seriously. Although he commissioned the economists Chuprov and Posnikov to undertake a study of Russian agriculture, when the two scholars produced a book that documented negative as well as positive aspects of capitalism in the Russian countryside, he never again invited them to undertake a similar investigation. In the 1890s, Chuprov was generally recognized as the dean of Russia's professional economists, but he was not appointed to Witte's blue-ribbon Commission On the Needs of Russian Agriculture in 1902.

In Witte's twentieth-century speeches and reports, previously cited data on the peasantry's constructive common efforts, traditions of sociability, and guarantees of security were replaced by new images and anecdotes demonstrating the stagnation and barbarism of the peasant commune. In his words, "Woe to the country that has not nurtured in its population a sense of law and of property, but on the contrary has established different forms of collective possession which have not been precisely defined by the law." Influenced by his predecessor N. Bunge, Witte eagerly cited John Stuart Mill's argument that a miraculous transformation from "desert to garden" took place when individuals acquired rights of property ownership.[47] However, his use of Mill to explain and predict the behavior of Russia's peasantry was not necessarily a sign of increased intellectual sophistication. It may have signified instead the degree of England's cultural triumph over progressive-minded Russians at the turn of the century.

Denmark: Peasants and Progress

> Amidst the orgy of fancies I remember coming across a placard, "The Land of the Happy Peasantry"; this, on examination, proved to come from an organization for propagating in Russia the excellent agricultural methods of Denmark.
> *(Bernard Pares on the February Revolution, 1917)*

In 1901, when P. C. Christiansen, a schoolteacher of peasant origin, became prime minister of Denmark, a number of departing members of the Danish Parliament vowed that they would never return to seats which had been soiled by the manure of peasants. And they turned out to be right. In the decades to come, Danish peasants took the lead in developing strategies for free trade and economic growth which were linked with a comprehensive network of agricultural cooperatives.[48] Christiansen's accession to power was the most dramatic twentieth-century example of a carefully crafted alliance between a liberal-oriented peasant party and Marxist Social Democrats who interpreted Marxism quite differently from Plekhanov and Lenin. In Russia, Marxists demanded a choice between rural backwardness and urban progress: to them, collaboration with peasants was out of the question. But in Denmark, a peasant/Marxist alliance was able to transform the economy and lay the foundations of a modern and democratic welfare state.

It was in the 1870s that Denmark embarked upon an economic development program intended to raise levels of agricultural expertise among the rural population, and to transform a wheat-based economy managed by private landowners into a dairy economy run by producer cooperatives. Although Russian historical economists were quite aware of the difference between tiny Denmark and the immense and sparsely populated Russian empire, they nevertheless found the Danish model particularly instructive. As the economist Chuprov observed, Denmark was, like Russia, predominantly a society of small producers whose economic decisions were shaped by nonprivate economic institutions and governed by an interventionist state.[49]

In contrast to late nineteenth-century Russia, Denmark reacted to domestic distress and international agrarian crisis by dramatically increasing both the reach and the scope of its educational institutions. In the 1880s and 1890s, the Danish public school system was reinforced by a comprehensive network of democratically organized "folk high schools," which emphasized free and cooperative learning, agrarian institutes for adults, and "popular" universities specifically designed for the sons and daughters of farmers and agricultural laborers.[50] Placing a high priority on improving the agricultural skills of the rural populace, Danish Social Democrats attempted to reach out to farmers with little formal schooling by establishing a system of traveling agricultural specialists who criss-crossed the countryside, providing information on the principles of scientific dairy production.[51]

According to Chuprov, Danish cooperatives were organized on local initiative, but generous government subsidies encouraged small farmers to take advantage of new techniques, to jointly enforce quality standards and jointly reap the profits of manufacturing and marketing. In order to finance the costly transition to dairy farming, cooperative credit associations provided farmers with generous mortgage loans.[52] Denmark's first cooperative dairy was established in 1882. By 1903, cooperatives processed over 80 percent of Denmark's milk production and became leading technological innovators and suppliers of capital for development. While agricultural production remained in the hands of independent farmers, processing was carried out in local farm industries run on a cooperative basis, with one vote for each cooperative member regardless of the size of individual holdings.[53]

Initially, Danish economic reforms disproportionately benefited prosperous peasants rather than cottagers or agricultural laborers. But under pressure from Danish Social Democrats, the cooperative system was extended to include the lower classes. Although a small minority of Danish Marxists held fast to the urban-oriented theories of Engels, Lenin, and Plekhanov, most supported reform strategies that resembled the economic programs proposed by Daniel'son and Vorontsov. Emphasizing the common interests of peasants, agricultural laborers, and urban proletarians as working people,[54] Social Democrats joined forces with a Liberal peasant party, which transformed Denmark into a cooperative-based economy devoted to free trade. As a major supplier of milk, cheese, and butter to Western European nations (and to England in particular), Denmark enjoyed an astonishing 50 percent increase in the number of its horned cattle between 1870 and 1905.[55]

In considering Denmark as an economic model, the Russian economist Chuprov contrasted the Danish government's emphasis on education and cooperatives with the Russian autocracy's reliance on massive tax increases to extract what was defined as "surplus grain" from subsistence peasants. According to Chuprov, the Russian government relied on grain sales as a source of capital and used coercion as an economic stimulus, while the Danish government subsidized massive projects for rural education, harvested twice as much grain per person compared to Russia and imported grain for home consumption.[56] As he saw it, the short-sightedness and cruelty of Russia's economic strategy were epitomized by the slogan attributed to Finance Minister Vyshnegradskii on the eve of the famine of 1891: "We shall eat less, but we shall export grain."

Although Chuprov's data on the Danish model was not disputed in the decades to come, not everyone agreed with his interpretations and recommendations. According to Lenin, the most important feature of Danish cooperatives was that they brought disproportionate benefits to wealthy proprietors at the expense of the small producer. The economist M. Ia. Gertzenshtein insisted that the essence of Denmark's economic success lay in the balance between the farmer's security of private ownership rights and the cooperative framework.[57] In general, Chuprov neither confronted nor denied such criticisms. He was interested above all in Denmark as an economic model for transformation, which avoided the massive poverty and social dislocation characteristic of England's Agricultural Revolution.

According to Chuprov, Danish efforts to help small producers establish viable small holdings by means of cooperatives, educational initiatives, and lenient credit policies were as instructive as England's economic example. The Danish model suggested that rural development required neither the total destruction of communal property arrangements nor the wholesale separation of small producers from the land. As he saw it, Russia might well learn from the example of a nation that prospered without economic polarization or revolutionary political violence. It is interesting to consider Chuprov's hopes for the small producer in the light of observations by a modern Danish scholar who argues that: "The petit bourgeoisie has served as a mediator of the working class' pursuit of its own interests, and its dominance has prevented class polarization and confrontation between the working class and a capitalist bourgeoisie from becoming the over-riding conflict of Danish society."[58] In many respects, such an outcome would have been Chuprov's dream come true.

German Paths: Order, Cooperatives, and Revisionism

To Russian policy-makers, scholars, and Marxists, Denmark's example was much less familiar than Germany's. Russians were more likely to have studied in Germany than in any other Western nation, and for over a century, Germany's economic example inspired both supporters and critics of the Russian autocracy. Conservative Russian critics of the commune admired the power and reach of the German state, as well as its staunch support for private-property rights. Viewing the task of Tsar Alexander III as a mission to root out and destroy the threat of anarchy in all of its terrifying manifestations, Konstantin Pobedonostsev denounced the commune as an anarchic institution. In the context of government-instituted pogroms against religious and ethnic minorities, Russian conservatives were drawn to an "iron," "Prussian-style" defense of property rights as a strategy to unify the "strongest," most truly Russian peasants against the dangers that threatened both from without and within.

One of the most uncompromising statements of this position appeared in a book entitled *Young Russia* by the Russian writer N. A. Bezobrazov, who adopted the revealing pseudonym "Evropeets" (the European).[59] According to Evropeets, Prussia's example could best teach Russian reformers how to deal with the anarchic backwardness of the peasant commune. As he saw it, communes permitted ignorant majorities to outvote the sober and hardworking peasants who comprised the minority in any democratic assembly. Evropeets contended that it was not unusual for communes to confiscate the cow of one member to pay the tax arrears of his drunken neighbor, or to force a father to bequeath his property to an ungrateful and disobedient son. And while there might be "people ready to die for their fatherland," he contended there were none who were willing "to work their life long to accumulate a fortune for their neighbors."[60] In place of the commune's lenience, inconsistency, and "senseless collectivism," Evropeets recommended the implementation of Prussian-style legislation that permitted watchmen, guards, and bailiffs to shoot to kill criminals who damaged forests, crops, and machinery, or encroached on the property of others. Inspired by the same impulse which led the Russian government to construct the military colonies of the 1800s, Evropeets longed above all for a world of orderly, stringently supervised peasant villages. Considering it just and rational to apportion voting rights on the basis of property ownership, he argued that Russia's future depended on the generous economic and political rewards provided to productive investors of capital, and on the impositions of harsh punishments for actions that threatened the security of property.[61]

A quite different German model appealed to the wide range of educated Russians who linked agricultural improvement with the supply of massive quantities of cheap credit to the peasantry. In the 1870s, the Imperial Free Economic Society recommended the establishment of cooperative credit associations on the German model created by Friedrich Wilhelm Raiffeisen in the middle decades of the nineteenth century. In the 1880s and 1890s, all of Tsar Alexander III's Ministers of Finance supported the expansion of Raiffeisen cooperatives. From an official point of view, such institutions—if they could avoid being taken over by Jews and other undesirables—could promote the accumulation of private capital, which would eventually eliminate the peasant commune.[62]

According to the more liberal Prince A. I. Vasil'chikov, credit cooperatives would offer essential support to "a person who has some property and trade, a piece of land, a cow or horse. . ." As he saw it, "on such a person will Russian democracy be based."[63] The economist Chuprov contended that by making use of the lessons of German and Danish experience, Russians might establish credit cooperatives which could encourage peasants to gain the habits, experience, and knowledge they needed to build a better future within the framework of a "mixed economy."[64]

In the late nineteenth century, Russian historical economists like Chuprov linked the issue of cooperatives with the cause of German Revisionism. In the publications of economists like Eduard David and Georg von Vollmar, they discovered evidence indicating that German peasants did not mindlessly reject new agricultural techniques and practices. Instead, peasants devised a complex system of mixed farming, which adapted the three-field system and other traditional practices to the demands of modern economic life. With substantial government assistance, they formed producers' cooperative associations, which were able to triumph over domestic and foreign competition at the turn of the century. According to David, peasant survival depended on the aid of such institutions, which provided the poor with access to credit previously available only to the wealthy.[65]

Indifferent to the question of whether or not Revisionism constituted "true" Marxism, historical economists wanted above all to incorporate peasants into an evolutionary economic strategy for development. Instead of demonizing peasants and defining the "essence" of Marxism as urban and proletarian, the economists Vorontsov and A. A. Isaev praised Revisionist Marxists for expanding the program of the SPD (*Sozialistische Partei Deutschlands*) to include the rural populace. Like his Danish counterparts, Vollmar contended that peasants were a potential Marxist constituency, and demanded that Social Democrats (1) call for the transfer of land to peasant communes or rural associations, and (2) support the formation of cooperatives to provide peasants with capital and machinery at minimal cost.[66] Inspired by German Revisionist proposals, the Russian economist Vorontsov hoped that this "modern trend of Marxism in the West" might become a source of support for Russian advocates of a peasant-based strategy for rural development.[67]

Thanks above all to the efforts of Karl Kautsky, Germany's SPD responded with unwavering hostility to the Revisionist challenge. Kautsky, whose efforts to exterminate ideological heresy won him the nickname the "Torquemada of Marxism," relied on the first volume of *Capital* to justify the exclusion of the peasant question from the SPD program. According to Kautsky, the separation of peasants from the land was already well underway; it was time, he said, for German agriculture to be organized according to an urban industrial model of production. In Kautsky's view, David, Vollmar, and Eduard Bernstein were simple opportunists who pretended that fundamental change was achievable without a violent and revolutionary social upheaval, and cynically promised historically obsolete social elements (i.e., the peasantry) a future under capitalism and even under socialism.

In his influential book *Die Agrarfrage* (1899), Kautsky argued that most peasants would refuse to join cooperatives because of their "property fanaticism," while those who did would soon discover that cooperatives were invariably controlled by rich peasants. Although he insisted that peasants were doomed, Kautsky also made the damaging admission that contemporary statistical data indicated that German small holdings were in fact currently on the rise.[68] He resolved this contradiction by arguing that peasants survived precisely because they were so primitive. Unlike more civilized and rational human beings, they were willing to engage in "superhuman" labor and accept "subhuman" levels of consumption. According to Kautsky, the increase in peasant holdings was in no way attributable to qualities of intelligence, flexibility, or common sense.[69]

Kautsky's arguments won the enthusiastic backing of those Marxists who were intent on drawing sharp distinctions between "progressive" urban proletarians and the backward and unreliable peasant petty bourgeoisie. With no hesitation, Friedrich Engels weighed in on the side of Kautsky, arguing that peasants could not become a Marxist political constituency until they had become landless proletarians. According to Engels "The peasants must recognize that they are lost beyond saving."[70] Along similar lines, August Bebel, the SPD's leading organizer, reminded David and Vollmar that they were not "the spokesmen for the Bavarian peasants but for the intelligent industrial workers and . . . duty bound to maintain our program pure and undefiled."[71]

At the Breslau convention of 1895, an overwhelming majority of Party delegates approved a resolution which refused to "pretend" that peasants could survive in the modern world. In the grip of what one scholar has described as "the cultural and emotional prejudices" of most German Marxists against the peasantry,[72] the convention refused to adopt an agrarian program. As the SPD rejected the notion that peasants could be allies of the urban working class, Junker conservatives took advantage of the political vacuum which thus opened up, and launched a successful campaign that appealed to the peasantry to form antisocialist "Peasant Leagues."

The SPD's decision to ignore the peasantry dismayed a number of Russian observers.[73] The economist A. A. Isaev berated German Social Democrats for leaving peasants to the mercy of national socialists, anti-Semites, and Junker landlords. How, he asked, could the SPD simply turn its back on the majority of the German population? How could they envision a "peasantless" future that bore so little relationship to the realities of the present day?[74] Isaev feared that Russians attempting to learn from the German experience would interpret the resolutions passed by the SPD as a sign that in formulating strategies for political or economic change, they too should ignore the peasant majority of the population.

From Theory to Practice: German Models and Russian Peasant Rebellion

Isaev was right to be so concerned. Kautsky's pronouncements were welcomed by Russian Minister of Agriculture Ermolov as a realistic appraisal of the peasantry. For his part, Lenin enthusiastically agreed that a peasant-based modern agriculture organized on a cooperative basis was "out of the question."[75] The 1898 manifesto of the first congress of the Russian Social Democratic Labor Party (written by P. B. Struve) contained only one reference to the peasant majority of the population. The impression left by the document was that peasants constituted such an insignificant component of the Russian scene that there was no need for extended discussion of their political or economic importance.[76]

However, the Russian Marxist consensus on the peasant majority's lack of significance was soon broken. In 1902, Marxists committed to the urban proletariat were confronted by a peasant-based "miniature revolution." The responses of Menshevik Marxists were particularly consistent. Citing statements by Marx and Kautsky on the inherent backwardness of small-scale production and the "property fanaticism" of small producers, they argued that Marxists could not promise land to the peasantry. As Plekhanov observed, in the more advanced region of the Russian countryside, "We stand with Kautsky." On the other hand, Lenin's response revealed the qualities of political flexibility that distinguished him from the Mensheviks and from many leading Bolsheviks. While remaining committed to the stage theories of historical development which Marx (and Comte) had earlier discovered in Western economic experience, Lenin unceremoniously abandoned earlier assertions of capitalism's triumph. In 1903, he began to argue that the Russian countryside was still rife with *feudal* economic relationships between serflike peasants and their landlords. In the light of Western European history, Lenin suggested that Russia was experiencing a phase similar to the French Revolution. Peasants were therefore behaving like revolutionaries because they were fighting against feudal backwardness. Lenin called on Social Democrats to support peasants in their revolutionary struggle to abolish survivals of feudalism in the Russian countryside.

In many respects, the political common sense that led Lenin to incorporate the peasantry into Marxist political strategy was at odds with his rigid insistence that the commune was a survival of feudalism. Like his Menshevik adversaries, Lenin continued to believe that the peasantry's best hope was to disappear as quickly as possible and to give up their communal institutions. Like his state capitalist counterparts within the tsarist regime, Lenin appealed to backward social elements at the foot of Civilization's ladder to ascend to a higher, more European level of advancement and abandon their communal practices, along with a host of retrograde friends and neighbors. In keeping with the compelling dynamic of this scenario, the "backward" possessed no rational or legitimate right to refuse, to search for less polarized alternatives, or to lay the ladder down.[77] As arguments of this sort gained currency in the years to come, they carried the clear suggestion that if a peasant populace turned out to be unduly backward, government leaders (or revolutionary vanguards) might be forced to impose coercive economic strategies in order to move the nation to higher levels of economic development.

Chapter Eight

THE DEMISE OF ECONOMIC PLURALISM

CONSTRUCTING A TWENTIETH-CENTURY MODEL

FOR PROGRESS AND DEVELOPMENT

> Feudalism is that rung, between which rung and capitalism,
> there are no intermediate rungs.
> *(V. I. Lenin)*

B Y 1900, THE KEY aspects of Russia's modernizing mindset were
securely in place, with Western models and historical categories
occupying center stage. On the positive side, a focus on the primacy of Western stages of historical development provided its advocates
with a comforting sense of intellectual coherence and clarity. From the
Right and Left of the ideological spectrum, progressives hastened to label
and classify the institutions and social elements that belonged either to
"feudal" or to "modern" periods of Russian history. To Westernizers of
this sort, it seemed obvious, for example, that the disappearance of historically obsolete communes was long overdue, and that the "man of property" symbolized the best hope for the nation's immediate future.

However, clarity was achieved at a high cost. Categories derived from
Western economic experience served not only to illuminate, but on occasion, to screen out realities for which Western analogies did not immediately spring to mind. In the countryside, economic behavior which was
judged anomalous—no matter how widespread—was neglected, or as-
similated through the use of an intricate array of terms like "pre-feudal,"
"semi-feudal," "pre-capitalist," "semi-capitalist," and "semi-bourgeois."
Judgments about the degree of feudalism present or absent in the Russian
countryside became increasingly commonplace among reforming government officials and Marxists.[1] But precise definitions of feudalism were
extremely rare.[2]

Ignoring the important differences between the medieval West's limited
monarchies and serfs on the one hand, and on the other, the free peasants
and decentralized monarchies of tenth-century Kiev or sixteenth-century
Muscovy's serf-dominated autocracy, they attempted to situate Imperial
Russia and the Russian people within a feudal stage of socioeconomic
development.[3] Using a variety of not very consistent measures, both Lenin

and Finance Minister Witte discovered feudalism in every aspect of Russian rural society that they considered backward, and tirelessly publicized evidence that a higher (capitalist) culture had come into being.

Lenin's Economics

Although many aspects of Lenin's life and work were controversial, it is significant that his economic writings were less so. *The Development of Capitalism in Russia* (1899) not only became the standard introduction to the Russian economy for later generations of Marxists; it was also welcomed by a number of policy-makers and scholars who despised Lenin's politics. As I have suggested elsewhere, Lenin's economic studies were in fact quite problematic—notable as much for their omissions as for their positive content.[4] From a reading of Lenin, it would have been difficult to discover, for example, that there were a large number of professional economists at work in late Imperial Russia.[5] By ignoring the research and judgments of the leading professional economists of his day, Lenin could more easily mask the foolishness of his claim that late-nineteenth-century Russia had already become a predominantly capitalist society. The topics which concerned contemporary Russian economists— among them, England's agrarian crisis, the complexity of the Russian peasant commune, the peasant as victim and actor—were not a central focus of Lenin's economic research. K. R. Kachorovskii, one of Russia's leading statisticians, suggested that Lenin's work reflected only the "sketchiest" knowledge of primary sources, with data arbitrarily selected in order to support *a priori* conclusions.[6]

In many respects, the Western lens through which Lenin viewed Russian economic history narrowed rather than expanded his perspectives on the Russian countryside. Relying on the English model set out by Marx in *Capital*, he argued that Russia was becoming "depeasantized," and that the peasant commune was already moribund. According to Lenin in 1894 and 1895, "the entire mass of the village folk work for capital," which was already "dominant in the countryside."[7] In *The Development of Capitalism in Russia*, he claimed that survivals of feudalism—including the peasant commune—were rapidly disintegrating. When the statistician Vikhliaev responded by presenting voluminous statistical data on the commune's persistence and spread, Lenin triumphantly accused Vikhliaev of being "mired in detail."[8]

While Lenin's work provided a valuable perspective on capitalist developments in the Russian countryside, it excluded the evidence contained in a wide range of contemporary statistical studies, which indicated that in fact, neither peasants nor their communes were dying out.[9] Although Lenin delighted in the contrast between his own "scientific" judgments and the "subjectivist" populism of his adversaries, his claim that the Russian countryside was capitalist in 1899 seemed quite impervious to empirical disproof.[10] As the events of 1905 demonstrated, it was the politics of peasant revolution rather than the weight of economic evidence that eventually convinced Lenin to abandon his foolish claims for the dominance of capitalism in the countryside, and to argue instead that the Russian rural economy was predominantly "feudal."

The Tsarist Regime's Version of "Leninist" Economics: C. A. Kofoed

At the other end of Russia's political spectrum, pro-Western advocates of state capitalism were equally eager to see the end of the "medieval" peasant commune. By the 1900s, Finance Minister Witte no longer referred to the constructive economic behavior by peasant communes, which had figured in his earlier speeches. Government reformers spoke of the commune's demise as a foregone conclusion, and were content to ignore both the data and the arguments of economists and statisticians like Chuprov, Posnikov, Manuilov, and Chernenkov. Among the most interesting architects of the government's narrowing empirical perspective was the Danish-born Carl Andreas Kofoed.

In many respects, Kofoed resembled the Danish legislators of the 1900s who refused to sit in the Parliamentary seats soiled by "the manure" of peasants.[11] One of the leading agricultural experts of his day, he downplayed the role of peasants and Marxists as key agents in Denmark's early twentieth-century "Agricultural Miracle," and called instead for decisive government action to break the back of peasant conservatism. When he became a Russian subject, Kofoed devoted his career to the proposition that commune peasants represented the chief obstacle to Russian economic advance.[12] Insisting that tenure reform was more important to Russia's future than any other kind of economic change, Kofoed argued that unless the outmoded techniques "stupidly" fostered by periodic repartition were eliminated once and for all, no serious improvement in Russian agriculture was possible. In his view, peasants could only hope to achieve a "Western" level of economic, social and cultural development *after* they were liberated from the constraints of the commune and supplied with consolidated and workable allotments of land as their private property.[13]

In Kofoed's writings, freedom of economic decision-making was dissociated from any other kind of freedom. Paying little attention to government "Russification" campaigns or pogroms against Jews, Greeks, Armenians, or other groups categorized as "alien," he warned instead against the threat that radical intellectuals posed to Russia's progress and stability. According to Kofoed, violence-prone radical ideologues also represented an obstacle to realistic and effective government economic policy. As portrayed by Kofoed, Russian intellectuals were misguided and immature. Romantic and populistic in their sympathies, they hated the West and ignored the realities of the Russian agricultural economy. Stubbornly insisting that communes were "sacrosanct," they refused to provide themselves with factual information about the disadvantages of communal tenure.[14] As in the case of Lenin, a reader of Kofoed would never have guessed that in reality, Western-trained Russian economists had carried out over a half century of economic research on the West, or that statisticians employed by local *zemstvo* institutions were engaged in massive empirical studies of peasant economic behavior within and outside of the commune.

It is difficult to believe that Kofoed was unfamiliar with the leading professional economists of the day or with the statistical data demonstrating, for example, that the "backward" practice of strip cultivation which he attributed to the commune was (1) equally prevalent within and outside the peasant commune and (2) quite common in France and Germany. But however one may wish to explain his omissions of fact and argument, it is undeniably true that Kofoed ignored the research carried out by Russia's professional economists on such topics as Western economic history, productivity rates, and levels of economic innovation within and outside the peasant commune. Their research findings did not form part of his selective account of the Russian agricultural economy.

In place of the "sentimentality" of Russia's peasant-loving intellectuals, Kofoed recommended to Russia's reading public the British journalist Donald MacKenzie Wallace's book entitled *Russia* (1877).[15] However, Kofoed's praise for Wallace was as misleading as it was revealing, because Kofoed ignored the substantial segments of the book that were at odds with his own view of the Russian countryside. For example, Wallace contended that such peasant customs as repartition were neither stupid nor irrational. Attributing loyalty to the commune to the material burdens of peasant life rather than to mindless conservatism, he cited the testimony of a peasant from Yaroslav province who became a rich merchant with several houses in St. Petersburg: "It is all very well to be free, and I don't want anything from the Commune now; but my old father lives there, my mother is buried there, and I like to go back to the old place sometimes. Besides, I have children, and our affairs are commercial. Who knows but that my children will be very glad some day to have a share of the communal land?"[16] According to Wallace, comments of this sort reflected a degree of common sense sorely lacking among both advocates and critics of the commune. In contrast to Kofoed—who never considered the possibility that peasants could weigh their economic options—Wallace suggested that peasants might quite understandably decide to reject the "either-or" choices between prosperity and commune backwardness that were posed for them by progressives of the Right and Left.

Wallace believed that both critics and defenders of the peasant commune were prone to exaggerate. On the one hand, landowners pining for the days of serfdom were eager to transform every frustrating encounter with a peasant into a proof of insuperable ignorance and commune backwardness. As he saw it, their "overwrought" complaints about commune rigidity and conservatism exerted undue influence on Russian public opinion.[17] On the other hand, Wallace believed that Russian intellectuals sympathetic to the peasantry tended to exaggerate the negative political impact of the commune's break-up. While the destruction of the English commons had indeed produced a numerous and impoverished class of wage laborers, the tough-minded Wallace pointed out that it had *not* produced a revolution by the dispossessed. It seemed to him peculiar that the commune's supporters

> fear the Proletariate far more than we do, who habitually live in the midst of it. Of course it is quite possible that their view of the subject is truer than ours, and that we may some day, like the people who live tranquilly on the slopes of a volcano, be rudely awakened from our fancied security. I am at present not endeavoring to justify our habitual callousness with regard to social dangers, but simply seeking to explain why the Russians, who have little or no practical acquaintance with pauperism, should have taken such elaborate precautions against it.[18]

In England—at least so far—even the most regrettable extremes of economic inequality had failed to produce a revolutionary upheaval. According to Wallace, peasants possessed a variety of virtues and defects, and their communes were sometimes flexible in responding to new challenges and opportunities.

In many respects, Wallace's judgment resembled the later views of Karl Marx. Writing in 1877, Wallace declared:

> Though it may confidently be asserted that the Commune will sooner or later undergo profound modifications, it is not easy to predict what form it will ultimately assume. Perhaps all of its peculiarities will disappear and it will become merely an organ of local self-government; but on the other hand, perhaps it will modify itself in accordance with new requirements, without abolishing its present fundamental characteristics, and succeed in partly realizing the sanguine expectations of its admirers. The facility with which it has hitherto adapted itself to circumstances, and the vigorous vitality which it everywhere displays, tends to justify these expectations; but it is still too soon to speak with confidence. Time alone can solve the problem.[19]

Four years later, Marx's letter to Vera Zasulich took a similar tack. In an argument which Russia's early Marxists prevented from reaching a wider audience,[20] Marx contended that the Russian peasant commune might be able to "shake off its primitive qualities and develop directly as an element of collective production on a national scale." Although he was by no means certain that such changes would in fact occur, Marx considered it possible that communes could be capable of assimilating the positive achievements of capitalism "without going through all its horrors."[21]

While it is highly unlikely that Kofoed knew of Marx's letter to Zasulich, it is hard to imagine that he had not read the parts of Wallace's book which contradicted his own view of the commune's role in Russia's future development. There is an uncanny resemblance between Kofoed's selective use of Wallace and Lenin's selective use of Marx's later writings. Just as "the true disciples of Marx" took it upon themselves to exclude Marx's letters from the Marxist "canon" and even to deny that the letters existed, Kofoed excluded from his writings and policy recommendations both the data and the judgments advanced by the British expert whose wisdom he praised. Subsequent debates and policy-making would be impoverished by such omissions.

Revolution and Reform: The Politics of Tenure Transformation

Russia's first twentieth-century revolution began on Bloody Sunday (January 22, 1905), when government troops attacked icon-carrying, unarmed demonstrators in the shadow of the Winter Palace. Between 1905 and 1907, worker and peasant unrest shook the political and economic foundations of society and the state. Among the peasantry, village communes emerged as a rallying point for a widespread demand for the abolition of private property in land.[22] In response to the epidemic of arson and land seizure which swept the countryside, even the most tradition-bound of Russia's landed gentry became convinced that communes were as politically dangerous as they were economically backward.[23] The fears produced by revolutionary upheaval achieved what more than a century of economic arguments against the commune had failed to accomplish.[24] Faced by overwhelming evidence that communes did not represent a conservative force in Russian society, the landed gentry decided to support government action to eliminate them.

To break the commune in the midst of a still escalating peasant *jacquerie*, Tsar Nicholas II appointed Peter Stolypin as Premier. A long-time commune critic and former provincial governor admired by conservatives for his brutally efficient methods of dealing with peasant unrest, Stolypin saw it as his mission to free the "stronger and healthier" sectors of the peasantry from commune-induced ignorance, indolence, and drunkenness. From the outset, his concerns were as much political as they were economic. Long before 1905, Stolypin warned that rural poverty provided fertile ground for revolutionary agitators, and advocated peasant landownership to save the country from the twin dangers of democracy and economic ruin.[25] As he saw it, only the rural entrepreneur could establish "a firm and stable foundation for the development of the country."[26]

In the context of 1905's revolutionary upheaval, Stolypin and his supporters argued that Russia needed above all a class of propertied peasants who aligned themselves with other landowners and with the government rather than with their "needy and drunken" village neighbors. As they broke away from the peasant "state," they would naturally look to the tsarist regime for support. According to Stolypin, "strong peasants" would no longer view the police and the magistrates as enemies. Instead, they would demand that powerful authorities protect their new property against trespass by their neighbors.

The Stolypin Reforms were intended to foster the formation of enclosed, self-contained farms (*khutory*); the *otrub* (a farm with land consolidated but with the owner's dwelling place still in the village) was viewed as a transitional economic unit.[27] Although reformers frequently contended that communes were weak institutions, it is significant that the government chose to rely on them to implement member requests for separation. In order to ease the departure process, the government issued decrees that made it progressively easier for peasant households to claim communal allotments as their private property. Initially, peasants with allotment land held in communal tenure were permitted to separate from the commune and claim a share of common land as their private property by a two-thirds vote of the commune assembly. Later, a simple majority and finally, a single request was decreed sufficient to dissolve a commune. Financial payments were offered to peasants attempting to establish a *khutor*, and generous subsidies were granted to *zemstvo* organizations that agreed to provide preferential treatment to "separators" over commune members.[28] In 1911, in order to foster the establishment of enclosed farms, communes were required (if requested) either to consolidate the scattered strips of a peasant allotment or to pay the peasant a financial indemnity for the land involved.

Believing that a political system which privileged private property would defuse political demands for fundamental changes in society and the state, Stolypin rewrote the electoral laws for the second and third state dumas in order to ensure that voting rights were confined to males who owned large quantities of private property. Like England's Reform Bill of 1834, the Stolypin decrees of 1906 and 1907 enfranchised the wealthy male landowner and disenfranchised the majority of the population.[29] The Russian state thus placed its political wager on "the magic of property."

RUSSIAN PROGRESSIVES RESPOND

To many of Russia's leading social scientists, the Stolypin-led counterrevolution was both short-sighted and disastrous. The liberal scholar Vinogradov argued that Russia's upper classes were behaving even more irresponsibly than the French nobility on the eve of 1789. Instead of reforming the conditions that drove peasants to violence, they were supporting destruction of the peasantry's traditional guarantees of security. According to Vinogradov, the Russian gentry were setting the stage for an explosion of violence, which would eventually engulf society and the state.[30] According to the medievalist A. N. Savin, destroying communal guarantees of security was akin to "planting gunpowder in the cellar of a house where you yourself live."[31] The sociologist Kovalevskii ridiculed the notion that tenure issues were both the cause and solution of Russia's economic problems; it made no sense to him to "extract from life a single fact [the commune] and make it responsible for all poverty." The economist Posnikov denounced the Stolypin reforms as "utopian," contending that nowhere in the world did successful economic programs rely so narrowly on tenure reform. The economist Chuprov pointed out that illiterate peasants did not miraculously acquire the capital and knowledge they needed in order to survive and prosper by the simple act of leaving the commune. According to Chuprov, "In their desire to equate Russian peasants with Western Europeans . . . our lawmakers forget the colossal differences between them."[32] In general, Russia's historical economists believed that the Stolypin reforms were more likely to produce impoverished and revolutionary proletarians than they were to create a class of politically conservative peasant property owners.

The spectacle of social revolution and government-sponsored economic reform confronted Russia's Marxists with a dilemma that challenged their political acumen as well as their socialist principles. Both Menshevik and Bolshevik responses were revealing. When an insurgent, All-Russian Peasant Union demanded the abolition of private property in land during the summer of 1905, the Menshevik Martov complained that peasants were failing to behave like the petty bourgeoisie described in the "Communist Manifesto." Convinced that peasants were either survivors of feudalism or defenders of capitalism, he was appalled rather than enthusiastic about commune-based demands for equal access to the land in 1905 and 1906. Wedded to a peasantophobic version of Marxism, Martov could only hope that peasants would abandon anarchist and utopian traditions of "leveling" and demand the right to become owners of private property.[33]

Mensheviks like Aksel'rod and Plekhanov argued that Marxian social-ists could support (but never ally themselves) with a peasant movement which was by definition bourgeois and capitalist in orientation. Insisting that Western historical categories and stages of socioeconomic develop-ment were universally valid, the Menshevik economist P. P. Maslov argued that in 1906, Marxists were forced to choose between "futile" support for an obsolete commune and its irrational peasant defenders, or a reluctant acceptance of a brutal government's policy of state capitalism. With many regrets and *caveats*, Maslov decided that Marxists were obliged to opt for capitalism, which at least had the merit of rapidly generating a numer-ous, class-conscious and revolutionary proletariat. As he saw it, the autoc-racy's efforts were more progressive than commune-based demands for a transfer of land to the peasantry.[34]

In contrast to the Mensheviks, Lenin attempted to align Russian Marx-ism with the peasant revolution currently underway. In order to carry off this maneuver, he engaged in a series of analytical shifts and manipula-tions comprehensible only to devotees of the most dogmatic version of Marxism. In keeping with the traditional Marxist argument that peasants could only be revolutionaries when they joined the bourgeois struggle against feudalism, and became conservative once a capitalist stage of de-velopment had been reached, Lenin abandoned his previous claims that Russia was capitalist. In 1905, he declared Russia an overwhelmingly feudal society. Intent on situating the countryside at a stage of economic development which could explain why peasants were behaving as revolu-tionaries, he contended that "proletarian" Bolshevik socialists were quite capable of leading peasants from feudalism to a higher stage of capital-ism.[35] To counter Stolypin's "Prussian" reforms, Lenin later proposed an "American-style" strategy for nationalization of the land. Arguing that it was necessary to clear the Russian countryside of feudal survivals (includ-ing the "medieval" commune), he contrasted Stolypin's "wager on the strong" to his own plan, which permitted a far greater number of peasants to become property-owners. According to Lenin, nationalization would more rapidly accelerate the capitalist transformation that constituted the next item on Russia's historical agenda.[36]

Although Lenin's decision to categorize Russia as a precapitalist society was triggered by the politics of revolution, he was *not*—for better or for worse—a simple opportunist. Willing to set aside his previous economic analysis, Lenin nevertheless drew the line at the idea of supporting the peasant commune. Dismissing the popularity of commune-based de-mands for the abolition of private property, Lenin insisted that in reality peasants wanted nothing more than to become private owners of land. Denouncing the "reactionaries" who responded to the Revolution of 1905 by forming a Socialist Revolutionary Party devoted to the cause of peasant socialism,[37] Lenin contended that peasants could not be socialists. Faithful to the Marxist dogmas established by the Emancipation of Labor group in 1883, Lenin consigned peasants and communes to a backward feudal past. Refusing to "pretend" that peasants could survive in the modern world, he was quite principled in his insistence that peasants would eventually be destroyed by the superior competitive forces of the large-scale agricultural entrepreneur.[38]

The ideological rigidity of Bolsheviks and Mensheviks on the subject of the commune frequently left them with a thankless choice between hypocrisy, opportunism, or political paralysis. The events of 1905 revealed that Bolsheviks and Mensheviks alike were inspired by Western and Russian traditions that positioned the modernizer as missionary, guide, guardian, and defender of progress against irrational and spontaneous "interventions" from below. In their responses to peasant revolution, both treated peasants as primitives *par excellence*. The Mensheviks believed that only a powerful, state capitalist government could move peasants forward. To Lenin, it was clear that Bolsheviks could lead a capitalist government that represented the peasantry and the proletariat.

Long before 1905, educated Russians to the Right and Left of the political spectrum were inspired by a heroic vision of leadership which owed as much to the elitist conceptions of August Comte as to the ideas of Karl Marx.[39] Like vanguards and "saviors of the people" in other times and places, they denied or ridiculed the socioeconomic relationships that peasants maintained with each other. Finding it difficult to establish their control over a social element which still possessed powerful ties to family, land, and community, Marxists concentrated their efforts on rootless urban proletarians who—unlike commune peasants—had nowhere else to turn. In the Russian case at least, both government reformers and Marxists saw the stubborn and recalcitrant commune peasant as a prime obstacle to their strategies for economic progress and development. Their responses suggest that the very existence of communal institutions whose power and influence were rooted in the geographic context and history of a thousand specific locales, may constitute a threat to any elite intent on imposing its values and institutions on "the backward."

The Impact of the Stolypin Reform: After 1906 and After 1917

THE COMMUNE'S SURVIVAL

In the attempt to eliminate an institution they stereotyped as wholly collectivist and conservative, Stolypin and his supporters argued in quite neoclassical fashion that Russia's future depended on the emergence of a rational "economic man" from the constraints of a medieval commune.

Even before 1905, A. A. Rittikh argued that the most energetic peasants abandoned their villages for the city in order to escape the power of the commune to confiscate the product of peasant labor. As he saw it, the creation of a modern rural economy depended on the establishment of firm guarantees for private property and rights of private accumulation.[40]

However, between 1906 and 1914, peasants made a mockery of the most cherished assumptions of government reformers. Although policy-makers played their "wager on the strong," it turned out that many of the peasants most eager to abandon the commune came from the more marginalized and impoverished groups within village society. In the Central Black Earth Region, for example, widows, the elderly, and declining families who foresaw a reduction in their allotments when it was time for a new repartition, came forward to claim their allotments as private property. Their willingness to sell communal allotments in order to meet short-term material needs enraged many of the younger and more able-bodied peasants, who described Stolypin's "wager on the strong" as a "wager on the elderly."[41]

In general, government reformers ignored the statistical data indicating that communes had devised intricate systems of reward and compensation for individual innovation.[42] Certain that private initiative could only be rewarded outside of the commune framework, they pressured local *zemstvos* to confine their education and assistance efforts to the "separators."[43] Local resistance to government efforts to stack the deck in favor of privatization came not only from commune peasants, but from agricultural specialists and economists (many of them trained or influenced by Chuprov and his students). In opposing government pressures, they did not claim that communes were preferable to the *khutor*. Instead, the Economic Bureau of the Moscow provincial zemstvo declared in 1909 that—given the scarcity of agronomists—it was easier and more practical to aid communes than to help individual farmers who usually needed case by case assistance. According to the Russian scholar Zyrianov, the collaboration between *zemstvo* agronomists and commune peasants who devised strategies for intensive cultivation may well have represented a grass-roots "counterproposal" to the principle of *khutorizatsiia*.[44]

From the outset, government reformers were aware that anticommunal strategies would fail unless fledgling property owners acquired easier access to credit. Recognizing that it would be too expensive for the government to provide direct subsidies in amounts sufficient to place the *khutor* on a sound financial footing, officials within the Ministry of Finance welcomed the growth of cooperatives as a way to ease the government's financial burden.[45] German and Danish cooperatives were avidly studied in the hope that they would provide cheap credit without undermining traditional hierarchies within society and the state.[46] However, not all conservatives were enthusiastic or optimistic about the formation of cooperatives. Provincial governors and officials in the Ministry of the Interior expressed the fear that "greedy Jews" or other "aliens" might seize control of them, or that Socialist Revolutionary activists would infiltrate cooperatives and radicalize the peasantry.[47]

Conservatives' suspicions were not in fact misplaced. In the post-1905 period, cooperatives became a beacon of hope to many whose motives were distinctly socialist. In Anita Baker's astute formulation, the cooperatives became a "conveniently ambiguous" ideological symbol, which could represent opportunities for private enterprise, or a hope for protection against market forces, or a balance between private against collective efforts, or even a way to preserve the peasant commune.[48] V. A. Kil'chevskii, a leading activist in the cooperative movement, contended that the success of the cooperative movement as a cultural force would be assured "only when its moving spirits are persons who in conscience are alien to any business interest."[49] For their part, both commune peasants and "separators" enthusiastically joined the new cooperatives. By any measure, the movement was extremely successful; on the eve of 1917, there were more cooperatives in Russia than in any Western European nation, including Germany. However, Russia's cooperatives utterly failed to fulfill the government's hope that they would undermine the powers of the commune. Available evidence suggests instead that cooperatives were extremely helpful to commune peasants.[50]

According to most scholarly assessments, the Stolypin Reforms produced only modest changes in rural tenure arrangements.[51] Although government initiatives accelerated a general trend toward intensive cultivation within and outside of the peasant commune,[52] only 10 percent of former commune peasants became Western-style proprietors of consolidated farms between 1910 and 1914.[53] In general, the amount of land area under cultivation rose, as did agricultural productivity rates. But peasants who became proprietors (1) did not do so voluntarily, (2) were no more likely to abandon traditional farming practices than their former commune neighbors, and (3) returned to the commune in increasing numbers on the eve of World War I. In fact, peasant violence against the "separators" became so severe that the reforms were suspended in 1916.[54]

Although David Macey has usefully described the Stolypin Reforms as an effort at "social engineering" intended to create the ideal rural entrepreneur, the Japanese scholar Kimitaka Matsuzato has insightfully portrayed the interaction between officials and peasants as something more like a "judo" bout: "if the government pushes the peasantry, the peasantry recedes but, hooking its leg over the rival's, it tries to circumvent the government; and vice versa."[55]

Peasant communes survived and became stronger in the course of the Revolutions of 1917, and this process continued well into the Soviet period. Particularly in 1917, when the central government's weakness shifted the balance of power in the direction of the peasantry, communes seized all private landed property (estates, church lands, and enclosed peasant farms), dividing it among their members according to traditional family labor principles. By 1918, only 2 percent of peasant households farmed arable land outside of the commune.[56] The new Soviet regime tried with little success to gain control over the countryside by calling on rural proletarians to join forces with Moscow against their village neighbors. In general, efforts to replace the peasant commune or even to affect its internal operations failed as well. Despite Soviet pressure on communes to adopt a principle of compensation according to investments of labor, many communes continued to follow the traditional commune practice of reward according to the number of family members (mouths to feed).[57] According to Orlando Figes, peasant behavior during this period was characterized by a high degree of flexibility and—Bolshevik stereotypes to the contrary—a persistent striving toward equitable treatment of all who wished to labor on the land.[58]

THE IDEOLOGICAL DEMISE OF THE COMMUNE: BEFORE 1917

Although the Stolypin Reforms failed to revolutionize existing systems of peasant land tenure, they were more successful in the area of public relations. A succession of government-sponsored journals (*Khutor, Khutorianin, Khutorskoe khoziaistvo*) provided much advice and moral support to peasants who separated from the commune. And as government officials like Krivoshein, Kofoed, and Rittikh celebrated the accomplishments of village entrepreneurs and repeatedly exposed the deficiencies of the commune, some of Stolypin's early critics began to give way. Although leading SR activists and liberal social scientists remained skeptical,[59] many educated Russians came to believe in the "magic of property," and succumbed to the appeal of the argument that universal laws of historical development annihilated communal institutions in every time and place.

Given their preexisting belief in "the idiocy of rural life," Russia's Marxists were among the most easily persuaded. On the eve of World War I, even Lenin came to fear that the Stolypin Reforms had taken deep root among ignorant and short-sighted peasants.[60] Liberals like Maxim Kovalevskii, the economists N. P. Oganovskii and I. V. Mozzukhin, and some members of the peasant-oriented Socialist Revolutionary Party also became convinced that millions were deserting the commune enthusiastically and *en masse*. On the eve of World War I, N. N. Sukhanov, a leading

Socialist Revolutionary turned Menshevik, contended that "no one" on the Left could any longer deny that Russia was replicating the economic experience of the West, as set out in the pages of *Capital*.[61]

Yet however confident Sukhanov and his *confrères* may have been about the direction of Russian rural development, their judgments were uniformly mistaken for the period before, during, and immediately after 1917. Sukhanov's former SR colleagues turned out to be right. As the scholar Richard Pipes observed over two decades ago: "As a matter of historical record, Russia did not follow the capitalist path, it did not emulate Britain. . . ."[62] While the triumph of inaccurate economic assessments which then went on to become the basis for policies that disastrously failed may well testify to the superior power of ideas, this is not the kind of triumph to which progressive-minded reformers or revolutionaries were likely to lay claim.

THE IDEOLOGICAL DEMISE OF THE COMMUNE: AFTER 1917

When the Bolsheviks came to power in 1917, they seized every available opportunity to declare their hatred for Russia's past and their intention to start anew. However, there was nothing new about their fear and loathing for a "dark," all too "Russian" peasantry, presumably untouched by Western reason, and incapable of understanding the conditions of their lives. Traditional Bolshevik suspicions of the peasantry as representatives of a primitive petty bourgeoisie were exacerbated by the experience of economic collapse, civil war, and foreign intervention that followed the October Revolution. In rural areas at least, the brutalities of "War Communism" and the onslaught of government representatives who sought simultaneously to uplift and constrain "the backward" must have seemed at least moderately familiar to the peasantry. Russian governments had for centuries viewed peasants with similar attitudes of condescension and contempt.

Marxists convinced that peasants were either members of the petty bourgeoisie or the wretched feudal survivals described in volume 1 of *Capital*, turned out to be wholly incapable of detecting the commune's resurgence and flexibility or the notions of distributive justice that bound its members. At a far remove from the realities of the Russian countryside, N. I. Bukharin and E. P. Preobrazhenskii's influential book *The ABC of Communism* (1918) foolishly asserted that the commune-dominated Russian countryside was in fact controlled by petty bourgeois proprietors of land.[63] Advocates for the abortive policy of War Communism routinely blamed greed, "Asiatic" peasant cruelty, and bigotry for their failures. According to Lenin, even revolutionary proletarians were weakened and brought low because they were "semi-peasant." Trotsky sometimes criticized peasants for their primitive, "herd instinct"; on other occasions, he faulted peasants for their unbridled, petty bourgeois individualism.

In the 1920s, even as Bolsheviks ousted Mensheviks from Soviet political life, both groups remained in agreement that peasants possessed no culture, no institutions worthy of note, and no future in the modern world. Even the followers of Bukharin who resisted Stalin's policy of forced collectivization, shared his assumption that in Russia as in the advanced capitalist nations of Western Europe, peasants and communes were obsolete.[64] As in centuries past, peasant resistance did not move members of the Soviet political elite to question their assumptions. Instead, the more tender-hearted of Soviet officials commiserated with each other over the tragic backwardness of Russia and of the peasantry in particular.

Soviet hopes for a prosperous agricultural economy rested on the fragile possibility that backward peasants could be induced—against all odds— to behave more rationally. From the writings of Lenin, Bukharin, Trotsky, and Preobrazhenskii, one might imagine an ideal peasant who behaved as follows:

> Hardworking, young, respectful toward the Soviet authorities and eager to learn, Nikolai or Matvei or Mikhail happily surrenders his grain to the Red Army's shock detachments and informs them of the secret hoard which his neighbor has buried in the dirt behind his *izba*. He eagerly leaves his land and community to work on a large-scale agricultural enterprise. As he studies Lenin, Trotsky, and Bukharin, he becomes more rational in his outlook and goes on to acquire the rudiments of Western culture. In this process, he begins to understand why he must sacrifice his material interests for an indefinite period of time, and repudiate his individual and collective past as an assortment of medieval horrors and stupidities.[65]

Such a Matvei or Nikolai or Mikhail would have delighted Lenin and Trotsky. But with minor modifications, he would have pleased the autocracy's conservative reformers just as well. Peasants who learned to despise their hideous past might have been equally eager to obey the decrees of pre-1917 "guardians" like Stolypin and Kofoed.

Chapter Nine

CULTURES OF MODERNIZATION ON THE EVE OF THE TWENTY-FIRST CENTURY

NOTES TOWARD A CONCLUSION

> At the heart of the myth of growth is the vision of the "cargo cult"—the arrival of all of the wondrous gifts of modernity in plentiful supply for all. In many places, however, there has been an intolerable delay in the arrival of the cargo-bearing ships. In other places, there has been questioning as to whether the cargo is worth the mess it has made on the beach. Needless to say, the latter question is unlikely to be raised by those still waiting for the appearance of the ships on the horizon.
>
> *(Peter Berger,* Pyramids of Sacrifice, *1974)*

> Like the Pacific islanders waiting for the White Man to return to landing strips in 'great birds,' the Russians were waiting for the White Man to return to Russia, bearing gifts and bringing the supposed prosperity that according to current lore, the West created during the pre-revolutionary tsarist period.
>
> *(David Lempert, "Changing Russian Political Culture in the 1990s," 1993)*

Traditions of Westernization

IN THE many stories that Western culture tells of itself, individual freedom and rights of ownership have played a leading role. But in Russian intellectual history, Westernizers seldom linked the twin ideals of freedom and private ownership; in general, early advocates of property rights were supporters of autocratic rule.[1] Agreeing with Voltaire's argument that serfdom was justified in Russia because Russian peasants were too backward and ignorant to survive on their own, Westernized serfowners defended bondage as a form of guardianship for the weak and defenseless. In the eighteenth and early nineteenth centuries, a tiny hereditary elite studied Adam Smith and J. B. Say and concluded that serfs were their most valuable and productive form of private property. At the same time, admirers of England's Agricultural Revolution implemented intrusive schemes for the establishment of more privatized systems of tenure which relied on "pitiless punishment" and unprecedented levels of regimentation as economic stimuli.[2]

It was not until the 1840s that a self-proclaimed "Westernizer" group would argue that Westernization meant opposition to serfdom and authoritarian rule. But it is revealing that even their courageous and principled challenge to Russia's police-ridden status quo was riddled with the same contempt and fear of backward peasants expressed by Russian serfowners from time immemorial. A love of Western culture bred in enthusiasts like Belinskii not only a commitment to emancipation but a visceral hatred for the "dark" world of commune peasants, whose every move was presumably brutal and callous and whose greatest pleasure was to watch beatings and executions. It was left to a Slavophile landed gentry to claim that peasants were already human beings with a culture and institutions of their own. As critics of Western liberalism, Slavophiles admired English Tories and German Romantics; they valued the peasant commune as a stabilizing element in the Russian countryside, and argued that communes might prove to be a potentially viable framework for economic activity.[3]

In the 1860s and 1870s, the German-trained scholars who came to dominate the field of Russian economics were inspired by liberal political ideals. Arguing that freedom, prosperity, and domestic peace were best guaranteed by a democratically oriented government and a mixed economy, Russia's historical economists rejected the notion that elimination of communal institutions, values, and practices was the West's supreme achievement. They argued instead that the West provided examples of effective action by both limited and activist governments, by private entrepreneurs, rural co-operatives, labor unions, and socialist parties in a rich and instructive array of changing configurations. Liberal economists contended that a representative government devoted to democratic reform, popular education, and the supply of cheap credit to the rural population was far more important than tenure reform.[4]

However, in the latter decades of the nineteenth century, as Russia's liberal economists insisted that tenure issues be considered within a broader framework of political, financial and educational reform, leading government officials were adopting a single-minded faith in the "magic of property." Although traditionalists in the Ministry of the Interior continued to rely on the commune as a conservative political force in the countryside, many in the Ministry of Finance called for the abolition of communal tenure. It was not until revolution erupted in 1905, and insurgent communes destroyed once and for all their conservative political image that government policy shifted decisively against them. Convinced that the salvation of society and the state lay in the establishment of a system of private ownership, conservatives who had previously supported the commune now feared its "dangerous" hold upon the peasant majority of the population. Popular resistance to anticommunal measures was denounced as a sign of peasant backwardness.

In 1917, when the Bolsheviks seized power and established a new Soviet state, the defects of "petty bourgeois greed" joined the familiar charge of backwardness as justifications for both the coercive policies of War Communism and the later, far more brutal, campaigns for Forced Collectivization. In Party debates and reports from the countryside, officials of the new Soviet state recounted their painful struggles to overcome the stubborn resistance of peasants they described as "Asiatic," "Oriental," cruel, apathetic, short-sighted, and stupid. In Party debates over the constraints of War Communism, Soviet leaders argued that coercion was unavoidably necessary to advance the cause of economic progress and the modernization of rural life.

Although the level of violence inflicted on the peasantry was incomparably higher during the Stalin era, it was significant that in his murderous campaigns in the countryside Stalin deployed a rhetoric familiar at least since the time of Catherine the Great. As in the past, peasants and their communes were not simply criticized as economically backward; their recalcitrance and resistance was denounced as a threat to the stability of society and the state. Viewing the peasant majority of the population as heavy burden inherited by the Soviet state, Stalinist functionaries described peasant opposition as both traitorous and counterrevolutionary. In the 1930s, as the goverment imposed a tenure transformation that moved peasants from commune to collective farm, Soviet officials viewed the localism and autonomy of the commune as a danger to the state's monopolistic claims to leadership, authority, and control.

Either/Or: The Triumph of Dichotomized Economic Perspectives

> There was the belief . . . that a place such as I came from could be returned to only at the price of intellectual death; cut off from the cultural springs of the metropolis, the . . . countryside is Circe and Mammon. Finally, there was the assumption that the life of the metropolis is the experience, the modern experience, and that the life of the rural town . . . is not only irrelevant to our time, but archaic as well, because unknown or unconsidered by the people who really matter—that is, the urban intellectuals.
>
> (Wendell Berry, The Long-Legged House, 1980)

Before 1917, government leaders and their Marxist adversaries portrayed the urbanized West as the source of all rational hopes for the future.[5] In contrast, Russia was a world of culture deficit, whose only assets were the phenomena which could be identified as at least potentially "Western." A wide array of crises and conflicts were attributed to the striking disparity between Russia and the cultures of the civilized and civil societies of Western Europe. The values that progressives attached to perceptions of "difference" are significant and revealing. Distinctions between the West and Russia, between communal and private institutions, and between the countryside and the city were not construed as complementary elements of human life, history and culture. Instead, they were interpreted as differences in worth, and reflective of a hierarchy in which Russia, the commune and the peasant occupied an extremely low ranking.

Engaged in a "culture war" that could only end when the inferior half of the dichotomous pair was obliterated by the other, both government reformers and Marxists denounced advocates of pluralism as the enemies of the West. The Westernizer was portrayed as an intelligent, progressive, and civilized person who looked to the immediate future and recognized only one form of tenure (private) and one mode of economic development (capitalist).[6] One fate—extinction—was prescribed for peasant communities the world over. To its advocates and defenders, the narrowness of such either/or economic perspectives was obscured by the claim that they were all universal in their application.

As we have seen, social scientists who called for more openness and flexibility on these points were attacked for taking up a sentimental, "Slavophile," or "populist" attitude toward patently "inferior," precapitalist and feudal institutions or social elements. Ridiculed for arguing that the choice between tradition and modernity was less than absolute, they were accused as well of claiming that Russia constituted an exception to laws of development that governed all the other peoples of the world. According to the precepts of the early twentieth-century progressive, to doubt that every people would eventually move from primitive feudalism to advanced capitalism was to reveal the doubter as a thoroughgoing enemy of Reason and Science. As voices to the Left and Right of the ideological spectrum issued calls to battle against the medieval "darkness" of the countryside, arguments for economic pluralism steadily lost ground. The contention that Russia's economic future depended on the outcome of a complex and variable interaction between Russia and the West did not seem to concentrate the mind nearly as well as the choice between progress and stagnation.

Although Russia's historical economists lost the "culture war," the demise of economic pluralism was not simply an example of complex perspectives losing out to those that were simpler. The political deficiencies and weakness of its leading proponents played a key role in their defeat. Whatever their virtues as scholars, Russia's historical economists were unable to devise alternative modes of analysis or reasonably coherent economic goals. Although they possessed important critical insights into the economic history of Russia and the West, made use of a far wider range of economic and statistical evidence than their adversaries, and rightly understood that Russia was not on the eve of a capitalist economic transformation either in 1905 or 1917, their wisdom did not lead them toward effective or principled action.

Perhaps most damaging to the cause of economic pluralism was the failure of its defenders to face up to the political implications of their economic judgments or to the dilemmas of liberalism in the Russian context. Despite the richness and complexity of their research and historical perspectives, liberal economists like Posnikov were paralyzed by the conflict between their hatred for state coercion and social injustice, and their—as it turned out—more deeply seated fear of a vengeance-ridden peasantry.[7] In 1917, when Posnikov became the Provisional Government's Minister of Agriculture and his colleague Manuilov was appointed Minister of Education, they were confronted by a peasantry that was—as they had long ago predicted—far more desperate, violent, and embittered than in 1905. Entrusted with the responsibility and power that had eluded them in earlier decades, they accomplished little. With his usual political acumen, Lenin pointed out that Russia's liberals found it far easier to sympathize with peasants *before* they had actually shown themselves capable of revolutionary violence.[8]

In contrast to Posnikov and Manuilov, Lenin braved the ironies of a capitalist revolution led by Social Democrats, and sought to mobilize the widest possible support for Bolshevik leadership.[9] Kofoed, the Danish-born adviser to the Russian government, chose autocracy and the authoritarian capitalist strategy of Stolypin. Under the leadership of P. N. Miliukov and the ex-Marxist Struve, the Kadet Party decided that peasant anarchy constituted an even greater evil than the survival of the Romanov dynasty, and forged alliances with the supporters of the old regime. An over-riding fear of peasant anarchy, when added to a lack of political courage or a coherent alternative vision, left Russia's historical economists trailing behind a rightward moving Kadet Liberal Party (which was in turn increasingly willing to compromise with more or less despicable military leaders, eager to restore order by any means necessary).[10]

The Intersecting Cultures of Russia and the West

Among the more unfortunate features of the twentieth century's dichotomized thinking about progress was a denial of the complexity of Russia's relationship to the West. In the eighteenth century, when the German-born Catherine the Great followed the economic advice of German Cameralists and Montesquieu, she was well aware that the cultural boundaries between Russia and the West were anything but clearcut. In the decades to come, German-born scholars created political economy as a Russian academic discipline, and the historical economist Wilhelm Roscher incorporated the research findings of Russian scholars into what he described as a "German-Russian" school of economics.[11] Marx praised Bervi's *Conditions of the Russian Working Class* as the best economic study since Engels's book on English factory workers, and the economists Daniel'son and Kablukov supplied him with the data and arguments which led Marx to confront—however belatedly—the issue of cultural difference. Vinogradov and Kovalevskii became leading participants in Western European debates over the origin of private-property rights, and the influential Belgian economist Laveleye cited Russian economic research and arguments in textbooks that were required reading for Harvard economics undergraduates at the turn of the century.[12]

Russian scholars, officials, and social critics battled each other through rival economic analyses and histories that were either derived from or legitimized by references to the work of Western economic thinkers.[13] In the 1850s, Moscow University's Vernadskii translated the work of Frederic Bastiat and Henry Carey, while Bervi cited Engels and Cliffe-Leslie. In the 1860s and 1870s, the economist Ziber became Russia's leading Ricardian economist, and Chuprov cited Marx as well as Wilhelm Roscher and John Stuart Mill. A substantial portion of Russian intellectual history was played out on the interdependent cultural terrains of the West and Russia.

Defining the Core Values of Western Culture

As we have seen, Russia's Westernizing efforts frequently highlighted institutions and values that did not become central to the Anglo-American cultural mainstream. While some admired such Western ideals as the dignity of persons, the popular accountability of institutions, and the right to challenge illegitimate authority,[14] many more were devotees of Western military technology and surveillance techniques. Westernizers of the latter sort considered Prussian police methods a major European cultural asset. The centuries-long history of Russia's hierarchical and authoritarian borrowings from the West tend to reinforce the twentieth-century claim of Michel Foucault that alongside the ideals of liberty and democracy, *Discipline and Punish* was a mindset quite central to Western culture.

From the Russian perspective, there were many "Wests" to choose from. And particularly for those of us who are inhabitants of England and the United States, it is extremely useful to consider whether Russians were wrong to believe that German historical economics, or Comte's notion of a vanguard elite destined to lift the world out of medieval backwardness were key components of Western culture. Did Russians become better "Westernizers" when they agreed with the most optimistic Western visions of a world dominated by liberal institutions? In the early twentieth century, Anglophiles like Peter Struve and Nikolai Ziber believed that the Golden Age of English capitalism would last forever. Like Lenin, the tsarist Minister of Agriculture Ermolov was quite certain that Russia and the West would follow similar historical trajectories. But they were wrong. The days of England's dominance are now long past, and over seventy years of Soviet history has demonstrated beyond question that Imperial Russia did not follow the paths marked out by England, France, Germany or other Western European nations.

As Russia's historical economists observed, Western nations achieved modernity by a variety of different paths, each one conditioned and shaped by a particular history and material environment. The history of Western economic theory includes neo-classical, historical, and socialist perspectives, and examples of economic success in which government, private enterprise, and/or co-operative institutions played a leading role. Russian perceptions of the West as a heterogeneous culture raise important questions about the West's "true" meaning, and about the standards by which its major features have been defined. The study of Russian efforts to make use of Western economic models can be both a sobering and an illuminating experience.

The Cruel Choice: To Be Civilized and "Western," or Backward and "Russian"

> Only those among you are welcome who can help us think of our problems on our own and bring to us information that is useful to us, and are yourselves willing to learn a lot from us.
> (Anisur M. D. Rahman, Society for International Development, 1981)

By 1900, Western nations held dominion over a third of the peoples of the world (some 560 millions). Their economic and political triumphs were routinely attributed to cultural, and in particular, to racial superiority. In this context, Western categories and definitions carried particular weight. Under conditions of colonial domination, nations that suffered economic and political defeat were invited—and often required—to accept cultural subordination as well. The Vietnamese of French Indochina were forced to celebrate Bastille day, and were praised and rewarded for learning French; a knowledge of English history and literature was equated with the advance of reason in schools established by the British to "civilize" Indian children. To many of the colonized, the process of Westernization went far beyond the transmission of particular skills; it involved as well an acceptance of the notion that indigenous cultures, institutions, and languages were backward and unworthy of study.[15] In the nineteenth and early twentieth centuries, as Russia suffered repeated military defeats and became the site of substantial Western economic investment, educated Russians learned to describe themselves—as well as those they sought to change—as "backward."[16]

Long before the age of Kipling, "Westernizers" like Belinskii were already describing their peasant compatriots as a dark and sullen people, who—like the Indians described by Kipling—were "half devil and half child."[17] In a late nineteenth-and early twentieth-century world of increasingly racist imperialism, the autocracy and its Soviet successors embarked on "civilizing missions," which were intended to introduce the Western light of modernity into the heart of darkness—the savagery of a communal peasant world. In the intensity with which educated Russians attempted to become "Western," it is difficult to avoid the suspicion that they were not simply trying to devise development strategies; they were engaged as well in an effort to demonstrate that—unlike the benighted peasantry—they deserved to be considered rational and civilized human beings.

Whether they were advocates for capitalism, socialism, or communism, progressive-minded Russians of the ninteenth and early twentieth centuries learned to lump the word "Russian" together with adjectives like "Asiatic," "Oriental," and "Eastern" in a pejorative rhetoric used to describe all manner of thoughts and actions considered despicable and backward. This was not a uniquely Russian phenomenon. References to "Oriental" darkness, despotism, and servility were a characteristic feature of modern thought.[18] In the Russian case, "Russia" was also identified with the peasantry, the commune, the tsarist regime, or the Orthodox church as an obstacle to progress. Few progressives were able to resist the temptation to prove how civilized they were by the degree of enthusiasm with which they denounced social elements, institutions, or values for being "all too Russian."

It is instructive to compare the defeat suffered by Russian advocates of economic pluralism with the cultures of modernization that emerged in some of the regions of the world colonized by the West. In Africa, India, and Latin America, there were of course many "Russian-style" progressives who sought liberation from what they viewed as the backwardness and absurdities of their country's non-Western and premodern culture. In the early twentieth century, the intimidating power of Westerners who humiliated the wisest of his people led Prince Modupe of Guinea to migrate to the United States and write a book entitled *I Was a Savage*;[19] in later years, the novelist V. S. Naipaul satirized admirers of the West, who became what he called *The Mimic Men*. But Naipaul affirmed nevertheless that Western civilization is the "universal civilization which fits all men."[20]

However, it is significant that resistance to colonialism also produced freedom fighters who affirmed the humanity of non-Western peoples, and political leaders whose strategies for change did not require the obliteration of every indigenous value and institution. In the twentieth century, Amilcar Cabral of Guinea-Bissau achieved a level understanding of the complexities of cultural borrowing which unfortunately never became dominant in the Russian context.[21] According to Cabral, who was trained as an agronomist, "while we scrap colonial culture and the negative aspects of our own culture, whether in our character or in our environment, we have to create a new culture, also based on our traditions but respecting everything that the world today has conquered for the service of mankind."[22] In Russia, the struggle to establish a cultural identity that incorporated Western expertise and knowledge proved to be a painful, difficult, and not very successful process.

Much earlier in Russia's intellectual history, Alexander Herzen argued that Russia had to learn from both the mistakes and achievements of the West. In his words:

> We have no reason to repeat the epic story of your emancipation, in the course of which your road has become so encumbered by the monuments of the past that you are hardly able to take a single step ahead. Your labors and your sufferings are our lessons. History is very unjust. The latecomers receive instead of the gnawed bones [the right] of precedence [at the table] of experience. All of the development of mankind is nothing else but [an expression of] that chronological ingratitude.[23]

However, in the twentieth century, Herzen's words led many Western scholars to describe him as a sentimental and anti-Western populist.[24] Although historical economists also took account of what they viewed as the light and shadow of the West, they were charged with similar failings. Prerevolutionary reformers and Marxists permitted only those who recognized the universal superiority of liberal Western culture to claim the mantle of "the Westernizer."

While in some of the colonized regions of Africa, India, and Latin America the defense of cultural integrity and indigenous institutions became the basis for struggles for equality, democracy, and national liberation, in Russia the most highly publicized defenders of Russian culture were a host of authoritarian and xenophobic nationalists. Although historical economists devised complex, Western-oriented perspectives on the issue of development, they lost the ideological and political battles of the early twentieth century (and failed to attract the attention of Soviet or

Western scholars or policy-makers in the post World War II era). In contrast to the leaders of twentieth-century anticolonial struggles, Russian Marxists and tsarist policy-makers who set the agenda for Western and Soviet scholarship for decades to come were quite successful in identifying "Russia" with all that was backward and contemptible.

At the end of the twentieth century, it is revealing that African leaders who face a variety of political and economic disasters do not routinely attribute them to the national character of the inhabitants of Zimbabwe, Eritrea, or South Africa. In contrast, liberal Russian leaders of the post-Soviet Union routinely denounce their opponents as "all too Russian,"— an ignorant, peasant-like mass, accustomed to stultifying guarantees of employment and health care.[25] In 1992, the US political scientist Francis Fukuyama described Russia's move toward capitalism as proof that all historical paths of development invariably led from backwardness to the pinnacle reached by the economic and political institutions of the West. Accompanied by the enthusiastic praise of the erstwhile president of Georgia Edward Shevarnadze (then a chief adviser to Gorbachev), Fukayama's book triumphantly declared that the end of History was at hand.[26]

However flattering it may be to Western sensibilities to argue that the economic, political, social, and cultural successes of the United State represent the highpoint of human achievement, there is a certain self-indulgent quality to Fukuyama's claims, and much that is both tragic and poignant about its embrace by Russians, Georgians, and other progressive-minded groups in the successor states of the Soviet Union. In the late 1990s, it is evident that the end of Russia's history has not yet been reached (and many in the United States fervently hope that we are not at the end of our own historical development).

In the period following the breakup of the USSR, a number of Westward-looking economic reformers constructed an image of the United States as the possessor of a national economy wonderfully devoid of substantial poverty or market failure. Contemporary observers like Boris Kagarlitsky reported that Russians enamored of the West contended that "good Americans" prospered; homelessness and unemployment were viewed as the well-deserved plight of lazy African Americans and other people of color.[27] In contrast, Soviet history was portrayed as a record of unrelieved irrationality, cruelty, and failure, devoid of achievements in science, mathematics, or space technology. In the US, the Soviet Union's espoused values of literacy, full employment, paid maternity leaves, and free health care are ridiculed as fraudulent, and blamed for the slowness of contemporary Russian economic growth and development. In the rush to embrace American-style capitalism, obstacles and difficulties were attributed to the elderly, unattractive women, "peasant-like" factory workers, bigoted, Stalinist, and anti-Western Communist hardliners, or even—

in one recent formulation—to the rigidity of Russian males who prefer suicide to the difficult task of adjusting to much-needed change.[28]

Shock Treatment in Historical Perspective

To deal with Russia's desperate need for change Western advisers and many Russian liberals of the 1980s and 1990s joined forces to advocate a "shock therapy" approach to economic development. Peculiarly indifferent to the symbolic significance of using this particular form of psychiatric terminology, they did not recall that shock therapy has been a controversial treatment in the West, typically used only after all other efforts to help the patient have failed. Just as psychiatrists have used electric shocks in the hope that they will obliterate the barriers to healthy behavior and perception constructed by the patient's badly functioning brain, Russia's economic advisers argued that the shock of material insecurity might restore Russians to more normal and rational patterns of economic behavior. Memory loss has frequently been a side effect of shock therapy, and contemporary proponents of this course of treatment for Russia believe that shock therapy will help Russians to forget the enervating social guarantees that were embedded in the Soviet past.

In some respects, the conception of change that inspired economist/ advocates of shock therapy in the 1990s recalls the mindset of earlier reformers in Russian and Soviet history who denounced an ungrateful and uncomprehending populace which refused to adopt their programs and policies, and advocated the use of coercion as an economic stimulus. Before the 1990s, the most striking example of shock therapy may well have been the Forced Collectivization campaigns of the 1930s. According to Stalin's arguments, he had no choice but to force peasants into a modern world they would never have entered on their own. Unless peasants were driven from their communes into large, state-run agricultural enterprises, Stalin argued that Russia would remain forever backward and weak, a prize easily conquered by predatory foreign nations.[29]

Although many scholars have since documented the viability and flexibility of the commune in the 1920s, Stalin—like Stolypin before him— reified and essentialized the commune as a wholly reactionary and rigid institution. While Stolypin ignored the wide range of *private* economic efforts permitted, fostered, and rewarded within the commune framework, Stalin ignored the commune's *collectivism* and portrayed it as the breeding ground for greedy kulaks bent on capitalist counterrevolution. Although Stalin's policies were incomparably more violent than Stolypin's, there is a disquieting resemblance between the repeated declarations by both leaders that there existed no middle ground between stagnation and progress. Stalin's response to peasant resistance recalled as well the reactions of the eighteenth-century agronomist Bolotov, who tortured his recalcitrant peasants to make them behave rationally, or the Anglophile reformer Admiral Mordvinov, who created totalitarian military colonies in order to enforce compliance with "rational" modes of economic and non-economic behavior. Like embattled Russian proponents of change in other times and places, Stalin commented, "It is sometimes asked whether it is not possible to slow down the tempo a bit, to put a check on the movements. No, comrades, it is not possible!"[30] According to Stalin's urgent, "either/or, backwardness or progress" scenario, forced collectivization represented the Soviet Union's only option in the struggle to achieve modernity.[31] Alternative strategies that were "easier" on peasants in the short run were dismissed as "half-measures," which postponed the inevitable and slowed the resolution of the Soviet Union's economic crises. As envisioned by its leading tsarist and Marxist proponents, change was not a process that created new economic institutions out of old ones; it required instead the wholesale obliteration of the past.[32]

In arguments that reverberate throughout the history of Russian economic thought, reformers of the 1990s have demanded that Russians must either obliterate the past or be enslaved by it. Encouraged by Western economic advisers to ignore the long-term historical processes that created the vast infrastructure upon which Western market economies were based, Russian economists proposed "500-day plans" for a total destatization and privatization of the Soviet economy.[33] As a majority of the population experienced change in the form of growing unemployment and a disintegrating social safety net, they argued that shock therapy constituted the only strategy which could move the country forward. Gradualism was denounced as a form of conservatism and reaction.

Although it took Margaret Thatcher a decade to privatize only 5 percent of England's state enterprises, the Russian economists Shatalin and Yavlinskii (counseled by US economist Jeffrey Sachs) contended that to reject their "500-day" privatization plans was to ignore "the laws of economic and social development" and to court unprecedented disaster.[34] Some historically minded liberal democrats who traced the origins of the Soviet collective/state farm system to the peasant commune, even resurrected the Stolypin reforms as a privatizing alternative to totalitarian collectivism.

To many Western-oriented reformers of the 1990s, destruction was number one on Russia's economic agenda. According to one US adviser, it was essential that Russian reforms be "disruptive on a historically unprecedented scale" in order to ensure that they were irreversible.[35] Since disruption meant homelessness, unemployment, a decline in levels of health care, and a rapid rise in infant and adult mortality rates, the shock therapist's callousness and lack of empathy is rather chilling. A Swedish adviser, balancing what he described as "wildly exaggerated" social costs against the benefits of reform, observed with a measure of satisfaction, "who could have believed that communism's demise would be so cheap?"[36] The tough solutions that US advisers recommended for Russia contrast sharply with the generous US government measures taken to prop up and restore banks in the early 1980s, and to keep large institutions from bankruptcy in the wake of the stock market failure of 1987. Long ago, one of the world's most renowned eighteenth-century cynics recognized the universal appeal of change that exempts the reformer from having to suffer through the process. In the words of La Rochefoucauld: "We have all of us sufficient courage to bear the pains of others."

Dichotomized choices between stagnation and progress have shaped the economic debates of the post-Soviet era. Although the English model admired in earlier times no longer carries much weight, the "either/or" economic mindset is clearly alive and well. The one idea which scarcely varied throughout the history of this approach to problems of economic development was that there was a "West" and a "Russia," each quite settled, clear, unassailably self-evident entities. Instead of promoting a fuller knowledge which included the mutual influences and entanglements of the two, Russia's Westernizers have tended instead to defend a stereotypical view of each. As a consequence, Russian culture was defined as wholly different from an essentialized West (and persistently demoted to a lesser status.[37]

Not long ago, the political scientist Robert Daniels suggested that it was ironic that at a time when Americans were agonizing over the ineffectiveness of US political and economic institutions, US economic advisers sought to convince educated Russians that all of their difficulties could be solved "by transforming themselves into clones of the USA." Although Russian reformers who embraced this position delighted US economic experts, in 1991 the Russian newspaper *Arguments and Facts* suggested a more tragic interpretation of Russia's admiration for the West: "You don't understand what our people see when they look at America. . . . These are hard economic times. The people need a myth to believe in. We can't be too critical of America for a simple reason. . . . We are going to be a colony."[38] By the late 1990s, many of the leading proponents of shock therapy have become convinced that it may have failed. With what may be a dawning awareness of the significance of cultural difference, US economist Jeffrey Sachs has admitted that in the case of Russia, he felt like a surgeon who sliced open a patient, only to discover nothing that was supposed to be there! As one US journalist observed, Sachs's experience suggests "that the surgeon not only had the wrong diagnosis but mistook the patient for someone else."[39] Why the Soviet patient should have been so unfamiliar to a Western surgeon also remains something of a mystery.

On the Russian side, the balance between self-respect and openness to learning from others seems as difficult to achieve at present as in earlier times. In the words of Daniels, "Perhaps we need to underscore for the former Communist countries themselves how their haste to change, slough off the past, and copy theoretical Western models, though understandable as a reaction against their discredited Communist regimes, may be doing more harm than good, while justified in the uncomfortably familiar terms of a radiant future."[40]

Although strategies for privatization were presented as a way to eliminate economic inefficiency, their most striking consequence in Russia and other former communist states has been to increase the political and economic power of some social groups—and in particular of former Soviet officials—over others. A case in point is Viktor Chernomyrdin, who was Minister of Natural Gas under the Soviet regime and became Russia's prime minister in 1992. Chernomyrdin is now the largest shareholder of the privatized company Gazprom, which controls between 20 and 35 percent of the world's natural gas reserves.[41]

Russia in the 1990s has seen the emergence of Russian millionaires and billionaires (many of them the same officials who devised the policy of shock therapy), as well as the persistent rejection of proposals for a mixed economy as "a return to the past." In a 1995 article for *Moscow Times*, Konstantin Zuyev wrote:

> [The Russian people] more and more attentively evaluate just who Russia's new rich are and how they got that way. If it had happened on the basis of talent, energy and business sense, it would not have produced the kind of envy that many commentators claim is our inheritance from the communist era. We do not see many self-made Henry Fords among our new rich. Instead, we see that the main tools for getting rich in Russia are insolence, moral compromise, abuse of one's position with the country's power structures, and crime.[42]

Communist advocates of a mixed economy and a measure of social welfare have since reemerged in Lithuania, Belarus, Poland, and Hungary. However, in Russia, these goals were monopolized until 1995 by extreme right-wing nationalists, who provided a respite from unremitting cultural self-hatred by encouraging the hatred of "un-Russian" social groups. It remains to be seen whether Russia's resurgent Communist Party or any other political group will emerge to fight for changes that reject the shock therapy of free marketeers as well as the shocks administered by Stalinists in the earlier decades of the twentieth century. But thus far, according to the economist Marshall Goldman, "the emerging Russian society may be for the benefit of only a few with connections in the government—in many ways even fewer than under the old communist regime."[43] Former Deputy Prime Minister Leonid Abalkin's fear that a disregard for the human costs of change was dismayingly similar to the attitude of Bolsheviks in 1917 has been rejected; arguments for social justice as an economic goal have been dismissed as Slavophile and conservative.[44]

"Lessons" and Questions

My investigation of Russian efforts to learn from the West represents only a preliminary effort to raise questions that deserve richer and more multifaceted responses than the ones I have provided. I should emphasize that the message of this study is not that we should abandon the use of economic models, distrust all intellectuals, or reject every aspect of Western culture. In general, the research findings contained in this book have heightened the value that I place upon (1) the search for less dichotomized and more historical approaches to urgent economic questions, and (2) the recognition that it is not unusual in the history of economic thought— and not necessarily a bad idea—for modern economists to take seriously the imperatives of social security and stability, which particularly concern participants in the struggle for modernity who are not entrepreneurs. Both the efforts and the fate of Russian historical economics are instructive in this regard.

Equally important is the light that Russian historical perspectives cast upon the West. As outsiders within Western culture, educated Russians paid attention to ideas and institutions which were extremely popular within and outside Western Europe but subsequently neglected in England, France, and the United States. For example, it is only during the past decade that the German historical school of economics which they studied has been rediscovered by Anglo-American scholars.[45] The survival, prosperity, and democratic orientation of the Scandinavian peasant economies to which educated Russians looked for models and examples in the 1900s is a topic which does not yet figure in the "grand scheme" of Western historical development. Although Russian scholars could not have guessed that German and Danish models would be excluded from the Western economic canon, it is worth considering whether the history of their encounters with heterogeneous Western economies might contribute to the creation of a more inclusive picture of the West, with far more complex lessons to offer to the rest of the world than have been previously suggested.[46]

In addition, Russian efforts to learn from Western economic experience illuminate the dilemmas that arise in the process of economic and noneconomic cultural borrowings. Like the Algerian intellectuals long ago described by Frantz Fanon, educated Russians were invited by the West to abandon every aspect of a supposedly despicable culture in order to be recognized as civilized, rational, and economically productive individuals. Driven by a quite understandable fear of backwardness, many took on the role of colonizers in their own country. Arguing that they were engaged in efforts either to strengthen the national economy or to further the cause of socialism, they adopted coercive methods, which established them in positions of power over the objects of their development strategies.

In the all-too-familiar modernization scenario, the majority become the obstacle to progress, with enlightened leaders finding themselves obliged to "force" peasants to engage in productive economic behavior. The history of so many efforts to re-create an idealized Western experience on Russian soil suggests that it may be useful to consider other possibilities. One of the most promising avenues for contemporary researchers and policy-makers may be found in the work of the nineteenth-century historically oriented economists and social scientists who looked Westward and saw not only individual freedom, but unlimited greed, opportunity, insecurity, cooperatives, and welfare states. Turning to Russia, they argued that the polarities of "backwardness" and "progress" did not explain why peasants adopted innovations either within or outside of the peasant commune.

The historic encounters between educated Russians and the West, and between Russian "high culture" and indigenous values and institutions suggest that it may also be useful to move away from efforts to understand the outcome of rural development strategies as a problem of backward peasants, and to look more closely at the relationship between the modernizer and the people to be "modernized." Whether we read the Marxist Plekhanov or the tsarist official Kofoed on the topic of "mindless peasants" and "barbaric communes," what stands out is their fervent hope that peasants might have the good sense to serve as a *tabula rasa* on which they and other educated Russians might eloquently write. (It is also worth noting that the language with which they describe the "backward" was frequently as crude as the behavior that they claim to be describing.)

As anthropologists who study other geographic areas have long been well aware, contempt for the object of change seldom fosters either real understanding or successful policy outcomes. Unfortunately, although cultural understanding is a practical necessity for the policy-maker, it has not yet found a secure place in the analysis of economic policy and practice.[47] There may well be a connection between the "modernizer's" certainty that peasants suffered from a profound and all-encompassing culture deficit and the history of peasant reluctance to accept strategies for rural development in which they functioned as "raw material" rather than as coparticipants in the change process. It is useful to consider, for example, how peasants might have responded to a Communist Party operative in 1919 reading the passage from the "Communist Manifesto" on "the idiocy of rural life." While some might be glad to recognize the evils set out by Marx, others might wonder why they were so despised.

In the course of the nineteenth and twentieth centuries, educated Russians who were appalled at the peasantry's alleged culture deficit also learned to view themselves as culturally deficient in relation to the West. Given the human cost of the policies inspired by deficit modes of thinking, it is worth considering the potential for "non-missionary" approaches to change, which might be based upon an account of Russian culture that includes, among others, historical economists, Marxists, Ricardians—and peasants who are pragmatists, or fearful of shock therapy, or fanatics of one sort or another, both within and outside of the commune. If Russian culture constitutes, to a far greater degree than has been previously realized, a part of, rather than an obstacle to what we call "development," one might envision a way of thinking about development that revises the traditional, hierarchical relationship between those who create and impose economic models and those who are presumably to benefit from them.[48]

The tumultuous events that led to the Soviet Union's break-up in 1993 provide a powerful and appropriately ambiguous scenario of cultural appropriation with which I would like to conclude:

> As Boris Yeltsin battled the members of Parliament who wanted to slow the pace of privatization, he seized on the same tactics that were earlier deployed by the U.S. Marines against Manuel Noriega in Panama in 1991. By blaring Western rock music at "hard-liners" holed up in the parliament building in Moscow, he hoped to disorient and demoralize them. Although this strategy did not succeed in driving out his opponents, it reflected still another example of Westernization as a weapon in Russia's continuing struggle against the survivals of the past.[49]

The complex challenges of Westernization remain. I hope that at this point the reader's questions are more numerous than they were at the beginning of this study.

NOTES

PREFACE

1. My first book, *Lenin and the Problem of Marxist Peasant Revolution* (Oxford: Oxford University Press, 1983), was a response to this question.

2. Many scholars in the field of US history have raised similar questions about the exclusion of particular institutions and social groups from mainstream scholarly research. See, for example, economists Lou Ferleger and Jay Mandle, who note that little attention has been paid to the history of the government's important role in promoting U.S. agricultural development, or Cary Nelson's study of literary critics of the 1950s who decided to exclude works by women and minorities from U.S. literature's literary "canon." See Ferleger and Mandle, "The Managerial Revolution and the Developmental State: The Case of U.S. Agriculture," *Business and Economic History* 22, no. 2 (1993): 68–101, and Cary Nelson, *Repression and Recovery: Modern American Poetry and the Politics of Cultural Memory, 1910–1945* (Madison, Wisc.: University of Wisconsin Press, 1989).

3. See Esther Kingston-Mann, "Three Steps Forward, One Step Back" Dilemmas of Upward Mobility," in Esther Kingston-Mann and Timothy Sieber, ed., *Achieving Against the Odds: Teaching and Learning at an Urban Commuter University in the Year 2000* (forthcoming).

4. Zack Deal, "Serf and State Peasant Agriculture: Kharkov Province, 1842–1861," Ph.D. diss., Vanderbilt University, 1978.

5. Helma Repczuk, "Nicholas Mordvinov (1754–1845): Russia's Would-Be Reformer," Ph.D. diss., Columbia University, 1962.

6. Steven Grant, "The Peasant Commune in Russian Thought, 1861–1905," Ph.D. diss., Harvard University, 1973.

7. Anthony Netting, "Russian Liberalism: The Years of Promise, 1842–55," Ph.D. diss., Columbia University, 1967; Allison Blakely, "The Socialist Revolutionary Party, 1901–1907: The Populist Response to the Industrialization of Russia," Ph.D. diss., University of California at Berkeley, 1971; Janet Vaillant, "Encountering the West: The Ideological Responses of Aleksei S. Khomiakov and Leopold S. Senghor," Ph.D. diss., Harvard University, 1969; and Boris Ischboldin, *History of the Non-Marxian Russian Socio-Economic Thought* (New Delhi: New Book Society of India, 1971).

8. Two influential explorations of the question of "partial" perspectives are James Clifford, "Introduction: Partial Truths," in *Writing Culture: The Poetics and Politics of Ethnography*, ed. James Clifford and George Marcus (Berkeley and Los Angeles: University of California Press, 1980), pp. 1–26, and *Out There: Marginalization and Contemporary Culture*, ed. R. Ferguson, M. Gever, Trinh Minh-ha, and Cornel West (Cambridge, Mass.: MIT Press, 1990).

9. See, especially, Patricia Hill Collins, "The Outsider Within," *Social Problems* 33, no. 6 (December 1986): 514–32.

10. See chapter 9, pp. 177–78.

11. See especially Cornel West, *Beyond Eurocentrism and Multiculturalism* (Monroe, Me.: Common Courage Press, 1993), and Edward Said, *Orientalism* (New York: Pantheon Books, 1978).

12. Although I had not read her work until my own research was virtually complete, the methods I have used closely resemble those of Dorothy Ross, and I have paraphrased and made use of a number of the formulations she sets out in the introduction to her book, *The Origins of American Social Science* (Cambridge: Cambridge University Press, 1991).

INTRODUCTION

1. The definition of culture used here reflects the influence of social scientists who argue that culture is not only what has been judged the "best," or highest achievement of a particular time period, but a complex of all of the symbols and values that create the ideological frame of reference through which people attempt to deal with the circumstances in which they find themselves. Culture is thus present in social institutions like the family, in creative expressions of art, and in patterns of economic and political activity. It is not composed of static, discrete traits that may be easily transferred from one locale to another. "Culture is constantly changing and transformed, as new forms are created out of old ones." See Clifford Geertz, "From the 'Native's Point of View': On the Nature of Anthropological Understanding," in Geertz, *Local Knowledge: Further Essays in Intrepetive Anthropology* (New York: Basic Books, 1985), pp. 55–70; and Betty J. Craige, *Laying the Ladder Down: The Emergence of Cultural Holism* (Amherst: University of Massachusetts Press, 1992).

2. See especially Teodor Shanin's ground-breaking *The Awkward Class: Political Sociology of Peasantry in a Developing Society, Russia, 1910–1925* (Oxford: Clarendon Press, 1974); and Robert Edelman's incisive discussion of these issues, *Proletarian Peasants: The Revolution of 1905 in Russia's Southwest* (Ithaca, N.Y.: Cornell University Press, 1988).

3. For many years, the classic study of the Russian peasantry was Geroid Robinson's *Rural Russia under the Old Regime* (Berkeley and Los Angeles: University of California Press, 1932), a work that portrayed peasants as an increasingly impoverished socal element, shattering into kulak and proletarian fragments as they encountered the modern capitalist world. Unfortunately, Robinson's book did not stimulate further research. Not a single major English-language investigation of the peasant question appeared until 1968, which saw the publication of *The Peasant in Nineteenth-Century Russia*, edited by W. S. Vucinich (Stanford, Cal.: Stanford University Press). See survey of Soviet and Western scholarship and other recent works cited in "Breaking the Silence," in Esther Kingston-Mann and Timothy Mixter, eds., *Peasant Economy, Culture, and Politics of European Russia, 1800–1921* (Princeton: Princeton University Press, 1992), pp. 1–5.

4. See discussion in Esther Kingston-Mann, *Lenin and the Problem of Marxist Peasant Revolution* (Oxford: Oxford University Press, 1983), pp. 48–54.

5. Alfred Shutz, "The Stranger: An Essay in Social Psychology," *American Journal of Sociology* 49 (1944):499–507.

6. Some interesting recent explorations of this issue are Robert Ellickson, "Property in Land," *Yale Law Journal* 6, no 102 (April 1993): 1317–1400; Michael Trebilcock, "Communal Property Right," *University of Toronto Law Journal* 34, no. 4 (November 1984): 377–420; and Richard Posner, "A Theory of Primitive Society, with Special Reference to Law," *Journal of Law and Economics* 23, no. 1 (1980): 1–53.

7. See Esther Kingston-Mann, "Peasant Communes and Economic Innovation: A Preliminary Inquiry," in Kingston-Mann and Mixter, eds., *Peasant Economy*, pp. 35–36.

CHAPTER ONE
THE TRUE WEST: ENGLAND, FRANCE, AND GERMANY

1. Although English writers of the day tended to avoid the word "peasant," I have nevertheless decided to use it here because to my mind it describes with some accuracy the economic experience of individuals who farmed with the help of their families and in keeping with decisions of a village community, and paid rent or dues to masters or landlords. Neither the term "farmer" nor "small producer" captures the complexity of such economic behavior. See discussion in Jeanette Neeson, "An Eighteenth-Century English Peasantry," in *Protest and Survival: Essays for E. P. Thompson*, J. Rule and R. Malcolmson, eds. (New York: New Press, 1993), pp. 24–26. The discussion that follows relies on a number of scholarly studies of the 1980s and 1990s; it differs significantly from the valuable work of scholars like Jerome Blum, who emphasize the stark dichotomy between backward peasants, communes, and serfs on the one hand, and the imperatives of progress on the other. See Neeson, *Commoners: Common Right, Enclosure and Social Change in England, 1799–1820* (Cambridge: Cambridge University Press, 1993); Mick Reed, "The Peasantry of Nineteenth-Century England: A Neglected Class?" *History Workshop Journal* 18 (1984): 53–76; Mick Reed and R.A.E. Welles, eds., *Class, Conflict and Protest in the English Countryside, 1700–1880* (Cambridge: Frank Cass, 1990); and Jerome Blum, *The End of the Old Order in Rural Europe* (Princeton: Princeton University Press, 1978).

2. See Nicholas Canny, "The Ideology of English Colonization: From Ireland to America," *William and Mary Quarterly* 30, no. 4 (October 1973): 585; David Quinn, *The Elizabethans and the Irish* (Ithaca, N.Y.: Cornell University Press, 1966), p. 161; Francis Jennings, *The Invasion of America: Indians, Colonialism and the Cant of Conquest* (New York: Norton, 1976), p. 7; and Thomas More, *Utopia* (New Haven: Yale University Press, 1964), p. 76.

3. See discussion in Esther Kingston-Mann, "Marxism and Russian Rural Development: Problems of Evidence, Experience and Culture," *The American Historical Review* 86 (October 1981): 731–52.

4. In addition to the works cited above and below, see John Berger, especially "Peasants and Progress," *New Society* 43, no. 796 (January 1978): 10–11, and *Pig Earth* (New York: Pantheon, 1985); Marc Bloch, *French Rural History* (Berkeley: University of California Press, 1966), and *Land and Work in Medieval*

Europe (London: Routledge & Kegan Paul, 1967); Michael Confino, *Systèmes agraires et progrès agricole: L'Assolement triennial en Russie au xvii-e–xix-e siècles* (Paris: Mouton, 1969); R. J. Evans and W. R. Lee, *The German Peasantry* (New York: St. Martin's Press, 1987); George Grantham, "The Persistence of Open-Field Farming in 19th-Century France, *Journal of Economic History* 40 (July 1980): 515–32; Daniel Faucher, "Routine et innovation dans la vie paysanne," *Journal de psychologie normale et pathologique* (1949): 89–103; Boguslaw Galeski, *Basic Concepts of Rural Sociology* (Manchester: Manchester University Press, 1972); Eric Kerridge, *The Agricultural Revolution* (London: Allen & Unwin, 1967); William Parker and Eric Jones, *European Peasants and Their Markets* (Princeton: Princeton University Press, 1975); Teodor Shanin, *The Rules of the Game: Cross-disciplinary Essays on Models in Scholarly Thought* (London: Tavistock Publications, 1972), and *Russia as a Developing Society* (New Haven: Yale University Press, 1985). See also the review articles by Barry Eichengreen, "*The Economic History of Britain Since 1700*: A Review," *Journal of European Economic History* 12, no. 2 (spring 1983): 437–44; Peter Lindert, "Remodeling British Economic History," *Journal of Economic History* 43, no. 4 (December 1983): 986–92; and Jonathan Prude, "Trouble with Economic History," *Comparative Studies in Society and History* 27 (October 1985): 744–54, and notes 5–6.

5. The operation of common and collective property systems as risk-spreading devices in colonial America, medieval England, and elsewhere is discussed in Robert Ellickson, "Property in Land," *Yale Law Journal* 102, no. 6 (April 1993): 1317–1400. See also D. N. McCloskey, "The Persistence of English Common Fields," in Parker and Jones, *European Peasants*, pp. 73–119, and "English Open Fields as Behavior Towards Risk," in *Research in Economic History*, ed. Paul Uselding, vol. 1 (Greenwich, Conn.: Jai Press, 1976), pp. 124–70; Grantham, "The Persistence of Open-Field Farming," pp. 529–31; and R. C. Hoffman, "Medieval Origins of the Common fields," in Parker and Jones, *European Peasants*, pp. 62–63.

6. There is much evidence to indicate that initially, fallow fields were freely used by all members of the community. Eventually, peasant communities established rules to regulate the number and type of animals permitted to graze at any given time, so that peasants with more livestock would not overgraze the area at the expense of their poorer neighbors. A useful discussion of pre-enclosure farming practices is contained in Warren Ault, *Open Field Farming in Medieval England: A Study of Village By-laws* (London: Allen & Unwin, 1972).

7. See, for example, Herman Rebel, *Peasant Classes: The Bureaucratization of Property and Family Relations under Early Habsburg Absolutism, 1511–1636* (Princeton: Princeton University Press, 1983), and David Sabean, *Power in the Blood: Popular and Village Discourse in Early Modern Germany* (Cambridge: Cambridge University Press, 1984).

8. Wolfgang Kaschuba, "Peasants and Others: The Historical Contours of Village Class Society," in *The German Peasantry*, ed. R. J. Evans and R. W. Lee, p. 203.

9. See especially Alan R. H. Baker and R. A. Butlin, *Studies of Field Systems in the British Isles* (Cambridge: Cambridge University Press, 1973), p. 628, cited

in Michael Mazur, "The Dispersion of Holdings in the Open Fields: An Interpretation in Terms of Property Rights," *Journal of European Economic History* 6, no. 2 (1977): 461–71.

10. These practices have been described as by-laws and implicit contracts by Carl Dahlman, *The Open Field System and Beyond: A Property Rights Analysis of an Economic Institution* (New York: Cambridge University Press, 1990), pp. 120–27.

11. See Garrett Hardin, "The Tragedy of the Commons," *Science* 162, no. 3859 (Dec. 13, 1968): 1243–48. The strategies that small producers devised to deal with this difficulty are discussed in Dahlman, *The Open Field System*. See also Ellickson, "Property in Land," pp. 1388–92.

12. Although the English became the standard-bearers of Europe's agricultural transformation, it was in fact the Dutch who pioneered many of the new systems of field use. See Ralph Davis, *The Rise of the Atlantic Economies* (Ithaca, N.Y.: Cornell University Press, 1973), pp. 118–19.

13. Even Jethro Tull's much-praised horse-drawn seed drill was not widely used in England until the very end of the eighteenth century. Stewart Richards, "Agricultural Science in Higher Education: Problems of Identity in Britain's First Chair of Agriculture, Edinburgh, 1790–1831," *Agricultural History Review* 33 (1985): 59.

14. M. A. Havinden, "Agricultural Progress in Open Field Oxfordshire," *Agricultural History Review* 9 (1961): 73–83.

15. G. E. Mingay, "Introduction," in *Arthur Young and His Times*, ed. G. E. Mingay (London: Macmillan, 1975), pp. 98–99.

16. See discussion of the links between community institutions and economic change in the floating of water meadows and "up and down husbandry" in Dahlman, *The Open Field System,* pp. 174–76.

17. Kerridge *The Agricultural Revolution*, p. 16

18. Christopher Hill, *The World Turned Upside Down: Radical Ideas During the English Revolution* (London: Temple Smith, 1972), pp. 103–105, 307; and see also Fenner Brockway, *Britain's First Socialists: The Levellers, Agitators and Diggers of the English Revolution* (New York: Quartet Books, 1980), and Henry Brailsford, *The Levellers and the English Revolution* (Stanford, Cal.: Stanford University Press, 1983).

19. To the tune that in England is called "God Save the Queen," Thomas Spence wrote lyrics to "The Jubilee Hymn," which included the following stanzas: "Hark! how the trumpet's sound / Proclaims the land around / The Jubilee! / Tells all the poor oppress'd / No more they shall be cess'd / Nor landlords more molest / Their property. / Rents t'ourselves now we pay / Dreading no quarter day / Fraught with distress. / Welcome that day draws near / For then our rents we share / Earth's rightful lords we are / Ordain'd for this." See O. D. Rudkin, *Thomas Spence and His Connections* (London: Allen & Unwin, 1927), P. M. Ashraf, *The Life and Times of Thomas Spence* (Newcastle: Frank Graham Publisher, 1983), and Malcolm Chase, *The People's Farm: England's Radical Agrarians 1775–1840* (Oxford: Clarendon Press, 1988).

20. According to P. J. Perry, "one of the remarkable features of high farming is its development by tenant farmers enjoying little or no security." See Perry, "High

Farming in Victorian Britain: Prospect and Retrospect," *Agricultural History* 55, no. 2 (April 1981): 156–66.

21. Quoted in Stuart MacDonald, "Agricultural Improvement and the Neglected Laborer," *Agricultural History Review* 31, part 2 (April 1983): 84.

22. According to MacDonald's intriguing essay, historians have tended to focus too narrowly on the invention as the only important aspect of an innovation process. His study indicates that successful innovation depends at least in part on (1) user modifications introduced by the laborer, and (2) at a later stage, upon the skills of the marketing manager. In the eighteenth century, the crucial role of the intelligent laborer in the innovation process was emphasized in the journal *The Rational Farmer* (1771). See MacDonald, "Agricultural Improvement," pp. 81–90, and E.J.T. Collins, "Harvest Technology and Labor Supply in Britain, 1790–1870," *Economic History Review* 22, series 2 (December 1969): 453–73.

23. See MacDonald, "Agricultural Improvement," p. 83.

24. Marc Bloch, quoted in Michael Confino, *Domaines et seigneurs en Russie vers la fin du xviii-e siècle; étude des structures agraires et de mentalités économiques* (Paris: Institut d'études slaves de l'Université de Paris, 1963), pp. 19 and 76.

25. According to one contemporary observer, farming instructions that targeted agriculturists were aimed at the "Upper extremity" of the educated classes. See discussion in Stewart Richards, "Agricultural Science in Higher Education," p. 59, and Nicholas Goddard, "The Development and Influence of Agricultural Periodicals and Newspapers, 1780–1880," *Agricultural History Review* 31, part 2 (1983): 116–31.

26. Quoted in Mingay, ed., "Introduction," *Arthur Young and His Times*, p. 9.

27. In the eighteenth century and afterward, discussions of enclosure frequently oversimplify the extraordinary complexities of traditional land use. According to Eric Kerridge, "The simple world in which all land was either common or enclosed turns out to be imaginary. Reality was far more complex. Often, large parcels in common fields were enclosed with quicksets (hedges) though no less subject to common rights. Conversely, much open land was not subject to common rights. Bringing the dispersed properties of each person into fewer pieces, freed from all rights of commonage, was called 'putting the land in severalty' in contradistinction to those subject to common rights. . . . Severalty lands were neither common nor enclosed." Kerridge, *The Agricultural Revolution*, pp. 16–17. See also Robert Allen, *Enclosure and the Yeoman* (Oxford: Oxford University Press, 1992), pp. 37–39, and see general discussion in Jerome Blum, "English Parliamentary Enclosures," *Journal of Modern History* 53 (July 1981): 477–504.

28. Ernlé, Lord Rowland, *English Farming: Past and Present* (London: Longmans, Green & Co., 1941), p. 46.

29. See Joyce Appleby, *Economic Thought and Ideology in Seventeenth-Century England* (Princeton: Princeton University Press, 1978), p. 57.

30. According to Humphries, ahistoric stereotypes about male breadwinners and dependent women and children obscured the realities of labor incumbent on every element of the peasant household. Young is quoted in Jane Humphries, "Enclosures, Common Rights, and Women: The Proletarianization of Families in the Late Eighteenth and Early Nineteenth Centuries," *Journal of Economic His-*

tory 50, no. 1 (March 1990): 22. See also Ivy Pinchbeck, *Women Workers and the Industrial Revolution* (New York: Routledge & Kegan Paul, 1972).

31. See Donald McCloskey, "The Prudent Peasant: New Findings on Open Fields," *Journal of Economic History* 51 (June 1991): 51.

32. Joan Thirsk, *Tudor Enclosures* (London: Routledge & Kegan Paul, 1970), p. 21.

33. See discussion in Neeson, "An Eighteenth-Century English Peasantry," pp. 58–59.

34. Neeson, *Commoners*, p. 130, and James Scott, *The Weapons of the Weak: Forms of Everyday Resistance in Peasant Life* (New Haven: Yale University Press, 1985).

35. See, for example, Havinden, "Agricultural Progress in Open Field Oxfordshire," pp. 73–83.

36. Mingay, *A Social History of the English Countryside* (London: Routledge, 1990), p. 50.

37. Young is here referring to Royston, near Hertfordshire. Quoted in Mingay, ed., *Arthur Young and His Times*, pp. 99–111.

38. According to Robert Allen, Young's data yielded similar conclusions for France and Ireland. As Allen demonstrates, Young's enthusiasm for enclosure was due to the use of new agricultural techniques, or to the payment of high rents, rather than crop yields. See Robert Allen and Cormac Ó Gráda, "On the Road with Arthur Young: English, Irish, and French Agriculture During the Industrial Revolution," *Journal of Economic History* 48 (March 1988): 116, and Allen, *Enclosure and the Yeoman: Agricultural Development of the South Midlands 1450–1850* (Oxford: Oxford University Press, 1992). In Russia, the enclosed private farms established a century later by the tsarist regime retained strip cultivation, and were not any more "improved" than the traditional peasant communes. See discussion in Dorothy G. Atkinson, *The End of the Russian Land Commune, 1905–1930* (Stanford, Cal.: Stanford University Press, 1983), pp. 71–100, and chapter 8, p. 177.

39. Quoted in Mingay, ed., *Arthur Young and His Times*, p. 111.

40. A similar kind of tunnel vision afflicted European colonists who ignored the complexities of the Indian farming practices they observed. Although Samuel de Champlain, Thomas Morton, and John Winthrop noted the use of fertilizer, crop rotation, and a three-field system by Indian cultivators, the image of Indians as lazy and indifferent to improvement would nevertheless prevail and served to justify dispossession. See Howard Russell, *Indian New England before the Mayflower* (Hanover, N.H.: University Press of New England, 1980), pp. 10, 11, 166; Peter Thomas, "Contrastive Subsistence Strategies and Land Use as Factors for Understanding Indian-White Relations in New England," *Ethnohistory* 23, no. 1 (winter 1976): 1–10; and William Cronon, *Changes in the Land: Indians, Colonists and the Ecology of New England* (New York: Hill and Wang, 1985), pp. 55–56.

41. According to the evidence put forward by the nineteenth-century historical economist T. E. Cliffe-Leslie, once traditional claims to land use were eliminated, tenants could easily farm themselves out of their holdings. Frequently, tenants

abided by the precept "Don't farm too well," and exhausted the land in pursuit of short-term gains in the last years before their leases expired. See Cliffe-Leslie, *Land Systems and Industrial Economy of Ireland, England and Continental Countries* (London: 1870), p. 133.

42. Adam Smith, *The Wealth of Nations* (New York: Modern Library, 1937), p. 187.

43. Smith, *Wealth*, p. 390.

44. Smith, *Wealth*, p. 783, and see also Paul McNulty, "Adam Smith's Concept of Labor," *Journal of the History of Ideas* 34, no. 3 (1973): 345–66.

45. According to Jacob Viner, "Smith recognized every possible impulse and motive to action included under self-interest except a deliberate intention to promote the welfare of others than one's self." Viner, *The Long View and the Short: Studies in Economic Theory and Policy* (Glencoe, Ill.: Free Press, 1958), pp. 227–28. See also *Wealth*, pp. 66–7.

46. Quoted in Shearer Davis Bowman, *Masters and Lords: Mid-19th-Century U.S. Planters and Prussian Junkers* (Oxford: Oxford University Press, 1993), p. 195.

47. The popularity of Ferguson's works continued well into the nineteenth century, with the appearance of an Italian edition in 1807, a Boston edition in 1890, an Edinburgh printing in 1814, and a Philadelphia printing in 1819. Russell's equally universalistic and private-property-oriented study of medieval Europe was reprinted thirty-nine times between 1779 and 1871 in the United Kingdom and United States. See discussion in Ronald Meek, *Social Science and the Ignoble Savage* (Cambridge: Cambridge University Press, 1976), pp. 152–53.

48. Quoted in Carol Rose, "The Comedy of the Commons: Custom, Commerce, and Inherently Public Property," *University of Chicago Law Review* 53 (summer 1986): 711.

49. See Humphries, "Enclosure," pp. 28–30, and especially K.D.M. Snell, *Annals of the Labouring Poor: Social Change and Agrarian England 1660–1900* (Cambridge: Cambridge University Press, 1985), pp. 170ff.

50. Neeson, "The Opponents of Enclosure in Eighteenth-Century Northhamptonshire," *Past and Present* 105 (November 1984): 134.

51. Quoted in Bob Heys, "John Clare and Enclosure," *John Clare Society Journal* 6 (July 1987): 10–18.

52. Arthur Young, *Travels in France During the Years 1787–1789* (Cambridge: Cambridge University Press, 1950), p. 292.

53. After the 1600s when the state joined the nobility as appropriator of peasant output, by imposing a heavy direct tax (the *taille*) and a tax on commodities like salt (the *gabelle*), peasant survival was frequently linked to the rent of land as a supplement to their meager holdings.

54. Patrick O'Brien and Caglar Keyder, *Economic Growth in Britain and France, 1780–1914: Two Paths to the Twentieth Century* (London: Allen & Unwin, 1978), p. 133 and passim. See also William Hagen, "Capitalism and the Countryside in Early Modern Europe: Interpretation, Models, Debates," *Agricultural History* 62, no. 1 (winter 1988): 13–50.

55. These figures were taken from a bibliography compiled in 1810. See Michel Morineau, "Y a-t-il une révolution agricole en France au xviiie siècle?" *Revue Historique* 239, part 2 (1968): 299.

56. Denis Diderot, *Dictionnaire philosophique* (London: 1824), p. 327. Voltaire's *Épitre sur l'Agriculture* (1761) portrayed the joys of the English countryside as a place where individuals could peacefully pursue new agricultural methods, enclose common lands, and in general contribute to the nation's wealth and prosperity. See discussion in Kingsley Martin, *French Liberal Thought in the 18th Century: A Study of Political Ideas from Bayle to Condorcet* (London: Phoenix House, 1962), p. 234. A. J. Bourde, *The Influence of England on the French Agronomes, 1750–1789* (Cambridge: Cambridge University Press, 1953), p. 187.

57. Quoted in Harvey Chisick, *The Limits of Reform in the Enlightenment* (Princeton: Princeton University Press, 1981), p. 70.

58. Quoted in Harry C. Payne, *The Philosophes and the People* (New Haven: Yale University Press, 1976), p. 96. Voltaire nevertheless established schools for peasants at his Ferney estate and occasionally expressed more moderate views. Toward the end of his life, he also noted: "the great misfortune of the peasantry is stupidity and another is neglect; no one thinks of them except when the plague devastates them and their herds."

59. Montesquieu, *Oeuvres Complètes*, vol. 3 (Paris: Nagel, 1950), p. 302; and Payne, *The Philosophes*, p. 28.

60. Quoted in Harry C. Payne, "Elite vs. Popular Mentality in the 18th Century," *Historical Reflections* 2, no. 2 (summer 1975): 79.

61. Quoted in Chisick, *The Limits of Reform*, p. 251. More positive comments on peasants occur in the writings of Rousseau; even Diderot advised Catherine the Great to search for wisdom in the huts of the people. But such suggestions did not usually touch the questions of rural development. See Diderot, *Mémoires pour Catherine II*, ed. Paul Verniere (Paris: Garnier Freres, 1966), pp. 129, 167.

62. Quoted in Albert Hirschmann's brilliant account of the apotheosis of middle-class values. As Hirschman has shown, this view of the middle class was itself the product of a dramatic ideological shift from earlier views of the bourgeois *gentilhomme* as clumsy, crass, and given to violence. Hirschmann, *The Passions and the Interests: Political Arguments for Capitalism before Its Triumph* (Princeton: Princeton University Press, 1979), p. 71.

63. Martin, *French Liberal Thought*, pp. 231–32.

64. Elizabeth Fox-Genovese, *The Origins of Physiocracy: Revolution and Social Order in Eighteenth-Century France* (Ithaca, N.Y.: Cornell University Press, 1976), p. 71.

65. Quoted in J.Q.C. Mackrell, *The Attack on "Feudalism" in Eighteenth-Century France* (London: Routledge & Kegan Paul, 1973), p. 112.

66. See discussion in Mackrell, *The Attack on "Feudalism,"* p. 14, and Georges Weulersse, *Le Mouvement physiocratique en France*, vol. 1 (Paris: Mouton, 1910), p. 408, and vol. 2, pp. 5, 731–34.

67. Quoted in Chisick, *The Limits of Reform*, p. 163.

68. Burke, *Reflections on the Revolution in France* (New York: Liberal Arts Press, 1985), p. 241.

69. See, for example, Quesnay's *General Maxims for the Economics of Government of an Agricultural Kingdom* in Ronald Meek, *The Economics of Physiocracy: Essays and Translations* (Cambridge, Mass.: Harvard University Press, 1963), p. 232. The Physiocrats argued that all would eventually benefit from such

changes. As the Physiocrat Roubaud pointed out, employers would need the services of wage laborers and would therefore pay them well. However, such questions were not Roubaud's primary concern. In his words, "Si les travaux des champs ne suffis pas a le nourrir, qu'il y ajoute quelque métier. Il n'a pas besoin d'être propriétaire." Quoted in Weulersse, *Le Mouvement physiocratique*, vol. 2, p. 466.

70. Quoted in Meek, *The Economics of Physiocracy*, p. 235. See also the illuminating discussion of Gianni Vaggi, *The Economics of Francois Quesnay* (Houndmills, Basingstoke, Hampshire: Macmillan, 1987).

71. Mackrell, *The Attack on "Feudalism,"* p. 112.

72. Vaggi, *The Economics of Francois Quesnay*, p. 144, and see also pp. 181–88.

73. O'Brien and Keyder, *Economic Growth in Britain and France*, pp. 128–33.

74. Pierre de Saint Jacob, *Les Paysans de la Bourgogne du nord au dernier siècle de l'ancien regime* (Dijon: Bernigaud et Privat, 1960), pp. 87–92, and Florence Gauthier, *La Voie paysanne dans la Revolution francaise: L'Exemple de picard* (Paris: F. Maspero, 1977), pp. 95–131. I am indebted to David Hunt for directing me toward the work of these scholars.

75. With each village maintaining its own common herd, peasants tried to ensure that the number of animals in the common herd remained the same throughout the period when they grazed on the fallow land. During this period (called the *parc*) the village rotated the herd so that the strips on which the *parc* began in a period of short summer nights and therefore of little manure would also be the ones on which the *parc* ended in the late autumn, when nights were at their longest. The purpose of this system was to ensure that all would benefit from the equal distribution of manure. Gauthier, *La Voie paysanne*, pp. 61–82, 95–99, and P. N. Jones, *The Peasantry in the French Revolution* (New York: Cambridge University Press, 1988), pp. 53–54 and 129–30.

76. Georges Lefebvre, *Les Paysans du Nord pendant la Revolution francaise* (Paris: A. Colin, 1972), pp. 201–2, 209–10; and see also the discussion of peasant efforts at agricultural improvement in Jones, *The Peasantry in the French Revolution*, pp. 53–54, 128.

77. See discussion in George Grantham, "The Persistence of Open-Field Farming," p. 23

78. Allen and Ó Gráda, "On the Road with Arthur Young," p. 116. See also Arthur Young, *Travels*, p. 291.

79. Marc Bloch, quoted in Bourde, *The Influence of England*, p. 35.

80. Bourde, *The Influence of England*, pp. 47ff.

81. See discussion in Emilio Willems, "Peasantry and City: Cultural Persistence and Change in Historical Perspective. A European Case," *The American Anthropologist* 72 (April 1970): 539–41, and B. H. Slicher Van Bath, *The Agrarian History of Western Europe* (London: E. Arnold, 1963), p. 240 and p. 244.

82. See general discussion in Heide Wunder, *Die bauerliche Gemeinde in Deutschland* (Göttingen: Vandenhoek & Ruprecht, 1985), pp. 20–24.

83. See Kaschuba, "Peasants and Others" in *The German Peasantry*, pp. 242–49, and W. R. Lee, "Family and 'Modernization': The Peasant Family and Social Change in Nineteenth-Century Bavaria," in *The German Family: Essays on the*

Social History of the Family in 19th- and 20th-Century Germany, ed. R. J. Evans and W. R. Lee (London: Croom Helm, 1981), p. 104, and especially, Martine Segalen, " 'Sein Teil haben': Geschwisterbeziehungen in einem egalitaren Vererbungssystem," in *Emotionen und materielle Interessen: Sozialanthropologische und historische Beitrage zur Familienforschung,* ed. Hans Medick and David Sabean (Göttingen: Vandenhoeck & Ruprecht, 1984), pp. 181–98, and Wilhelm Abel, *Geschichte der deutschen Landwirtschaft vom fruhen Mittelalter bis zum 19 Jahrhundert* (Stuttgart: E. Ulmer, 1967).

84. Heide Wunder, "Peasant Organization and Class Conflict in East and West Germany," *Past and Present* 78 (February 1978): 48–49.

85. See H. E. Bodeker, "Das staatswissenschaftliche Fächersystem in 18. Jahrhundert," in *Wissenschaften im Zeitalter der Aufklärung,* ed. R. Vierhaus (Göttingen: Vandenhoeck & Ruprecht, 1985), pp. 142–62, Albion Small, *The Cameralists: The Pioneers of German Social Policy* (New York: Burt Franklin, 1909), pp. 5–20, and Erhard Dittrich, *Die Deutschen und österreichischen Kameralisten* (Darmstadt: Wissenschaftliche Buch Geselleschaft, 1974).

86. See especially Theodor von den Goltz, *Geschichte der deutschen Landwirtschaft,* vol. 1 (Aalen: Scientia, 1963), pp. 319–20, and Hans Rosenberg, *Bureaucracy, Aristocracy and Autocracy: The Prussian Experience, 1660–1815* (Cambridge, Mass.: Harvard University Press, 1966).

87. J. G. Gagliardo, *From Pariah to Patriot: The Changing Image of the German Peasant, 1770–1840* (Lexington: University Press of Kentucky, 1969), pp. 128–31. Karl Friedrich's Physiocratic adviser, Johann August Schlettwein, struggled with little success to promote both free trade and free labor, but soon abandoned these politically explosive issues for the less controversial question of technological improvement. See Helen Liebel, *Enlightened Bureaucracy vs. Enlightened Despotism in Baden, 1750–1792* (Philadelphia: American Philosphical Society, 1965), p. 49.

88. See discussion in Kenneth Carpenter, *Dialogue in Political Economy: Translations from and into German in the 18th Century* (Boston: Kress Library of Business and Economics, 1977), pp. 3–8, 52.

89. Gagliardo, *From Pariah to Patriot,* pp. 128–31.

90. Carl William Hasek, *The Introduction of Adam Smith's Doctrines into Germany* (New York: Columbia University Press, 1925), p. 87.

91. Quoted in Klaus Epstein, *The Genesis of German Conservatism* (Princeton: Princeton University Press, 1966), p. 181. Susan Mahoney, "A Good Constitution: Social Science in Eighteenth-Century Göttingen" (Ph.D. diss., University of Chicago, 1982), p. 155.

92. By 1777, *The Wealth of Nations* had already been reviewed in the Göttingen *Anzeigen.* See discussion of Smith's impact in W. Trene, "Adam Smith in Deutschland," in *Deutschland und Europa: Festschrift fur Hans Rothfels,* ed. W. Conze (Dusseldorf: Droste-Verlag, 1951), pp. 101–33, and Mahoney, "A Good Constitution," pp. 34 and 66.

93. Mahoney, "A Good Constitution," p. 133.

94. Quoted in Gagliardo, *From Pariah to Patriot,* p. 133.

95. An extremely useful study of German responses to Western economics is contained in Keith Tribe, *Governing Economy: The Reformation of German Eco-*

nomic Discourse, 1760–1840 (Cambridge: Cambridge University Press, 1988). See also W. Trene, "Adam Smith," pp. 101–133.

96. See Hasek, *The Introduction of Adam Smith's Doctrines*, p. 112, and Mahoney, "A Good Constitution," p. 186.

97. See John Gagliardo, *From Pariah to Patriot*, p. 33, and discussion of Justi in Tribe, *Governing Economy*, pp. 55–99, and Small, *The Cameralists*, p. 458.

98. Small, *The Cameralists*, pp. 514, 545–46.

99. Schumpeter, *A History of Theoretical Analysis* (New York: Routledge, 1974), p. 172.

100. Marc Raeff, "The Well-Ordered Police State and the Development of Modernity in 17th-and 18th-Century Europe: An Attempt at a Comparative Approach," *The American Historical Review* 80 (December 1975): 1230.

101. See the insightful discussion in Tribe, *Governing Economy*, p. 69.

102. Frederick did not view such constraints as a threat to property rights; an individual without private property rights was in his view no better than a slave. See Walther Hubatsch, *Frederick the Great of Prussia: Absolutism and Administration* (London: Thames and Hudson, 1975), pp. 170–73.

103. Gagliardo, *From Pariah to Patriot*, pp. 274–76.

104. The book's editor was H. C. Hirzel, a physician from Zurich and a member of the local *Natürforschende Gesellschaft*. The book's original title was *Die Wirtschaft eines philosophischen Bauers*. It was translated into French in 1762 under the title *Le Socrate rustique*. P. Johnstone, "Turnips and Romanticism," *Agricultural History* 12 (July 1938): 224–55; 11 (April 1937): 80–95.

105. Mirabeau's statement appeared in *Le Socrate rustique*, vol. 1 (1777), pp. 305–6. See Paul Johnstone, "Turnips and Romanticism," pp. 224–55.

106. The complex historical background of the "German" position cannot be elaborated here. A useful discussion of the intellectual and cultural shifts that generated positive evaluations of the peasantry is contained in Gagliardo's *From Pariah to Patriot*.

107. Mack Walker, *German Home Towns, Community, State and General Estate, 1648–1871* (Ithaca, N.Y.: Cornell University Press, 1971), pp. 186–87.

108. Even German conservatives tended to attribute the peasantry's defects to ignorance and brutal treatment rather than natural inferiority. See Klaus Epstein, *The Genesis of German Conservatism*, p. 210

109. See discussion in Esther Kingston-Mann, *Lenin and the Problem of Marxist Peasant Revolution* (Oxford: Oxford University Press, 1983), and "Marxism and Russian Rural Development," pp. 731–52.

110. See Gagliardo, *From Pariah to Patriot*. It is interesting to compare Gagliardo's study with Clive Dewey's essay on a later period in European economic history, entitled "The Rehabilitation of the Peasant Proprietor in Nineteenth-Century Economic Thought," *History of Political Economy* 6, no. 1 (spring 1974): 17–47.

111. I am grateful to Keith Tribe for sharing with me his view of the utopian character of both liberal and Cameralist theory in the eighteenth and early nineteenth centuries. (Personal communication, August 14, 1989).

112. Georges Sorel, *Reflections on Violence* (New York: B. W. Huebsch, 1908). See discussion in Peter Berger, *Pyramids of Sacrifice: Political Ethics and Social Change* (New York: Basic Books, 1974), p. 17.

113. See, for example, Emily Rosenberg, *The Spreading of the American Dream: American Economic and Cultural Expansion, 1890–1945* (New York: Hill and Wang, 1982).

CHAPTER TWO
IN THE LIGHT AND SHADOW OF THE WEST:
PROGRESS IN THE AGE OF ENLIGHTENMENT

1. This chapter is not intended to survey the whole of eighteenth-century Russian intellectual history, even on the topic of rural development. My goal is to illuminate some aspects of Westernization in the Russian context which have not been explored by other scholars. I have benefited from the scholarly achievements of Michael Confino and Marc Raeff, and my view of eighteenth-century social and political history has been much influenced by the work of John LeDonne and by a valuable dissertation by T. Wilson Augustine, "The Economic Attitudes and Opinions Expressed by the Russian Nobility in the Great Commission of 1767" (Ph.D. diss., Columbia University, 1969). See especially, Michael Confino, *Domaines et seigneurs en Russie vers la fin du xviii-e siècle; étude des structures agraires et de mentalités économiques* (Paris: Institut d'études slaves de l'Université de Paris, 1963), and *Systèmes agraires et progrès agricole: L'assolement triennial en Russia aux xviii-e–xix-e siècle; étude d'économie et de sociologie rurales* (Paris: Mouton, 1969); and also Marc Raeff, *The Well-Ordered Police State: Social and Institutional Change through Law in the Germanies and Russia, 1600–1800* (New Haven: Yale University Press, 1983), and *Political Ideas and Institutions in Imperial Russia* (Boulder, Col.: Westview Press, 1994); Augustine, "Notes Toward a Portrait of the Eighteenth-Century Russian Nobility," *Canadian Slavic Studies* 4, no. 3 (fall 1970): 373–425.

2. It is exceedingly rare to find a major work of modern English-language, Russian or Soviet scholarship dealing with the pre-Emancipation era which fails to identify "Westernization" with beneficial change. Arcadius Kahan's two essays ("The Costs of 'Westernization' in Russia: The Gentry and the Economy in Russian History," in *The Structure of Russian History: Interpretive Essays*, ed. Michael Cherniavsky [New York: Random House, 1970], pp. 224–50; and "Continuity in Economic Activity and Policy during the Post-Petrine Period in Russia," *Journal of Economic History* 25, no.1 [March 1965]: 61–85) do not focus on the impact of Western economics. Marc Raeff's complex and instructive discussion, *The Well-Ordered Police State*, does not center on the issue of "Westernization" and is not primarily concerned with economic issues.

3. Arcadius Kahan, *The Plow, the Hammer, and the Knout: An Economic History of Eighteenth-Century Russia* (Chicago: University of Chicago Press, 1985), p. 45.

4. Nina Cornell, "The Role of the Nobility in Agricultural Change in Russia during the Reign of Catherine II" (Ph.D. dissertation, University of Illinois, 1972), pp. 55–7, and Ester Boserup, *The Conditions of Agricultural Growth: The Economics of Agrarian Change under Population Pressure* (Chicago: Aldine Pub. Co., 1965).

5. According to N. S. Rubinshtein, the area under cultivation expanded by 60–100% between 1775–1800. See *Sel'skoe khoziastvo Rossii vo vtoroi polovine xviii v.* (Moscow: 1957), pp. 321–22.

212 NOTES TO PAGES 35-40

6. Confino, *Domaines et seigneurs*, pp. 139–41; see also John LeDonne, *Ruling Russia: Politics and Administration in the Age of Absolutism* (Princeton: Princeton University Press, 1984), pp. 130–31.

7. Peasants in these areas made use of the short growing season to clear the land of trees and to enrich it with wood ash from the timber they had cut. Peasants then planted grain (usually rye) and farmed their fields until the soil was exhausted. At that point, they went on to cultivate other burnt-out patches of land, which were prepared beforehand.

8. See general discussion of subsistence/crisis strategies in Steven Hoch, *Serfdom and Social Control in Russia* (Chicago: University of Chicago Press, 1986), pp. 15–64.

9. The Russian term for commune is *mir* or *obschina*. See the useful discussion by Steven A. Grant, "*Obshchina* and *Mir*," *Slavic Review* 35, no. 4 (1976): 636–51, and Carsten Goehrke, *Die Theorien über die Entstehung und Entwicklung des "Mir"* (Wiesbaden: O. Harassowitz, 1964).

10. The internecine conflicts of peasant communities are emphasized in Hoch, *Serfdom and Social Control*, pp. 133–86, and see also the introductory chapters of Stephen Frank, "Cultural Conflict and Criminality in Rural Russia, 1861–1900" (Ph.D. dissertation, Brown University, 1987).

11. Under the *barshchina* system, only a portion of the estate's land (usually the smaller portion) was used by peasants for their own needs. On the bulk of the estate (the *demesne*) they performed labor for a time period set by their masters.

12. Robert E. Jones, *Provincial Development in Russia: Catherine II and Jakob Sievers* (New Brunswick, N.J.: Rutgers University Press, 1984), p. 68.

13. See the valuable discussion by Edgar Melton, "Enlightened Seignorialism and Its Dilemmas in Serf Russia, 1750–1830," *Journal of Modern History* 62 (December 1990): 681–82. Melton emphasizes the overriding concern of serfowners with the maintenance of order. He argues that they were well aware that in order to achieve this end, they needed to provide peasants with protection as well as some minimum level of economic security. But see also Wallace Daniel, "Conflict Between Economic Vision and Economic Reality: The Case of M. M. Shcherbatov," *Slavonic and East European Review* 67, no. 1 (January 1989): 47–48.

14. Existing property law and records of ownership were in any case quite murky until the last decades of the eighteenth century. See discussion in A. V. Romanovich-Slavatinskii, *Dvorianstvo v Rossii ot nachala xviii veka do otmeny krepostnogo prava* (Kiev: 1912), pp. 244–60; Jones, *Provincial Development*, 110–111; and Ralph Blanshard, "A Proposal for Social Reform in the Reign of Catherine II" (Ph.D. diss., SUNY-Binghamton, 1972), pp. 191–92.

15. Confino, *Domaines*, pp. 139–41.

16. See Michael Confino, "La Politique du tutelle: Des seigneurs russes envers leur paysans vers la fin du xvii siècle," *Revue des études Slaves* 37 (1960): 47–49.

17. In 1808, one of serfowner P. A. Koshkarov's harem girls, caught running away with a groom, was severely beaten and forced to sit on a chair for a whole month, an iron collar with spokes around her neck preventing her from turning her head. There is no indication that the groom survived the severe beating he received. In the late eighteenth and early nineteenth centuries, serfowners in increasing numbers freely sold families and individual family members—particu-

larly young girls and boys—at slave markets in St. Petersburg and Moscow, and escalated their financial demands with relative indifference to peasant ability to pay. As Rodney Bohac has shown, the serfowner N. S. Gagarin increased *obrok* obligations by 400 percent on his massive Manuilov estate in Tver province between 1810 and 1814; payments were doubled between 1813 and 1814 alone. See V. I. Semevskii, *Krest'ianskii vopros v Rossii v xviii i pervoi polovine xix veka* vol. 1 (St. Petersburg: 1888), pp. 22, 198; Peter Kolchin, *Unfree Labor: American Slavery and Russian Serfdom* (Cambridge, Mass.: Belknap Press of Harvard University Press, 1987), pp. 124–25; and Bohac, "Everyday Forms of Resistance: Serf Opposition to Gentry Exactions, 1800–1861," in *Peasant Economy*, p. 244.

18. E. Denisoff, "Aux origines de l'église russe autocéphale," *Revue des études Slaves* 23 (1947): 66–88, and the insightful observations of J. H. Billington, *The Icon and the Axe: An Interpretive History of Russian Culture* (New York: Random House, 1970), pp. 69–71.

19. P. I. Alefirenko, *Krest'ianskoe dvizhenie i krest'ianskii vopros* (Moscow: 1958), p. 519. An interesting discussion of the popular legends that related to the reign of Peter the Great is Michael Cherniavsky's *Tsar and People: Studies in Russian Myths* (New York: Random House, 1969). For a careful discussion of the unremitting government emphasis on regulation and regimentation during this period, see also E. V. Anisimov, *The Reforms of Peter the Great: Progress Through Coercion in Russia*, trans. John T. Alexander (Armonk, N.Y.: M. E. Sharpe, 1993).

20. From the time of Peter I, every Russian empress except Alexander III's Danish bride was of German origin.

21. See discussion of Schlözer and the University of Göttingen in chapter 1, pp. 27-28; and S. L. Peshtich, *Russkaia istoriografiia xvii veka*, vol. 3 (Leningrad: 1965), pp. 210–42.

22. J. L. Black, *Citizens for the Fatherland: Education, Educators and Pedagogical Ideals in Eighteenth-Century Russia* (New York: Columbia University Press, 1979), p. 57.

23. See, for example, Raeff, "Les Slaves, les Allemands et les 'Lumières,' " *Canadian Slavic Studies* 1, no. 4 (1967): 521–51; and Raeff, "The Well-Ordered Police State," 1221–43.

24. See discussion of Justi in chapter 1, p. 28.

25. Pososhkov's views are discussed in A. Brikner, "Pososhkov kak ekonomist," in *Ivan Pososhkov: Sochinenie*, vol. 1 (St. Petersburg: 1876), pp. 258–78; L. R. Lewitter, "Ivan Tikhonovich Pososhkov and the 'Spirit of Capitalism,' " *Slavic and East European Review* 51 (1973): 524–53; C. B. O'Brien, "Ivan Pososhkov: Russian Critic of Mercantilist Principles," *American Slavic and East European Review* 14 (1955): 503–11; and Blanshard, "A Proposal for Social Reform in the Reign of Catherine II," p. 52.

26. See discussion in Alefirenko, *Krest'ianskoe dvizhenie i krest'ianskii vopros*, pp. 512–13, and Brikner, "Pososhkov kak ekonomist," p. 267.

27. Brikner, "Pososhkov kak ekonomist," pp. 260–61.

28. P. I. Alefirenko, "Ekonomicheskie vzgliady V. N. Tatishcheva," *Voprosy istorii* 12 (1948): 89–97; Blanshard, "A Proposal for Social Reform," pp. 49–50; and I. S. Bak, "Ekonomicheskie vozzreniia V. N. Tatishcheva," *Istoricheskie zapiski* 54 (1955): 362–81.

29. See I. S. Bak, "Ekonomicheskie vozzreniia M. V. Lomonosova," *Problemy ekonomiki* 4 (1940): 131–43; and P. N. Berkov, "Lomonosov i Lifliandskaia ekonomiia," in *Lomonosov: Sbornik statei i materialov,* ed. A. I. Andreev and L. B. Modzalevskii, vol. 2 (Moscow-Leningrad: 1946), pp, 271–76.

30. Even the would-be English tutor enjoyed significant economic advantages. According to one émigré to Russia, "In summer I be clerk to a butcher at Cronstadt, and in winter I teaches English to the Russian nobility's children." Ernest J. Simmons, *English Literature and Culture in Russia (1553–1840)* (New York: Octagon Books, 1935), p. 33.

31. The plays and poems of Denis Fonvizin satirized the fascination with French style among Russia's Francophile upper classes. See discussion in Shchipanov, *Izbrannye proizvedeniia russkikh myslitelei vtoroi poloviny xviii veka,* vol. 1 (Moscow: 1952), p. 30, and Dukes, *Catherine the Great and the Russian Nobility,* p. 32–33; see also Raeff, "Les Slaves," pp. 521–31, and David J. Welsh, *Russian Comedy 1765–1823* (The Hague: Mouton, 1966), pp. 49–50.

32. Andrei Bolotov, *Zhizn' i prikliucheniia Andreia Bolotova, opisannye samim im dlia svoikh potomkov,* 4 vols. (St. Petersburg: 1870–73), vol. 2, p. 318.

33. See discussion in Georg Säcke, "Der Einfluss Englands auf die politische Ideologie der russischen Gesellschaft in der 2. Halfte des xviii Jahrhunderts," *Archiv für Kulturgeschichte* 39 (1941): 85–86.

34. Erich Donnert, "Russische Studenten an Englischen Universitäten im 18. Jahrhundert," *Wegenetz Europaischen Geistes,* ed. R. G. Plaschka and K. Mack (Munich: R. Oldenbourg, 1987), pp. 127–33, and Georg Säcke, "Die Moskauer Nachschrift der Vorlesungen von Adam Smith," *Zeitschrift für Nationaloekonomie* 9 (1939): 351–56. See also A. G. Cross, *"By the Banks of the Thames": Russians in Eighteenth-Century Britain* (Newtonville, Mass.: Oriental Research Partners, 1980).

35. John Halit Brown, "A Provincial Landowner: A. T. Bolotov, 1738–1833" (Ph.D. diss., Princeton University, 1976), pp. 109–12.

36. See Philip Clendenning, "Eighteenth-Century Russian Translations of Western Economic Works," *Journal of European Economic History* 1 (winter 1972): 745–53.

37. The following discussion is much influenced by Michael Confino's brilliant essay, "La Politique du tutelle," *Revue des études Slaves* 37 (1960): 39–69. A useful discussion of the Imperial Free Economic Society's later activities is contained in Joan Pratt, "The Russian Free Economic Society" (Ph.D. diss., University of Missouri–Columbia, 1983).

38. Shchipanov, *Izbrannye proizvedeniia,* vol. 2, p. 549.

39. Shchipanov, *Izbrannye proizvedeniia,* vol. 2, pp. 8–9. See also *Sbornik imperatorskogo russkogo istoricheskago obshchestva* 32 (St. Petersburg: 1867–1916): 87–89, cited hereafter as *SIRIO*; V. V. Oreshkin, *Vol'noe ekonomicheskoe obshchestvo 1765–1917* (Moscow: 1963), pp. 62–6; and see also Säcke, "Der Einfluss Englands," p. 93.

40. Golitsyn, quoted in A. I. Pashkov, *Istoriia russkoi ekonomicheskoi mysli,* vol. 1 (Moscow: 1955), p. 532, and see also I. S. Bak, "Dmitrii Alekseevich Goli-

tsyn (Filosofskie, obshchestvenno-politicheskie i ekonomicheskie vozzreniia)."
Istoricheskie zapiski 16 (1948): 258–72.

41. Quoted in A. I. Khodnev, *Istoriia imperatorskogo vol'nogo ekono-micheskogo obshchestva* (St. Petersburg: 1865), pp. 24–25, and see also V. I. Semevskii, *Krest'ianskii vopros*, vol. 1, p. 48.

42. Quoted in V. V. Mavrodin, *Klassovaia bor'ba i obshchestvanno-politicheskaia mysl' v Rossii v xviii v* (Leningrad: 1964), p. 170; and see also *Trudy imperatorskogo vol'nogo ekonomicheskogo obshchestva* (cited hereafter as *TIVEO*) 8 (1765): 51–52.

43. Neither Catherine nor her advisers had read Mercier before he arrived. After their first (and last) meeting with him, Mercier waited in vain for another audience and eventually left Russia unnoticed by Catherine or her adviser Count Panin. See I. K. Luppol, "The Empress and the Philosophe," *Catherine the Great*, ed. Marc Raeff (New York: Hill and Wang, 1972), pp. 53–54, and Albert Lortholary, *Les "Philosophes" du xviii-e siècle et la Russie* (Paris: Editions contemporains, Boivic, 1951), pp. 25–26, pp. 181–83.

44. See chapter 1, pp. 19–20, 28–29. The work of Justi was translated by Denis Fonvizin, who was secretary to Count Panin. See discussion in Conrad Grau, "Zur Ideologie Geschichte in Russland und zu den deutsch-russischen Beziehungen in den sechziger/siebziger Jahren des 18 Jh.," *Jahrbuch für Geschichte der sozialistischen Länder Europas* 23, no. 2 (April 1979): 83–97.

45. Quoted in W. F. Reddaway, ed., *Documents of Catherine the Great: The Correspondence with Voltaire and the Instruction of 1767 in the English Text of 1768* (Cambridge: Cambridge University Press, 1931), p. xxiii.

46. Thomas Masaryk, *The Spirit of Russia: Studies in History, Literature and Philosophy* (London: Allen & Unwin, 1919), p. 72.

47. Many of these ideas came from the writings of Bielefeld. See, for example, articles 296 and 297, in B. D. Dmytryshyn, "The Economic Content of the 1767 'Nakaz' of Catherine II," *Slavic Review* 19, no. 1 (February 1960): 1–9; Nicholas V. Riasanovsky, *A Parting of the Ways: Government and the Educated Public in Russia, 1801–1855* (Oxford: Oxford University Press, 1976), p. 17; and Säcke, "Die Einfluss Englands," pp. 85–86.

48. Among the useful discussions of the Assembly and the provincial instructions collected by its delegates is Robert Givens, "Supplication and Reform in the Instructions of the Nobility," *Canadian-American Slavic Studies* 11, no. 4 (1977): 483–502.

49. David Ransel has suggested that the response to Catherine's 1767 effort to "test the waters" for possible reform convinced her how politically dangerous it was to risk alienating conservatives among the middle and lesser ranks of the nobility. Ransel, *The Politics of Catherinian Russia* (New Haven: Yale University Press, 1975), p. 194. See also N. M. Druzhinin, *Absoliutizm v Rossii xvii–xviii vv: Sbornik statei k semidesiatiletiiu so dnia rozhdeniia i sorokopiatiletiiu nauchnoi pedagogicheskoi deiatel'nosti V. V. Kafengauza* (Moscow: 1964), p. 442.

50. Donald Van Lare, "Tula Province in the Eighteenth Century: The Deputy Instructions to the Legislative Commission of 1767 as a Source of Local History" (Ph.D. diss., University of Kansas, 1978), pp. viii, 102.

51. Quoted in Augustine, "Notes Toward a Portrait," p. 392, and see also pp. 390–91.

52. See discussion in Donnert, "Russische Studenten," p. 133, and Säcke, "Der Einfluss Englands," p. 97. Desnitskii cautiously suggested that under certain circumstances, some peasant rights to ownership of moveable property might be desirable. Donnert, and Shchipanov, *Izbrannye proizvedeniia*, vol. 1, p. 319.

53. Augustine, "Notes Toward a Portrait," pp. 392, 409; and see *SIRIO*, vol. 4, pp. 249, 315, and vol. 14, p. 273.

54. *SIRIO*, vol. 32, pp. 53–55, 77–80.

55. Shchipanov, *Izbrannye proizvedeniia*, vol. 2, pp. 26–27, and *SIRIO*, vol. 68, p. 13 and vol. 14, p. 402.

56. Dukes, *Catherine the Great and the Russian Nobility*, pp. 123–24; and N. V. Pchelin, *Ekaterinskaia kommissiia "o sochineniia proekta novogo ulozhen-iia" i sovremennoe ei russkoe zakonodatel'stvo* (Moscow: 1915), p. 82.

57. Quoted in A. V. Kokorev, *Khrestomatiia po russkoi literature XVIII veka*, 4th ed. (Moscow: 1965), p. 258.

58. Confino, "La Politique du tutelle," pp. 60–62.

59. Jones, *Provincial Development*, pp. 152–56, and Roger Bartlett, "J. J. Sievers and the Russian Peasants under Catherine II," *Jahrbücher für geschichte Osteuropas* 32, no. 1 (1984): 28–30.

60. See chapter 1, p. 14.

61. At other times, Bolotov conceded that peasants were "more inclined to industriousness than to laziness and sloth." See discussion in Thomas Newlin, "The Voice in the Garden: Andrei Bolotov and the Anxieties of Russian Pastoral 1738–1833" (Ph.D. diss., Columbia University, 1994), p. 138.

62. Quoted in Semevskii, *Krest'ianskii vopros*, vol. 1, p. 59.

63. Quoted in K. V. Sivkov, *Ocherki po istorii krepostnago khoziaistva i krest'ianskogo dvizheniia v Rossii v pervoi polovine xix veka* (Moscow: 1952), pp. 575–76; Confino, "La Politique du tutelle," pp. 45–47, and *Domaines et seigneurs*, p. 132.

64. Brown, "A Provincial Landowner," pp. 109–12; V. I. Semevskii, *Krest'iane v tsarstvovanie*, vol. 1, p. 309; and Kahan, *The Plow, the Hammer and the Knout*, p. 66.

65. See, for example, Klingshtedt, *TIVEO* 16 (1770): 238–39, and Rychkov, *TIVEO* 16 (1770): 16–17, 23–24, 56–57; and Augustine, "Notes Toward a Portrait," pp. 373–425.

66. For this and other examples of his methods, see Bolotov, *Zhizn' i prikliucheniia Andreia Bolotova* (a supplement to *Russkaia starina*), pp. 434, 475, 477, 549–50, 637; and *TIVEO* 16 (1770): 76–77, 82, 185, 203.

67. Bolotov wrote most of the forty-two combined volumes of both journals. See discussion in Brown, "A Provincial Landowner," pp. 105–6.

68. Bolotov himself complained that peasants lived from day to day, and reproached the gentry for preferring short-term profits over long-term investment in the land. However, his biases made it impossible for him to draw parallels between the short-sightedness of serfs and their masters.

69. In 1767, Pastor Eisen was invited by Catherine to devise a plan to transform peasants into tenants on an estate owned by the brothers Orlov, but he was

abruptly dismissed on the eve of the Legislative Assembly. See Roger Bartlett, "J. J. Sievers and the Russian Peasants."

70. See A. S. Prugavin, *Zaprosy naroda i obiazannosti intelligentsii v oblasti prosveshcheniia i vospitaniia* (St. Petersburg: 1895), pp. 31–52; and the recent study by Ben Eklof, *Russian Peasant Schools: Officialdom, Village Culture, and popular pedagogy* (Berkeley and Los Angeles: University of California Press, 1988), pp. 84–86.

71. V. I. Semevskii, *Krest'iane v tsarstvovanie Imperatritsy* vol. 1, p. 281.

72. See chapter 1, p. 23.

73. M. M. Shcherbatov, *Sochineniia kniaza*, vol. 1 (St. Petersburg: 1896–98), p. 618.

74. Confino, "La Politique du tutelle," p. 48.

75. Quoted in Confino, *Domaines*, p. 256.

76. A. N. Radishchev, *Polnoe sobranie sochinenii* (cited hereafter as *PSS*), vol. 2 (Moscow-Leningrad: 1938), p. 186

77. Blanshard, "A Proposal," pp. 219–22, 262.

78. See discussion in Semevskii, *Krest'ianskii vopros*, vol. 1, pp. 62–3, and in Blanshard, "A Proposal," p. 262.

79. A. N. Radishchev, *A Journey from St. Petersburg to Moscow*, trans. Leo Wiener (Cambridge, Mass.: Harvard University Press, 1958), p. 209.

80. Radishchev, *PSS*, 1, p. 319.

81. See discussion in Allen McConnell, *Alexander Radishchev: A Russian Philosphe 1749–1802* (The Hague: Martinus Nijhoff, 1964), pp. 303–5.

82. Radishchev, *PSS*, 1, p. 312, and see discussion of Adam Smith, chapter 1, pp. 18–19.

83. See discussion of Shcherbatov in Andrzej Walicki, *The Slavophile Controversy: History of a Conservative Utopia in Nineteenth-Century Russian Thought* (Oxford: Clarendon Press, 1975), p. 26, Marc Raeff, "State and Nobility in the Ideology of M. M. Shcherbatov," *American Slavic and East European Review* 19 (1960): 363–79, and in Erich Donnert, "Mikhail Shcherbatov als politischer Ideologe des russischen Adels in der zweiten Hälfte des 18 Jahrhundert," *Zeitschrift für Slawistik* 18, no. 3 (1973): 411–12.

84. In Shcherbatov's words, "Nature had determined some to be leaders, others to be willing accomplices, and still a third [class] to be blind obeyers." Shcherbatov, *Sochineniia*, vol. 1, p. 222.

85. Shcherbatov, *Neizdannye sochineniia* (Moscow: 1935), pp. 8 and 12.

86. Quoted in N. M. Druzhinin, "Gosudarstvennye krest'iane v dvorianskikh i pravitel'stvennykh proektakh 1800–1833," *Istoricheskie zapiski* 7 (1940): 153.

87. LeDonne, *Ruling*, p. 135.

88. LeDonne, *Ruling*, pp. 95–101; see also Augustine, "Notes Toward a Portrait," p. 402.

89. Decrees of this sort meant that when, for example, peasants of the serfowner Olsufiev's estates sent a petitioner to Moscow to protest their brutal treatment, an infantry regiment was sent to knout them and carry off 130 villagers to prison. See Semevskii, *Krest'iane*, vol. 1, p. 434, and Robert Givens "Supplication and Reform," pp. 485–87.

90. This was particularly the view of Count Panin. See Semevskii, *Krest'iane*, vol. 1, p. 22, and LeDonne, *Ruling Russia*, pp. 135–36.

91. Robert E. Jones, "Jacob Sievers, Enlightened Reform, and the Development of a 'Third Estate' in Russia," *Russian Review* 36 (October 1977): 430–33; LeDonne, *Ruling Russia*, pp. 120–22.

92. In the course of the eighteenth century, state peasants had begun to engage in the purchase, sale, and rent of their allotments. Although some were enriched by this process, many were impoverished to the point where they could no longer pay their taxes. In the more stratified communities, state peasants demanded new and more egalitarian redistribution of the land, and a government in need of revenue agreed with them.

93. Catherine's approach to the colonists as proprietors was much like Frederick the Great's. See chapter 1, p. 29, and discussion in Roger Bartlett, *Human Capital: The Settlement of Foreigners in Russia, 1762–1804* (New York: Cambridge University Press, 1979), pp. 34–75, 112.

94. Hoch, *Serfdom and Social Control*, pp. 184–86.

95. Some scholars have described peasant dissimulation and work slowdowns as a form of "everyday resistance" by which peasants countered pressures imposed by ruling elites. Rodney Bohac discusses this concept in "Everyday Forms of Resistance," pp. 236–60.

96. LeDonne, *Ruling Russia*, p. 135; Geroid Robinson, *Rural Russia*, pp. 48–50; and Kolchin, *Unfree Labor*, pp. 242–43, 278–84.

97. The concept of "moral economy" discussed by the English historian E. P. Thompson and further developed in the work of James Scott and others, suggests that non-elite groups possess values and strategies which they use in an effort to affect or modify the rules and practices imposed upon them. See James Scott, *Moral Economy of the Peasant* (New Haven: Yale University Press, 1976), and Michael Adas, "From Footdragging to Fight: The Elusive History of Peasant Avoidance Protest in South and Southeast Asia," *Journal of Peasant Studies* 13, no. 2 (January 1986): 76–96.

98. See Chapter 4, pp. 108–9.

99. Bolotov, *Zhizn'*, vol. 3, pp. 445–46.

100. Romanovich-Slavatinskii, *Dvorianstvo v Rossii*, pp. 256–57.

101. This was a political strategy which was quite Cameralist in its outlook, and in general, I would agree with Marc Raeff that Catherine the Great was one of the great Cameralist rulers. "The Well-Ordered Police State," p. 1236.

102. Roger Bartlett, "J. J. Sievers and the Russian Peasants," 19–33; and see the general discussion in Jones, *Provincial Development*, pp. 152–56.

CHAPTER THREE
THE LESSONS OF WESTERN ECONOMICS:
SUPPORT OR CHALLENGE TO THE STATUS QUO?

1. Semevskii, *Krest'ianskii vopros*, vol. 1, p. 252 and pp. 270–75.

2. See James Flynn, *The University Reforms of Tsar Alexander I* (Washington, D.C.: Catholic University of America Press, 1988), pp. 218–19; and Elmar Jarvesoo, "Early Agricultural Education at Tartu University," *Journal of Baltic Studies* 11, no. 4 (1980): 341–55.

3. See discussion of the efforts by the rector of the University of St. Petersburg to defend statistician-economists like Karl Hermann and K. T. Arseniev in E. M. Kosachevskaia, *Mikhail Andreevich Balugianskii i Petersburgskii universitet v pervoi chetverti xix veka* (Leningrad: 1971), pp. 6–12. See also Flynn, *The University Reforms*, pp. 303–4.

4. In the words of Schlözer, "Göttingen kommt hier immer mehr und mehr in Mode." See general discussion in N. K. Karataev, *Ekonomicheskie nauki v Moskovskom universitete, 1755–1955* (Moscow: 1956), pp. 45–48; and Conrad Grau, "Zur Ideologie Geschichte in Russland," pp. 83–97.

5. Among the economists they most frequently cited were Adam Smith, Turgot, J. B. Say, Justi, and Beielefeld. See Karataev, *Ekonomicheskie nauki*, pp. 45–48.

6. E. M. Kosachevskaia, *M. A. Balugianskii*, pp. 52–55.

7. Quoted in Semevskii, *Krest'ianskii vopros*, vol. 1, pp. 313–15, 319; and see also *Trudy imperatorskogo vol'nogo ekonomicheskogo obshchestva* (Proceedings of the Imperial Free Economic Society, cited hereafter as *TIVEO*), vol. 66 (1814), pp. 82, 85–86. It is useful to compare Jakob's statement with D. A. Golitsyn's eighteenth-century argument that property "gives rise to security and spiritual peace, from this peace develops curiosity, and curiosity encourages all forms of knowledge of the arts, trade and the sciences." See chapter 2, p. 44–45.

8. Similar notions were advanced by the economist Balugianskii; see Kosachevskaia, *M. A. Balugianskii*, pp. 52–55. Jakob was invited to join the Ministry of Finance after the appearance of his book *Grundsätze der Policeygezetsebung und der Policeyanstalten* (1809). See discussion in chapter 1, pp. 27–33.

9. Henri Storch, *Cours d'économie politique en exposition des principes qui déterminent la prosperité des nations*, vol. 6 (Paris: 1815): 18–19. (Cited hereafter as *Cours*.)

10. Storch, *Cours*, vol. 3, pp. 248–58. Although it has been suggested that there were other liberal-minded economists of the day who advocated political reform, my own research suggests that Storch's caution was quite typical. But for a different view, see Roderick McGrew, "Dilemmas of Development: Baron Heinrich Friedrich Storch (1766–1835), on the Growth of Imperial Russia," *Jahrbücher für Geschichte Osteuropas* 24 (1976): 71.

11. According to Storch, farm labor could not be easily routinized, and environmental and other factors could always prevent the farmer from being rewarded in proportion to his investments of labor, capital or ingenuity.

12. See general discussion in John LeDonne, *Ruling Russia*, pp. 54, 95–101, 109, 186–89, and 347–48, and chapter 2, pp. 57–58.

13. See M. V. Nechkina, *Dvizhenie Dekabristov* (Moscow: 1955), pp. 13–14; and Ivan Pnin, *Sochineniia*, ed. I. K. Luppol (Moscow: 1934), p. 121.

14. Turgenev, *Opyt teorii nalogov* (Moscow: 1937). See discussion of Turgenev's economic perspectives in E. I. Tarasov, *Dekabrist Nikolai Ivanovich Turgenev: Ocherkii po istorii liberalizma v Rossi* (Samara: 1923).

15. A. S. Pushkin, *Eugene Onegin*, vol. 1, trans. V. N. Nabokov (New York: Pantheon Books, 1964), p. 98.

16. See discussion in I. G. Bliumin, *Ocherki ekonomicheskoi mysli v Rossii v pervoi polovine xix veka* (Moscow: 1940), pp. 50–51.

17. The liberal slave-owner interpretation of Adam Smith is carefully set out in Allen Kaufman, *Capitalism, Slavery and Republican Values: Antebellum Political Economists, 1819–1848* (Austin: University of Texas Press, 1982).

18. According to William O'Goode, "We go out of a state of nature into a state of society to render certain our personal security and the right to acquire and enjoy private property . . . the right of property exists before society [and] . . . the Legislature cannot deprive a citizen of his property in a slave." See discussion in James Oakes, *Slavery and Freedom: An Interpretation of the Old South* (New York: Vintage Books, 1990), pp. 72–77.

19. Mordvinov advocated tax reduction and the elimination of governmental restrictions and regulations in the industrial and commercial sector. At the same time, he rather inconsistently argued that the government should subsidize literacy and agricultural education, and the building of roads, railways, and factories for the manufacture of agricultural machinery. See the extremely valuable investigation of Mordvinov's views by Helma Repczuk, "Nicholas Mordvinov (1754–1845): Russia's Would-Be Reformer."

20. A. G. Cross, "By the Banks," p. 85.

21. While the material benefit of such moves to the peasantry is unknown, the profits to Mordvinov were substantial. In one instance involving the transfer of 300 serfs to his Saratov property, he was able to increase his income from 2,000 to 13,000 rubles annually. Repczuk, *Nicholas Mordvinov*, p. 25.

22. N. K. Shilder, *Imperator Aleksandr pervyi, ego zhizn' i tsarstvovanie*, vol. 4 (St. Petersburg: 1904–5), pp. 103–4.

23. Repczuk, *Nicholas Mordvinov*, p. 206; and Bliumin, *Ocherki*, pp. 79–80, 99.

24. Quoted in Repczuk, *Nicholas Mordvinov*, p. 111. The tenor and tone of Mordvinov's arguments are quite consistent with Blackstone's *Commentaries*, an eighteenth-century work that had been translated into Russian during the time of Catherine the Great. See chapter 1, p. 20.

25. M. M. Speranskii, *Proekty i zapiski* (Moscow-Leningrad: 1961), pp. 42, 90–91, pp. 123–25, and p. 186; and see M. Raeff, *Michael Speranskii: Statesman of Imperial Russia* (The Hague: Martinus Nijhoff, 1957), pp. 303–6, 363–64.

26. The Prussian reforms provided land at no charge to peasants who agreed to relinquish to their masters half to a third of the land they had previously cultivated. The reforms thus substantially enlarged the estates of the Junkers (who were also provided with a landless labor force which could hired and fired at will). See discussion in Shearer Bowman, "Antebellum Planters and Vormärz Junkers in Comparative Perspective," *American Historical Review* 74 (October 1980): 779–808; and Speranskii, *Proekty*, pp. 234–42, 239.

27. According to the terms of the new Imperial decrees, peasants were required to conclude rental agreements in order to use the land that was previously granted to them. *Dvizhenie Dekabristov*, pp. 77–82.

28. See A. El'nitskii, "Rostopchin," *Russkii biograficheskii slovar'* 27 (Moscow: 1918): 238–305.

29. See M. V. Dovnar-Zapolskii, "Krepostniki v pervoi chetverti xix v.," in *Velikaia reforma: Russkoe obshchestvo i krest'ianskii vopros v proshlom i nastoiashchem*, vol. 2, ed. A. Dzhivelegov, et al. (Moscow: 1911), pp. 130–38; and Romanovich-Slavatinskii, *Dvorianstvo v Rossii*, pp. 383–85.

30. Bliumin, *Ocherki*, pp. 91–95.

31. See general discussion in Eugene Genovese and Elizabeth Fox-Genovese, "The Slave Economies in Political Perspective," *Journal of American History* 66 (1979): 88–89.

32. Thomas Raikes, *A Visit to St. Petersburg in the Winter of 1829–1830* (London: R. Bentley, 1838), p. 29.

33. See discussion in Richard Pipes, "The Russian Military Colonies, 1810–1831," *Journal of Modern History* 22 (October 1950): 205–19.

34. Quoted in Eugene Genovese, *The World the Slaveholders Made* (New York: Pantheon Books, 1969), p. 162.

35. A useful comparison between such notions of discipline and later industrial theories of "Taylorism" appears in R. Keith Aufhauser, "Slavery and Scientific Management," *Journal of Economic History* 33, no. 4 (October 1973): 811–24.

36. Pipes, "The Russian Military Colonies," pp. 205–19.

37. Quoted in *Russkii arkhiv*, vol. 8 (1893), p. 535; *Russkaia starina*, vol. 4 (1904), p. 14.

38. In general, the Decembrists wrote little about economics and their economic views were not widely known. Decembrist leader Pavel Pestel's book *Russkaia pravda* (Russian Justice) was considered so inflammatory that it was buried underground until after the Emancipation of 1861. In his discussion of rural economic policy, Pestel proposed that the Russian countryside be divided into a commune region for the ordinary and unadventurous majority and a private-property-oriented region for the more energetic peasant entrepreneurs. Although the Decembrist economist N. I. Turgenev did not develop a general economic program for change, he saw England as an example of the wealth and power achievable under conditions of freedom, i.e., noncommunal economic institutions and limited government. Useful discussions of the Decembrist movement are contained in Marc Raeff, *The Decembrists* (Englewood Cliffs, N.J.: Prentice-Hall, 1966); and *Dvizhenie Dekabristov*.

39. Mordvinov's proposal is discussed in Repczuk, *Nicholas Mordvinov*, pp. 37–38.

40. During the thirty-year reign of Nicholas I, ten different secret committees were established to debate the question of emancipation reform. For an account of their work, see I. S. Bak, "Istoricheskaia zapiska o raznykh predpolozheniiakh po predmetu osvobozhdeniia krest'ian," in *Deviatnadtsatyi vek: Istoricheskii sbornik*, vol. 2, ed. P. Bartenev (Moscow: 1872), pp. 145–208; and Druzhinin, *Gosudarstvennye krest'iane*, vol. 1, pp. 165–96.

41. See the valuable discussion of Kankrin's mindset and policies in Walter Pintner's, *Russian Economic Policy under Nicholas I* (Ithaca, N.Y.: Cornell University Press, 1967).

42. Pintner, *Russian Economic Policy*, p. 23.

43. See discussion in Frederick Kaplan, "Du développement des idées révolutionnaire en Russie," *American Slavic and East European Review* 17, no. 2 (April 1958): 170–71.

44. A valuable discussion of Kiselev's intellectual background is contained in Henry Hirscheibel, "The District Captains of the Ministry of State Domains in the Reign of Nicholas I: A Case Study of Russian Provincial Officialdom, 1830–

1856" (Ph.D. diss., New York University, 1978), p. 49; and see also the account written by one of Kiselev's associates, the statistician-economist A. P. Zablotskii-Desiatovskii, *Graf P.D. Kiselev i ego vremia* (St. Petersburg: 1882).

45. It has been estimated that the indebtedness of state peasants increased by 65% between 1834 (when the Ministry of State Domains was created) and 1847. In contrast, general state taxes increased less than 10% during this period. See M. N. Druzhinin, *Gosudarstvennaia krest'ianskaia reforma P.D. Kiseleva*, 2 vols. (Moscow: 1946–58), vol. 2, pp. 91–128, 131, 135.

46. Alexander M. Herzen, *My Past and Thoughts: The Memoirs of Alexander Herzen*, trans. Constance Garnett, vol. 1 (New York: Knopf, 1968), pp. 257–58.

47. Hirscheibel, "The District Captains," p. 73.

48. Quoted in P. A. Zaionchkovskii, *The Abolition of Serfdom in Russia*, ed. and trans. Susan Wobst (Gulf Breeze, Fla.: Academic International Press, 1978), p. 120.

49. *Dvizhenie Dekabristov*, pp. 244–55; and see discussion in Kahan, *Jahrbücher Geschichte Osteuropas* 7 (1960): 362.

50. Quoted in W. Bruce Lincoln, *In the Vanguard of Reform: Russia's Enlightened Bureaucrats 1825–1861* (Dekalb: Northern Illinois University Press, 1982), p. 32.

51. Kiselev proposed voluntary gentry agreements to accord peasants a right to land use in return for the fulfillment of "reasonable" obligations. The gentry were to retain ownership of the land but were prohibited from evicting its peasant occupants.

52. Kiselev began his reforms with 80 surveyors; by the 1850s, there were 1500 such officials, many of whom were notorious for their corrupt and coercive methods. See discussion in Hirscheibel, "The District Captains," pp. 39–40.

53. Hirscheibel, "The District Captains," p. 258.

54. As Priscilla Roosevelt has noted, Slavophiles and "Westernizers" were equally contemptuous of "Official Nationalists" like F. V. Bulgarin, N. P. Grech, M. P. Pogodin, and S. P. Shevyrev. See Priscilla Roosevelt, *Apostle of Russian Liberalism: Timofei Granovsky* (Newtonville, Mass.: Oriental Research Partners, 1986), pp. 46 and 74.

55. In the words of the Slavophile A. I. Koshelev, "All of us, and particularly Khomiakov and Aksakov, were nicknamed Slavophiles, but this term absolutely fails to express the essential nature of our philosophical orientation." Quoted in Andrzej Walicki's scholarly study and philosophical reflection, *The Slavophile Controversy: History of a Conservative Utopia in Nineteenth-Century Russian Thought* (Oxford: Clarendon Press, 1975), p. 395–96. On balance, Walicki decisively rejects the Slavophile disclaimer. In his view, the Slavophiles were fundamentally reactionary and anti-Western. If liberalism is defined as the essence of Western culture, Walicki's judgment is clearly accurate. However, Walicki's argument is rooted in a denial that English Tory, German Romantic, and Prussian statist traditions were significant components of Western culture.

56. See Roosevelt, *Apostle of Russian Liberalism*, p. 112; and P. V. Annenkov, *Zamechatel'noe desiatiletie*, ed. V. P. Dorofeev, vol. 2 of Annenkov's *Literaturnye vospominaniia*, pp. 135–376.

57. The scholarly literature on the Slavophiles is extremely rich. See, for example, Edward Chmielewski, *Tribune of the Slavophiles: Konstantin Aksakov*

(Gainesville: University of Florida Press, 1961); Peter Christoff, *An Introduction to Nineteenth-Century Russian Slavophilism*, vol. 1, *A. S. Khomiakov* (The Hague: Mouton, 1961); vol. 2, *I. V. Kireevskii* (The Hague: Mouton, 1972); vol. 3, *K. S. Aksakov* (Princeton: Princeton University Press, 1982); A. G. Dement'ev, *Ocherki po istorii russkoi zhurnalistiki 1840–50gg* (Moscow-Leningrad: 1951); Abbott Gleason, *European and Muscovite: Ivan Kireevskii and the Origins of Slavophilism* (Cambridge, Mass.: Harvard University Press, 1971); Stephen Lukashevich, *Ivan Aksakov 1823–1886: A Study in Russian Thought and Politics* (Cambridge, Mass.: Harvard University Press, 1965); A. N. Pypin, *Kharakteristika literaturnykh mnenii ot 20-ykh do 50-ykh godov* (St. Petersburg: 1890); and Nicholas Riasanovsky, *Russia and the West in the Teaching of the Slavophiles* (Cambridge, Mass.: Harvard University Press, 1952).

58. See Walicki's detailed discussion of German philosphical influences on the Slavophiles in *The Slavophile Controversy*, especially pp. 287–336.

59. See the broader discussion of this phenomenon in E. J. Hobsbawm and Terence Ranger, *The Invention of Tradition* (New York: Cambridge University Press, 1983).

60. See the insightful discussion in Janet Vaillant, "Encountering the West: The Ideological Responses of Aleksei S. Khomiakov and Leopold S. Senghor" (Ph.D. diss., Harvard University, 1971), pp. 270–75.

61. A. S. Khomiakov, *Polnoe sobranie sochinenii (cited hereafter as PSS)*, vol. 3, 4th ed. (Moscow: 1914), pp. 105, 115–16, 185; and see discussion in Peter Christoff, "A. S. Khomiakov on the Agricultural and Industrial Problem in Russia," in *Essays in Russian History*, ed. A. Fergusson and A. Levin (Hamden, Conn.: Archon Books, 1964), p. 156.

62. Khomiakov, *PSS*, vol. 1, pp. 90–92, 117.

63. Khomiakov, *PSS*, vol. 1, pp. 187–88, and vol. 3, pp. 408–9.

64. Quoted in B. E. Nolde, *Iurii Samarin i ego vremia* (Paris: Impr. de Navarre, 1926), pp. 54–55; and see also E. Muller, "Lorenz von Stein und Jurij Samarins Vision des absoluten Sozialstaates," *Jahrbücher für Geschichte Osteuropas* 15 (1967): 575–96.

65. Khomiakov hoped that the formation of cooperatives might eventually check or at least provide some balance against the power of English property-owners. *PSS*, vol. 8, pp. 262–63.

66. I. S. Aksakov, *Sochineniia*, vol. 2 (Moscow: 1886–87), pp. 462–63; and see also Marc Raeff, "The Peasant Commune in the Political Thinking of Russian Publicists; Laissez Faire Liberalism in the Reign of Alexander II" (Ph.D. thesis, Harvard University, 1950), p. 84.

67. Khomiakov, *PSS*, vol. 3, pp. 464–68.

68. Khomiakov, *PSS*, vol. 3, pp. 458–59, 462–65. Khomiakov went on to speculate that free peasant communes might become the basis for an economy which combined industry and agriculture instead of placing these two necessary economic pursuits in geographic, social, and economic conflict. An industrial revolution of this sort would not require an "English-style" (1) expulsion of peasants from the land, (2) subordination of the countryside to the city, or (3) the depersonalization of human relations produced by a system that assessed individuals only according to the value of the skills they could buy and sell in the labor market.

69. Khomiakov, *PSS*, vol. 3, pp. 464–68.

70. I. V. Kireevskii, *Polnoe sobranie sochinenii Ivana Vasil'evicha Kirieevskago* (Ann Arbor, Mich.: Ardis, 1983), pp. 267–68.

71. Khomiakov, *PSS*, vol. 1 (Moscow: 1900–11), p. 249, and vol. 2, pp. 241–45. See also Riasanovsky, *Russia and the West*, p. 45. It has been estimated that Khomiakov's reform proposals would have reduced by a third the size of the average allotments that most peasants already cultivated; holdings above the average were to revert to the estate-owner. In the years immediately preceding the Emancipation of 1861, Khomiakov argued that communes should enforce demands for redemption payments "with the greatest severity" and in cases of extreme delinquency, he recommended the expulsion of whole villages to Siberia, accompanied by the sale of their allotments of land. In this matter, Khomiakov argued, "inexorable and seemingly cruel strictness is true mercy." Khomiakov, *PSS*, vol. 3, pp. 305–8; and see also Semevskii, *Krest'ianskii vopros*, vol. 2, pp. 398–401.

72. Vaillant, "Encountering," pp. 270–75.

73. See discussion in Thomas Masaryk, *The Spirit of Russia: Studies in History, Literature and Philosophy* (London: Allen & Unwin, 1919), p. 270.

74. Gary Hamburg, *Boris Chicherin and Early Russian Liberalism, 1828–1866* (Stanford, Cal.: Stanford University Press, 1993), pp. 60–61.

75. Anthony Netting, "Russian Liberalism: The Years of Promise, 1842–55" (Ph.D. diss., Columbia University, 1967), p. 249.

76. See Konstantin Aksakov, *Vospominanie studentsva 1832–4 godov* (St. Petersburg: 1911), pp. 21–24; and Roosevelt, *Apostle*, pp. 59–61.

77. V. G. Belinskii, *Polnoe sobranie sochineniia*, vol. 7 (Moscow: 1955), pp. 434–35. The Slavophile Khomiakov indignantly denounced such declarations as arrogant and elitist. However, according to Andzej Walicki, Belinskii's arguments reflected his opposition to government-sponsored glorifications of nationalism in the reign of Nicholas I. See Walicki, *The Slavophile Controversy*, p. 420 and chapter 1, pp. 32–33.

78. Herzen, *PSS*, vol. 3 (Paris: 1915), p. 117.

79. Priscilla Roosevelt, "Granovskii at the Lectern: A Conservative Liberal's Vision of History," *Forschungen zur osteuropaischen Geschichte* 219 (Berlin: 1981): 61–192.

80. See Belinskii, *PSS*, vol. 12, pp. 444–53, pp. 467–68.

81. V. A. Miliutin, *Izbrannye proizvedeniia* (Moscow: 1946), p. 162.

82. The comments of the Westernizer V. Botkin are revealing. In his words: "I am by no means an admirer of the bourgeoisie; its crudeness, its prosaic vulgarity offend me as much as anyone else; but for me it is facts that count. . . . my whole sympathy is undoubtedly on the side of the workers, as the downtrodden class. And yet I cannot help adding—God grant us such a bourgeoisie!" Quoted in P. V. Annenkov, *P. V. Annenkov i ego druz'ia: literaturnyia vospominaniia i perepiska 1835–1885 godov* (St. Petersburg: 1982), p. 551.

83. Netting, "Russian Liberalism," p. 612.

84. Herzen, *PSS*, vol. 3, p. 117.

85. Quoted in Roosevelt, *Apostle*, p. 61.

86. See discussion in Roosevelt, *Apostle*, pp. 74–75.

87. T. N. Granovskii, *Sochineniia T. N. Granovskago. S portretom avtora*, 2nd ed., vol. 1 (Moscow: 1866), p. 445.

88. When a *Rural Reader* attracted 30,000 readers between 1843 and 1848 with catechisms on proper agricultural methods and abridged and simplified versions of Pushkin, Belinskii declared himself "amazed" and delighted, but he continued nevertheless to maintain that the peasantry constituted a "dark," inert, and conservative force. Belinskii's comments on the *Rural Reader* are contained in *PSS*, vol. 6, pp. 681–90, vol. 8, pp. 153–58, and vol. 9, pp. 301–5. See also vol. 23, pp. 467–68.

89. Quoted in Roosevelt, *Apostle*, p. 161.

90. Quoted in Walicki, *The Slavophile Controversy*, p. 275.

91. Khomiakov, *PSS*, vol. 1, p. 92.

92. Belinskii, *PSS*, vol. 10, p. 369.

93. Aksakov, quoted in Raeff, "The Peasant Commune," p. 86.

94. See discussion of Aksakov's view of the "servility of mind and body" among Russia's Westernizers in Stephen Lukashevich, *Aksakov*, p. 13.

95. It is interesting that Khomiakov held the landed gentry rather than Peter the Great primarily responsible for Russia's backwardness. See *PSS*, vol. 3, pp. 16–19.

96. Gleason, *The Slavophiles*, pp. 262–63; Khomiakov, *PSS*, vol. 1, p. 22; and N. P. Koliupanov, *Biografiia Aleksandra Ivanovicha Kosheleva*, 2 vols. (Moscow: 1889–92), Appendix, vol. 2, p. 317.

97. Quoted in Christoff, "A. S. Khomiakov," *Essays in Russian History*, pp. 152–53.

98. According to Kavelin, the reign of Ivan IV marked the beginning of a rational historical process of state-building, with the dreaded *oprichnina* as the policing mechanism for the development of a political system which was based upon merit rather than hereditary privilege. Kavelin, *Sobranie sochinenii* (St. Petersburg: 1897), vol. 1, pp. 45, 247.

99. Quoted in Vetrinskii (pseudonym of V. E. Cheshikhin), *T. N. Granovskii i ego vremia* (St. Petersburg: 1905), pp. 364–65.

100. See Semevskii, *Krest'ianskii vopros*, vol. 2, p. 427; and Walicki, *The Slavophile Controversy*, p. 272.

101. See Richard Schweder's intriguing discussion of the links between romanticism and the beginnings of modern anthropology, "Anthropology's Romantic Rebellion Against the Enlightenment," *Culture Theory*, ed. R. A. Schweder and Robert LeVine (Cambridge: Cambridge University Press, 1984), pp. 32 and 48; and Clifford Geertz, "On the Nature of Anthropological Understanding," *American Scientist* 63 (January/February 1975): 47–53.

102. Haxthausen, *The Russian Empire: Its People, Institutions and Resources* (London: Chapman & Hall, 1856), vol. 1, pp. 125 146; vol. 2, p. 407.

103. Haxthausen, *The Russian Empire*, vol. 1, p. 125–8, and vol. 2, pp. 234, 240.

104. Haxthausen, *The Russian Empire*, vol. 1, p. 348.

105. S. Frederick Starr, "August von Haxthausen and Russia," *Slavonic and East European Review* 46 (July 1968): 463.

106. Quoted in Hamburg, *Boris Chicherin*, pp. 70–71.

107. Alexander M. Herzen, *Polnoe sobranie sochinenii i pisem*, vol. 13 (Petrograd: 1919), p. 302.

108. Alexander M. Herzen, *My Past and Thoughts: The Memoirs of Alexander Herzen*, trans. Constance Garnett, vol. 4 (New York: Knopf, 1968), p. 1661.

109. Herzen, *O razvitii revoliutsionnykh idei v Rossii* (Moscow: 1958), p. 47.

110. Herzen, *My Past and Thoughts*, vol. 2, p. 526.

111. Herzen, *Polnoe sobranie sochinenii i pisem*, vol. 7, p. 151.

112. Herzen, *My Past and Thoughts*, vol. 2, p. 528; vol. 4, pp. 1572–73. See also Franco Venturi's empathic discussion of Herzen, *Roots of Revolution* (New York: Knopf, 1960), pp. 34–35.

113. A. V. Stankevich, *T. N. Granovskii i ego perepiska* (Moscow: 1897), vol. 2, pp. 448 and 477.

114. George Fisher, *Russian Liberalism from Gentry to Intelligentsia* (Cambridge, Mass.: Harvard University Press, 1958), p. 18.

115. Herzen, *My Past and Thoughts*, vol. 4, p. 1683, and p. 1573. It is useful to compare Herzen's view with Tolstoi's early short story "A Landlord's Morning." Tolstoi recounts the efforts of a repentant serfowner who decides to share with the simple peasant the fruits of his superior knowledge of agriculture. When he attempts to teach peasants to work the land more effectively, he is thwarted at every turn. Portrayed by Tolstoi as an ignorant reformer who considers peasants a blank slate upon which he could benevolently write, the landlord fails. Although—unlike Tolstoi—Herzen remained an admirer of Western culture, he was as skeptical as Tolstoi about the degree to which upper-class reformers possessed practical skills or knowledge about peasants. "A Landlord's Morning," in *Leo Tolstoy: Short Novels*, vol. 1, ed. Ernest J. Simmons (New York, 1965) p. 71–126.

116. Herzen, *Memoirs*, vol. 3, chapter 4, p. 1084.

117. Herzen, *My Past and Thoughts*, vol. 2, p. 354.

CHAPTER FOUR
UNIVERSALISM AND ITS DISCONTENTS:
THE LAWS OF HISTORY, ECONOMICS, AND HUMAN PROGRESS

1. For an introduction to Comte's ideas and their impact, see Raymond Aron, "Auguste Comte," *Main Currents in Sociological Thought*, vol. 1, trans. Richard Howard and Helen Weaver (New York: Basic Books, 1960), pp. 73–143; *Positivism and Sociology*, ed. Anthony Giddens (London: Heineman, 1975); Georges Gurvitch, *Les fondateurs de la sociologie contemporaine: pour le centenaire de la mort d'Auguste Comte (1857–1957); Auguste Comte, Karl Marx et Herbert Spencer*, 2 vols. (Paris: Centre de Documentation Universitaire, 1957), pp. 1–48; and Leszek Kolakowski, "Auguste Comte: Positivism in the Romantic Age," in *The Alienation of Reason: A History of Positivist Thought* (Garden City, N.Y.: Doubleday, 1968), pp. 47–72.

2. B. G. Safronov, *M. M. Kovalevskii kak sotsiolog* (Moscow: 1960), pp. 45–50; and P. S. Shkurinov, *Pozitivizm v Rossii xix veka* (Moscow: 1980), pp. 44–63.

3. Quoted in Émile de Laveleye, *De la propriété et de ses formes primitives* (Paris: Germer, 1901), p. xxviii.

4. See Ben Seligman, "The Impact of Positivism on Economic Thought," *History of Political Economy* 1, no. 2 (1969): 258, 268; and discussion of the hierar-

chical notions of progress which inspired Comte's disciples in Jerzy Szacki, *History of Sociological Thought* (London: Aldwych Press, 1979), pp. 176–79.

5. Quoted in Theodore Porter, *The Rise of Statistical Thinking, 1820–1900* (Princeton: Princeton University Press, 1986), pp. 46–47.

6. See chapter 1, pp. 28–29.

7. Comte wrote a similar letter to the grand vizier of the Ottoman Empire. See Auguste Comte, *Système de politique positive, ou, Traité de sociologie, instituant la religion de l'humanité*, vol. 3 (Paris: L. Mathias, 1853), pp. xxix–xlix; and general discussion in J. H. Billington, "The Intelligentsia and the Religion of Humanity," *American Historical Review* 65, no. 4 (July 1960): 807–21.

8. V. P. Bezobrazov, *Aristokratiia i interesy dvorianstva* (Moscow: 1866).

9. See, for example, I. P. Vernadskii: *Politicheskoe ravnovesie i Angliia* (Moscow: 1855), *Ocherk istorii politicheskoi ekonomii* (St. Petersburg: 1858), and *Prospekt politicheskoi ekonomii* (St. Petersburg: 1858).

10. See, for example, Maria Vernadskaia, *Sobranie sochinenii* (St. Petersburg: 1862), pp. 76 and 306.

11. See general discussion in V. N. Rozental', "Obshchestvenno-politicheskaia programma russkogo liberalizma v seredine 50-kh godov xix veka," *Istoricheskie zapiski* 70 (1961): 197–222; and V. A. Tvardovskaia, *Ideologiia poreformennogo samoderzhaviia (M. N. Katkov i ego izdaniia)* (Moscow: 1978).

12. Quoted in S. Frederick Starr, *Decentralization and Self-Government in Russia* (Princeton: Princeton University Press, 1972), p. 80; and see S. Nevedenskii, who writes: "For Katkov, contemporary England was the new Rome, embodying all the positive forces of modern life." See *Katkov i ego vremia* (St. Petersburg: 1888), p. 114; and see V. A. Kitaev, *Ot frondy k okhranitel'stvu: Istoriia russkoi liberal'noi mysli 50–60kh godov xix veka* (Moscow: 1972), pp. 144–50.

13. Quoted in Kitaev, *Ot frondy*, pp. 142–43.

14. Karataev, *Ekonomicheskie nauki*, p. 93.

15. Although they are seldom studied today, Bastiat and Carey took the mid-nineteenth-century educated reading public by storm, their writings even outsold *The Wealth of Nations*. Brief descriptions of their work are included in Joseph Schumpeter, *History of Economic Analysis*, pp. 499–500, 515–18, 553–54; Lewis Haney, *History of Economic Thought* (New York: Macmillan, 1949), pp. 337, 419, 513, 515, and 846. See also N. K. Karataev, *Russkaia ekonomicheskaia mysl' v period krizisa feodal'nogo khoziaistva (40–60-kh gody xix veka* (Moscow: 1957), pp. 139, 188–99.

16. In addition to the aforementioned I. N. Linovskii, this "old-style" liberal argument was supported by A. D. Zheltukhin, the founder of *Zhurnal semlevladel'tsev*. Like Mordvinov and other economic thinkers of the 1820s and 1830s, Linovskii claimed that serfdom was more humane than the "freedom" which left laborers to starve in the streets of London and Manchester. See earlier discussion in chapter 3, p. 73, and Karataev, *Ekonomicheskie nauki*, pp. 79–80.

17. See E. Maslov, *O vlianii razlichnykh vidov pozemel'noi sobstvennosti na narodnoe bogatstvo* (Kazan: 1860).

18. N. Kh. Bunge, "Garmoniia khoziaistvennykh otnoshenii," *Otechestvennye zapiski* 11 (1859): 1–42.

19. B. N. Chicherin, *Vospominaniia*, 4 vols. (Moscow: 1929–34), vol. 1, p. 12 and vol. 4, pp. 169ff; see also Hamburg, *Boris Chicherin*, p. 72.

20. A. I. Koshelev, *Zapiski (1812–1883)* (Berlin: 1884), p. 37.

21. See, for example, Zaionchkovskii, *The Abolition of Serfdom in Russia*; and Terence Emmons, *The Russian Landed Gentry and the Peasant Emancipation of 1861* (Berkeley and Los Angeles: University of California Press, 1968); recent Soviet and Western research on emancipation appears in *The Great Reforms in Russia*, L. G. Zakharova and John Bushnell, eds. (Bloomington: Indiana University Press, 1994).

22. See general discussion in N. A. Tsagalov, *Ocherki russkoi ekonomicheskoi mysli perioda padeniia krepostnogo prava* (Moscow: 1956), pp. 357–62; Karataev, *Russkaia ekonomicheskaia mysl'*, pp. 81–82; and Lincoln, *In the Vanguard of Reform*, p. 123.

23. Chicherin, *Sobstvennost' i gosudarstvo*, vol. 1 (Moscow: 1882), p. 457.

24. See Kitaev, *Ot frondy*, pp. 188–89; general discussion in Raeff, "The Peasant Commune in the Political Thinking of Russian Publicists," pp. 166–88; Hamburg, *Boris Chicherin*, pp. 85–88; and the relatively sympathetic account of Chicherin's position in Walicki, *Legal Philosophies of Russian Liberalism* (Oxford: Clarendon Press, 1987), pp. 125–26.

25. See discussion in Grant, "The Peasant Commune in Russian Thought, 1861–1905," p. 36–37.

26. Quoted in Chernyshev, *Agrarno-krest'ianskaia politika Rossii za 150 let* (Petrograd: 1918), pp. 86, 91.

27. K. D. Kavelin, *Sobranie Sochinenii*, vol. 4 (St. Petersburg: 1897), p. 255. Kavelin was an extremely complex thinker, whose work deserves further study. In the 1830s and 1840s, he was the only member of the "Westernizer" group who was not hostile to the peasant commune. In the decades to come, he was increasingly convinced of the commune's political and social significance. In the last years of his life, Karl Marx found Kavelin's work of great interest. See chapter 6, pp. 136–38.

28. Kavelin, *Sochineniia*, vol. 2, pp. 182–83, and vol. 4, pp. 268–79.

29. See discussion in Koshelev, "Obshchinnoe pozemel'noe vladenie," *Sel'skoe blagoustroistvo* 8 (1858): 107–13, and Abbott Gleason, *Young Russia: The Genesis of Russian Radicalism in the 1860s* (Chicago: University of Chicago Press, 1983), p. 192.

30. Iu. F. Samarin, "Uprazdnenie krepostnogo prava i ustroistvo otnoshenii mezhdu pomeshchikami i krest'ianami v Prussii," *Sel'skoe blagoustroistvo* 1, no. 4 (1858): 37–92, and vol. 2 (1858), 103–28, vol. 4, pp. 24–27, and vol. 8, pp. 117–18.

31. A. I. Koshelev, *Sel'skoe blagoustroistvo* 4, nos. 7–9 (1858): 107–43.

32. I have not been able to discover any writings by liberal economists that respond directly to Slavophile descriptions of the commune's operations or diverse functions.

33. Iu. F. Samarin, *Sochineniia*, vol. 2 (Moscow: 1878), p. 115.

34. Tengoborskii was a statistician who served for years as an adviser to the autocracy's Ministry of Finance. Ludwig Tengoborskii, *Commentaries on the Productive Forces of Russia*, vol. 1 (London: Longman, Brown, Green, and Longmans, 1855–56), p. 320.

35. Tengoborskii, *Commentaries*, vol. 1, p. 331, pp. 231, 315, 336, 392–93; and see the careful study by Zack Deal, "Serf and State Peasant Agriculture: Kharkov Province, 1842–1861" (Ph.D. diss., Vanderbilt University, 1978).

36. In the 1970s, Robert Fogel and Stanley Engerman's study of the profitability of slavery set off a lengthy debate among American economic historians. See *Time on the Cross: The Economics of American Negro Slavery* (Boston: Little, Brown, 1974); and responses by Herbert Gutman, *Slavery and the Numbers Game: A Critique of "Time on the Cross"* (Urbana: University of Illinois Press, 1975); and Paul David, Herbert Gutman, et al., *Reckoning with Slavery* (New York: Oxford University Press, 1976).

37. Tengoborskii, *Commentaries*, vol. 1, pp. 378–79, and see also pp. 362–65, 377.

38. See Vernadskii's introduction to Tengoborskii's *Commentaries*, "Predislovie," in *O proizvoditel'nykh silakh v Rossii* (Moscow: 1857), pp. 1–4.

39. There is a substantial scholarly literature devoted to Chernyshevskii. See, for example, B. P. Kozmin, *Iz istorii revoliutsionnoi mysli v Rossii* (Moscow: 1961); Evgenii Lampert, *Sons Against Fathers* (Oxford: Clarendon Press, 1965); Norman G. O. Pereira, *The Thought and Teachings of N. G. Chernyshevskij* (The Hague: Mouton, 1975); Venturi, *Roots of Revolution*; E. S. Vilenskaia, *Revoliutsionnoe podpol'e v Rossii (60-e gody xix v.)* (Moscow: 1965); and William Woehrlin, *Chernyshevskii: The Man and the Journalist* (Cambridge, Mass.: Harvard University Press, 1971).

40. Quoted in Iurii Steklov, *N. G. Chernyshevskii: Ego zhizn' i deiatel'nost 1828–89*, vol. 1 (Moscow: 1928), p. 110.

41. With equal bluntness, N. A. Dobroliubov referred to Vernadskii as both a symbol and a source of Russia's intellectual bankruptcy. Dobroliubov, *Sobranie sochinenii*, vol. 4 (Moscow: 1962), p. 336.

42. See p. 100–01.

43. Chernyshevskii, *Izbrannye ekonomicheskoi proizvedenii*, vol. 1 (Moscow: 1948), pp. 317–30.

44. Chernyshevskii, *Izbrannye*, vol. 1, pp. 111–18, 228–30.

45. Chernyshevskii, *Polnoe sobranie sochinenii* (cited hereafter as *PSS*), vol. 5 (Moscow: 1939–53), p. 84

46. Chernyshevskii, *Izbrannye*, vol. 1, pp. 153, 167, and vol. 2, pp. 298–99.

47. Chernyshevskii, *Izbrannye*, vol. 1, pp. 229–30, 383, and vol. 2, pp. 285, 295; and see discussion in chapter 1.

48. Quoted in Venturi, *Roots*, p. 160.

49. Chernyshevskii, *Izbrannye*, vol. 2, p. 179, and vol. 1, pp. 202–3.

50. Chernyshevskii, *Izbrannye*, vol. 2, p. 285.

51. Quoted in Venturi, *Roots*, p. 381.

52. Chernyshevskii, *PSS*, vol. 7, p. 864.

53. Katkov's shift astonished contemporaries like Prince Cherkasskii, who predicted (correctly) that Katkov would "soon confess his errors and turn back onto the opposite path." Kitaev, *Ot frondy* , pp. 190–92.

54. N. Kh. Bunge, "Garmoniia," *Otechestvennye zapiski* 11 (1859): 1–42.

55. Quoted in Daniel Field, *The End of Serfdom: Nobility and Bureaucracy in Russia, 1855–1861* (Cambridge, Mass.: Harvard University Press, 1976), p. 444. A complex figure in Russian intellectual life, Cherkasskii was described by Richard Wortman as a Slavophile and by Marc Raeff as a "Manchester liberal." He began as an admirer of the Slavophile Ivan Kireevskii and shared the latter's fear of the dangerous excesses of Western capitalism. By the 1850s, Cherkasskii came

to believe that capitalism represented a brutal but necessary phase of Russia's future development. In his words, "Capital is a bloodsucker, and this is how it ought to be. It is better to draw a little blood in order to preserve the remainder." However, such tough-minded remarks did not prevent him from supporting the retention of the commune as a conservative force when the time came to frame the Emancipation statutes. Raeff, "The Peasant Commune in the Political Thinking of Russian Publicists," p. 25.

56. Quoted in Field, *The End of Serfdom*, p. 23, and see also p. 40.

57. See discussion in Zablotskii-Desiatovskii, *Graf Kiselev i ego vremia*, vol. 4, p. 207.

58. One of the best of the many valuable accounts of the reforms is still Zaionchkovskii, *The Abolition of Serfdom*.

59. Shearer Bowman, *Masters and Lords: Mid-Nineteenth-Century U.S. Planters and Prussian Junkers* (Oxford: Oxford University Press, 1993), pp. 18–19.

60. I am grateful to Heather Hogan for the reminder that Russian unskilled workers were called *chernorabochie* (black workers).

61. See discussion in Oakes, *Slavery and Freedom*, pp. 3–8, and pp. 36–37. Bowman's study of Prussia's bound labor force suggests a far greater similarity in the conditions and opportunities of Prussian and Russian peasants. See especially, *Masters and Lords*, p. 19, p. 48.

62. Peasants possessed a wide repertoire of oppositional strategies ranging from evasion to petitions to the master or official, work stoppages, the more confrontational *volnenie* in which a group of serfs decided on collective protest or outright rebellion. These activities were almost invariably collective and communal rather than individual. See discussion in Peter Kolchin, *Unfree Labor: American Slavery and Russian Serfdom* (Cambridge, Mass.: Belknap Press of Harvard University Press, 1987), pp. 257–71.

63. See Eric Foner, *Reconstruction: American's Unfinished Revolution, 1863–1877* (New York: Harper & Row, 1988). For a quite different perspective which emphasizes the superiority of the American emancipation reform, see Peter Kolchin, "The Tragic Era? Interpreting Southern Reconstruction in Comparative Perspective," in *The Meaning of Freedom: Economics, Politics and Culture after Slavery*, ed. Frank McGlynn and Seymour Drescher (Pittsburgh: University of Pittsburgh Press, 1992), pp. 291–311.

64. Lou Ferleger, "Share-Cropping Contracts in the Late Nineteenth-Century South," *Agricultural History* 7, no. 3 (summer 1993): 31–46; Roger L. Ransom and Richard Sutch, *One Kind of Freedom: The Economic Consequences of Emancipation* (Cambridge: Cambridge University Press, 1977); Jay R. Mandle, *The Roots of Black Poverty: The Southern Plantation Economy after the Civil War* (Durham, N.C.: Duke University Press, 1978), and *Not Slave Not Free: The African American Economic Experience Since the Civil War* (Durham, N.C.: Duke University Press, 1992).

65. See discussion in Olga Crisp, "Peasant Land Tenure and Civil Rights: Implications Before 1906," *Civil Rights in Imperial Russia* (Oxford: The Clarendon Press, 1989), ed. Olga Crisp and Linda Edmondson, pp. 33–64. For more detailed discussion of this process, see the classic discussions in Gerold T. Robinson, *Rural Russia under the Old Regime* (Berkeley and Los Angeles: University of California

Press, 1932), pp. 65–66; and Jerome Blum, *Lord and Peasant in Russia* (Princeton: Princeton University Press, 1960), pp. 592–98.

66. Because many Junkers opted to receive compensation in kind and cash as well as land, the German scholar Sigmund Neumann concluded that the Stein-Hardenberg reform "resulted less in the freeing of the peasants than in the victory of the large estate" through a *de facto* enclosure movement. In this process, the economic position of the Junkers was further strengthened by government aid to those landlords who consolidated scattered strips of land and adopted new systems of crop rotation. See Bowman, *Masters and Lords*, pp. 69–70, and "Antebellum Planters," p. 292.

67. Lazar Volin, *A Century of Russian Agriculture: From Alexander II to Khrushchev* (Cambridge, Mass.: Harvard University Press, 1970), pp. 50–53.

68. Quoted in Leon Litwack, *Been in the Storm So Long: The Aftermath of Slavery* (New York: Knopf, 1979), p. 399; LaWanda Cox, "The Promise of Land for the Freedmen," *Mississippi Valley Historical Review* 45 (December 1958): 429; and McPherson, *The Struggle for Equality*, p. 409.

69. Quoted in E. V. Tarle, "Imperator Nikolai I i krest'ianskii vopros v Rossii, po neizdannym doneseniiam frantsuzikh diplomatov 1842–47," in *Zapad i Rossiia: Stat'i i dokumenty iz istorii xvii–xx vekov* (Petrograd: 1918), pp. 17 and 27.

70. Aksakov believed that the gentry should be compensated by the government rather than by the peasantry. See Ivan Aksakov, *Sochineniia 5*, p. 374.

71. "Pismo I. S. Aksakova v Orlovskuiu derevniu," *Russkii arkhiv* 6 (1901): 299.

72. S. B. Okun and K. V. Sivkov, *Krest'ianskoe dvizhenie v Rossii v 1857–1861gg: Sbornik dokumentov* (Moscow: 1963), p. 498.

73. Douglas Hay, *Albion's Fatal Tree: Crime and Society in Eighteenth-Century England* (New York: Pantheon Books, 1975) p. 74.

CHAPTER FIVE
INTERSECTIONS OF WESTERN AND RUSSIAN CULTURE:
RUSSIAN HISTORICAL ECONOMICS

1. Although a distinction should be made between historical economics and economic history, both fields became increasingly marginal to the study of economics in the United States and Great Britain after World War I. The exclusion of German economics was particularly notable. In 1983, a survey of seven leading economic journals revealed that seventy percent of the articles dealt with British economists. See Neil De Marchi and John Lodewijks, "HOPE and the Journal Literature in the History of Economic Thought," *History of Political Economy* 15, no. 3 (fall 1983): 321–43. Among the scholarly works to address this issue since the 1980s are Gerard Koot, *English Historical Economics, 1870–1926: The Rise of Economic History and Neomercantilism* (New York: Cambridge University Press, 1987); D. C. Coleman, *History and the Economic Past: An Account of the Rise and Decline of Economic History* (Oxford: Oxford University Press, 1987); and Alon Kadish, *Historians, Economists and Economic History* (New

York: Routledge, 1989). English language studies of German historical economics are rare. See Nicholas Balabkins, *Not By Theory Alone: The Economics of Gustav von Schmöller and His Legacy to America* (Berlin: Duncker & Humblot, 1988); and n. 11 below.

2. Useful discussions of this period are contained in Abbott Gleason, *Young Russia: The Genesis of Russian Radicalism in the 1860s* (Chicago: University of Chicago Press, 1983); A. A. Kornilov, *Obshchestvennoe dvizhenie pri Aleksandre II, 1855–1881 istoricheskie ocherki* (Paris: Société nouvelle de librairie et d'édition, 1905); N. M. Pirumova, *Zemskoe liberal'noe dvizhenie* (Moscow: 1977); Richard Stites, *The Women's Liberation Movement in Russia* (Princeton: Princeton University Press, 1978); Venturi, *Roots of Revolution*; and Vilenskaia, *Revoliutsionnoe.*

3. According to the economist Henry Sidgwick, writing in 1885: "Some 35 years ago both the theory of political economy and its main outlines, and the most important applications of it, were considered as finally settled by the great number of educated persons in England." Dewey, "The Rehabilitation of the Peasant Proprietor," pp. 42–44; and see Erin O'Brien, "Neglected but not Forgotten: The English Historical Economists," undergraduate honors paper, Department of History, University of Massachussets, Boston, 1988.

4. Quoted in John Stuart Mill, *Principles of Political Economy With Some of Their Applications to Social Philosophy*, ed. Sir William Ashley (Fairfield, N.J.: A. M. Kelley, 1976), p. 773. See discussion of Mill's position in Dewey, "The Rehabilitation," pp. 17–47; and David Martin, "The Rehabilitation of the Peasant Proprietor in Nineteenth-Century Economic Thought: A Comment," *History of Political Economy* 8, no.2 (1976): 297–302.

5. T. E. Cliffe-Leslie, *Essays in Moral and Political Philosophy* (London: 1879), p. 212.

6. Quoted in Joseph Dorfman, "The Role of the German Historical School in American Economic Thought," *Proceedings of the American Economic Association* 45 (May 1955): 21.

7. In the 1870s and 1880s, the work of Ingram and Rogers became popular texts for English trade unions and for socialist-sponsored educational activities, and appeared in a wide range of foreign translations. See Koot, *English Historical Economics*, pp. 39–59, 63–82, 135–55, 142–50; and D. C. Coleman, *History and the Economic Past*, pp. 38, 43–48, 57–58, 85–86.

8. Dewey, "The Rehabilitation," p. 38.

9. Quoted in John Cunningham Wood, *British Economists and the Empire* (New York: St. Martin's Press, 1983), p. 71.

10. Alfred Marshall, *The Present Position of Economics* (London: Macmillan and Company, 1885), p. 12.

11. Cliffe-Leslie, *Essays*, pp. 148–66.

12. An important early study of Roscher and his school is William Cherin's "The German Historical School of Economics: A Study in Methodology of the Social Sciences" (Ph.D. diss., University of California at Berkeley, 1933).

13. Wilhelm Roscher, *Principles of Political Economy*, vol. 1 (Chicago: Callaghan and Company, 1882), from the 13th 1877 German edition, p. 113.

14. Cherin, "The German Historical School," pp. 9–10.

15. See general discussion in Ulla Schafer, *Historische Nationaloekonomie und Sozialstatistik als Gesellschaftswissenschaften* (Vienna: Bohlau, 1971); and Gottfried Eisermann, *Die Grundlagen des Historismus in der deutschen Nationaloekonomie* (Stuttgart: F. Enke, 1956); and Nicholas Balabkins, *Not by Theory*.

16. According to Knies, the liberal economists J. B. Say and David Ricardo stubbornly insisted on the universal applicability of their theories despite their willingness to recognize a variety of "exceptions." See Knies, *Politische Oekonomie vom geschichtlichen Standpunkte* (Braunschweig: C. A. Schwetschke, 1883), p. 424.

17. Bruno Hildebrand, *Die Nationaloekonomie der Gegenwart und Zukunft und andere gesammelte Schriften*, ed. H. Gehrig (Jena: G. Fischer, 1922), pp. 27–29 (published in Russian translation in 1860).

18. Schmöller's *Grundrisse* went through seven German editions. An accessible introduction to his work is Schmöller, "The Idea of Justice in Political Economy," trans. Carl Schurz, *Annals of the American Academy of Political and Social Sciences* 4 (1894): 697–736. For an extremely positive assessment of Schmöller's greatness as an economist, see Joseph Schumpeter, "Gustav von Schmöller und die Probleme von Heute," *Schmöllers Jahrbuch für Gesetzgebung, Verwaltung und Volkswirtschaft* 50 (1926): 1–52.

19. Quoted in Paul Lambert, "Emile de Laveleye," *History of Political Economy*, vol. 1, no. 2 (1970): 272.

20. See the useful general discussion in Dieter Lindenlaub, *Richtungskämpfe in Verein für Sozialpolitik* (Wiesbaden: F. Steiner, 1967).

21. For Wagner, and even more for "agrarian" writers like Rätzel, Treitschke, and Haekel, the defense of peasants as "true Germans" was linked with ideologies of racism and imperialism. See Kenneth Barkin, *The Controversy over German Industralization 1880–1902* (Chicago: University of Chicago Press, 1970), pp. 138–47; and especially Woodruff Smith, *The Ideological Origins of Nazi Imperialism* (New York: Oxford University Press, 1986), pp. 21–30.

22. See Heinz Barthel, et al., "Karl Bücher: Seine politische und wissenschaftliche Stellung," in Ernst Engelberg, ed., *Karl-Marx-Universität Leipzig, 1409–1959*, vol. 2 (Leipzig: Verlag Enzyklopedie, 1959), pp. 78–91; and *International Encyclopedia of the Social Sciences*, vol. 2, pp. 163–66.

23. Roscher, *The Principles of Political Economy*, pp. 71–75, 176–77, 239.

24. Laveleye, *De la propriété*, pp. xiii–xiv.

25. According to the Russian Marxist Plekhanov, the *kathedersozialisten* wanted a prosperous bourgeoisie without an exploited proletariat (a clear impossibility from his point of view). See discussion in Barkin, *The Controversy over German Industrialization*, pp. 183–47.

26. While they recognized the importance of economic security, is is significant that *kathedersozialisten* were by no means unanimous in their support for a more democratic or inclusive political system. Cliffe-Leslie, *Essays*, pp. 444–45.

27. For a more detailed discussion of classical Marxism, see Esther Kingston-Mann, *Lenin and the Problem of Marxist Peasant Revolution*, pp. 9–18.

28. See chapter 6, pp. 132–35.

29. Eisermann, *Die Grundlagen*, p. 172; and see especially Roscher, *Ansichten der Volkswirtschaft aus dem geschichtlichen Standpunkte* (Leipzig and Heidelberg: 1861), pp. 1–6.

30. See chapter 4, pp. 93–95.

31. Karl Marx, *Capital* (London: W. Glaisher, 1909), vol. 1, p. 13.

32. Although it has been rightly argued that *Capital* contained a number of useful comments about land nationalization and associations of small producers, they are sparse, and exerted relatively little influence upon his nineteenth-century admirers. *Capital*, vol. 3, pp. 945–46; and chapter 6, pp. 140–46.

33. See *Capital*, vol. 3, p. 739.

34. *Capital*, vol. 3, p. 938.

35. *Capital*, vol. 1, p. 835.

36. See Chicherin, "Die Leibeigenschaft in Russland," *Deutsche-Staats-wort-erbuch*, vol. 6 (Stuttgart: J. C. Bluntschli and K. Brater, 1861), pp. 393–411; and Kavelin "Einiges über die russische Dorfgemeinde," *Tübingen Zeitschrift* 1 (1864): 1–53. Kavelin's essay "Obshchinnoe vladenie" (1876) was translated into German and published in book form as *Der bauerliche Gemeindebesitz in Russland* (Leipzig: 1877).

37. Roscher was particularly impressed by Kavelin's article in the *Tübingen Zeitschrift*. The "German-Russian" school is discussed in volume 2 of Wilhelm Roscher's *Die System der Volkswirtschaft: Nationaloekonomik des Ackerbaues und der verwandten Urproductionen*, 4th ed. (Stuttgart: 1865). I have also used the 13th edition (Stuttgart: J. G. Cotta, 1903) to trace the changing references to Russian data. See also Roscher "Die Deutsch-Russische Schule der Nationaloekonomik," *Berichte über die Verhandlungen der königlich Sächsischen Gesellschaft der Wissenschaften zu Leipzig Philologisch-Historische Klasse* (1870): 139–180.

38. Maurer, *Einleitung zur Geschichte des Mark-, Hof-, Dorf-, und Stadt-Verfassung und der öffentlichen Gewalt* (Munich: 1854). This work was translated into Russian in 1880 as *Vvedenie v istoriiu obshchinnogo podvornogo, sel'skogo i gorodskogo ustroistva i obshchestvennoi vlasti* (Moscow: 1880); and see also A. I. Danilov, *Problemy agrarnoi istorii rannego Srednevekov'ia v nemetskoi istoriografiia kontsa xix–nachala xx v.* (Moscow: 1958), pp. 161–62.

39. See discussion in Cliffe-Leslie, *Essays*, p. 206.

40. Maine, *Ancient Law: Its Connection with the Early History of Society, and Its Relation to Modern Ideas* (New York: H. Holt and Company, 1875), pp. 258–59.

41. B. E. Lippincott, *Victorian Critics of Democracy: Carlyle, Ruskin, Arnold, Stephen, Maine, Lecky* (Minneapolis: University of Minnesota Press, 1938), pp. 167–206.

42. Laveleye, *De la propriété*, pp. 28–29. Along similar lines, Henry Maine spoke of Haxthausen's account of the Russian peasant commune as "the revelation of a new social order, having no counterpart in the West." Quoted in George Stocking, *Victorian Anthropology* (New York: Free Press, 1987), p. 121.

43. Laveleye, *De la propriété*, p. 41.

44. Laveleye, *De la propriété*, p. 23.

45. See discussion of Smith's position in chapter 1, pp. 18–19.

46. Laveleye, *De la propriété*, pp. 30–31, 41.

47. Laveleye, *De la propriété*, pp. xiii–xiv.

48. Laveleye, "Land Systems of Belgium and Holland," in *Systems of Land Tenure in Various Countries. A Series of Essays Published under the Sanction of the Cobden Club*, edited by J. W. Probyn (London, New York: Cassell, Petter, Galpin, 1881), p. 444.

49. Quoted in Eisermann, *Die Grundlagen*, p. 202; Balabkins, *Not by Theory*, p. 40,

50. Kautsky, "Schmöller über den Fortschritt der Arbeiterklass," *Die Neue Zeit* 22 (1904): 229–31, 236.

51. See Warren Samuels, "Ashley's and Taussig's Lectures on the History of Economic Thought at Harvard, 1895–1897," *History of Political Economy* 9 (October 1977): 384–411.

52. In a survey of 116 American economists and sociologists carried out between 1873 and 1905, 53 out of the 80 who were considered the most influential identified themselves with the German historical school of economics. Jurgen Herbst, *The German Historical School in American Scholarship: A Study in the Transfer of Culture* (Ithaca, N.Y.: Cornell University Press, 1965), pp. 128–29.

53. Joseph Dorfman, "The Role of the German Historical School in American Economic Thought," *Proceedings of the American Economic Association* 45 (May 1955): 17.

54. Taussig studied with Adolph Wagner, Ely with Karl Knies, and Small with Roscher himself. In 1940, Small was elected president of the Economic History Association. Balabkins, *Not By Theory*, pp. 102–4. In the words of Taussig, German scholarship had achieved "a degree of perfection that astonishes the world." Dorfman, "The Role of the German Historical School," pp. 21–22.

55. After the Russian revolution of 1917, Taussig's (and Harvard's) enthusiasm diminished. In a textbook that became the standard introduction to economics for American economics students in the 1920s, Taussig criticized the historical economist Ingram as "somewhat radical" and Roscher as "unfortunate in taking Germany as the center" of his work. See Dorfman, "Role of German Historical School," p. 27; Jurgen Herbst, *German Historical School*, pp. 148–59; and Samuels, "Ashley's and Taussig's Lectures," p. 411.

56. Karataev, *Ekonomicheskie nauki v Moskovskom universitete*, pp. 115–16.

57. See for example, Cliffe-Leslie, *Vladenie i pol'zovanie zemlieu v razlichnykh stranakh* (St. Petersburg: 1871); and discussion by I. D. Ivaniukov, "Sintez ob uchenii ekonomicheskoi politike," *Russkaia mysl'* 2 (1880): 28–29; and N. K. Karataev, ed., *Narodnicheskaia ekonomicheskaia literatura. Izbrannye proizvedeniia* (Moscow: 1958), pp. 88–89, 131–58.

58. A. P. Shchapov, *Sochineniia* 4 (England: Farnborough, Gregg, 1971), pp. 201, 238–40; and see also Tvardovskaia, *Ideologiia poreformennogo*, pp. 62–63.

59. A number of populist writers, most notably Chernyshevskii and Shelgunov, were equally contemptuous of the relativism of the German Historical School and of Roscher in particular. According to Chernyshevskii, one could prove either the benefits or defects of slavery, torture or the workings of the market by a judicious quotation from the voluminous works of Roscher. For a Soviet account that emphasizes Schmöller's effort to eliminate Social Democratic influence on the masses, see A. I. Danilov, *Problemy agrarnoi istorii*, pp. 26–27.

60. V. V. Sviatlovskii, *Politicheskaia ekonomiia* (Moscow: 1900), pp. 124–25.

61. In the 1870s, Mikhailov published a series of articles in *Sovremennik*, which attempted to refute European and Russian notions of the physical, mental, and moral inferiority of women. See, for example, M. L. Mikhailov, *Zhenshchiny* (St. Petersburg: 1903).

62. Bervi, *Polozhenie rabochego klassa v Rossii* (St. Petersburg: 1869), 217–18.

63. See discussion in A. I. Pashkov and N. A. Tsagalov, *Istoriia russkoi ekonomicheskoi mysli* (Moscow: 1955), pp. 317 and 251.

64. See, for example, Peter Berger and Thomas Luckmann, *The Social Construction of Reality* (Garden City, N.Y.: Anchor Books, 1966); Berger, *Pyramids of Sacrifice*; and Denis Goulet, *The Cruel Choice: A New Concept in the Theory of Development* (Lanham, Md.: University Press of America, 1985).

65. See discussion of "tutelage" and "pitiless punishment" by reformers in the reign of Catherine II in chapter 2, pp. 49–52; and the observations of Khomiakov in chapter 3, pp. 80–81.

66. Quoted in Alexander Vucinich, *Science in Russian Culture* (Stanford, Cal.: Stanford University Press, 1970), p. 13; and see Shkurinov, *Pozitivizm v Rossii xix veka*, pp. 119–226.

67. A. F. Shchapov, *Sochineniia* 4, pp. 8–9. See Roger Bartlett's valuable discussion "A. F. Shchapov, the Commune, and Chernyshevskii," *Russian Thought and Society 1800–1917: Essays in Honour of Eugene Lampert*, ed. Bartlett (Keele: University of Keele Press, 1984), pp. 67–91.

68. G. E. Eliseev, in Karataev, ed., *Narodnicheskaia ekonomicheskaia literatura*, p. 153.

69. N. K. Mikhailovskii, *Sochineniia*, vol. 1 (St. Petersburg: 1906), pp. 905–6, vol. 2, p. 293, and vol. 3, pp. 285–86. See also discussion in Vucinich, *Science in Russian Culture*, pp. 24–30.

70. The government responded to the publication of this book by arresting the publishers and attempting—unsuccessfully—to seize all available copies.

71. Bervi, *Polozhenie rabochego klassa*, p. 207.

72. Bervi, in Karataev, ed., *Narodnicheskaia ekonomicheskaia literatura*, pp. 201 and 213.

73. *Polozhenie,* pp. 207, 218, and N. Bervi, "Sokhranitsiia li obshchinnoe vladenie?" *Otechestvennye zapiski* 1 (1877): 213–38.

74. This phrase is Teodor Shanin's, from unpublished comments at The First International Conference on the Peasants of European Russia, Boston, June 1990.

75. *Trudy imperatorskogo vol'nogo ekonomicheskogo obshchestva* (Proceedings of the Imperial Free Economic Society, cited hereafter as *TIVEO*) 4 (February 1866): 328.

76. I. I. Kudritskii, *S'ezd sel'skikh khoziaev v Sankt Peterburge v. 1865* (St. Petersburg: 1866), pp. 195–96.

77. *TIVEO* 1 (February 1866): 316; and see also V. A. Panaev, A. I. Astaurov, *TIVEO* 4 (October 1866): 1–17; and 4 (December 1866): 522–38.

78. See the careful analysis of the debates and investigations of the 1870s in Steven Grant, "The Peasant Commune in Russian Thought," pp. 192–272 (especially pp. 198–99).

79. A perceptive comparison between their efforts and the activities of the American students who participated in the Mississippi "freedom summer" of the 1960s was drawn by Abbott Gleason in *Young Russia*, pp. 123, 135–36.

80. Chuprov, *Rechi*, vol. 1, pp. 48–50.

81. Karataev, *Ekonomicheskie nauki*, p. 163. See the introduction by N. A. Kablukov to Chuprov, *Rechi*, vol. 1, pp. xxxvi–xxxvii.

82. Kingston-Mann, "Breaking the Silence," *Peasant Economy*, and "Understanding Peasants, Understanding the Experts: Zemstvo Statisticians in Pre-revolutionary Russia," paper presented at the First International Conference on Peasant Culture and Consciousness, Bellagio, Italy, January 1992."

83. Chuprov, *Rechi*, vol. 1, pp. 12–17; and Chuprov, *Istoriia politicheskoi ekonomii* (Moscow: 1913), p. 213.

84. See, for example, A. L. Reuel, *Russkaia ekonomicheskaia mysl' 60–70-khgodov xix veka i marksizm* (Moscow: 1956), p. 287; and Karataev, *Istoriia*, vol. 2, p. 57.

85. N. I. Ziber, *David Rikardo i Karl Marks v ikh obshchestvenno-ekonomicheskikh issledovaniiakh* (St. Petersburg: 1885). Ziber's view was shared by the eminent economist Joseph Schumpeter, who described Marx as a Ricardian economist. Schumpeter, *History of Economic Analysis*, pp. 390. 649, 682.

86. See discussion in Reuel, *Russkaia ekonomicheskaia mysl' 60–70-kho godov xix veka i marksizm* (Moscow: 1956), pp. 295–311.

87. Ziber, "O kollektivnom kharaktere pervonachal'noi nedvizhnoi sobstvennosti," *Sobranie sochinenii*, vol. 1 (St. Petersburg: 1900), p. 47.

88. See especially Ziber, *David Rikardo i Karl Marks*, pp. 140–41.

CHAPTER SIX
CAPTURING THE "ESSENCE" OF MARX:
THE EMERGENCE OF ORTHODOX MARXISM

1. Quoted in Haruki Wada, "Marx and Revolutionary Russia," in *Late Marx and the Russian Road: Marx and the Peripheries of Capitalism*, ed. Teodor Shanin (New York: Monthly Review Press, 1983), pp. 40–76.

2. Quoted in Karl Marx and Friedrich Engels, *Sochineniia*, vol. 32 (Moscow: 1961), p. 358, and see also Shanin, "Late Marx: Gods and Craftsmen," in *Late Marx*, pp. 3–39.

3. Kingston-Mann, *Lenin*, p. 16–17

4. See discussion of Enlightenment attitudes toward the peasantry in chapter 1, pp. 22–24.

5. Marx, in Karl Marx and Friedrich Engels, *Selected Works*, vol. 1 (Moscow: 1969), pp. 494–99; Kingston-Mann, *Lenin*, pp. 16–17; Edward Said, *Orientalism*, pp. 153–56; and *Karl Marx: Surveys from Exile*, ed. David Fernbach (London: Penguin Books, 1973), pp. 306–7, 320.

6. See discussion in Danilov, *Problemy agrarnoi istorii* , p. 205.

7. See Shanin, ed., *Late Marx and the Russian Road*, pp. 15, 18–110; and chapter 5, pp. 117–19.

8. Quoted in *Karl Marx über Formen vorkapitalistischen Produktion: Vergleichende Studien zur Geschichte d. Grundeigentums 1879–1880*, ed. P. Harstick (Frankfurt am Main; New York: Campus-Verlag, 1977), p. 88.

9. Quoted in *Karl Marx über Formen vorkapitalistischen Produktion*, pp. 106, 150.

10. Throughout this chapter, I have been deeply indebted to the extraordinarily valuable discussion of Marx's changing views in James White, "Marx and the Russians: The Romantic Heritage," *Scottish Slavonic Review* 7 (October 1987): 51–81.

11. According to Marx, the People's Will (*Narodnaia Volia*) was "the leading detachment of the revolutionary movement in Europe." Quoted in V. Ia. Iakovlev (V. Bogucharskii), *Iz istorii politicheskoi bor'by v 70-kh i 80-kh gg. xix veka: Partiia narodnoi voli, eia proizkhozhdenie, sud'by i gibel'* (Moscow: 1912), p. 470.

12. Letter to Sorge, Karl Marx and Friedrich Engels, *Werke* (Berlin: Dietz, 1966), vol. 34, p. 477.

13. Safronov, *M. M. Kovalevskii*, pp. 23–24.

14. Karl Marx and Friedrich Engels, *Selected Correspondence 1846–1895: A Selection with Commentary and Notes* (London: Lawrence, 1934), pp. 282–83; Marx and Engels, *Sochineniia*, vol. 32, p. 358; and Reuel, *Russkaia ekonomicheskaia*, p. 185.

15. Quoted in M. Rubel and M. Manale, *Marx Without Myth: A Chronological Study of His Life and Work* (Oxford: Basil Blackwell, 1975), p. 252; and see also T. Shanin, ed., *Late Marx*, p. 14.

16. Marx was referring to Adolph Wagner, a *kathedersozialist* who began his career at the University of Dorpat. Wagner published a book critical of the peasant commune, entitled *Die Abschaffung des privaten Eigentums* (1871). As a professor at the University of Berlin, he sided with Chicherin and dismissed Beliaev, Haxthausen, and Alexander Herzen as Slavophiles, conservatives, and communists respectively. *Perepiska K. Marksa i F. Engel'sa s russkimi politicheskimi deiatel'iami* (Leningrad: 1951), vol. 2, p. 93. See chapter 5, p. 116.

17. In the Slavophile/"Westernizer" controversy of the 1840s, Kavelin was the only "Westernizer" who maintained an open mind on the future of the commune. Writing from a vantage point far closer to the center of power in Russian society than Daniel'son or Chuprov, he served briefly as the tutor of the young Alexander II. See chapter 5, p. 120.

18. Kavelin's "Obshchinnoe vladenie." A review essay of the work of A. S. Posnikov, *Obshchinnoe zemlevladenie* (Yaroslavl and Odessa: 1875), E. Iakushkin, *Obychnoe pravo* (Yaroslavl: 1875), Laveleye, *De la propriété et de ses formes primitives*, and Johannes Keussler, *Zur Geschichte und Kritik des bauerlichen Gemeindebesitzes in Russland* (Riga: 1876–87). See especially "Obshchinnoe vladenie," *Nedelia*, nos. 3–5 (1877): 130–45 and nos. 6–7 (1878): 210–28.

19. Kavelin, "Obshchinnoe vladenie," *Nedelia* nos. 3–5 (1877): 128–29, and nos. 6–7 (1878): 210, 217, 219, 223. Such arguments were, of course, identical with those advanced by German historical economists of the *Verein für Sozialpolitik*: "Obshchinnoe vladenie," *Nedelia* (1877–78): 123–33, 210–28, and 134.

20. Quoted in White, "Marx and the Russians," p. 72.

21. Marx "Letter to Mikhailovskii" (1877) in *Selected Correspondence of Karl Marx and Friedrich Engels, 1846–1895* (New York: International Publisher, 1944), pp. 354–55.

22. The following discussion of Daniel'son's position is based largely on *Ocherki nashego poreformennogo khoziaistve* (St. Petersburg: 1893), especially pp. 342–45; and his "Apologiia vlast' deneg, kak priznak vremeni," *Russkoe bogatstvo* (January 1895 and February 1895), especially January, pp. 168–69 and February, pp. 30–34.

23. Daniel'son, *Ocherki*, p. 323.

24. In general, social critics (both Marxist and non-Marxist) were more likely than economists and statisticians to debate the "possibility" or "impossibility" of capitalism. For a fuller discussion of their debates, see Walicki, *The Controversy over Capitalism*; and Arthur Mendel, *Dilemmas of Progress in Tsarist Russia: Legal Marxism and Legal Populism* (Cambridge, Mass.: Harvard University Press, 1961).

25. Daniel'son, *Ocherki*, p. 113.

26. T. I. Grin, *K. Marks, F. Engel's i revoliutsionnaia Rossiia: K. 160-letiiu so dnia rozhdeniia K. Marksa: Rek. ukaz. lit.* (Moscow: 1978), p. 437. See Kingston-Mann, *Lenin*. A useful and carefully nuanced discussion of Daniel'son that does not make use of Russian language sources is contained in Athar Hussain and Keith Tribe, *Marx and Engels on the Agrarian Crisis*, vol. 2 (London: Macmillan, 1981), pp. 16–50.

27. See S. Mitskevich, *Na grani dvukh epokh* (Moscow: 1937), p. 128; *Katorga i ssylka*, no. 1 (1934): 78, and discussion in Richard Pipes's magisterial *Struve*, pp. 79–80, 83.

28. Shanin, ed., *Late Marx*, p. 14.

29. Marx and Engels, *Selected Correspondence*, p. 412. Marx worked very carefully on this formulation. For earlier drafts of this passage, see *Late Marx*, pp. 99–123. See also Walicki, *Controversy*, pp. 179–94.

30. *Capital*, vol. 3, pp. 945–46.

31. In contrast to Plekhanov, Orlov himself attributed inequalities between rich and poor in Moscow province to the influence of factors external to the commune. Like most of the leading statisticians of his day, Orlov considered the commune to have some potential as an economic institution. A detailed and valuable discussion of Orlov and his colleagues is contained in Steven Grant, "The Peasant Commune in Russian Thought," pp. 269–72; and see also Kingston-Mann, "Peasant Communes and Economic Innovation," pp. 23–51.

32. In 1887, Plekhanov angrily declared that Russian revolutionaries had tried to minister to the needs of the peasantry, but had met with no peasant support, sympathy, or understanding. *Sochineniia*, ed. D. Riazanov (Moscow: 1923), vol. 2, pp. 221–22.

33. Engels sent a copy to Zasulich in 1884 (the year after Marx's death). The letter finally appeared in 1886 in the radical journal *Vestnik narodnoi voli*, shortly after Engels sent a copy of it to Daniel'son. White, "Marx and the Russians," p. 75.

34. See D. B. Riazanov, "Briefwechsel zwischen Vera Zasulich und Marx," *Marx-Engels Archiv: Zeitschrift des Marx-Engels-Instituts in Moskau*, vol. 2 (Frankfurt am Main: Marx-Engels-Archiv verlagsgesellschaft m.b.h., 1927), pp. 309–10.

35. G. V. Plekhanov, *Sochineniia*, vol. 10, p. 129.

36. Plekhanov, *Sochineniia*, vol. 2, p. 221–22 and p. 271; see also Samuel Baron's study, *Plekhanov: The Father of Russian Marxism* (Stanford, Cal.: Stanford University Press, 1966), pp. 99–106.

37. See discussion in Kingston-Mann, *Lenin*, pp. 33–34.

38. Plekhanov's 1879 statement appears in *Sochineniia*, vol. 1, p. 61. His later comment is cited in B. N. Kozmin, "Neizdannye pis'ma G. V. Plekhanova i P. L. Lavrova," *Literaturnoe nasledstvo*, nos. 19–21 (1935): 293.

39. Pipes, *Struve*, pp. 91–92; Peter B. Struve, *Kriticheskiia zametki k voprosu ob ekonomicheskom razvitii Rossii*, vol. 1 (St. Petersburg: 1894), p. 124.

40. Struve's "Manchesterite" leanings were discussed in K. Golovin, *Russkii Vestnik* (December 1894): 311–29.

41. A. A. Manuilov, "K voprosu o mobilizatsii zemel. sobst.," *Russkoe bogatstvo* 6 (1897): 34–41.

42. Daniel'son was extremely critical of Struve's scholarship, accusing him of ignoring 99 percent of the statistical studies published in the past twenty years in order to support the "prejudices of Plekhanov and Skvortsov about the predominant and progressive role of capitalism in the Russian countryside." *Russkoe Bogatstvo* 3 (March 1895): 54.

43. See discussion in Pipes, *Struve*, p. 61, pp. 90–91.

44. See Pipes, *Struve*, p. 326; and P. B. Struve, "Karl Marks i sud'by marksizmy," *Segodnia* (Riga: 1921): 130–31.

45. For a discussion of the data compiled by Vorontsov and others, see Kingston-Mann, "Peasant Communes and Economic Innovation," pp. 36–40.

46. Quoted in Richard Pipes, "Russian Marxism and Its Populist Background: The Late Nineteenth Century," *Russian Review* 19, no. 4 (October 1960): 319; and Pipes, *Struve*, pp. 85–86. See also A. S. Martynov, "Glavneishye momenty v istorii russkogo marksizma," *Obshchestvennoe dvizhenie v Rossii v nachale xix veka*, vol. 2, part 2 (St. Petersburg: 1909–14), p. 286.

47. G. V. Plekhanov, *Sochineniia*, vol. 9, p. 156.

48. See Pipes, *Struve*, p. 64; V. I. Lenin, *Polnoe sobranie sochinenii* (PSS), vol. 3 (Moscow: 1958), pp. 185–87, pp. 191–98; and Plekhanov, *Sochineniia*, vol. 10, p. 129.

49. Quoted in *Reminiscences of Marx and Engels* (Moscow: 1962), p. 320.

50. Daniel'son to Engels, *Perepiska k. marksa i f. engel'sa s russkimi politicheskimi deiatel'iami* (Leningrad: 1951), cited hereafter as *Perepiska*, p. 156.

51. Engels to Daniel'son, *Perepiska*, p. 168.

52. Daniel'son to Engels, *Perepiska*, p. 118.

53. Daniel'son to Engels, *Perepiska*, p. 183.

54. Engels to Daniel'son, *Perepiska*, p. 184.

55. See discussion in chapter 7.

56. See chapter 8, p. 171.

57. At the same time, Plekhanov conceded that such arguments might have been valid in the early 1880s. See Plekhanov to Engels, *Perepiska*, p. 329.

58. Engels to Daniel'son, *K. Marks, F. Engels i revoliutsionnaia Rossiia*, pp. 712–13. Engels to Daniel'son, *Perepiska*, p. 340.

59. It was revealing that in 1905, Mensheviks and Bolsheviks would debate endlessly over the question of whether Russia was in fact experiencing a bour-

geois-democratic revolution. See discussion in Kingston-Mann, *Lenin*, p. 85, and chapter 8, pp. 173–76.

60. See discussion of the uses of late-nineteenth-century *zemstvo* statistical data in Kingston-Mann and Mixter, eds., *Peasant Economy, Culture, and Politics*, pp. 11–12.

CHAPTER SEVEN
IN SEARCH OF THE TRUE WEST:
ENGLAND, DENMARK, AND GERMANY

1. Pipes, *Struve*, p. 39.

2. See discussion in Pipes, *Struve*, p. 106, and the careful analysis by Steven Grant, "The Peasant Commune in Russian Thought," pp. 332–39. Among the *zemstvo* statisticians whose evidence indicated that the commune in their respective regions was surviving and capable of performing at least as well as private agricultural proprietors are: A. A. Dudkin, N. Dobrotvorskii, V. N. Grigoriev, I. M. Krasnoperov, L. S. Lichkov, V. I. Orlov, V. Prugavin, N. N. Romanov, F. A. Shcherbina and K. Ermolinskii, and S. N. Iuzhakov. Many of these researchers were sympathetic to the peasantry (which made them, in Marxist terms, "subjective"). But they were not uncritical enthusiasts. Most believed that the commune was a viable institution, at least for the time being. Only a few argued that the commune was the best economic arrangement for the peasantry for the indefinite future. See the discussions of *zemstvo* statistics by A. F. Fortunatov, "Obshchii obzor zemskoi statistikikrest'ianskogo khoziaistva," in *Itogi ekonomicheskogo issledovaniia Rossii po dannym zemskoi statistiki* (Moscow: 1892), vol. 2; N. A. Svavitskii, *Zemskie podvornye perepisi (obzor metodologii)* (Moscow: 1961); and Esther Kingston-Mann, "Understanding Peasants, Understanding the Experts: Zemstvo Statisticians in Pre-revolutionary Russia," paper presented at the First International Conference on Peasant Culture and Consciousness, Bellagio, Italy, January 1992.

3. See general discussion in B. G. Mogil'nitskii, *Politicheskie i metodologicheskie idei russkoi liberal'noi medievistiki serediny 70-x godov xix v.—nachala 900-x godov* (Tomsk: 1969), pp. 51–53; and Danilov, *Problemy agrarnoi istorii*, pp. 36–39.

4. Paul Vinogradoff, *Villeinage in England: Essays in English Medieval History* (Oxford: Clarendon Press, 1892), p. vi.

5. Fustel's work was translated into Russian as *Istoriia obshchestvennogo stroia drevnei Frantsii* (St. Petersburg: 1901–10), 6 vol. Frederick Seebohm's *The English Village Community* (London: 1896), went through five editions in thirteen years. See discussion in Mogil'nitskii, *Politicheskie*, pp. 134–35. The works of Maitland and Seebohm were generously cited by Baron Firks (Schedo-Ferrati) in his *Études sur l'Avenir de la Russie* (Berlin: 1868).

6. See, for example, Paul Vinogradov, *Istoriia srednikh vekov* 2d ed. (Moscow: 1899–1900), addendum, p. 3, p. 318; and *Politicheskie*, p. 39.

7. See discussion of Kovalevskii's view of Maurer in B. G. Safronov, *M. M. Kovalevskii kak sotsiolog*, pp. 79–80.

8. Luchitskii, who wrote the first archival study of communes in Spain, concluded that they did not disappear due to internal contradications or antagonisms. See Ivan Luchitskii, "Pozemel'naia obshchina v Pireneiakh," *Otechestvennye zapiski 1883*, nos. 9, 10, 12. Kareev, in a series of studies that were enthusiastically praised by the great French historian Marc Bloch, documented the government's role in determining the survival or demise of communal practices in prerevolutionary France. See N. Kareev, "Zametka o raspadenii pozemel'noi obshchiny na Zapade," *Znanie* 4 (1876): 1–14.

9. Mogil'nitskii, *Politicheskie*, pp. 476–79.

10. See Vinogradoff, *English Society in the Eleventh Century: Essays in English Medieval History* (Oxford: Clarendon Press, 1908), pp. 476–79.

11. Seebohm was in fact an active opponent of land reform proposals in late-nineteenth-century England, arguing that there could be no justification for government encroachment upon an Englishman's right to control his property. See Frederick Seebohm, "Villeinage in England," *English Historical Review* 7 (July 1892): 444–65.

12. See for example M. M. Kovalevskii, *Angliiskaia konstitutsiia i eia istorik* (Moscow: 1880), *Modern Customs and Ancient Laws of Russia* (London: D. Nutt, 1891), and *Obshchinnoe zemlevladenie, prichiny, khod i posledstviia: ego razlozheniia, chast'* 1 (Moscow: Tip. F. B. Millera, 1879).

13. See, for example, M. M. Kovalevskii, "Le passage historique de la propriété individuelle," *Annales de l'Institut International de Sociologie* 2 (1895): 175–230. Kovalevskii and liberals like P. N. Miliukov hoped that the disappearance of the Russian peasant commune would be followed by the emergence of English-style parliamentary government. See P. F. Laptin, *Obshchina v russkoi istoriografii poslednei treti xix-nachala xx v.* (Kiev: 1971); and James White, "Marx and the Russians," p. 67.

14. The contradictions in Kovalevskii's work were first noted by P. A. Sokolovskii, "O prichinakh raspadeniia pozemel'noi obshchiny," *Slovo* 10 (1887): 139. See also Mogil'nitskii *Politicheskie*, p. 64.

15. See, for example, M. M. Kovalevskii, *Razvitie narodnogo khoziaistva v zapadnoi evrope* (St. Petersburg: 1899), p. 166 and *Obshchestvennyi stroi Anglii v kontse srednikh vekov* (Moscow: 1880), p. 134.

16. It is worth noting that Posnikov's judgments are supported by the research of twentieth-century English and US scholars, who have pointed out how little attention has been paid to the economic activity of tenants. See Perry, "High Farming in Victorian Britain," pp. 156–66; and William Harbaugh, "Tenancy and Soil Conservation," A paper presented at the Agricultural History Society, Washington, D.C., 1991, p. 2.

17. Posnikov observed as well that the government's role in subsidizing and funding irrigating and drainage projects was far greater, and equally effective, in the states of Germany. Chuprov pointed out that no serious transformation of either large or small farming had ever been undertaken in the West by farmers using their own capital; in England, the state established mortgage credit systems to aid the large-scale proprietor. In Germany, France, and Denmark, credit cooperatives supplemented the state's immense investment in land improvement and in the granting of low-interest loans to small producers. See Posnikov, *Obshchinnoe*

zemlevladenie (Yaroslavl and Odessa: 1875), p. 70; and Chuprov, *Krest'ianskii vopros* (Moscow: 1909), pp. 89–90. See also A. I. Vasil'chikov's earlier work, *Zemlevladenie i zemledelie v Rossii i v drugikh evropeiskikh gosudarstvakh*, 2 vols. (St. Petersburg: 1876).

18. See chapter 4, pp. 103–4.

19. This judgment is supported by a variety of twentieth-century scholars, but see for example, W. W. Rostow, "Investment and the Great Depression in 19th-Century England," *Economic History Review* 9 (May 1939): 145–58.

20. N. A. Kablukov, *Ob usloviiakh razvitiia krest'ianskogo khozaiastva v Rossii* (Moscow: 1899), pp. 13–15.

21. A. A. Manuilov, *Pozemel'nyi vopros v Rossii* (Moscow: 1905), pp. 72–73; and *Arenda v Irlandii* (Moscow: 1895), 221; and see also Julian McQuiston, "Tenant Right: Farmer Against Landlord in Victorian England 1847–1884," *Agricultural History* 47 (April 1973): 95–113.

22. Kingston-Mann, "Peasant Communes and Economic Innovation," p. 45.

23. Quoted in Carsten Pape, "The Peasant Zemstvo," *Russian History* 11, nos. 2–3 (1984): 234.

24. N. I. Ziber, *Izbrannye ekonomicheskie proizvedeniia* (Moscow: 1959), p. 683.

25. Uspenskii and Skaldin did not undertake any systematic empirical studies. They carefully observed some of the more poverty-stricken commune villages of the post-Emancipation era and viewed them as typical. See, for example, Gleb Uspenskii, *Polnoe sobranie sochinenii 5* (Moscow: 1940): 124–50; and Skaldin (F. P. Elenev), *V zakholusti i v stolitse* (St. Petersburg: 1870).

26. An uncle of the more famous P. A. Stolypin, who devised the anticommune reforms of 1906–11, D. A. Stolypin published a number of pamphlets promoting the abandonment of strip cultivation, as well as *Uchenie Konta i primenenie ego k resheniiu voprosa ob organizatsii zemel'noi sobstvennosti* (Moscow: 1891).

27. Plekhanov, *Sochineniia*, vol. 2, p. 225.

28. M. I. Tugan-Baranovskii, *Promyshlennye krizisy; ocherk iz sotsial'noi istorii Anglii* (St. Petersburg: 1894), 1.2.

29. Lenin, *PSS*, vol. 3, p. 7.

30. Quoted in Chernyshev, *Agrarno-krest'ianskaia politika Rossii za 150 let*, pp. 238–39.

31. See, for example, A. S. Ermolov's *Neurozhai i narodnoe bedstvie* (St. Petersburg: 1892), a book that helped to raise him to the post of Minister of Agriculture; A. A. Rittikh, *Krest'ianskii pravoporiadok* (St. Petersburg: 1903); and V. I. Gurko, *Ustoi narodnogo khoziaistva Rossii: Agrarno-ekonomicheskie etiudy* (St. Petersburg: 1902), a study of Russian agriculture, which concentrated on the economic virtues of large, privately owned, landed estates and devoted only 12 out of 201 pages to the peasantry.

32. K. P. Pobedonostsev, *Kurs grazhdanskogo prava*, 3 vols. (St. Petersburg: 1896), vol. 2, pp. 543–44.

33. Vorontsov-Dashkov, quoted in Chernyshev, *Agrarno-krest'ianskaia politika*, pp. 232–35.

34. See chapter 1, p. 20.

35. See A. S. Ermolov, *Nash zemel'nyi vopros* (St. Petersburg: 1906), pp. 187–89.

36. Plekhanov, *Sochineniia*, vol. 2, pp. 203 and 344.

37. A. I. Skvortsov, *Ekonomicheskie prichiny golodovok v Rossii i mery k ikh ustranenii: Ekonomicheskie etiudy*, vol. 1 (St. Petersburg: 1894), p. 114.

38. Plekhanov, *Sochineniia*, vol. 9, pp. 161, 180, and 190.

39. Struve, *Kriticheskiia zametki*, pp. 243–44.

40. See Snell, *Annals of the Labouring Poor*; and the detailed discussion of England's agrarian crisis in Ping-ti Ho's neglected but still valuable *Land and State in Great Britain 1873–1910: A Study of Land Reform Movements and Land Policies* (Ann Arbor: University of Michigan Press, 1973), pp. 103–5, 292.

41. Struve, "Moim kritikam," in *Materialy k kharakteristike nashego khoziaistvennogo razvitiia: Sbornik statei* (St. Petersburg, Moscow: 1895), p. 174.

42. Ziber, quoted in N. K. Mikhailovskii, *Polnoe sobranie sochinenii*, vol. 9 (St. Petersburg: 1903), p. 327.

43. Plekhanov, *Sochineniia*, vol. 2, p. 271.

44. See Ngo Vinh Long, *Before the Revolution: The Vietnamese Peasants under the French* (Cambridge, Mass.: MIT Press, 1973), pp. 3–43; and see also Milton Osbourne, *The French Presence in Cochin China and Cambodia* (Ithaca, N.Y.: Cornell University Press, 1969).

45. See R. H. Bates, *Essays on the Political Economy of Rural Africa* (Cambridge: Cambridge University Press, 1983), pp. 98–99. According to another study, it was the negation of "Europe's faith in the universality of its own economic and technical norms that forced European governments to take responsibility for potentially strategic tropical territories." Ralph Austen, *Northwest Tanzania under German and British Rule* (New Haven: Yale University Press, 1968), p. 3. See also David Kimble, *A Political History of Ghana: The Rise of Gold Coast Nationalism* (Oxford: Oxford University Press, 1963); and R. C. Pratt, "Administration and Politics in Uganda, 1919–1945," in Vincent Harlow and E. M. Chilvers, eds., *History of East Africa*, vol. 2 (Oxford: Oxford University Press, 1965), pp. 476–542.

46. Quoted in Chernyshev, *Agrarno-krest'ianskaia politika*, pp. 251–52.

47. S. Iu. Witte, *Agrarnyi vopros v sovete ministrov* (Moscow: 1924), pp. 70–82. See also Francis Wcislo, *Reforming Rural Russia: State, Local Society and National Politics 1855–1914* (Princeton: Princeton University Press, 1990), pp. 122–41.

48. In the discussion which follows, I have focused on Denmark and Germany, because Denmark represents the most instructive contrast to the English example, and German models were the most influential among Russian conservatives, Marxists, and historical economists. However, the United States, Italy, and France were also much discussed in Russia's development debates. See Kingston-Mann, "Understanding Peasants."

49. Chuprov, *Krest'ianskii vopros*, pp. 78–83.

50. A similar phenomenon occurred in Italy, where Social Democrats of the early 1900s established rural syndicates to lease out machinery to farmers on a short-term basis and sent teachers to the provinces to provide technical information and to promote the organization of a wide variety of rural cooperatives. These efforts were described by Chuprov in *Melkoe zemledelie i ego osnovnyia nuzhdy* (Moscow: 1913), pp. 84–88, and *Krest'ianskii vopros*, p. 194.

51. See general discussion in Uffe Östergaard, "Peasants and Danes: The Danish National Identity and Political Culture," *Comparative Studies in Society and History* 34 (January 1992): 3–22; and T. Kjaergaard, "The Farmers' Interpretation of Danish History," *Scandinavian Journal of History* 10, no. 1 (1985): 97–118.

52. In general, later scholarship confirms Chuprov's description of Danish farm policy. See, for example, Karen J. Friedman, "Danish Agricultural Policy, 1870–1970," *Food Research Institute Studies* 13 (October 1974): 226–28. See also H. Faber, *Cooperation in Danish Agriculture*, trans. Hans Hertel (London: Longmans, Green & Co., 1918).

53. Chuprov, *Krest'ianskii vopros*, pp. 80–88.

54. See especially N. F. Christiansen, "Reformism within Danish Social Democracy until the Nineteen Thirties," *Scandinavian Journal of History* 3 (1978): 297–322; and P. Christiansen, "Peasant Adaptation to Bourgeois Culture?" *Ethnologia Scandinavica* (1978): 98–152.

55. Chuprov, *Krest'ianskii vopros*, pp. 81–82; and see also M. Ia. Gertzenshtein, *Agrarnyi vopros v programmakh razlichnykh partii* (Moscow: 1906), pp. 23–26.

56. V. P. Vorontsov, *Gosudarstvennye dolgi Rossii* (Moscow: 1908), p. 86.

57. See Gertzenshtein, *Agrarnyi vopros*, p. 13.

58. N. F. Christiansen, "Reformism within Danish Social Democracy," p. 322.

59. Unrelated to the economist and official V. P. Bezobrazov, "Evropeets" edited the journal *Vest'* and spent many years in Germany, where he published *Molodaia Rossiia* (Berlin: 1871).

60. Evropeets, *Molodaia Rossiia*, p. 37.

61. Evropeets, *Molodaia Rossiia*, p. 55. It is interesting to compare Evropeets's version of a "Prussian model" with Lenin's. See chapter 8, pp. 174–75.

62. See Anita Baker, "Community and Growth: Muddling Through with Russian Credit Cooperatives," *Journal of Economic History* 37 (March 1977): 139–60, 148–50; and see general discussion in S. N. Prokopovich, *Kooperativnoe dvizhenie v Rossii* (Moscow: 1918).

63. Quoted in P. A. Sokolovskii, *Ssud-sberegatel'nye tovarishchestva po otzyvam literatury* (St. Petersburg: 1889), p. 221. See also A. I. Vasil'chikov and A. V. Iakovlev, *Melkii zemel'nyi kredit v Rossii* (St. Petersburg: 1876), p. 45; and Vasil'chikov's much discussed study, *Zemlevladenie i zemledelie v Rossii i v drugikh evropeiskikh gosudarstvakh*.

64. Chuprov, *Krest'ianskii vopros*, pp. 85–88.

65. See R. G. Moeller, "Peasants and Tariffs in the Kaisserreich: How Backward Were the *Bauern*?" *Agricultural History* 55 (December 1981): 371–84; and Gertzenshtein, *Agrarnyi vopros*, pp. 12–13.

66. See discussion in Peter Gay, *The Dilemma of Democratic Socialism* (New York: Collier Books, 1962), pp. 162–63, 194–95.

67. See discussion in V. P. Vorontsov, *Novoe Vremia*, February 19, 1899; and Eduard David, *Sozializmus und Landwirtschaft*, vol. 1 (Berlin: Verlag der Sozialistischen Monatshefte, 1903), pp. 49, 698–99. It is interesting to compare David's effort with Lenin's unsuccessful attempt to convince the second party congress of the RSDLP (1903) to adopt an agrarian program.

68. At the same time, he was careful to point out that their efforts were less successful than those of Danish peasants. See Farr, " 'Tradition' and the Peasantry," p. 24.

69. While peasants were reproached by many European progressives of an earlier era for their mindless apathy, Kautsky considered their primitive enthusiasm for work and self-denial the proof of their inherent irrationality. The negative stereotype remained, but its content was reversed.

70. Quoted in Alexander Gerschenkron, *Bread and Democracy in Germany* (Ithaca, N.Y.: Cornell University Press, 1989), p. 29. See discussion of Engels's arguments over this issue with the Russian economist Danielson in chapter 6, pp. 144–46.

71. Quoted in William Maehl, "German Social Democratic Agrarian Policy, 1890–1895, Reconsidered," *Central European History* 13 (June 1980): 143.

72. Gary Steenson, *Karl Kautsky 1854–1938: Marxism in the Classical Years* (Pittsburgh: University of Pittsburgh Press, 1978), p. 111.

73. Other European Marxists were more flexible. See note 51. In addition to the Danish Marxists, Italian Marxists also adopted constructive policies toward the peasantry. See Giuliano Procacci, "Geografia e struttura del movimento contadino della Valle padana nel suo periodo formativo (1901–1906)," *Studi storici* 5 (1964): 40–120.

74. A. A. Isaev, *O sotsializm nashikh dnei* (Stuttgart: 1902), p. 125. According to Maehl, "Not until the Kiel convention in 1927 did the SPD make a sadly belated attempt to forestall the efforts of reactionaries to herd the farmers into the Nationalist and Nazi camps." "German Social Democratic Agrarian Policy, 1890–1895," p. 157.

75. V. I. Lenin, *Polnoe sobranie sochineniia*, vol. 3, p. 338.

76. V. M. Chernov, who emerged as a leader of the peasant-oriented Socialist Revolutionary Party (SR) after 1905, provided an incisive analysis of the Marxist dilemma in *K voprosu o kapitalizme i krest'ianstve* (Moscow: 1904), pp. 26–28.

77. A valuable discussion of the image of the "ladder" in Western thought and its attendant hierarchical implications, is contained in Betty J. Craige, *Laying the Ladder Down: The Emergence of Cultural Holism* (Amherst: University of Massachusetts Press, 1992), p. xv.

CHAPTER EIGHT
THE DEMISE OF ECONOMIC PLURALISM: CONSTRUCTING A TWENTIETH-CENTURY MODEL FOR PROGRESS AND DEVELOPMENT

1. This terminology became extremely widespread in the course of the twentieth century. A useful discussion of antifeudal arguments used in modern Pakistan is contained in Ronald Herring, "Zulfikar Ali Bhutto and the Eradication of Feudalism in Pakistan," *Comparative Studies in Society and History* 21, no. 4 (spring 1979): 521–22.

2. The vagueness and inconsistency of the progressives' generalizations about feudalism mirrored Lenin's tortuous efforts to fit peasants into a Marxian class analysis. In Lenin's writings, peasants were serfs, or members of the bourgeoisie, petty bourgeoisie, semi-proletariat, or proletariat who moved back and forth from one category to another with dizzying rapidity. See Boguslaw Galeskii, *Basic Concepts of Rural Sociology* (Manchester: Manchester University Press, 1972), p. 107; and discussion in Kingston-Mann, *Lenin*, pp. 50–51.

3. A still valuable cross-cultural discussion of feudalism is Rushton Coulborn's *Feudalism in History* (Hamden, Conn.: Archon Books, 1965).

4. For a fuller discussion of Lenin's research and the evolution of his thinking on the peasant question, see Kingston-Mann, *Lenin*.

5. Lenin's only extended reference to economists occurred in *What Is To Be Done?* (1902), a polemical work that denounced "economists" as Marxist turncoats who supported the German Revisionism of Eduard Bernstein. See the critical contemporary response to Lenin's book by the former Marxist N. S. Rusanov, "Evoliutsiia russkoi sotsialisticheskoi mysli," *Vestnik* 3 (March 1903): 23–34.

6. K. R. Kachorovskii, *Bor'ba za zemliu* (St. Petersburg: 1908), p. xlviii.

7. See also Lenin's writings of the 1894 and 1895 in *Polnoe sobranie sochineniia* 1, pp. 278, 237–38, and 395.

8. Lenin's use of economic data is discussed in Kingston-Mann, *Lenin*, pp. 48–54.

9. The work of Posnikov, Kablukov, and A. A. Kaufman were particularly influential, as were the statistical findings of researchers like N. N. Chernenkov, N. Karyshev, L. S. Lichkov, V. Trirogov, F. A. Shcherbina, A. F. Fortunatov, and A. A. Karelin. See Kingston-Mann, "Peasant Communes and Economic Innovation," pp. 23–51.

10. Among the many scholarly studies that deal with issues ignored by Lenin, see Elvira Wilbur, "Was Russian Peasant Agriculture Really that Impoverished?: Evidence from Case Study from the 'Impoverished Center' at the End of the Nineteenth Century," *Journal of Economic History* (March 1983): 137–44; Judith Pallot, "Agrarian Modernization on Peasant Farms in the Era of Capitalism," in *Studies in Russian Historical Geography*, vol. 2 (London, New York: Academic Press, 1983), pp. 432–49; Jeffrey Burds, "The Social Control of Peasant Labor in Russia: The Response of Village Communities to Labor Migration in the Central Industrial Region, 1861–1905," in *Peasant Economy, Culture, and Politics*, ed. Kingston-Mann and Mixter, pp. 52–100; Leonard Friesen, "Bukkers, Plows, and Lobogreikas: Peasant Acquisition of Agricultural Implements in New Russia before 1900," *Russian Review* 53, no. 3 (July 1994): 399–418; and Teodor Shanin, *Russia as a Developing Society*, 2 vols. (New Haven: Yale University Press, 1985).

11. See chapter 7, p. 158.

12. Kofoed was sent abroad to study European land reform policies and returned to publish a book on the topic, which appeared (in Russian) in 1906. He would serve as an adviser to A. A. Rittikh, the chief administrator of the Stolypin Reforms, and to A. V. Krivoshein, who was Russia's Minister of Agriculture between 1908 and 1915. A useful account of his role in the reform effort is contained in N. Karpov, *Agrarnaia politika Stolypina* (Leningrad: 1925). See also David Macey, *Government and Peasant in Russia, 1861–1906: The Pre-history of the Stolypin Reforms* (DeKalb: Northern Illinois University Press, 1987).

13. See C. A. Kofoed, *My Share in the Stolypin Agrarian Reforms* ed. Bend Jensen (Odense, Denmark: Odense University Press, 1985), p. 17, and *Krest'ianskie khutory na nadel'noi zemle* (Moscow: 1909), pp. 40–45.

14. Kofoed, *My Share*, pp. 18–19.

15. Wallace was a journalist for the *London Times*, whose book was the product of a six-year stay in Russia, during which time he participated in the work of

the government-appointed Valuev Commission on the state of Russian agriculture. Wallace was quite critical of the Commission's work and biased recommendations. In his words, "the conclusions of the committee are far from giving a complete and thoroughly trustworthy picture of the present agrarian condition of Russia." See Kofoed, *My Share*, p. 18; Donald MacKenzie Wallace, *Russia* (New York: H. Holt and Co., 1970), p. 511; and the critical comments on the Valuev Commission by A. I. Koshelev, *Ob obshchinnom zemlevladenii v Rossii* (Berlin: 1875).

16. Wallace, *Russia*, p. 101.

17. Wallace, *Russia*, p. 542.

18. Wallace, *Russia*, p. 142.

19. Wallace, *Russia*, p. 148.

20. See chapter 6, pp. 145–46.

21. In order to realize such a positive outcome, Marx warned that it would be necessary to eliminate "the deleterious influences which assail it [the commune] from every quarter . . ." Marx, "Letter to Zasulich," *Selected Correpondence of Karl Marx and Friedrich Engels*, p. 412. Marx worked very carefully on this formulation; earlier drafts of this passage are included in ibid., pp. 400–421. An important series of discussions of the significance of Marx's later writings is contained in *Late Marx and the Russian Road*, ed. T. Shanin, pp. 1–9; and see also chapter 6 above, pp. 141–46.

22. See discussion in Teodor Shanin, *Russia, 1905–07: Revolution as a Moment of Truth* (New Haven: Yale University Press, 1986), pp. 171–73.

23. For a useful discussion of gentry responses to peasant violence, see Roberta Manning, *Crisis of the Old Order in Russia: Gentry and Government* (Princeton: Princeton University Press, 1982), pp. 145–48, 219–21.

24. See, for example, the arguments of Prince Menshikov on the eve of Emancipation, discussed in Chapter 4, p. 107.

25. Anita Baker, "Community and Growth," p. 144.

26. See P. A. Stolypin, *Poezdka v sibir i povolzhe* (St. Petersburg: 1911), p. 117.

27. Among the wide range of valuable studies of the Stolypin Reforms, see V. S. Diakin, *Krizis samoderzhaviia v Rossii 1895–1917* (Leningrad: 1904), and *Samoderzhavie, burzhuaziia, i dvoriantsvo v 1907–1911 gg* (Leningrad: 1978); S. M. Dubrovskii, *Stolypinskaia zemel'naia reforma: Iz istorii sel'skogo khoziaistva i krest'ianstva Rossii v nachale xx veka* (Moscow: 1963); David A. J. Macey, *Government and Peasant in Russia, 1861–1906*; George L. Yaney, *The Systematization of Russian Government* (Urbana: University of Illinois Press, 1973), and *The Urge to Mobilize: Agrarian Reform in Russia 1861–1930* (Urbana: University of Illinois Press, 1982); P. N. Zyrianov, "Stolypin i sud'by russkoi derevni," *Obshchestvennye nauki i sovremennost'* 4 (1991): 117–18.

28. At one point, the Ministry of the Interior proposed that a large sum of cash be given to *khutor* peasants for "the unsubtle political purpose of 'increasing the number of individuals who wanted to leave communal land tenure.' " Eventually, this reward for choosing the *khutor* was offered at 50 rubles each. Baker, "Community and Growth," pp. 152–53.

29. The desire to ensure that progressive economic reform served the interests of a conservative political system was not a uniquely Russian phenomenon. In

early-twentieth-century Egypt, reformist policy-makers were equally convinced that far-reaching agricultural and industrial change could distract and pacify egalitarian or democratically oriented critics of traditional authority and privilege. See Charles Smith, "The Intellectual and Modernization; Definitions and Reconsiderations: The Egyptian Experience," *Comparative Studies in Society and History* 22 (1980): 524–25. Some late-nineteenth-century examples are discussed in Mariusz Dobek, *The Political Logic of Privatization: Lessons from Great Britain and Poland* (Westport, Conn.: Praeger, 1993), p. 70.

30. Vinogradov, *Politicheskie pis'ma* (St. Petersburg: 1905), p. 114.

31. A. N. Savin, "Russkie razrushiteli obshchiny i angliiski ogorazhivateli," *Moskovskii ezhenedel'nik*, no. 2 (1909): 38.

32. Chuprov, *Krest'ianskii vopros*, pp. 320–33. See also A. N. Savin, "Russkie razrushiteli obshchiny i angliiski ogorazhivateli," p. 38; and I. V. Chernyshev, *Agrarno-krest'ianskaia*, pp. 353–54, and *Obshchina posle 9 noiabria 1906 g* (Petrograd: 1917).

33. Mogil'nitskii, *Politicheskie i ekonomicheskie*, p. 72. Martov, *Iskra* 93 (March 17, 1905); and see also Martov's later comments in *Londonskii s'ezd Rossiiskoi Sots.-demokr. Rab. Partii aprel'–mai 1907 g.; Polnyi text protokolov* (Paris: Izd. Tsentral'nogo komiteta, 1909), pp. 301–3.

34. P. P. Maslov, *Agrarnyi vopros v Rossii* (St. Petersburg: 1906), vol. 2, p. 341.

35. Kingston-Mann, *Lenin*, p. 67.

36. For a detailed discussion of Lenin's nationalization strategy, see Kingston-Mann, *Lenin*, pp. 105, 151.

37. Because the major focus of this book is the pre-1905 period and because SR ideas were demonized and excluded from high-level ideological and policy debates, I have not emphasized the SR role in the foregoing discussion. But see Allison Blakely's valuable "The Socialist Revolutionary Party, 1901–1907: The Populist Response to the Industrialization of Russia" (Ph.D. diss., University of California at Berkeley, 1971); and Grant, "The Peasant Commune in Russian Thought: 1861–1905."

38. An extended discussion of this point is contained in Kingston-Mann, *Lenin*, pp. 101–27.

39. See chapter 4, pp. 93–95.

40. Useful discussions of the pervasive assumptions about peasants and their communes on the part of Russia's governing elite are contained in Yanni Kotsonis, "Agricultural Cooperatives and the Agrarian Question in Russia, 1861–1914" (Ph.D. diss., Columbia University, 1994); and Frank, "Cultural Conflict and Criminality in Rural Russia."

41. P. N. Zyrianov, *Krest'ianskaia obshchina evropeiskoi Rossii 1907–1914* (Moscow: 1992), pp. 162–68, 243–53; and see also V. S. Diakin, *Krizis samoderzhaviia v Rossii 1895–1917* (Leningrad: 1984).

42. Nineteenth-century *zemstvo* statistical data indicated that in a number of widely distant provinces, peasants who fertilized their allotments received either special monetary payments or the right to retain their original allotment. In Western Siberia, the statistician-economist A. A. Kaufman could not discover a single instance in which peasants failed to receive compensation at the time of repartition

for any investments of labor or capital that were out of the ordinary. Kaufman, *Obshchina i uspekhi sel'skogo khoziaistva v Sibirii* (St. Petersburg: 1894), pp. 133–42; and Kingston-Mann, "Peasant Communes and Economic Innovation," pp. 42–46.

43. Stolypin's telegram of 1909 urging provincial and district *zemstvos* to grant preferential treatment to peasants who attempted to establish consolidated private farms is discussed in B. B. Veselovskii, *Istorii zemstvo za sorok let*, vol. 4 (St. Petersburg: 1909–11), p. 121; and see also Kimitaka Matsuzato, "The Fate of Agronomists in Russia: Their Quantitative Dynamics from 1911 to 1916," *Russian Review* 55 (April 1996): 181–82.

44. Kimitaka Matsuzato, "Stolypinskaia reforma i Russkii tekhnologicheskii perevorot," *Acta Slavica Iaponica* 10 (1992): 33–42; and general discussion in P. Zyrianov, *Krest'ianskaia obshchina*, pp. 93–140, 227.

45. The standard work on cooperatives remains E. Kayden and A. Antsiferov, *The Cooperative Movement During the War* (New Haven: Yale University Press, 1927); and George Pavlovsky, *Agricultural Russia on the Eve of the Revolution* (New York: H. Fertig, 1968), but see also the works cited below.

46. Baker, "Community and Growth," p. 154; and see also Dominic Lieven, *Russia's Rulers under the Old Regime* (New Haven: Yale University Press, 1989); and Richard Robbins, *The Tsar's Viceroys: Russia's Provincial Governors in the Last Years of the Empire* (Ithaca, N.Y.: Cornell University Press, 1987).

47. As Baker has noted, the rapid development of cooperatives after 1906 in fact took place with a relatively small amount of government financial support. Baker, "Community and Growth," pp. 154–56.

48. See Baker, "Community and Growth," pp. 149–53; Catherine Salzman, "Consumer Cooperative Societies in Russia, Goals v. Gains 1900–1918," *Cahiers du monde Russe et Soviètique* 23, nos. 3–4 (1982): 351–69; and Yanni Kotsonis's study "Agricultural Cooperatives."

49. Quoted in Scott J. Seregny, "Teachers and Rural Cooperatives: The Politics of Education and Professional Identities in Russia, 1908–1917," *The Russian Review* 55, no. 4 (October 1996): 570.

50. Baker, "Community and Growth," p. 153.

51. See David Macey's useful discussion of "individualization" vs. "privatization" in the Stolypin Reforms, *Government and Peasant in Russia*; the detailed discussion in Atkinson, *The End of the Russian Land Commune*, pp. 79–82; and Kimitaka Matsuzato, "Stolypinskaia reforma i rossiiskaia agrotechnologicheskaia revoliutsiia," *Otechestvennaia istoriia* 6 (1992): 194–200.

52. According to Matsuzato, the years between 1906 and 1914 saw the development of an "Agro-technical Revolution," which affected commune and non-commune peasants, and went far beyond the tenure-oriented conceptions of the Stolypin Reforms. See Matsuzato, "Stolypinskaia reforma," 194–200.

53. An additional 15 percent became *otrubniki*. Diakin, *Krizis*, pp. 367–68; S. M. Dubrovskii, *Stolypinskaia zemel'naia reforma*; P. N. Zyrianov, "Stolypin i sud'by russkoi derevni," pp. 117–18.

54. As was the case during England's enclosure movement, peasant opposition frequently took the form of "everyday resistance" rather than outright re-

bellion. One of the more typical patterns of government/peasant interaction was evident in the village of Bolotovo in Tambov province, where wealthier peasants claimed their allotments as private land in 1909. Over the explicit opposition of the commune assembly, local officials allowed these peasants to claim some of the commune's best land as private property. When assembly complaints to the provincial governor brought no response, peasants began pulling up the boundary posts that marked off the newly established private property and proceeded to break into the houses of the "separators." The district police officer was driven away and when more police were sent in, jeering peasants cried, "Kill the bloodsuckers!" The police opened fire, killing eight and wounding thirteen. Cossacks were then dispatched to conduct a three-day search of the village, and seventy-seven peasants were arrested. Throughout 1910 mysterious fires broke out at the homes of separators, and boundary signs continued to disappear. M. Egorov, "Krest'ianskoe dvzhenie v tsentral'noi chernozemnoi oblasti v 1907–1914 godakh," *Voprosy istorii* 5 (1948): 14–15. See also the discussion of English resistance to enclosure, chapter 1, p. 16, and Scott, *The Weapons of the Weak*.

55. Kimitaka Matsuzato, "New Dimensions in the Studies of Russian Agrarian History," unpublished paper, 1994, p. 23.

56. V. P. Danilov, "Ob istoricheskikh sud'bakh krest'ianskoi obshchiny v Rossii," in *Ezhegodnik po agrarnoi istorii*, vol. 6, *Problemy istorii russkoi obshchiny* (Vologda: 1976), pp. 106–8.

57. Hiroshi Okuda, "The Emergence of the Kolkhoz: The End of Communes in Russia" (unpublished paper), p. ix.

58. See Orlando Figes, "Peasant Farmers and the Minority Groups of Rural Society: Peasant Egalitarianism and Village Social Relations during the Russian Revolution (1917–1921)," in Kingston-Mann and Mixter, eds., *Peasant Economy*, pp. 378–402; and Figes, *Peasant Russia, Civil War: The Volga Countryside in Revolution, 1917–1921* (Oxford: Clarendon Press, 1989).

59. See especially the journals *Russkoe bogatstvo* and *Vestnik sel'skogo khoziaistva* between 1906 and 1914, and the work of contemporary scholars like N. P. Makarov, *Krest'ianskoe kooperativnoe dvizhenie v zapadnoi Sibirii* (Moscow: 1910).

60. Kingston-Mann, *Lenin*, p. 123.

61. N. N. Sukhanov, *Marksizm i narodnichestvo* (Berlin: 1915), p. 28; and see Atkinson, *The End of the Russian Land Commune*, pp. 112–13.

62. Pipes, *Struve*, p. 43

63. N. I. Bukharin and E. P. Preobrazhenskii, *The ABC of Communism* (Ann Arbor: University of Michigan Press, 1988), pp. 165–66.

64. See the valuable discussion of the agrarian economic debates of the 1920s in Susan Gross Solomon, *The Soviet Agrarian Debates: A Controversy in the Social Sciences* (Boulder, Colo.: Westview Press, 1977); and Stephen Cohen, *Bukharin and the Bolshevik Revolution: A Political Biography 1888–1938* (New York: Knopf, 1973).

65. Kingston-Mann, "The Majority as an Obstacle to Progress: Radicals, Peasants and the Russian Revolution," *Radical America* 6, nos. 4–5 (1982): 85.

CHAPTER NINE
CULTURES OF MODERNIZATION ON THE EVE OF THE
TWENTY-FIRST CENTURY: NOTES TOWARD A CONCLUSION

1. A similar phenomenon occurred among Indian intellectuals who supported authoritarian rule, as well as modernization and development. See Edward Shils, "The Intellectual between Tradition and Modernity: The Indian Situation," *Comparative Studies in Society and History* Supplement 1 (The Hague: Mouton, 1961), pp. 16–18, pp. 24–25.

2. See chapter 2, pp. 48–50, and chapter 3, pp. 74–76.

3. See chapter 3, pp. 78–80.

4. A. I. Chuprov, *Krest'ianskii vopros*, pp. 189–90 and p. 287.

5. The following discussion reflects the influence of Patricia Hill Collins, "Learning from the Outsider Within," *Social Problems* 33, no.6 (December 1986): 514–532. See also the extremely useful discussion of the role of dichotomized thinking in Western intellectual history in Betty J. Craige, *Laying the Ladder Down: The Emergence of Cultural Holism* (Amherst: University of Massachusetts Press, 1992), pp. 3–4.

6. In the decades that followed the Bolshevik seizure of power, the dichotomized thinking of Soviet policy-makers produced a variety of ironies and contradictions. In 1917, Soviet leaders began by denying the commune's existence, and then astonished the world with the spectacle of a socialist government pursuing a New Economic Policy that promoted privatized economic activity in a commune-dominated countryside.

7. See William Rosenberg's study, *Liberals and the Russian Revolution*.

8. See Lenin's discussion of the transformation of Russian liberalism after 1904 in *Polnoe sobranie sochinenii* 5th edition, vol. 25, p. 34. The contradictions that plagued liberals within the peasant-oriented Socialist Revolutionary Party, which emerged in the aftermath of the Revolution of 1905, have been amply documented in Oliver Radkey's extremely hostile study, *The Agrarian Foes of Bolshevism: Promise and Default of the Russian Socialist Revolutionaries* (New York: Columbia University Press, 1958).

9. A detailed discussion of Lenin's arguments for Bolshevik leadership of a capitalist revolution in the pre-1917 period is contained in Kingston-Mann, *Lenin and the Problem of Marxist Peasant Revolution*, pp. 103–5.

10. The economists who supported the SR party, which emerged after 1905, were afflicted by similar misgivings. Their economic thinking deserves further study. See Allison Blakely's valuable dissertation, "The Socialist Revolutionary Party, 1901–1907: The Populist Response to the Industrialization of Russia."

11. See the economist N. A. Kablukov, "Russkie issledovatelei kak istochniki nemetskoi uchenosti," pp. 427–37

12. See discussion in chapter 5, pp. 121–22.

13. Among the many studies that reveal the pervasiveness of Western influences on nineteenth-and early twentieth-century Russians who differed widely in ideals, aims, and behavior, see Laura Engelstein's *The Keys to Happiness: Sex and the Search for Modernity in Fin-de-Siècle Russia* (Ithaca, N.Y.: Cornell University Press, 1992).

14. A classic example of this definition of Western culture is Gabriel Almond, "Capitalism and Democracy," pp. 467–73.

15. See general discussion in Edward Said, *Culture and Imperialism* (New York: Knopf, 1993).

16. This formulation owes much to the discussion contained in Peter Berger, *Pyramids of Sacrifice*, pp. 10–11.

17. Kipling, "Take up the white man's burden— / Send forth the best ye breed— / Go bind your sons to exile / To serve your captives' need; / To wait in heavy harness / On fluttered folk and wild / You new-caught, sullen peoples, / Half devil and half child." "The White Man's Burden," in *The Portable Kipling* (New York: Penguin, 1982), p. 602; and chapter 3, pp. 82–84.

18. See especially Said, *Orientalism*, pp. 2–4.

19. Prince Modupe, *I Was a Savage* (New York: Praeger, 1957), pp. 62–72.

20. Quoted in Samuel Huntington, in "The Clash of Civilizations?" in *Foreign Affairs* 72 (1993): 40. See also V. S. Naipaul, *The Mimic Men* (Harmondsworth, England: Penguin Books, 1969).

21. See, for example, Amilcar Cabral, *Return to the Source* (New York: African Information Service, 1973); Albert Memmi, *The Colonizers and the Colonized* (Boston: Beacon Press, 1967); and Asgedet Stefanos, "African Women and Revolutionary Change: A Freirian and Feminist Perspective," in Jim Fraser, et al., editors, *Mentoring the Mentor: A Critical Dialogue with Paulo Freire* (New York: Peter Lang, 1997).

22. Cabral, quoted in Basil Davidson, *The Search for Africa: History, Culture, Politics* (New York: Times Books, 1994), p. 223; and see also Julius Nyerere, *Freedom and Development* (New York: Oxford University Press, 1973); John Charles Hatch, *Two African Statesmen: Kaunda of Zambia and Nyerere of Tanzania* (London: Secker & Warburg, 1976); and the work of Denis Goulet, *The Cruel Choice*, and *The Uncertain Promise: Value Conflicts and Technological Transfer* (New York: New Horizons Press, 1989).

23. See discussion in chapter 3, pp. 82–92.

24. See especially Martin Malia, *Alexander Herzen and the Birth of Russian Socialism, 1812–1855* (Cambridge, Mass.: Harvard University Press, 1961).

25. See, e.g., the article by Gavril Popov, "The Dangers of Democracy," *New York Review of Books* (April 16, 1990): 27–28.

26. Francis Fukuyama, *The End of History and the Last Man* (New York: Free Press, 1992).

27. See, for example, the Boris Kagarlitsky essay, "Back in the USA/USSR," *Socialist Review* (1991): 33–39; and Patricia Williams, "Disorder in the House," *Theorizing Black Feminisms*, ed. Stanlie James and Abena Busia (London: Routledge & Kegan Paul, 1993), p. 121.

28. See Michael Specter, "Deep in the Russian Soul, a Lethal Darkness," *New York Times* (June 8, 1997): 1; Patricia Williams, "Disorder in the House," pp. 115–20. See Anders Aslund, *Post-Soviet Economy*, p. 288.

29. In the 1930s and afterward, Stalin ascribed the necessity for forced collectivization to peasant backwardness. One of the clearest later pronouncements is quoted in Richard Lauterbach, "Stalin at 65," *Life* (January 2, 1945): 67.

30. Stalin, *Problems of Leninism*, p. 356.

31. An interesting recent study which emphasizes the rationalist justifications for coercion during the Stalin era is Stephen Kotkin, *Magnetic Mountain: Stalinism as a Civilization* (Berkeley and Los Angeles: University of California Press, 1995).

32. A recent study which examines growth, change, and development without dichotomizing past and present is Robert Putnam's brilliant and quite unsentimental study of medieval traditions of community as a source of vitality and strength in building democratic institutions and promoting productive economic behavior. *Making Democracy Work: Civic Traditions in Modern Italy* (Princeton: Princeton University Press, 1994).

33. See the valuable but neglected study by Mariusz Dobek, *The Political Logic of Privatization* (Westport, Conn: Praeger, 1993).

34. Quoted in Edgar Feige, "The Transition to a Market Economy in Russia: Property Rights, Mass Privatization and Stabilization," in *A Fourth Way? Privatization, Property and the Emergence of New Market Economies*, ed. Gregory Alexander and Grazyna Skapska (London: Routledge, 1993), p. 67.

35. Richard Ericson, "The Classical Soviet-Style Economy: Nature of the System and Implications for reform," *Journal of Economic Perspectives* 5 (1991): 11.

36. Anders Aslund, *How Russia Became a Market Economy* (Washington DC: Brookings Institution, 1995), pp. 314–16.

37. This discussion owes much to the formulations of Edward Said's exploration of questions of East and West in his *Orientalism*, p. 32–34.

38. Quoted in David Lempert, "Changing Russian Political Culture in the 1990s: Parasites, Paradigms and Perestroika," *Comparative Studies in Society and History* 35, no. 3 (July 1993): 628–46.

39. Quoted in William Pfaff, "Bad Advice from the West Has Imperiled Russia," *The Baltimore Sun* (December 2, 1996): 11a.

40. Quoted in "The State of the Field" (an abridged version of Robert Daniels's presidential address, presented November 20, 1992, at the AAASS convention), *Newsletter of the American Association for the Advancement of Slavic Studies* 33, no. 1 (January 1993): 3.

41. See Dobek, *Political Logic of Privatization*, pp. 4–5, and David Kotz and Fred Weir, *Revolution from Above: The Demise of the Soviet System* (London: Routledge, 1997).

42. Quoted in Marshall Goldman, "The Pitfalls of Russian Privatization," *Challenge: A Magazine of Economic Affairs* 40, no. 3 (May–June 1997): 47. See also Goldman's critique of the "quick fix," shock therapy approach, *Lost Opportunity: Why Economic Reforms in Russia Have Not Worked* (New York: W. W. Norton &. Co., 1994).

43. Goldman, "Pitfalls," *Challenge*, p. 49.

44. Yitshak Brudny, "The Heralds of Opposition to Perestroyka," *Soviet Economy* 5, no. 2 (1989): 162–200.

45. See discussion in chapter 5, note 1, pp. 231–32.

46. See the brilliant discussion of the political and cultural construction of marginality in Anna Lowenhaupt Tsing, *In the Realm of the Diamond Queen: Mar-*

ginality in an Out-of-the-Way Place (Princeton: Princeton University Press, 1993), pp. 5–37.

47. A valuable discussion of this issue as it relates to education is contained in Robert LeVine and Merry White, *Human Conditions*, p. 13.

48. See the general discussion in Stephen Gudeman, *Economics as Culture: Models and Metaphors of Livelihood* (Boston: Routledge & Kegan Paul, 1986).

49. See discussion in Patricia Williams, "Disorder," pp. 118–23.

SELECTED BIBLIOGRAPHY

THE FOLLOWING list of sources is not intended to provide an exhaustive listing of the literature relevant to the topic of this book, but to provide guidance to further exploration of the many "Wests" encountered by non-Western observers; a sampling of materials that provide insights into the Russian experience, and for comparison, some valuable conceptual approaches to the culture or economic development.

CONCEPTUAL AND COMPARATIVE APPROACHES TO ECONOMIC DEVELOPMENT AND CULTURAL CHANGE

Adas, Michael. "From Footdragging to Fight: The Elusive History of Peasant Avoidance Protest in South and Southeast Asia." *Journal of Peasant Studies* 13, no. 2 (January 1986): 76–96.

Almond, Gabriel. "Capitalism and Democracy." *Political Science and Politics* 24, no. 3 (1991): 467–73.

Austen, Ralph. *Northwest Tanzania under German and British Rule.* New Haven: Yale University Press, 1968.

Bates, R. H. *Essays on the Political Economy of Rural Africa.* Cambridge: Cambridge University Press, 1983.

Berger, John. "Peasants and Progress." *New Society* 43, no. 796 (January 1978): 10–11.

———. *Pig Earth.* New York: Pantheon, 1985.

———. *Ways of Seeing.* London: Penguin Books, 1995.

Berger, Peter. *Pyramids of Sacrifice: Political Ethics and Social Change.* New York: Basic Books, 1974.

———, and Thomas Luckmann. *The Social Construction of Reality.* Garden City, N.Y.: Anchor Books, 1966.

Billington, James H. "The Intelligentsia and the Religion of Humanity." *American Historical Review* 65, no. 4 (July 1960): 807–21.

Boserup, Ester. *The Conditions of Agricultural Growth.* Chicago: Aldine Pub. Co., 1965.

Bowman, Shearer Davis. "Antebellum Planters and Vormärz Junkers in Comparative Perspective." *American Historical Review* 74 (October 1980): 779–808.

———. *Masters and Lords: Mid-Nineteenth-Century U.S. Planters and Prussian Junkers.* Oxford: Oxford University Press, 1993.

Cabral, Amilcar. *Return to the Source.* New York: African Information Service, 1973.

Clifford, James, and George Marcus, eds. "Introduction: Partial Truths." In *Writing Culture: The Poetics and Politics of Ethnography.* Berkeley and Los Angeles: University of California Press, 1980.

Collins, Patricia Hill. "Learning from the Outsider Within." *Social Problems* 33, no. 6 (December 1986): 514–32.

Craige, Betty J. *Laying the Ladder Down: The Emergence of Cultural Holism.* Amherst: University of Massachusetts Press, 1992.

Dahlman, Carl. *The Open Field System and Beyond: A Property Rights Analysis of an Economic Institution.* New York: Cambridge University Press, 1990.

Davidson, Basil. *The Search for Africa: History, Culture, Politics.* New York: Times Books, 1994.

Davis, Ralph. *The Rise of the Atlantic Economies.* Ithaca, N.Y.: Cornell University Press, 1973.

De Marchi, Neil, and John Lodewijks. "HOPE and the Journal Literature in the History of Economic Thought." *History of Political Economy* 15, no. 3 (fall 1983): 321–43.

Dobek, Mariusz. *The Political Logic of Privatization: Lessons from Great Britain and Poland.* Westport, Conn.: Praeger, 1993.

Ellickson, Robert. "Property in Land." *Yale Law Journal* 6, no. 102 (April 1993): 1317–1400.

Ferguson, Russell, Martha Gever, Trinh Minh-ha, and Cornel West, eds. *Out There: Marginalization and Contemporary Culture.* Cambridge, Mass.: MIT Press, 1990.

Fernbach, David, ed. *Karl Marx: Surveys from Exile.* New York: Penguin Books, 1973.

Fukuyama, Francis. *The End of History and the Last Man.* New York: Free Press, 1992.

Fustel de Coulanges, N. D. *The Origin of Property in Land.* Translated by M. Ashley. London: 1891.

Galeskii, Boguslaw. *Basic Concepts of Rural Sociology.* Manchester: Manchester University Press, 1972.

Geertz, Clifford. "From the 'Native's Point of View': On the Nature of Anthropological Understanding." In Geertz, *Local Knowledge: Further Essays in Interpretive Anthropology.* New York: Basic Books, 1983.

———. "On the Nature of Anthropological Understanding." *American Scientist* 63 (January/February 1975): 47–53.

Genovese, Eugene, and Elizabeth Fox-Genovese. "The Slave Economies in Political Perspective." *Journal of American History* 66 (1979): 7–23.

Georgescu-Roegen, N. "Economic Theory and Agrarian Economics." *Oxford Economic Papers* 12, no. 1 (February 1960): 1–40.

Giddens, Anthony, ed. *Positivism and Sociology.* London: Heineman, 1975.

Goulet, Denis. *The Cruel Choice: A New Concept in the Theory of Development.* Lanham, Md.: University Press of America, 1985.

———. *The Uncertain Promise: Value Conflicts and Technological Transfer.* New York: New Horizons Press, 1989.

Gudeman, Stephen. *Economics as Culture: Models and Metaphors of Livelihood.* Boston: Routledge & Kegan Paul, 1986.

Gusfield, Joseph. "Tradition and Modernity: Misplaced Polarities in the Study of Social Change." *American Journal of Sociology* 71 (1965): 461–472.

Haney, Lewis. *History of Economic Thought.* New York: Macmillan, 1949.

Hatch, John Charles. *Two African Statesmen: Kaunda of Zambia and Nyerere of Tanzania*. London: Secker & Warburg, 1976.

Herring, Ronald. "Zulfikar Ali Bhutto and the Eradication of Feudalism in Pakistan." *Comparative Studies in Society and History* 21, no. 4 (spring 1979): 519–57.

Hill, Polly. *Studies in Rural Capitalism in West Africa*. Cambridge: Cambridge University Press, 1970.

Hobsbawm, E. J., and Terence Ranger. *The Invention of Tradition*. New York: Cambridge University Press, 1983.

Hussain, Athar, and Keith Tribe. *Marx and Engels on the Agrarian Crisis*. 2 vols. London: Macmillan, 1981.

Hutchinson, T. W. *On Revolutions and Progress in Economic Knowledge*. Cambridge: Cambridge University Press, 1978.

Kimble, David. *A Political History of Ghana: The Rise of Gold Coast Nationalism*. Oxford: Oxford University Press, 1963.

Kolchin, Peter. "The Tragic Era? Interpreting Southern Reconstruction in Comparative Perspective." In *The Meaning of Freedom: Economics, Politics and Culture after Slavery*. Edited by Frank McGlynn and Seymour Drescher. Pittsburgh: University of Pittsburgh Press, 1992. Pp. 291–311.

———. *Unfree Labor: American Slavery and Russian Serfdom*. Cambridge, Mass.: Belknap Press of Harvard University Press, 1987.

Kuhn, Thomas. *The Structure of Scientific Revolutions*. Chicago: University of Chicago Press, 1970.

LeVine, Robert, and Merry White. *Human Conditions: The Cultural Basis of Educational Development*. New York: Routledge & Kegan Paul, 1986.

Maine, Henry. *Ancient Law: Its Connection with the Early History of Society, and Its Relation to Modern Ideas*. New York: H. Holt and Company, 1875.

Mazur, Michael. "The Dispersion of Holdings in the Open Fields: An Interpretation in Terms of Property Rights." *Journal of European Economic History* 6, no. 2 (1977): 461–72.

Meek, Ronald. *Social Science and the Ignoble Savage*. Cambridge: Cambridge University Press, 1976.

Memmi, Albert. *The Colonizers and the Colonized*. Boston: Beacon Press, 1967.

Modupe, Prince. *I Was a Savage*. New York: Praeger, 1957.

Naipaul, V. S. *The Mimic Men*. Harmondsworth, Middlesex, England: Penguin Books, 1969.

Ngo, Vinh Long. *Before the Revolution: The Vietnamese Peasants under the French*. Cambridge, Mass.: MIT Press, 1973.

Nyerere, Julius. *Freedom and Development*. Nairobi; New York: Oxford University Press, 1973.

O'Brien, Patrick, and Caglar Keyder. *Economic Growth in Britain and France, 1780–1914: Two Paths to the Twentieth Century*. London: Allen & Unwin, 1978.

Osbourne, Milton. *The French Presence in Cochin China and Cambodia*. Ithaca, N.Y.: Cornell University Press, 1969.

Porter, Theodore. *The Rise of Statistical Thinking, 1820–1900*. Princeton: Princeton University Press, 1986.

Posner, Richard A. "A Theory of Primitive Society, with Special Reference to Law." *Journal of Law and Economics* 23, no. 1 (1980): 1–53.

Pratt, R. C. "Administration and Politics in Uganda, 1919–1945." In *History of East Africa*. Vol. 2. Edited by Vincent Harlow and E. M. Chilvers. Oxford: Oxford University Press, 1965. Pp. 476–542.

Prude, Jonathan. "Trouble with Economic History." *Comparative Studies in Society and History* 27 (October 1985): 744–54.

Quinn, David. *The Elizabethans and the Irish.* Ithaca, N.Y.: Cornell University Press, 1966.

Rose, Carol. "The Comedy of the Commons: Custom, Commerce, and Inherently Public Property." *University of Chicago Law Review* 53 (summer 1986): 711–81.

Ruttan, V. W. "Social Science Knowledge and Institutional Change." *American Journal of Agricultural Economics* 66 (1984): 549–59.

Said, Edward. *Culture and Imperialism.* New York: Knopf, 1993.

———. *Orientalism.* New York: Pantheon Books, 1978.

Schweder, Richard A. "Anthropology's Romantic Rebellion Against the Enlightenment." In *Culture Theory.* Edited by Richard A. Schweder and Robert Levine. Cambridge: Cambridge University Press, 1984.

Scott, James. *Moral Economy of the Peasant.* New Haven: Yale University Press, 1976.

———. *The Weapons of the Weak: Forms of Everyday Resistance in Peasant Life.* New Haven: Yale University Press, 1985.

Seligman, Ben. "The Impact of Positivism on Economic Thought." *History of Political Economy* 1, no. 2 (1969): 256–78.

Shils, Edward. "The Intellectual between Tradition and Modernity: The Indian Situation." *Comparative Studies in Society and History,* Supplement 1. The Hague: Mouton, 1961.

Shutz, Alfred. "The Stranger: An Essay in Social Psychology." *American Journal of Sociology* 49, no. 6 (1944): 499–507.

Smith, Charles. "The Intellectual and Modernization; Definitions and Reconsiderations: The Egyptian Experience." *Comparative Studies in Society and History* 22 (1980): 513–53.

Steele, E. D. "J. S. Mill and the Irish Question: The Principles of Political Economy 1848–1865." *Historical Journal* 13, no. 2 (1970): 216–36.

Stefanos, Asgedet. "African Women and Revolutionary Change: A Freirian and Feminist Perspective." In *Mentoring the Mentor: A Critical Dialogue with Paulo Freire.* Edited by Jim Fraser, et al. New York: Peter Lang, 1997.

Tönnies, Ferdinand. *Community and Society.* Translated by C. Loomis. East Lansing: Michigan State University Press, 1957.

Trebilcock, Michael. "Communal Property Right." *University of Toronto Law Journal* 34, no. 4 (November 1984): 377–420.

Tsing, Anna Lowenhaupt. *In the Realm of the Diamond Queen: Marginality in an Out-of-the-Way Place.* Princeton: Princeton University Press, 1993.

Viner, Jacob. *The Long View and the Short: Studies in Economic Theory and Policy.* Glencoe, Ill.: Free Press, 1958.

West, Cornel. *Beyond Eurocentrism and Multiculturalism.* Monroe, Maine: Common Courage Press, 1993.

Williams, Patricia. "Disorder in the House." In *Theorizing Black Feminisms.* Edited by Stanlie James and Abena Busia. London: Routledge & Kegan Paul, 1993, 118–23.

CONTINENTAL EUROPE

Abel, Wilhelm. *Geschichte der deutschen Landwirtschaft vom fruhen Mittelalter bis zum 19 Jahrhundert.* Stuttgart: E. Ulmer, 1967.

Aron, Raymond. "Auguste Comte." In *Main Currents in Sociological Thought.* Translated by Richard Howard and Helen Weaver. New York: Basic Books, 1960. Pp. 73–143.

Balabkins, Nicholas. *Not By Theory Alone: The Economics of Gustav von Schmöller and His Legacy to America.* Berlin: Duncker & Humblot, 1988.

Barkin, Kenneth. *The Controversy over German Industralization 1880–1902.* Chicago: University of Chicago Press, 1970.

Barthel, Heinz, et al. "Karl Bücher: Seine politische und wissenschaftliche Stellung." In *Karl-Marx-Universität Leipzig, 1409–1959.* 2 vols. Edited by Ernst Engelberg. Leipzig: Verlag Enzyklopedie, 1959.

Bath, B. H. Slicher Van. *The Agrarian History of Western Europe.* London: E. Arnold, 1963.

Bloch, Marc. *French Rural History.* Berkeley and Los Angeles: University of California Press, 1966.

———. *Land and Work in Medieval Europe.* London: Routledge & Kegan Paul, 1967.

Blum, Jerome. *The End of the Old Order in Rural Europe.* Princeton: Princeton University Press, 1978.

Bodeker, H. E. "Das staatswissenschaftliche Fachersystem in 18. Jahrhundert." In *Wissenschaften im Zeitalter der Aufklärung.* Edited by R. Vierhaus. Göttingen: Vandenhoeck & Ruprecht, 1985.

Bourde, A. J. *The Influence of England on the French Agronomes, 1750–1789.* Cambridge: Cambridge University Press, 1953.

Burke, Edmund. *Reflections on the Revolution in France.* New York: Liberal Arts Press, 1985.

Carpenter, Kenneth. *Dialogue in Political Economy: Translations from and into German in the 18th Century.* Boston: Kress Library of Business and Economics, 1977.

Cherin, William. "The German Historical School of Economics: A Study in Methodology of the Social Sciences." Ph.D. diss., University of California at Berkeley, 1933.

Chisick, Harvey. *The Limits of Reform in the Enlightenment.* Princeton: Princeton University Press, 1981.

Christiansen, N. F. "Reformism within Danish Social Democracy until the Nineteen Thirties." *Scandinavian Journal of History* 3 (1978): 297–322.

Christiansen, P. "Peasant Adaptation to Bourgeois Culture?" *Ethnologia Scandinavica* (1978): 98–152.

Comte, Auguste. *Système de politique positive, ou, Traité de sociologie, instituant la religion de l'humanité.* 4 vols. Paris: L. Mathias, 1851–54.

Coulborn, Rushton. *Feudalism in History.* Hamden, Conn.: Archon Books, 1965.

David, Eduard. *Sozializmus und Landwirtschaft*. Berlin: Verlag der Sozialistischen Monatshefte, 1903.

Dewey, Clive J. "The Rehabilitation of the Peasant Proprietor in Nineteenth-Century Economic Thought." *History of Political Economy* 6, no. 1 (spring 1974): 17–47.

Diderot, Denis. *Dictionnaire philosophique*. London: 1824.

———. *Mémoires pour Catherine II*. Edited by Paul Verniere. Paris: Garnier Freres, 1966.

Dittrich, Erhard. *Die Deutschen und Österreichischen Kameralisten*. Darmstadt: Wissenschaftliche Buch Gesellschaft, 1974.

Dorfman, Joseph. "The Role of the German Historical School in American Economic Thought." *Proceedings of the American Economic Association* 45 (May 1955): 21.

Eisermann, Gottfried. *Die Grundlagen des Historismus in der deutschen Nationaloekonomie*. Stuttgart: F. Enke, 1956.

Epstein, Klaus. *The Genesis of German Conservatism*. Princeton: Princeton University Press, 1966.

Evans, R. J., and W. R. Lee, eds. *The German Family: Essays on the Social History of the Family in 19th-and 20th-Century Germany*. London: Croom Helm, 1981.

———. *The German Peasantry*. New York: St. Martin's Press, 1987.

Faber, H. *Cooperation in Danish Agriculture*. Translated by Hans Hertel. London: Longmans, Green & Co., 1918.

Farr, Ian. " 'Tradition' and the Peasantry: On the Modern Historiography of Rural Germany." In *The German Peasantry*. Edited by R. J. Evans and W. R. Lee. New York: St. Martin's Press, 1987.

Faucher, Daniel. "Routine et innovation dans la vie paysanne." *Journal de Psychologie Normale et pathologique* (1949): 89–103.

Fox-Genovese, Elizabeth. *The Origins of Physiocracy: Revolution and Social Order in Eighteenth-Century France*. Ithaca, N.Y.: Cornell University Press, 1976.

Friedman, Karen J. "Danish Agricultural Policy, 1870–1970." *Food Research Institute Studies* 13 (October 1974): 226–28.

Gagliardo, J. G. *From Pariah to Patriot: The Changing Image of the German Peasant, 1770–1840*. Lexington: University Press of Kentucky, 1969.

Gauthier, Florence. *La Voie paysanne dans la Revolution francaise: L'Exemple de picard*. Paris: F. Maspero, 1977.

Gay, Peter. *The Dilemma of Democratic Socialism*. New York: Collier Books, 1962.

Gerschenkron, Alexander. *Bread and Democracy in Germany*. Ithaca, N.Y.: Cornell University Press, 1989.

Goltz, Teodor von den. *Geschichte der deutschen Landwirtschaft*. Vol. 1. Aalen: Scientia, 1963.

Grantham, George. "The Persistence of Open-Field Farming in 19th-Century France." *Journal of Economic History* 40 (July 1980): 515–32.

Gurvitch, Georges. *Les fondateurs de la sociologie contemporaine: pour le centenaire de la mort d'Auguste Comte (1857–1957); Auguste Comte, Karl Marx et Herbert Spencer*. 2 vols. Paris: Centre de Documentation Universitaire, 1957.

Hagen, William. "Capitalism and the Countryside in Early Modern Europe: Interpretation, Models, Debates." *Agricultural History* 62, no. 1 (winter 1988): 13–47.

Harstick, P., ed. *Karl Marx über Formen vorkapitalistischen Produktion: Vergleichende Studien zur Geschichte d. Grundeigentums 1879–1880.* Frankfurt am Main; New York: Campus-Verlag, 1977.

Hasek, Carl William. *The Introduction of Adam Smith's Doctrines into Germany.* New York: Columbia University Press, 1925.

Herbst, Jurgen. *The German Historical School in American Scholarship: A Study in the Transfer of Culture.* Ithaca, N.Y.: Cornell University Press, 1965.

Hildebrand, Bruno. *Die Nationaloekonomie der Gegenwart und Zukunft und andere gesammelte Schriften.* Edited by H. Gehrig. Jena: G. Fischer, 1922 (published in Russian translation in 1860).

Hirschmann, Albert. *The Passions and the Interests: Political Arguments for Capitalism before Its Triumph.* Princeton: Princeton University Press, 1977.

Hubatsch, Walther. *Frederick the Great of Prussia: Absolutism and Administration.* London: Thames and Hudson, 1975.

Huntington, Samuel. "The Clash of Civilizations?" *Foreign Affairs* 72 (1993): 22–49.

Jones, P. N. *The Peasantry in the French Revolution.* New York: Cambridge University Press, 1988.

Kaschuba, Wolfgang. "Peasants and Others: The Historical Contours of Village Class Society." In *The German Peasantry.* Edited by R. J. Evans and R. W. Lee. New York: St. Martin's Press, 1987.

Kautsky, Karl. "Schmöller über den Fortschritt der Arbeiterklass." *Die Neue Zeit* 22 (1904): 229–31, 236.

Kjaergaard, T. "The Farmers' Interpretation of Danish History." *Scandinavian Journal of History* 10, no. 1 (1985): 97–118.

Knies, Karl. *Die Politische Oekonomie vom geschichtlichen Standpunkte.* Braunschweig: C. A. Schwetschke, 1883.

Kolakowski, Leszek. "Auguste Comte: Positivism in the Romantic Age." In *The Alienation of Reason: A History of Positivist Thought.* Garden City, N.Y.: Doubleday, 1968.

Lambert, Paul. "Emile de Laveleye." In *History of Political Economy* 1, no. 2 (1970): 263–83.

Laveleye, Emile de. *De la propriété et de ses formes primitives.* Paris: Germer, 1901.

———. "Land Systems of Belgium and Holland." In *Systems of Land Tenure in Various Countries. A Series of Essays Published under the Sanction of the Cobden Club.* Edited by J. W. Probyn. London, New York: Cassell, Petter, Galpin, 1881.

Lefebvre, Georges. *Les Paysans du Nord pendant la Revolution francaise.* Paris: A. Colin, 1972.

Liebel, Helen. *Enlightened Bureaucracy vs. Enlightened Despotism in Baden, 1750–1792.* Philadelphia: American Philosphical Society, 1965.

Lindenlaub, Dieter. *Richtungskämpfe in Verein für Sozialpolitik.* Wiesbaden: F. Steiner, 1967.

Mackrell, J.Q.C. *The Attack on "Feudalism" in Eighteenth-Century France.* London: Routledge & Kegan Paul, 1973.

Maehl, William. "German Social Democratic Agrarian Policy, 1890–1895, Reconsidered." *Central European History* 13 (June 1980): 121–57.

Mahoney, Susan. "A Good Constitution: Social Science in Eighteenth-Century Göttingen." Ph.D. diss., University of Chicago, 1982.

Martin, David. "The Rehabilitation of the Peasant Proprietor in Nineteenth-Century Economic Thought: A Comment." *History of Political Economy* 8, no. 2 (1976): 297–302.

Martin, Kingsley. *French Liberal Thought in the 18th Century: A Study of Political Ideas from Bayle to Condorcet.* London: Phoenix House, 1962.

Marx, Karl. *Capital: A Critical Analysis of Capitalist Production.* London: W. Glaisher, 1909.

———. and Friedrich Engels. *Perepiska K. Marksa i F. Engel'sa s russkimi politicheskimi deiatel'iami.* Leningrad: 1951.

———. *Reminiscences of Marx and Engels.* Moscow: 1962.

———. *Selected Correspondence of Karl Marx and Friedrich Engels, 1846–1895: A Selection with Commentary and Notes.* London: Lawrence, 1934.

———. *Selected Works.* 3 vols. Moscow: Progress Publishers, 1969.

———. *Sochineniia.* Vol. 32. Moscow: 1961.

———. *Werke.* Berlin: Dietz, 1966.

Maurer, Ludwig von. *Einleitung zur Geschichte der Mark-, Hof-, Dorf-, und Stadt-Verfassung und der öffentlichen Gewalt.* Munich: 1854. Appeared in Russian as *Vvedenie v istoriiu obshchinnogo, podvornogo, sel'skogo i gorodskogo ustroistva i obshchestvennoi vlasti.* Moscow: 1880.

Meek, Ronald. *The Economics of Physiocracy: Essays and Translations.* Cambridge, Mass.: Harvard University Press, 1963.

Moeller, R. G. "Peasants and Tariffs in the Kaisserreich: How Backward Were the *Bauern*?" *Agricultural History* 55 (December 1981): 371–84.

Morineau, Michel. "Y A-t-il une révolution agricole en France au xviiie siècle?" *Revue Historique* 239, part 2 (1968): 289–326.

Muller, E. "Lorenz von Stein und Jurij Samarins Vision des absoluten Sozialstaates." *Jahrbücher für Geschichte Osteuropas* 15 (1967): 575–96.

Östergaard, Uffe. "Peasants and Danes: The Danish National Identity and Political Culture." *Comparative Studies of Society and History* 34 (January 1992): 3–22.

Parker, William, and Eric Jones, eds. *European Peasants and Their Markets.* Princeton: Princeton University Press, 1975.

Payne, Harry C. "Elite vs. Popular Mentality in the 18th Century." *Historical Reflections* 2, no. 2 (summer 1975): 183–200.

———. *The Philosophes and the People.* New Haven: Yale University Press, 1976.

Procacci, Giuliano. "Geografia e struttura del movimento contadino della Valle padana nel suo periodo formativo (1901–1906)." *Studi storici* 5 (1964): 40–120.

Putnam, Robert. *Making Democracy Work: Civic Traditions in Modern Italy.* Princeton: Princeton University Press, 1994.

Rebel, Herman. *Peasant Classes: The Bureaucratization of Property and Family Relations under Early Habsburg Absolutism, 1511–1636.* Princeton: Princeton University Press, 1983.

Reill, Peter. *German Enlightenment and the Rise of Historicism.* Berkeley and Los Angeles: University of California Press, 1975.

Roll, Eric. *A History of Economic Thought*. New York: Prentice Hall, 1950.

Roscher, Wilhelm. *Ansichten der Volkswritschaft aus dem geschichtlichen Standpunkte*. Leipzig and Heidelberg: 1861.

Roscher, Wilhelm. "Die Deutsch-Russische Schule der Nationaloekonomik." *Berichte über die Verhandlungen der königlich Sächsischen Gesellschaft der Wissenschaften zu Leipzig Philologisch-Historische Klasse* 22 (1870): 139–80.

——— *Die System der Volkswirtschaft*. Vol. 2. *Nationaloekonomik des Ackerbaues und der verwandten Urproductionensweige*. Stuttgart: J. G. Cotta, 1903.

———. *Principles of Political Economy*. 2 vols. Chicago: Callaghan and Company, 1882.

Rosenberg, Hans. *Bureaucracy, Aristocracy and Autocracy: The Prussian Experience, 1660–1815*. Cambridge, Mass.: Harvard University Press, 1966.

Ross, Denman. *Studies in Mediaeval History I: The Mark and the Manor*. Cambridge: Wilson, 1879.

Rubel, Maximilien, and M. Manale. *Marx Without Myth: A Chronological Study of His Life and Work*. Oxford: Basil Blackwell, 1975.

Sabean, David. *Power in the Blood: Popular and Village Discourse in Early Modern Germany*. Cambridge: Cambridge University Press, 1984.

Sagarra, Eda. *A Social History of Germany 1648–1914*. London: Methuen Press, 1977.

Saint Jacob, Pierre de. *Les Paysans de la Bourgogne du nord au dernier siècle de l'ancien regime*. Dijon: Bernigaud et Privat, 1960.

Schafer, Ulla. *Historische Nationaloekonomie und Sozialstatistik als Gesellschaftswissenschaften*. Vienna: Bohlau, 1971.

Schmöller, Gustav von. "The Idea of Justice in Political Economy." Translated by Carl Schurz. *Annals of the American Academy of Political and Social Sciences* 4 (1894): 697–736.

Schumpeter, Joseph. "Gustav von Schmöller und die Probleme von Heute." *Schmöllers Jahrbuch fur Gesetzgebung, Verwaltung und Volkswirtschaft* 50 (1926): 1–52.

——— *History of Economic Analysis*. New York; London: Routledge, 1974.

Segalen, Martine. " 'Sein Teil haben': Geschwisterbeziehungen in einem egalitaren Vererbungssystem." In *Emotionen und materielle Interessen: Sozialanthropologische und historische Beitrage zur Familienforschung*. Edited by Hans Medick and David Sabean. Göttingen: Vandenhoeck & Ruprecht, 1984.

Small, Albion. *The Cameralists: The Pioneers of German Social Policy*. New York: Burt Franklin, 1909.

Smith, Woodruff. *The Ideological Origins of Nazi Imperialism*. New York: Oxford University Press, 1986.

Sorel, Georges. *Reflections on Violence*. New York: B. W. Huebsch, 1908.

Spragens, Thomas. *The Irony of Liberal Reason*. Chicago: University of Chicago Press, 1981.

Steenson, Gary. *Karl Kautsky 1854–1938: Marxism in the Classical Years*. Pittsburgh: University of Pittsburgh Press, 1978.

Storch, Henri. *Cours d'économie politique ou exposition des principes qui déterminent la prosperité des nations*. 6 vols. St. Petersburg: 1815.

Szacki, Jerzy. *History of Sociological Thought*. London: Aldwych Press, 1979.

Tribe, Keith. *Governing Economy: The Reformation of German Economic Discourse, 1760–1840*. Cambridge: Cambridge University Press, 1988.

Vaggi, Gianni. *The Economics of Francois Quesnay*. Houndmills, Basingstoke, Hampshire: Macmillan, 1987.

Wagner, Adolph. *Die Abschaffung des privaten Eigentums*. Berlin: 1871.

Walker, Mack. *German Home Towns: Community, State and General Estate, 1648–1871*. Ithaca, N.Y.: Cornell University Press, 1971.

Weulersse, Georges. *Le Mouvement physiocratique en France*. 2 vols. Paris: Mouton, 1910.

Willems, Emilio. "Peasantry and City: Cultural Persistence and Change in Historical Perspective. A European Case." *The American Anthropologist* 72 (April 1970): 528–44.

Wunder, Heide. *Die bauerliche Gemeinde in Deutschland*. Göttingen: Vandenhoek & Ruprecht, 1985.

———. "Peasant Organization and Class Conflict in East and West Germany." *Past and Present* 78 (February 1978): 47–58.

ENGLAND

Allen, Robert. *Enclosure and the Yeoman: Agricultural Development of the South Midlands 1450–1850*. Oxford: Oxford University Press, 1992.

———, and Cormac Ó Gráda. "On the Road with Arthur Young: English, Irish, and French Agriculture During the Industrial Revolution." *Journal of Economic History* 48 (March 1988): 93–116.

Appleby, Joyce. *Economic Thought and Ideology in Seventeenth-Century England*. Princeton: Princeton University Press, 1978.

Ashraf, P. M. *The Life and Times of Thomas Spence*. Newcastle: Frank Graham Publisher, 1983.

Ault, Warren. *Open Field Farming in Medieval England: A Study of Village Bylaws*. London: Allen & Unwin; New York, Barnes & Noble, 1972.

Baker, Alan R. H., and R. A. Butlin. *Studies of Field Systems in the British Isles*. Cambridge: Cambridge University Press, 1973.

Blum, Jerome. "English Parliamentary Enclosures." *Journal of Modern History* 53 (July 1981): 477–504.

Brailsford, Henry. *The Levellers and the English Revolution*. Stanford, Cal.: Stanford University Press, 1983.

Brockway, Fenner. *Britain's First Socialists: The Levellers, Agitators and Diggers of the English Revolution*. New York: Quartet Books, 1980.

Canny, Nicholas. "The Ideology of English Colonization: From Ireland to America." *William and Mary Quarterly* 30, no. 4 (October 1973): 575–98.

Chase, Malcolm. *The People's Farm: England's Radical Agrarians 1775–1840*. Oxford: Clarendon Press, 1988.

Cliffe-Leslie, T. E. *Essays in Moral and Political Philosophy*. London: 1879.

———. *Land Systems and Industrial Economy of Ireland, England and Continental Countries*. London: 1870. [Reprint New York: A. M. Kelley, 1968.]

————. *Vladenie i pol'zovanie zemlieu v razlichnykh stranakh*. St. Petersburg: 1871.

Coats, A. W. "The Historist Reaction in English Political Economy 1870–90." *Economica* 21 (1954): 145–53.

Coleman, D. C. *History and the Economic Past: An Account of the Rise and Decline of Economic History*. Oxford: Oxford University Press, 1987.

Collins, E.J.T. "Harvest Technology and Labor Supply in Britain, 1790–1870." *Economic History Review* 22, series 2 (December 1969): 453–73.

Eichengreen, Barry. "*The Economic History of Britain Since 1700*: A Review." *Journal of European Economic History* 12, no. 2 (spring 1983): 437–44.

Ernlé, Lord Rowland. *English Farming: Past and Present*. London: Longmans, Green & Co., 1941.

Goddard, Nicholas. "The Development and Influence of Agricultural Periodicals and Newspapers, 1780–1880." *Agricultural History Review* 31, part 2 (1983): 116–31.

Hardin, Garrett. "The Tragedy of the Commons." *Science* 162, no. 3859 (Dec. 13, 1968): 1243–48.

Havinden, M. A. "Agricultural Progress in Open Field Oxfordshire." *Agricultural History Review* 9 (1961): 73–83.

Hay, Douglas. *Albion's Fatal Tree: Crime and Society in Eighteenth-Century England*. New York: Pantheon Books, 1975.

Heys, Bob. "John Clare and Enclosure, *John Clare Society Journal* 6 (July 1987): 10–18.

Hill, Christopher. *The World Turned Upside Down: Radical Ideas During the English Revolution*. London: Temple Smith, 1972.

Ho, Ping-ti. *Land and State in Great Britain 1873–1910: A Study of Land Reform Movements and Land Policies*. Ann Arbor: University of Michigan Press, 1973.

Humphries, Jane. "Enclosures, Common Rights, and Women: The Proletarianization of Families in the Late Eighteenth and Early Nineteenth Centuries." *Journal of Economic History* 50, no. 1 (March 1990): 17–41.

Johnstone, P. "Turnips and Romanticism." *Agricultural History* 12 (July 1938): 224–55; 11 (April 1937): 80–95.

Kadish, Alon. *Historians, Economists and Economic History*. New York: Routledge, 1989.

Kerridge, Eric. *The Agricultural Revolution*. London: Allen & Unwin, 1967.

Kipling, Rudyard. "The White Man's Burden." In *The Portable Kipling*. New York: Penguin Books, 1982.

Koot, Gerard. *English Historical Economics, 1870–1926: The Rise of Economic History and Neomercantilism*. New York: Cambridge University Press, 1987.

Lindert, Peter. "Remodeling British Economic History." *Journal of Economic History* 43, no. 4 (December 1983): 986–92.

Lippincott, B. E. *Victorian Critics of Democracy: Carlyle, Ruskin, Arnold, Stephen, Maine, Lecky*. Minneapolis: University of Minnesota Press, 1938.

McCloskey, Donald N. "English Open Fields as Behavior Towards Risk." In *Research in Economic History*. Vol. 1. Edited by Paul Uselding. Greenwich, Conn.: Jai Press, 1976. Pp. 124–70.

———. "The Prudent Peasant: New Findings on Open Fields." *Journal of Economic History* 51 (June 1991): 343–56.

MacDonald, Stuart. "Agricultural Improvement and the Neglected Laborer." *Agricultural History Review* 31, part 2 (April 1983): 81–90.

McNulty, Paul. "Adam Smith's Concept of Labor." *Journal of the History of Ideas* 34, no. 3 (1973): 345–66.

McQuiston, Julian. "Tenant Right: Farmer Against Landlord in Victorian England 1847–1884." *Agricultural History* 47 (April 1973): 95–113.

Marshall, Alfred. *The Present Position of Economics*. London: Macmillan and Company, 1885.

Mill, John Stuart. *Principles of Political Economy With Some of Their Applications to Social Philosophy*. Edited by Sir William Ashley. Fairfield, N.J.: A. M. Kelley, 1976.

Mingay, G. E. "Introduction." In *Arthur Young and His Times*. Ed. G. E. Mingay. London: Macmillan, 1975.

———. *A Social History of the English Countryside*. London: Routledge, 1990.

More, Thomas. *Utopia*. New Haven: Yale University Press, 1964.

Neeson, Jeanette. *Commoners: Common Right, Enclosure and Social Change in England, 1799–1820*. Cambridge: Cambridge University Press, 1993.

———. "The Opponents of Enclosure in Eighteenth-Century Northhamptonshire." *Past and Present* 105 (November 1984): 114–39.

O'Brien, Erin. "Neglected But Not Forgotten: The English Historical Economists." Undergraduate honors paper. Department of History, University of Massachussets, Boston, 1988.

Orwin, Charles. *The Open Fields*. Oxford: Clarendon Press, 1938.

Perry, P. J. "High Farming in Victorian Britain: Prospect and Retrospect." *Agricultural History* 55, no. 2 (April 1981): 156–66.

Pinchbeck, Ivy. *Women Workers and the Industrial Revolution*. New York: Routledge & Kegan Paul, 1972.

Reed, Mick. "The Peasantry of Nineteenth-Century England: A Neglected Class?" *History Workshop Journal* 18 (1984): 53–76.

———, and R.A.E. Welles, eds. *Class, Conflict and Protest in the English Countryside, 1700–1880*. Cambridge: Frank Cass, 1990.

Richards, Stewart. "Agricultural Science in Higher Education: Problems of Identity in Britain's First Chair of Agriculture, Edinburgh, 1790–1831." *Agricultural History Review* 33 (1985): 59–65.

Rostow, W. W. "Investment and the Great Depression in 19th-Century England." *Economic History Review* 9 (May 1939): 145–58.

Rudkin, O. D. *Thomas Spence and His Connections*. London: Allen & Unwin, 1927.

Rule, J., and R. Malcolmson, eds. *Protest and Survival: Essays for E. P. Thompson*. New York: New Press, 1993.

Seebohm, Frederick. *The English Village Community (Examined in its relations to the manorial & tribal systems and to the common or open field system of husbandry)*. London: Longmans, Green, & Co., 1896.

———. "Villeinage in England." *English Historical Review* 7 (July 1892): 444–65.

Smellie, K. B. "Sir Henry Maine." *Economica* 8 (1928): 64–94.

Smith, Adam. *The Wealth of Nations*. New York: Modern Library, 1937.

Snell, K.D.M. *Annals of the Labouring Poor: Social Change and Agrarian England 1660–1900*. Cambridge: Cambridge University Press, 1985.

Stocking, George. *Victorian Anthropology*. New York: Free Press, 1987.

Thirsk, Joan. *Tudor Enclosures*. London: Routledge & Kegan Paul, 1970.

Timmer, C. Peter. "The Turnip, The New Husbandry, and the English Agricultural Revolution." *The Quarterly Journal of Economics* 83, no. 3 (1969): 375–95.

Wood, John Cunningham. *British Economists and the Empire*. New York: St. Martin's Press, 1983.

Young, Arthur. *Travels in France During the Years 1787–1789*. Cambridge: Cambridge University Press, 1950.

UNITED STATES

Aufhauser, r. Keith. "Slavery and Scientific Management." *Journal of Economic History* 33, no. 4 (October 1973): 811–24.

Berry, Wendell. *The Long-legged House*. New York: Harcourt Brace & World, 1969.

Cox, LaWanda. "The Promise of Land for the Freedmen." *Mississippi Valley Historical Review* 45 (December 1958): 413–40.

Cronon, William. *Changes in the Land: Indians, Colonists and the Ecology of New England*. New York: Hill and Wang, 1985.

David, Paul, and Herbert Gutman, et al. *Reckoning with Slavery*. New York: Oxford University Press, 1976.

———, and Jay Mandle. "The Managerial Revolution and the Developmental State: The Case of U.S. Agriculture." *Business and Economic History* 22, no. 2 (1993): 68–101.

Ferleger, Lou. "Share-Cropping Contracts in the Late Nineteenth-Century South." *Agricultural History* 7, no. 3 (summer 1993): 31–46.

Fogel, Robert, and Stanley Engerman. *Time on the Cross: The Economics of American Negro Slavery*. Boston: Little, Brown, 1974.

Foner, Eric. *Reconstruction: American's Unfinished Revolution, 1863–1877*. New York: Harper & Row, 1988.

Genovese, Eugene. *The World the Slaveholders Made*. New York: Pantheon Books, 1969.

Gutman, Herbert. *Slavery and the Numbers Game: A Critique of "Time on the Cross."* Urbana: University of Illinois Press, 1975.

Harbaugh, William. "Tenancy and Soil Conservation." A paper presented at the Agricultural History Society, Washington, D.C., 1991.

Jennings, Francis. *The Invasion of America: Indians, Colonialism and the Cant of Conquest*. New York: Norton, 1976.

Kaufman, Allen. *Capitalism, Slavery and Republican Values: Antebellum Political Economists, 1819–1848*. Austin: University of Texas Press, 1982.

Litwack, Leon. *Been in the Storm So Long: The Aftermath of Slavery*. New York: Knopf, 1979.

McPherson, James. *The Struggle for Equality: Abolitionists and the Negro in the Civil War and Reconstruction.* Princeton: Princeton University Press, 1964.

Mandle, Jay R. *The Roots of Black Poverty: The Southern Plantation Economy after the Civil War.* Durham, N.C.: Duke University Press, 1978.

———. *Not Slave Not Free: The African American Economic Experience Since the Civil War.* Durham, N.C.: Duke University Press, 1992.

Nelson, Cary. *Repression and Recovery: Modern American Poetry and the Politics of Cultural Memory, 1910–1945.* Madison: University of Wisconsin Press, 1989.

Oakes, James. *Slavery and Freedom: An Interpretation of the Old South.* New York: Vintage Books, 1990.

Ransom, Roger L., and Richard Sutch. *One Kind of Freedom: The Economic Consequences of Emancipation.* Cambridge: Cambridge University Press, 1977.

Rosenberg, Emily. *The Spreading of the American Dream: American Economic and Cultural Expansion, 1890–1945.* New York: Hill and Wang, 1982.

Ross, Dorothy. *The Origins of American Social Science.* Cambridge: Cambridge University Press, 1991.

Russell, Howard. *Indian New England before the Mayflower.* Hanover, N.H.: University Press of New England, 1980.

Samuels, Warren. "Ashley's and Taussig's Lectures on the History of Economic Thought at Harvard, 1895–1897." *History of Political Economy* 9 (October 1977): 384–411.

Thomas, Peter. "Contrastive Subsistence Strategies and Land Use as Factors for Understanding Indian-White Relations in New England." *Ethnohistory* 23, no. 1 (winter 1976): 1–18.

IMPERIAL RUSSIA / SOVIET UNION / RUSSIA

Acton, Edward. *Alexander Herzen and the Role of the Intellectual Revolutionary.* Cambridge: Cambridge University Press, 1979.

Aksakov, I. S. *Sochineniia, 1860–1886.* 7 vols. Moscow: 1886–87.

Aksakov, Konstantin. *Vospominanie studentsva 1832–4 godov.* St. Petersburg: 1911.

Alefirenko, P. I. "Ekonomicheskie vzgliady V. N. Tatishcheva." *Voprosy istorii* 12 (1948): 89–97.

———. *Krest'ianskoe dvizhenie I krest'ianski vopros v Rossii v 30-50kh godakh xvii veka.* Moscow: 1958.

Anisimov, E. V. *The Reforms of Peter the Great: Progress Through Coercion in Russia.* Translated by John T. Alexander. Armonk, N.Y.: M. E. Sharpe, 1993.

Annenkov, P. V. *Literaturnye vospominaniia.* Edited by V. P. Dorofeev. Moscow: 1989.

———. *P. V. Annenkov i ego druz'ia: literaturnyia vospominaniia i perepiska 1835–1885 godov.* St. Petersburg: 1982.

Aslund, Anders. *How Russia Became a Market Economy.* Washington, D.C.: Brookings Institution, 1995.

————. *The Post-Soviet Economy: Soviet and Western Perspectives.* New York: Pinter Publishers, 1992.

Atkinson, D. G. *The End of the Russian Land Commune.* Stanford, Cal.: Stanford University Press, 1983.

Augustine, T. Wilson. "The Economic Attitudes and Opinions Expressed by the Russian Nobility in the Great Commission of 1767." Ph.D. diss., Columbia University, 1969.

————. "Notes Toward a Portrait of the Eighteenth-Century Russian Nobility." *Canadian Slavic Studies* 4 (fall 1970): 373–425.

Bak, I. S. "Dmitrii Alekseevich Golitsyn (Filosofskie, obshchestvenno-politicheskie i ekonomicheskie vozzreniia)." *Istoricheskie zapiski* 16 (1948): 258–72.

————. "Ekonomicheskie vozzreniia M. V. Lomonosova." *Problemy ekonomiki* 4 (1940): 131–43.

————. "Ekonomicheskie vozzreniia V. N. Tatishcheva." *Istoricheskie zapiski* 54 (1955): 362–81.

————. "Istoricheskaia zapiska o raznykh predpolozheniiakh po predmetu osvobozhdeniia krest'ian." In *Deviatnadtsatyi vek: Istoricheskii sbornik.* Vol. 2. Edited by P. Bartenev. Moscow: 1872.

Baker, Anita. "Community and Growth: Muddling Through with Russian Credit Cooperatives." *Journal of Economic History* 37 (March 1977): 139–60.

Baron, Samuel. *Plekhanov: The Father of Russian Marxism.* Stanford, Cal.: Stanford University Press, 1966.

Bartlett, Roger. "A. F. Shchapov, the Commune, and Chernyshevskii." In *Russian Thought and Society 1800–1917: Essays in Honour of Eugene Lampert.* Edited by Roger Bartlett. Keele: University of Keele Press, 1984. Pp. 67–91.

————. *Human Capital: The Settlement of Foreigners in Russia, 1762–1804.* New York: Cambridge University Press, 1979.

————. "J. J. Sievers and the Russian Peasants under Catherine II." *Jahrbücher für geschichte Osteuropas* 32, no. 1 (1984): 19–33.

Belinskii, V. G. *Polnoe sobranie sochineniia.* 13 vols. Moscow: 1955.

Berkov, P. N. "Lomonosov i Liflandaia ekonomiia." In *Lomonosov: Sbornik statei i materialov.* Vol. 2. Edited by A. I. Andreev and L. B. Modzalevskii. Moscow-Leningrad: 1946.

Bervi, N. *Izbrannye ekonomicheskie proizvedeniia.* 2 vols. Moscow: 1958, 1959.

————. *Polozhenie rabochego klassa v Rossii* St. Petersburg: 1869.

————. "Sokhranitsiia li obshchinnoe vladenie?" *Otechestvennye zapiski* 1 (1877): 213–38.

Bezobrazov, N. A. (Evropeets). *Molodaia Rossiia.* Berlin: 1874.

Bezobrazov, V. P. *Aristokratiia i interesy dvorianstva.* Moscow: 1866.

Billington, James H. *The Icon and the Axe: An Interpretive History of Russian Culture.* New York: Random House, 1970.

Black, J. L. *Citizens for the Fatherland: Education, Educators and Pedagogical Ideals in Eighteenth-Century Russia.* New York: Columbia University Press, 1979.

Blakely, Allison. "The Socialist Revolutionary Party, 1901–1907: The Populist Response to the Industrialization of Russia." Ph.D. diss., University of California at Berkeley, 1971.

Blanshard, Ralph. "A Proposal for Social Reform in the Reign of Catherine II." Ph.D. diss., SUNY-Binghamton, 1972.

Bliumin, I. G. *Ocherki ekonomicheskoi mysli v Rossii v pervoi polovine xix veka*. Moscow: 1940.

Blum, Jerome. *Lord and Peasant in Russia*. Princeton: Princeton University Press, 1960.

Bohac, Rodney. "Everyday Forms of Resistance: Serf Opposition to Gentry Exactions, 1800–1861." In *Peasant Economy, Culture, and Politics of European Russia, 1800–1921*. Edited by Esther Kingston-Mann and Timothy Mixter. Princeton: Princeton University Press, 1991. Pp. 236–60.

Bolotov, Andrei. *Zhizn' i prikliucheniia Andreia Bolotova, opisannye samim im dlia svoikh potomkov*. 4 vols. St. Petersburg: 1870–73.

Brikner, A. "Pososhkov kak ekonomist." In *Ivan Pososhkov: Sochinenie*. St. Petersburg: 1876.

Brown, John Halit. "A Provincial Landowner: A. T. Bolotov, 1738–1833." Ph.D. diss., Princeton University, 1976.

Brudny, Yitshak. "The Heralds of Opposition to Perestroyka." *Soviet Economy* 5, no. 2 (1989): 162–200.

Bukharin, N. I., and E. P. Preobrazhenskii. *The ABC of Communism*. Ann Arbor: University of Michigan Press, 1988.

Burds, Jeffrey. "The Social Control of Peasant Labor in Russia: The Response of Village Communities to Labor Migration in the Central Industrial Region, 1861–1905." In *Peasant Economy, Culture, and Politics of European Russia, 1800–1921*. Edited by Esther Kingston-Mann and Timothy Mixter. Princeton: Princeton University Press, 1991. Pp. 52–100.

Chaianov, A. V. *The Theory of Peasant Economy*. Edited by D. Thorner, et al. Homewood, Ill.: R. D. Irwin, for American Economic Association, 1966.

Cherniavsky, Michael. *Tsar and People: Studies in Russian Myths*. New York: Random House, 1969.

Chernov, V. M. *K voprosu o kapitalizme i krest'ianstve*. Moscow: 1904.

Chernyshev, I. V. *Agrarno-krest'ianskaia politika Rossii za 150 let*. Petrograd: 1918.
———. *Obshchina posle 9 noiabria 1906 g*. Petrograd: 1917.

Chernyshevskii, N. G. *Izbrannye ekonomicheskoi proizvedenii*. 3 vols. Moscow: 1948.
———. *Polnoe sobranie sochinenii*. 10 vols. St. Petersburg: 1906.

Chicherin, B. N. "Die Leibeigenschaft in Russland." *Deutsche-Staats-worterbuch*. Vol. 6. Stuttgart: J. C. Bluntschli and K. Brater, 1861. Pp. 393–411.
———. *Sobstvennost' i gosudarstvo*. 2 vols. Moscow: 1882.
———. *Vospominaniia*. 4 vols. Moscow: 1929–34.

Chmielewski, Edward. *Tribune of the Slavophiles: Konstantin Aksakov*. Gainesville: University of Florida Press, 1961.

Christoff, Peter. *An Introduction to Nineteenth-Century Russian Slavophilism*. Vol. 1, *A. S. Khomiakov* (The Hague: Mouton, 1961); vol. 2, *I. V. Kireevskii* (The Hague: Mouton, 1972); vol. 3, *K. S. Aksakov* (Princeton: Princeton University Press, 1982).
———. "A. S. Khomiakov on the Agricultural and Industrial Problem in Russia." In *Essays in Russian History*. Edited by A. Fergusson and A. Levin. Hamden, Conn.: Archon Books, 1964.

Chuprov, A. I. *Istoriia politicheskoi ekonomii*. Moscow: 1913.

———. *Krest'ianskii vopros*. Moscow: 1909.

———. *Melkoe zemledelie i ego osnovnyia nuzhdy*. Moscow: 1913.

———. *Ocherki po istorii politicheskoi ekonomii*. Moscow: 1918.

———. *Rechi i Stati*. Vol. 1. Moscow: 1909.

———. *Statistika*. Moscow: 1898.

Chuprov, A. I. and A. S. Posnikov, eds. *Vliianie urozhaev i khlebnykh tsen na nekotorye storony narodnogo khoziaistva*. 2 vols. St. Petersburg: 1897.

Clendenning, Philip. "Eighteenth-Century Russian Translations of Western Economic Works." *Journal of European Economic History* 1 (winter 1972): 745–53.

Cohen, Stephen. *Bukharin and the Bolshevik Revolution: A Political Biography 1888–1938*. New York: Knopf, 1973.

Confino, Michael. *Domaines et seigneurs en Russie vers la fin du xviii-e siècle; étude des structures agraires et de mentalités économiques*. Paris: Institut d'études slaves de l'Université de Paris, 1963.

———. "La Politique du tutelle: Des seigneurs russes envers leur paysans vers la fin du xvii siècle." *Revue des études Slaves* 37 (1960): 39–69.

———. *Systèmes agraires et progrès agricole: L'Assolement triennial en Russie au xvii-e–xix-e siècles*. No. 14 of a series: Études sur l'économie et la sociologie des pays slaves. Paris: Mouton, 1969.

Cornell, Nina. "The Role of the Nobility in Agricultural Change in Russia During the Reign of Catherine II." Ph.D. diss., University of Illinois, 1972.

Crisp, Olga. "Peasant Land Tenure and Civil Rights: Implications Before 1906." In *Civil Rights in Imperial Russia*. Edited by Olga Crisp and Linda Edmondson. New York: Oxford University Press, 1989.

Cross, A. G. ""An Oxford Dean in Catherine the Great's Russia." *Journal of European Studies* 1 (1975): 166–74.

———. *"By the Banks of the Thames": Russians in Eighteenth-Century Britain*. Newtonville, MA: Oriental Research Partners, 1980.

Daniel, Wallace. "Conflict Between Economic Vision and Economic Reality: The Case of M. M. Shcherbatov." *Slavonic and East European Review* 67, no. 1 (January 1989): 42–67.

Daniels, Robert. "The State of the Field." *Newsletter of the American Association for the Advancement of Slavic Studies* 33, no. 1 (January 1993): 3.

Daniel'son, N. F. "Apologiia vlast' deneg, kak priznak vremni." *Russkoe bogatstvo* (January 1895 and February 1895): 155–87.

———. *Ocherki nashego poreformennogo khoziaistve*. St. Petersburg: 1893.

Danilov, A. I. *Problemy agrarnoi istorii rannego Srednevekov'ia v nemetskoi istoriografiia kontsa xix–nachala xx v*. Moscow: 1958.

Danilov, V. P. "Ob istoricheskikh sud'bakh krest'ianskoi obshchiny v Rossii." In *Ezhegodnik po agrarnoi istorii*, vol. 6, *Problemy istorii russkoi obshchiny*. Vologda: 1976.

Deal, Zack. "Serf and State Peasant Agriculture: Kharkov Province, 1842–1861." Ph.D. diss., Vanderbilt University, 1978.

Dement'ev, A. G. *Ocherki po istorii russkoi zhurnalistiki 1840–50gg*. Moscow-Leningrad: 1951.

Denisoff, E. "Aux origines de l'église russe autocéphale." *Revue des études Slaves* 23 (1947): 66–88.

Deutscher, Isaac. *Stalin: A Political Biography.* New York: Oxford University Press, 1949.

Diakin, V. S. *Krizis samoderzhaviia v Rossii 1895–1917.* Leningrad: 1984.

———. *Samoderzhavie, burzhuaziia, i dvoriantsvo v 1907–1911 gg.* Leningrad: 1978.

Dmytryshyn, B. D. "The Economic Content of the 1767 'Nakaz' of Catherine II." *Slavic Review* 19, no. 1 (February 1960): 1–9.

Dobroliubov, N. A. *Sobranie sochinenii.* 9 vols. Leningrad: 1964.

Donnert, Erich. "Mikhail Shcherbatov als Politischer Ideologe des russischen Adels in der zweiten Hälfte des 18 Jahrhundert." *Zeitschrift für Slawistik* 18, no. 3 (1973): 411–12.

———. "Russische Studenten an Englischen Universitäten im 18. Jahrhundert." In *Wegenetz Europaischen Geistes.* Edited by R. G. Plaschka and K. Mack. Munich: R. Oldenbourg, 1987.

Dovnar-Zapolskii, M. V. "Krepostniki v pervoi chetverti xix v." In *Velikaia reforma: Russkoe obshchestvo i krest'ianskii vopros v proshlom i nastoiashchem.* 6 vols. Edited by A. Dzhivelegov, et al. Moscow: 1911.

Druzhinin, N. M. *Absoliutizm v Rossii xvii–xviii vv: Sbornik statei k semidesiatiletiiu so dnia rozhdeniia i sorokopiatiletiiu nauchnoi, pedagogicheskoi deiatel'nosti. V. V. Kafengauza. Moscow: 1964.*

———. *Gosudarstvennaia krest'ianskaia reforma P. D. Kiselëva.* 2 vols. Moscow: 1946–58.

———. "Gosudarstvennye krest'iane v dvorianskikh i pravitel'stvennykh proektakh 1800–1833." *Istoricheskie zapiski* 7 (1940): 149–81.

Dubrovskii, S. M. *Stolypinskaia zemel'naia reforma: iz istorii sel'skogo khoziaistva i krest'ianstva Rossii v nachale xx veka.* Moscow: 1963.

Dudzinskaia, E. A. "Burzhuaznye tendentsii v istorii i praktike slavianofilov." *Voprosy istorii* 1 (1972): 49–64.

Dukes, Paul. *Catherine the Great and the Russian Nobility.* Cambridge: Cambridge University Press, 1967.

Edelman, Robert. *Proletarian Peasants: The Revolution of 1905 in Russia's Southwest.* Ithaca, N.Y.: Cornell University Press, 1987.

Egorov, M. "Krest'ianskoe dvzhenie v tsentral'noi chernozemnoi oblasti v 1907–1914 godakh." *Voprosy istorii* 5 (1948): 3–19.

Eklof, Ben. *Russian Peasant Schools: Officialdom, Village Culture, and Popular Pedagogy.* Berkeley and Los Angeles: University of California Press, 1986.

Eliseev, G. Z. *Sochineniia.* 2 vols. Moscow: 1894.

El'nitskii, A. "Rostopchin." *Russkii biograficheskii slovar'* 27 (Moscow: 1918): 238–305.

Emmons, Terence. *The Russian Landed Gentry and the Peasant Emancipation of 1861.* Berkeley and Los Angeles: University of California Press, 1968.

Engelstein, Laura. *The Keys to Happiness: Sex and the Search for Modernity in Fin-de-Siècle Russia.* Ithaca, N.Y.: Cornell University Press, 1992.

Ericson, Richard. "The Classical Soviet-Style Economy: Nature of the System and Implications for Reform." *Journal of Economic Perspectives* 5 (1991): 11–28.

Ermolov, A. S. *Mémoire sur la production agricole de la Russie*. St. Petersburg: 1878.

———. *Nash zemel'nyi vopros*. St. Petersburg: 1906.

———. *Neurozhai i narodnoe bedstvie*. St. Petersburg: 1892.

Feige, Edgar. "The Transition to a Market Economy in Russia: Property Rights, Mass Privatization and Stabilization." In *A Fourth Way? Privatization, Property and the Emergence of New Market Economies*. Edited by Gregory Alexander and Grazyna Skapska. London: Routledge, 1993.

Field, Daniel. *The End of Serfdom: Nobility and Bureaucracy in Russia, 1855–1861*. Cambridge, Mass.: Harvard University Press: 1976.

Figes, Orlando. "Peasant Farmers and the Minority Groups of Rural Society: Peasant Egalitarianism and Village Social Relations During the Russian Revolution (1917–1921)." In *Peasant Economy, Culture, and Politics ofEuropean Russia, 1800–1921*. Edited by Esther Kingston-Mann and Timothy Mixter. Princeton: Princeton University Press, 1991. Pp. 378–401.

———. *Peasant Russia, Civil War: The Volga Countryside in Revolution, 1917–1921*. Oxford: Clarendon Press, 1989.

Firks, Baron (Schedo-Ferrati). *Études sur l'Avenir de la Russie*. Berlin: 1868.

Fischer, H. A. *Paul Vinogradoff: A Memoir*. Oxford: Clarendon Press, 1927.

Fisher, George. *Russian Liberalism from Gentry to Intelligentsia*. Cambridge, Mass.: Harvard University Press, 1958.

Flynn, James. *The University Reforms of Tsar Alexander I*. Washington, D.C.: Catholic University of America Press, 1988.

Fortunatov, A. F. "Obshchii obzor zemskoi statistiki krest'ianskogo khoziaistva." In *Itogi ekonomicheskogo issledovaniia Rossii po dannym zemskoi statistiki*. 2 vols. Moscow: 1892.

———. "Raspredelenie pozemel'noi sobstvennosti v evropeiskoi Rossii." *Russkaia mysl'* 7 (July 1886): 110–35.

Frank, Stephen. "Cultural Conflict and Criminality in Rural Russia, 1861–1900." Ph.D. diss., Brown University, 1987.

Friesen, Leonard. "Bukkers, Plows, and Lobogreikas: Peasant Acquisition of Agricultural Implements in New Russia before 1900." *Russian Review* 53, no. 3 (July 1994): 399–418.

Gatrell, Peter. *The Tsarist Economy 1850–1917*. London: Batsford, 1986.

Gertzenshtein, M. Ia. *Agrarnyi vopros v programmakh razlichnykh partii*. Moscow: 1906.

Getzler, Israel. *Martov: A Political Biography of a Russian Social Democrat*. London: Cambridge University Press, 1967.

Givens, Robert. "Supplication and Reform in the Instructions of the Nobility." *Canadian-American Slavic Studies* 11, no. 4 (1977): 483–502.

Gleason, Abbott. *European and Muscovite: Ivan Kireevskii and the Origins of Slavophilism*. Cambridge, Mass.: Harvard Universty Press, 1971.

———. *Young Russia: The Genesis of Russian Radicalism in the 1860s*. Chicago: University of Chiacgo Press, 1983.

Goehrke, Carsten. *Die Theorien über die Entstehung und Entwicklung des "Mir."* Wiesbaden: O. Harassowitz, 1964.

Goldman, Marshall. *Lost Opportunity: Why Economic Reforms in Russia Have Not Worked*. New York: W. W. Norton & Co., 1994.

———. "The Pitfalls of Russian Privatization." *Challenge: A Magazine of Economic Affairs* 40, no. 3 (May–June 1997): 35–49.

Granovskii, T. N. *Sochineniia T. N. Granovskago. S portretom avtora.* 2 vols. 2nd ed. Moscow: 1866.

Grant, Steven. "*Obshchina* and *Mir.*" *Slavic Review* 35, no. 4 (1976): 636–51.

———. "The Peasant Commune in Russian Thought, 1861–1905." Ph.D. diss., Harvard University, 1973.

Grau, Conrad. "Zur Ideologie Geschichte in Russland und zu den deutsch-russischen Beziehungen in den sechziger/siebziger Jahren des 18 Jh." *Jahrbuch für Geschichte der sozialistischen Länder Europas* 23, no. 2 (April 1979): 83–97.

Griffiths, David. "Eighteenth-Century Perceptions of Backwardness: Projects for the Creation of a Third Estate in Catherinian Russia." *Journal of Canadian-American Slavic Studies* 13/14 (1979): 452–72.

Grin, T. I. *K. Marks, F. Engel's i revoliutsionnaia Rossiia: K. 160-letiiu so dnia rozhdeniia K. Marksa: Rek. ukaz. lit.* Moscow: 1978.

Gurko, V. I. *Ustoi narodnogo khoziaistva Rossii: Agrarno-ekonomicheskie etiudy.* St. Petersburg: 1902.

Hamburg, Gary. *Boris Chicherin and Early Russian Liberalism, 1828–1866.* Stanford, Cal.: Stanford University Press, 1992.

Haxthausen, Baron August von. *The Russian Empire: Its People, Institutions and Resources.* Translated by R. Farie. 2 vols. London: Chapman & Hall, 1856.

Herzen, Alexander M. *My Past and Thoughts: The Memoirs of Alexander Herzen.* 4 vols. Translated by Constance Garnett. New York: A. A. Knopf, 1968.

———. *O razvitii revoliutsionnykh idei v Rossii.* Moscow: 1958.

———. *Polnoe sobranie sochinenii i pisem.* 22 vols. Petrograd: 1919–25.

Hirscheibel, Henry. "The District Captains of the Ministry of State Domains in the Reign of Nicholas I: A Case Study of Russian Provincial Officialdom, 1830–1856." Ph.D. diss., New York University, 1978.

Hoch, Steven. *Serfdom and Social Control in Russia.* Chicago: University of Chicago Press, 1986.

Iakovlev. V. Ia. (V. Bogucharskii). *Iz istorii politicheskoi bor'by v 70-kh i 80-kh gg. xix veka: Partiia narodnoi voli, eia proizkhozhdenie, sud'by i gibel'.* Moscow: 1912.

Iakushkin, E. I. *Obychnoe pravo.* Yaroslavl: 1875.

Indova, E. I. "Voprosy zemledeliia v 'Trudakh vol'nogo ekonomicheskogo obshchestva,' vo vtoroi polovine xvii veka." *Ezhegodnik po agrarnoi istorii Vostochnoi Evropy* (1980): 114–23.

Isaev, A. A. *O sotsializm nashikh dnei.* Stuttgart: 1902.

Ischboldin, Boris. *History of the Russian Non-Marxian Socio-Economic Thought.* New Delhi: New Book Society of India, 1971.

Ivaniukov, I. D. "Sintez ob uchenii ekonomicheskoi politike." *Russkaia mysl'* 2 (1880): 28–29.

Jarvesoo, Elmar. "Early Agricultural Education at Tartu University." *Journal of Baltic Studies* 11, no. 4 (1980): 341–55.

Jones, Robert E. "Jacob Sievers, Enlightened Reform, and the Development of a 'Third Estate' in Russia." *Russian Review* 36 (October 1977): 424–37.

————. *Provincial Development in Russia: Catherine II and Jakob Sievers*. New Brunswick, N.J.: Rutgers University Press, 1984.

Kablukov, N. A. *Ob usloviiakh razvitiia krest'ianskogo khoziaistva v Rossii*. Moscow: 1899.

————. "Russkie issledovatelei kak istochniki nemetskoi uchenosti." *Russkaia mysl'* 9 (September 1881): 427–437.

Kachorovskii, K. R. *Bor'ba za zemliu*. St. Petersburg: 1908.

————. *Russkaia obshchina. Vozmozhno li, zhelatel'no li eia sokhranenie i razvitie?: Opyt tsifrogo i fakticheskogo issledovaniia*. St. Petersburg: 1900.

Kagarlitsky, Boris. "Back in the USA/USSR." *Socialist Review* (1991): 33–39.

Kahan, Arcadius. "Continuity in Economic Activity and Policy During the Post-Petrine Period in Russia." *Journal of Economic History* 25, no. 1 (March 1965): 61–85.

————. "The Costs of 'Westernization' in Russia: The Gentry and the Economy in Russian History." In *The Structure of Russian History: Interpretive Essays*. Edited by Michael Cherniavsky. New York: Random House, 1970.

————. *The Plow, the Hammer, and the Knout: An Economic History of Eighteenth-Century Russia*. Chicago: University of Chicago Press, 1985.

Kaplan, Frederick. "Du développement des idées révolutionnaire en Russie." *American Slavic and East European Review* 17, no. 2 (April 1958):161–72.

Karataev, N. K. *Ekonomicheskie nauki v Moskovskom universitete, 1755–1955*. Moscow: 1956.

————. *Russkaia ekonomicheskaia mysl' v period krizisa feodal'nogo khoziaistva (40–60-kh gody xix veka)*. Moscow: 1957.

————, ed. *Narodnicheskaia ekonomicheskaia literatura. Izbrannye proizvedeniia*. Moscow: 1958.

Kareev, N. "Zametka o raspadenii pozemel'noi obshchiny na Zapade." *Znanie* 4 (1876): 1–14.

Karpov, N. *Agrarnaia politika Stolypina*. Leningrad: 1925.

Kaufman, A. A. *Obshchina i uspekhi sel'skogo khoziaistva v Sibirii*. St. Petersburg: 1894.

Kavelin, K. D. "Einiges über die russische Dorfgemeinde." *Tübingen Zeitschrift* 1 (1864): 1–53.

————. "Obshchinnoe vladenie." *Nedelia*, nos. 3–5 (1877): 130–35; nos. 6–7 (1878): 210–28; appeared in German in book form as *Der bauerliche Gemeindebesitz in Russland*. Leipzig: 1877.

————. *Sobranie sochinenii*. 4 vols. St. Petersburg: 1897.

Kayden, E., and A. Antsiferov. *The Cooperative Movement in Russia During the War*. New Haven: Yale University Press, [1929] 1927.

Keussler, Johannes. *Zur Geschichte und Kritik des bauerlichen Gemeindebesitzes in Russland*. 3 vols. Riga: 1876–1887.

Khodnev, A. I. *Istoriia imperatorskogo vol'nogo ekonomicheskogo obshchestva*. St. Petersburg: 1865.

Khomiakov, A. S. *Polnoe sobranie sochinenii*. 2 vols. Moscow: 1907.

————. *Polnoe sobranie sochinenii*. 4th edition. 8 vols. Moscow: 1914.

Kingston-Mann, Esther. "Breaking the Silence: An Introduction." In *Peasant Economy, Culture, and Politics of European Russia, 1800–1921*. Edited by Esther Kingston-Mann and Timothy Mixter. Princeton: Princeton University Press, 1991. Pp. 3–19.

———. "In the Light and Shadow of the West: The Impact of Western Economics in Pre-Emancipation Russia." *Comparative Studies in Society and History* 33, no. 1 (1991): 86–105.

———. "In Search of the True West: Western Economic Models and Russian Rural Development." *Journal of Historical Sociology* 3, no. 2 (1990): 23–49.

Kingston-Mann, Esther. *Lenin and the Problem of Marxist Peasant Revolution.* New York: Oxford University Press, 1983.

———. "The Majority as an Obstacle to Progress: Radicals, Peasants and the Russian Revolution." *Radical America* 6, nos. 4–5 (1982): 85.

———. "Marxism and Russian Rural Development: Problems of Evidence, Experience and Culture." The *American Historical Review* 86 (October 1981): 731–52.

———. "Peasant Communes and Economic Innovation: A Preliminary Inquiry." In *Peasant Economy, Culture, and Politics of European Russia, 1800–1921.* Edited by Esther Kingston-Mann and Timothy Mixter. Princeton: Princeton University Press, 1991. Pp. 23–51.

———. "Pre-Emancipation Russian Economists Interpret Western Liberal Economics." In *Proceedings of the History of Economics Society.* Middletown, Conn.: 1989.

———. "Understanding Peasants, Understanding the Experts: Zemstvo Statisticians in Pre-revolutionary Russia." Paper presented at the First International Conference on Peasant Culture and Consciousness. Bellagio, Italy, January 1992.

———, and Timothy Mixter, eds. *Peasant Economy, Culture, and Politics of European Russia, 1800–1921.* Princeton: Princeton University Press, 1991.

Kireevskii, I. V. *I. V. Kireevskogo v dvukh tomakh.* Moscow: 1911.

———. *Polnoe sobranie sochinenii Ivana Vasil'evicha Kirieevskago.* Ann Arbor, Mich.: Ardis, 1983.

Kitaev, V. A. *Ot frondy k okhranitel'stvu: Istoriia russkoi liberal'noi mysli 50–60kh godov xix veka.* Moscow: 1972.

Kofoed, C. A. *Bor'ba s chrezpolositsiu v Rossii i za granitseiu.* St. Petersburg: 1906.

———. *Krest'ianskie khutory na nadel'noi zemle.* Moscow: 1909.

———. *My Share in the Stolypin Agrarian Reforms.* Edited and translated by Bend Jensen. Odense, Denmark: Odense University Press, 1985.

Kokorev, A. V. *Khrestomatiia po russkoi literature xviii veka.* 4th edition. Moscow: 1965.

Koliupanov, N. P. *Biografiia Aleksandra Ivanovicha Kosheleva.* 2 vols. Moscow: 1889–92.

Kopyl, I. F. "Iz istorii russkoi agronomii xviii v." In *Materialy po istorii sel'skogo khoziaistva i krest'ianstva SSSR* 7. Moscow: 1969. Pp. 84–98.

Kornilov, A. A. *Obshchestvennoe dvizhenie pri Aleksandre II, 1855–1881 istoricheskie ocherki.* Paris: Société nouvelle de librairie et d'edition, 1905.

Kosachevskaia, E. M. *Mikhail Andreevich Balugianskii i Petersburgskii universitet v pervoi chetverti xix veka*. Leningrad: 1971.

Koshelev, A. I. *Ob obshchinnom zemlevladenii v Rossii*. Berlin: 1875.

————. *Zapiski (1812–1883)*. Berlin: 1884.

Kotkin, Stephen. *Magnetic Mountain: Stalinism as Civilization*. Berkeley and Los Angeles: University of California Press, 1995.

Kotsonis, Yanni. "Agricultural Cooperatives and the Agrarian Question in Russia, 1861–1914." Ph.D. diss., Columbia University, 1994.

Kotz, David, with Fred Weir. *Revolution from Above: The Demise of the Soviet System*. London: Routledge, 1997.

Kovalevskii, M. M. *Angliiskaia konstitutsiia i eia istorik*. Moscow: 1880.

————. *Modern Customs and Ancient Laws of Russia*. London: D. Nutt, 1891.

————. *Obshchestvennyi stroi Anglii v kontse srednikh vekov*. Moscow: 1880.

————. *Obshchinnoe zemlevladenie, prichiny, khod i posledstviia: ego razlozheniia, chast' 1*. Moscow: Tip. F. B. Millera, 1879.

————. "Le passage historique de la propriété individuelle." *Annales de l'Institut Internationale de Sociologie* 2 (1895): 175–230.

————. *Razvitie narodnogo khoziaistva v zapadnoi evrope*. St. Petersburg: 1899.

Kozmin, B. N. "Neizdannye pisma G. V. Plekhanova i P. L. Lavrova." *Literaturnoe nasledstvo*, nos. 19–21 (1935): 272–96.

Kozmin, B. P. *Iz istorii revoliutsionnoi mysli v Rossii; Izbrannye trudy*. Moscow: 1961.

Lampert, Evgenii. *Sons Against Fathers*. Oxford: Clarendon Press, 1965.

Laptin, P. F. *Obshchina v russkoi istoriografii poslednei treti xix-nachala xx v.* Kiev: 1971.

Lauterbach, Richard. "Stalin at 65." *Life* (January 2, 1945): 67.

LeDonne, John. *Ruling Russia: Politics and Administration in the Age of Absolutism*. Princeton: Princeton University Press, 1984.

Leikina-Svirskaia, Vera Romanova. *Intelligentsiia v Rossii vo vtoroi polovine xix veka*. Moscow: 1971.

Lempert, David. "Changing Russian Political Culture in the 1990s: Parasites, Paradigms and Perestroika." *Comparative Studies in Society and History* 35, no. 3 (July 1993): 628–46.

Lenin, V. I. *Polnoe sobranie sochinenii*. 5th ed. 55 vols. Moscow: 1958–65.

Lewitter, L. R. "Ivan Tikhonovich Pososhkov and the 'Spirit of Capitalism.' " *Slavic and East European Review*, 51 (1973): 524–53.

Lieven, Dominic. *Russia's Rulers under the Old Regime*. New Haven: Yale University Press, 1989.

Lincoln, W. Bruce. "Count P. D. Kiselev: A Reformer in Imperial Russia." *Australian Journal of Politics and History* 16, no. 2 (August 1970): 177–88.

————. *In the Vanguard of Reform: Russia's Enlightened Bureaucrats 1825–1861*. Dekalb: Northern Illinois University Press, 1982.

Litvak, B. G. *Russkaia derevnia v reforme 1861 goda: Chernozemnyi tsentr 1861–1895*. Moscow: 1972.

Lortholary, Albert. *Les "Philosophes" du xviii-e siècle et la Russie*. Paris: Editions contemporains, Boivic, 1951.

Luchitskii, Ivan. "Pozemel'naia obshchina v Pireneiakh." *Otechestvennye zapiski* 1883. Nos. 9, 10, 12.

Lukashevich, Stephen. *Ivan Aksakov 1823–1886: A Study in Russian Thought and Politics.* Cambridge, Mass.: Harvard University Press, 1965.

Luppol, I. K. "The Empress and the Philosophe." In *Catherine the Great; a Profile.* Edited by Marc Raeff. New York: Hill and Wang, 1972.

Macey, David A. J. *Government and Peasant in Russia, 1861–1906: The Prehistory of the Stolypin Reforms.* DeKalb: Northern Illinois University Press, 1987.

Madariaga, Isabel. *Catherine the Great: A Short History.* New Haven: Yale University Press, 1993.

Malia, Martin. *Alexander Herzen and the Birth of Russian Socialism, 1812–1855.* Cambridge, Mass.: Harvard University Press, 1961.

Manning, Roberta. *Crisis of the Old Order in Russia: Gentry and Government.* Princeton: Princeton University Press, 1982.

Manuilov, A. A. *Arenda v Irlandii.* Moscow: 1895.

———. "K voprosu o mobilizatsii zemel. sobst." *Russkoe bogatstvo* 6 (1897): 34–41.

———. *Pozemel'nyi vopros v Rossii.* Moscow: 1905.

Martynov, A. S. "Glavneishye momenty v istorii russkogo marksizma." In *Obshchestvennoe dvizhenie v Rossii v nachale xix veka.* Vol. 2, part 2. St. Petersburg: 1909–14.

Masaryk, Thomas. *The Spirit of Russia: Studies in History, Literature and Philosophy.* London: Allen & Unwin, 1919.

Maslov, E. *O vlianii razlichnykh vidov pozemel'noi sobstvennosti na narodnoe bogatstvo.* Kazan: 1860.

Maslov, P. P. *Agrarnyi vopros v Rossii.* Vol. 2. St. Petersburg: 1906.

Matsuzato, Kimitaka. "The Fate of Agronomists in Russia: Their Quantitative Dynamics from 1911 to 1916." *Russian Review* 55 (April 1996): 172–200.

———. "New Dimensions in the Studies of Russian Agrarian History." Unpublished paper, 1994.

———. "Stolypinskaia reforma i rossiiskaia agrotechnologicheskaia revoliutsiia." *Otechestvennaia istoriia* 6 (1992): 194–200.

———. "Stolypinskaia reforma i rossiikoi agrotekhnologicheskii perevorot." *Acta Slavica Iaponica* 10 (1992): 33–42.

Mavrodin, V. V. *Klassovaia bor'ba i obshchestvenno-politicheskaia mysl' v Rossii v xviii v.* Leningrad: 1964.

McConnell, Allen. *Alexander Radishchev: A Russian Philosphe 1749–1802.* The Hague: Martinus Nijhoff, 1964.

McGrew, Roderick. "Dilemmas of Development: Baron Heinrich Friedrich Storch (1766–1835), on the Growth of Imperial Russia." *Jahrbücher fur Geschichte Osteuropas* 24 (1976): 31–71.

Melton, Edgar. "Enlightened Seignorialism and Its Dilemmas in Serf Russia, 1750–1830." *Journal of Modern History* 62 (December 1990): 675–708.

Mendel, Arthur. *Dilemmas of Progress in Tsarist Russia: Legal Marxism and Legal Populism.* Cambridge, Mass.: Harvard University Press, 1961.

Mikhailov, M. L. *Zhenshchiny.* St. Petersburg: 1903.

Mikhailovskii, N. K. *Polnoe sobranie sochinenii.* St. Petersburg: 1903.

———. *Sochineniia.* 3 vols. St. Petersburg: 1906.

Miliutin, V. A. *Izbrannye proizvedeniia.* Moscow: 1946.

Mitskevich, S. *Na grani dvukh epokh.* Moscow: 1937.

Mogil'nitskii, B. G. *Politicheskie i metodologicheskie idei russkoi liberal'noi medievistiki serediny 70-x godov xix v.—nachala 900-x godov.* Tomsk: 1969.

Muller, E., "Lorenz v. Stein und Jurij Samarins Vision des absoluten Sozialstaates." *Jahrbücher für Geschichte Osteuropas* 15 (1967): 575–606.

Nechkina, M. V. *Dvizhenie Dekabristov.* Moscow: 1955.

———. "O 'voskhodiashchei' i 'niskhodiashchei' stadiiakh feodal'noi formatsii." *Voprosy istorii* 7 (1958): 86–108.

Netting, Anthony. "Russian Liberalism: The Years of Promise, 1842–55." Ph.D. diss., Columbia University, 1967.

Nevedenskii, S. *Katkov i ego vremia.* St. Petersburg: 1888.

Newlin, Thomas. "The Voice in the Garden: Andrei Bolotov and the Anxieties of Russian Pastoral 1738–1833." Ph.D. diss., Columbia University, 1994.

Nolde, B. E. *Iurii Samarin i ego vremia.* Paris: Impr. de Navarre, 1926.

O'Brien, C. B. "Ivan Pososhkov: Russian Critic of Mercantilist Principles." *American Slavic and East European Review* 14 (1955): 503–11.

Oganovskii, N. P. *Individualizatsiia zemlevladeniia v Rossii i eia posledstviia.* Moscow: 1917.

Okenfuss, Max. "Education and Empire: School Reform in Enlightened Russia." *Jahrbücher für geschichte Osteuropas* 27, no. 1 (1979).

Okuda, Hiroshi. "The Emergence of the Kolkhoz: The End of Communes in Russia." Unpublished paper.

———. "On Some Aspects of the Final Stages of the Russian Peasant Commune: Village Ramen'e and the Strategy of Collectivization." Paper presented at the Conference on the Russian Commune, University of Longdon, 1986.

Okun, S. B., and K. V. Sivkov. *Krest'ianskoe dvizhenie v Rossii v 1857–1861gg: Sbornik dokumentov.* Moscow: 1963.

Oreshkin, V. V. *Vol'noe ekonomicheskoe obshchestvo 1765–1917.* Moscow: 1963.

Orlovsky, Daniel. *The Limits of Reform: The Ministry of Internal Affairs in Imperial Russia, 1802–1881.* Cambridge, Mass.: Harvard University Press, 1981.

Pallot, Judith. "Agrarian Modernization on Peasant Farms in the Era of Capitalism." In *Studies in Russian Historical Geography.* 2 vols. London; New York: Academic Press, 1983.

Pashkov, A. I., and N. A. Tsagalov. *Istoriia russkoi ekonomicheskoi mysli.* 3 vols. Moscow: 1955–60.

Pavlovsky, George. *Agricultural Russia on the Eve of the Revolution.* New York: H. Fertig, 1968.

Pchelin, N. V. *Ekaterinskaia kommissiia "o sochineniia proekta novogo ulozheniia" i sovremennoe ei russkoe zakonodatel'stvo.* Moscow: 1915.

Pereira, Norman G. O. *The Thought and Teachings of N. G. Cernyshevskij.* The Hague: Mouton, 1975.

Peshtich, S. L. *Russkaia istoriografiia xviii veka.* 3 vols. Leningrad: 1965.

Pestel, P. I. *Russkaia pravda.* Moscow: 1893.

Petrushevskii, D. M. *Vosstanie Wat Tailera.* St. Petersburg: 1897.

Pfaff, William. "Bad Advice from the West Has Imperiled Russia." *The Baltimore Sun* (November 25, 1996): 11a.

Pintner, Walter. *Russian Economic Policy under Nicholas I.* Ithaca, N.Y.: Cornell University Press, 1967.

Pipes, Richard. "Russian Marxism and Its Populist Background: The Late Nineteenth Century." *The Russian Review* 19, no. 4 (October 1960): 316–77.

———. "The Russian Military Colonies, 1810–1831." *Journal of Modern History* 22 (October 1950): 205–19.

———. *Struve: Liberal on the Left.* Cambridge, Mass.: Harvard University Press, 1970.

Pirumova, N. M. *Zemskaia intelligentsiia i eë rol' v obshchestvennoi bor'be.* Moscow: 1986.

Plekhanov, G. V. *Sochineniia.* Edited by D. Riazanov. 24 vols. Moscow: 1923.

Pnin, Ivan. *Sochineniia.* Edited by I. K. Luppol. Moscow: 1934.

Pobedonostsev, K. P. *Kurs grazhdanskogo prava.* 3 vols. St. Petersburg: 1896.

Popov, Gavril. "The Dangers of Democracy." *New York Review of Books* (August 16, 1990): 27–28.

Posnikov, A. S. *Obshchinnoe zemlevladenie.* Yaroslavl and Odessa: 1875.

Postnikov, V. Ye. *Iuzhno-russkoe krest'ianskoe khoziaistvo.* Moscow: 1891.

Pratt, Joan. "The Russian Free Economic Society." Ph.D. diss., University of Missouri–Columbia, 1983.

Prokopovich, S. N. *Kooperativnoe dvizhenie v Rossii.* Moscow: 1918.

Prugavin, A. S. *Zaprosy naroda i obiazannosti intelligentsii v oblasti prosveshcheniia i vospitaniia.* St. Petersburg: 1895.

Prugavin, V. S. *Russkaia zemel'naia obshchina v trudakh eë mestnykh issledovatelei.* Moscow: 1888.

Pushkin, A. S. *Eugene Onegin.* Trans. V. N. Nabokov. New York: Pantheon Books, 1964.

Pypin, A. N. *Kharakteristika literaturnykh mnenii ot 20-ykh do 50-ykh godov.* St. Petersburg: 1890.

Radishchev, A. N. *A Journey from St. Petersburg to Moscow.* Translated by Leo Wiener. Cambridge, Mass.: Harvard University Press, 1958.

———. *Polnoe sobranie sochinenii.* 3 vols. Moscow-Leningrad: 1938.

Radkey, Oliver. *The Agrarian Foes of Bolshevism: Promise and Default of the Russian Socialist Revolutionaries.* New York: Columbia University Press, 1958.

Raeff, Marc. *The Decembrists.* Englewood Cliffs, N.J.: Prentice-Hall, 1966.

———. "The Peasant Commune in the Political Thinking of Russian Publicists: Laissez Faire Liberalism in the Reign of Alexander II." Ph.D. diss., Harvard University, 1950.

———. *Political Ideas and Institutions in Imperial Russia.* Boulder, Col.: Westview Press, 1994.

———. "State and Nobility in the Ideology of M. M. Shcherbatov." *American Slavic and East European Review* 19 (1960): 363–79.

———. "Les Slaves, les Allemands et les 'Lumières.' " *Canadian Slavic Studies* 1, no. 4 (1967): 521–51.

———. *The Well-Ordered Police State: Social and Institutional Change through Law in the Germanies and Russia, 1600–1800.* New Haven: Yale University Press, 1983.

Raeff, Marc. "The Well-Ordered Police State and the Development of Modernity in 17th-and 18th-Century Europe: An Attempt at a Comparative Approach." *The American Historical Review* 80 (December 1975): 1221–43.

Raikes, Thomas. *A Visit to St. Petersburg in the Winter of 1829–1830.* London: R. Bentley, 1838.

Ramer, Samuel C. "Traditional Healers and Peasant Culture in Russia, 1861–1917." In *Peasant Economy, Culture, and Politics ofEuropean Russia, 1800–1921.* Edited by Esther Kingston-Mann and Timothy Mixter. Princeton: Princeton University Press, 1991. pp. 207–32.

———. "The Traditional and the Modern in the Writings of Ivan Pmin." *Slavic Review* 34 (1975): 538–59.

Ransel, David. *The Politics of Catherinian Russia.* New Haven: Yale University Press, 1975.

Reddaway, W. F., ed. *Documents of Catherine the Great: The Correspondence with Voltaire and the Instruction of 1767 in the English Text of 1768.* Cambridge: Cambridge University Press, 1931.

Repczuk, Helma. "Nicholas Mordvinov (1754–1845): Russia's Would-Be Reformer." Ph.D.diss., Columbia University, 1962.

Reuel, A. L. *Russkaia ekonomicheskaia mysl' 60–70-kh godov xix veka i marksizm.* Moscow: 1956.

Riasanovsky, Nicholas V. *A Parting of the Ways: Government and the Educated Public in Russia, 1801–1855.* Oxford: Oxford University Press, 1976.

———. *Russia and the West in the Teaching of the Slavophiles.* Cambridge, Mass.: Harvard University Press, 1952.

Riazanov, D. B. "Briefwechsel zwischen Vera Zasulich und Marx." *Marx-Engels Arkhiv: Zeitschrift des Marx-Engels-Instituts in Moskau.* Vol. 2. Frankfurt am Main: Marx-Engels-Archiv verlagsgesellschaft m.b.h., 1927.

Rittikh, A. A. *Krest'ianskii pravoporiadok.* St. Petersburg: 1903.

———. *Zavisimost' krest'ian ot obshchiny i mir.* St. Petersburg: 1903.

Robbins, Richard. *The Tsar's Viceroys: Russia's Provincial Governors in the Last Years of the Empire.* Ithaca, N.Y.: Cornell University Press, 1987.

Robinson, Geroid T. *Rural Russia under the Old Regime.* Berkeley and Los Angeles: University of California Press, 1932.

Romanovich-Slavatinskii, A. V. *Dvorianstvo v Rossii ot nachala xviii veka do otmeny krepostnogo prava.* Kiev: 1912.

Roosevelt, Priscilla. *Apostle of Russian Liberalism: Timofei Granovsky.* Newtonville, Mass.: Oriental Research Partners, 1986.

———. "Granovskii at the Lectern: A Conservative Liberal's Vision of History." *Forschungen zur osteuropaischen Geschichte* 219 (Berlin, 1981): 61–192.

Rosenberg, William. *Liberals and the Russian Revolution: The Constitutional Democratic Party, 1917–1921.* Princeton: Princeton University Press, 1974.

Rozental', V. N. "Obshchestvenno-politicheskaia programma russkogo libe-ralizma v seredine 50-kh godov xix veka." *Istoricheskie zapiski* 70 (1961):197–222.

Rubinshtein, N. S. *Sel'skoe khoziaistvo Rossii vo vtoroi polovine xviii v.* Moscow: 1957.

Rusanov, N. S. "Evoliutsiia russkoi sotsialisticheskoi mysli." *Vestnik* 3 (March 1903): 23–34.

Rusanov, N. S. *Noveishaia literatura po obshchinnomu zemlevladenii v Rossii.* Moscow: 1879.

———. "Sovremennye proiavleniia kapitalizma v Rossii." *Russkoe bogatstvo* (January 1, 1880): 79–108; (February 2, 1880): 49–61.

Säcke, Georg. "Der Einfluss Englands auf die politische Ideologie der russischen Gesellschaft in der 2. Halfte des xviii Jahrhunderts." *Archiv für Kulturge-schichte* 39 (1941): 85–105.

———. "Die Moskauer Nachschrift der Vorlesungen von Adam Smith." *Zeit-schrift für Nationalokonomie* 9 (1939): 351–56.

Safronov, B. G. *M. M. Kovalevskii kak sotsiolog.* Moscow: 1960.

Salzman, Catherine. "Consumer Cooperative Societies in Russia, Goals v. Gains 1900–1918." *Cahiers du monde Russe et Soviètique* 23, nos. 3–4 (1982): 351–69.

Samarin, Iu. F. *Sochineniia.* 12 vols. Moscow: 1877–1911.

———. "Uprazdnenie krepostnogo prava i ustroistvo otnoshenii mezhdu pome-shchikami i krest'ianami v Prussii." *Sel'skoe blagoustroistvo* 1, no. 4 (1858): 37–92; 2 (1858): 103–28; vol. 4, 24–27; and vol. 8, 117–18.

Savin, A. N. "Russkie razrushiteli obshchiny i angliiski ogorazhivateli." *Moskov-skii ezhenedel'nik*, no. 2 (1909): 38–51.

Semevskii, V. I. *Krest'ianskii vopros v Rossii v xviii i pervoi polovine xix veka.* 2 vols. St. Petersburg: 1888.

———. *Krest'iane v tsarstvovanie imperatritsy ekateriny ii.* 2 vols. St. Petersburg: 1901.

———. *Politicheskaia i obshchestvennye idei Dekabristov.* St. Petersburg: 1909.

Seregny, Scott J. "Teachers and Rural Cooperatives: The Politics of Education and Professional Identities in Russia, 1908–1917." *The Russian Review* 55, no. 4 (October 1996): 567–90.

Shanin, Teodor. *The Awkward Class: Political Sociology of Peasantry in a Devel-oping Society, Russia, 1910–1925.* Oxford: Clarendon Press, 1974.

———. *The Rules of the Game: Cross-disciplinary Essays on Models in Scholarly Thought.* London: Tavistock Publications, 1972.

———. *Russia, 1905–07: Revolution as a Moment of Truth.* New Haven: Yale University Press, 1986.

———. *Russia as a Developing Society.* 2 vols. New Haven: Yale University Press, 1985.

———, ed. *Late Marx and the Russian Road: Marx and the "Peripheries of Capi-talism."* New York: Monthly Review Press, 1984.

Shchapov, A. P. *Sochineniia.* England: Farnborough, Gregg, 1971.

Shcherbatov, M. M. *Neizdannye sochineniia.* Moscow: 1935.

———. *On the Corruption of Morals in Russia.* Translated by A. Lentin. Cam-bridge: Cambridge University Press, 1969.

————. *Sochineniia kniaza M. M. Shcherbatov*. 2 vols. (St. Petersburg: 1896–98).

Shchipanov, I. Ia., ed. *Izbrannye proizvedeniia russkikh myslitelei vtoroi poloviny xviii veka*. 2 vols. Moscow: 1952.

Shelgunov, N. V., L. P. Shelgunova, and M. L. Mikhailov. *Vospominaniia*. 2 vols. Moscow: 1967.

Shilder, N. K. *Imperator Aleksandr pervyi, ego zhizn' i tsarstvovanie*. 4 vols. St. Petersburg: 1904–5.

Shkurinov, P. S. *Pozitivizm v Rossii xix veka*. Moscow: 1980.

Simmons, Ernest J. *English Literature and Culture in Russia (1553–1840)*. New York: Octagon Books, 1935.

Simonova, M. S. "Bor'ba techenii v pravitel'stvennom lagere po voprosam agrarnoi politika v kontse xix veka." *Istoriia SSSR*, no. 1 (1968): 65–82.

Sivkov, K. V. *Ocherki po istorii krepostnago khoziaistva i krest'ianskogo dvizheniia v Rossii v pervoi polovine xix veka*. Moscow: 1952.

Skaldin [F. P. Elenev, pseud.]. *V zakholusti i v stolitse*. St. Petersburg: 1870.

Skvortsov, A. I. *Ekonomicheskie prichiny golodovok v Rossii i mery k ikh ustranenii: Ekonomicheskie etiudy*. Vol. 1. St. Petersburg: 1894.

Sokolovskii, P. A. "O prichinakh raspadeniia pozemel'noi obshchiny." *Slovo* 10 (1887): 139–45.

————. *Ssud-sberegatel'nye tovarishchestva po otzyvam literatury*. St. Petersburg: 1889.

Solomon, Susan Gross. *The Soviet Agrarian Debates: A Controversy in the Social Sciences*. Boulder, Colo.: Westview Press, 1977.

Speranskii, M. M. *Proekty i zapiski*. Moscow-Leningrad: 1961.

Stalin, Josef. *Problems of Leninism*. Moscow: 1945.

Stankevich, A. V. *T.N. Granovskii i ego perepiska*. Moscow: 1897.

Starr, S. Frederick. "August von Haxthausen and Russia." *Slavonic and East European Review* 46 (July 1968): 462–78.

————. *Decentralization and Self-Government in Russia*. Princeton: Princeton University Press, 1972.

Steklov, Iurii. *N. G. Chernyshevskii: Ego zhizn' i deiatel'nost 1828–89*. 2 vols. Moscow: 1928.

Stites, Richard. *The Women's Liberation Movement in Russia*. Princeton: Princeton University Press, 1978.

Stolypin, D. A. *Uchenie Konta i primenenie ego k resheniiu voprosa ob organizatsii zemel'noi sobstvennosti*. Moscow: 1891.

Stolypin, P. A. *Poezdka v sibir i povolzhe*. St. Petersburg: 1911.

Struve, Peter B. "Karl Marks i sud'by marksizmy." *Segodnia* (Riga, 1921): 130–31.

————. *Kriticheskiia zamitki k voprosu ob ekonomicheskom razvitii Rossii*. Vol. 1. St. Petersburg: 1894.

————. "Moim kritikam." In *Materialy k kharakteristike nashego khoziaistvennogo razvitiia: Sbornik statei*. St. Petersburg; Moscow: 1895.

Sukhanov, N. N. *Marksizm i narodnichestvo*. Berlin: 1915.

Svavitskii, N. A. *Zemskie podvornye perepisi (obzor metodologii)*. Moscow: 1961.

Sviatlovskii, V. V. *Politicheskaia ekonomiia*. Moscow: 1900.

Tarasov, E. I. *Dekabrist Nikolai Ivanovich Turgenev: Ocherkii po istorii liberalizma v Rossi*. Samara: 1923.

Tarle, E. V. "Imperator Nikolai I i krest'ianskii vopros v Rossii, po neizdannym doneseniiam frantsuzkikh diplomatov 1842–47." In *Zapad i Rossiia: Stat'i i dokumenty iz istorii xvii–xx vekov.* Petrograd: 1918.

Tengoborskii, Ludwig. *Commentaries on the Productive Forces of Russia.* 2 vols. London: Longman, Brown, Green, and Longmans, 1855–56.

———. *O proizvoditel'nykh silakh v Rosii.* Perevod i predislovie I. P. Vernadskogo. Moscow: 1854.

Tolstoy, Leo. "A Landlord's Morning." In *Leo Tolstoy: Short Novels.* Vol. 1. Edited by Ernest J. Simmons. New York: Random House, 1965.

Trene, W. "Adam Smith in Deutschland." In *Deutschland und Europa: Historische Studien zur Volker-un Staatenordnung des Abendlandes (Festschrift fur Hans Rothfels).* Edited by W. Conze. Dusseldorf: Droste-Verlag, 1951.

Trudy imperatorskogo vol'nogo ekonomicheskogo obshchestva.

Tsagalov, N. A. *Ocherki russkoi ekonomicheskoi mysli perioda padeniia krepostnogo prava.* Moscow: 1956.

Tugan-Baranovskii, M. I. *Promyshlennye krizisy; Ocherk iz sotsial'noi istorii Anglii.* St. Petersburg: 1894.

Turgenev, N. S. *Opyt teorii nalogov.* Moscow: 1937.

Tvardovskaia, V. A. *Ideologiia poreformennogo samoderzhaviia (M. N. Katkov i ego izdaniia).* Moscow: 1978.

Uspenskii, Gleb. *Polnoe sobranie sochinenii.* 14 vols. Moscow: 1940.

Utkina, N. F. *Pozitivizm, antropologicheskii materializm i nauka v Rossii.* Moscow: 1975.

Vaillant, Janet. "Encountering the West: The Ideological Responses of Aleksei S. Khomiakov and Leopold S. Senghor." Ph.D. diss., Harvard University, 1971.

Valuev, P. A. *Dnevnik P. A. Valueva ministra vnutrennikh del 1877–1884.* Moscow: 1919.

Van Lare, Donald. "Tula Province in the Eighteenth Century: The Deputy Instructions to the Legislative Commission of 1767 as a Source of Local History." Ph.D. diss., University of Kansas, 1978.

Vasil'chikov, A. I. *Zemlevladenie i zemledelie v Rossii i v drugikh evropeiskikh gosudarstvakh.* 2 volumes. St. Petersburg: 1876.

———, and A. V. Iakovlev. *Melkii zemel'nyi kredit v Rossii.* St. Petersburg: 1876.

Venturi, Franco. *Roots of Revolution.* New York: Knopf, 1960.

Vernadskaia, Maria. *Sobranie sochinenii.* St. Petersburg: 1862.

Vernadskii, I. P. *Ocherk istorii politicheskoi ekonomii.* St. Petersburg: 1858.

———. *Politicheskoe ravnovesie i Angliia.* Moscow: 1855.

———. *Prospekt politicheskoi ekonomii.* St. Petersburg: 1858.

Veselovskii, B. B. *Istoriia zemstva za sorok let.* 4 vols. St. Petersburg: 1909–11.

———. *Krest'ianskii vopros i krest'ianskoe dvizhenie.* Moscow: 1958.

Vetrinskii (V. E. Cheshikhin). *T. N. Granovskii i ego vremia.* St. Petersburg: 1905.

Vikhliaev, P. A. *Ocherki iz russkoi sel'sko-khoziaistvennoi deistvitel'nosti* St. Petersburg: 1901.

Vilenskaia, E. S. *Revoliutsionnoe podpol'e v Rossii (60-e gody xix v.).* Moscow: 1965.

Vinogradoff, Paul. *English Society in the Eleventh Century: Essays in English Medieval History.* Oxford: Clarendon Press, 1908.

———. *Villeinage in England: Essays in English Medieval History*. Oxford: Clarendon Press, 1892.

Vinogradov, Paul. *Istoriia srednikh vekov*. Moscow: 1899–1900.

———. *Politicheskie pis'ma*. St. Petersburg: 1905.

Volin, Lazar. *A Century of Russian Agriculture: From Alexander II to Khrushchev*. Cambridge, Mass.: Harvard University Press, 1970.

Vorontsov, V. P. *Gosudarstvennye dolgi Rossii*. Moscow: 1908.

Vorontsov, V. P. *Progressivnyia techeniia v krest'ianskom khoziaistve*. St. Petersburg: 1892.

Vucinich, Alexander. *Science in Russian Culture*. Stanford, Cal.: Stanford University Press, 1970.

———. *Social Thought in Tsarist Russia*. Chicago: University of Chicago Press, 1976.

Vucinich, W. S., ed. *The Peasant in Nineteenth-Century Russia*. Stanford, Cal.: Stanford University Press, 1968.

Wada, Haruki. "Marx and Revolutionary Russia." In *Late Marx and the Russian Road: Marx and the Peripheries of Capitalism*. Edited by Teodor Shanin. New York: Monthly Review Press, 1983.

Walicki, Andrzej. *The Controversy over Capitalism: Studies in the Social Philosophy of the Russian Populists*. Notre Dame, Ind.: University of Notre Dame Press, 1989.

———. *Legal Philosophies of Russian Liberalism*. Oxford: Clarendon Press, 1987.

———. *The Slavophile Controversy: History of a Conservative Utopia in Nineteenth-Century Russian Thought*. Oxford: Clarendon Press, 1975.

Wallace, Donald MacKenzie. *Russia*. New York: H. Holt and Co., 1970.

Wcislo, Francis. *Reforming Rural Russia: State, Local Society and National Politics 1855–1914*. Princeton: Princeton University Press, 1990.

Welsh, David J. *Russian Comedy 1765–1823*. The Hague: Mouton, 1966.

White, James. "Marx and the Russians: The Romantic Heritage." *Scottish Slavonic Review* 7 (October 1987): 51–81.

Wilbur, Elvira. "Was Russian Peasant Agriculture Really that Impoverished?: Evidence from Case Study from the 'Impoverished Center' at the End of the Nineteenth Century." *Journal of Economic History* (March 1983): 137–44.

Witte, S. Iu. *Agrarnyi vopros v sovete ministrov*. Moscow: 1924.

———. *Zapiska po krest'ianskomu delo*. St. Petersburg: 1904.

Woehrlin, William F. *Chernyshevskii: The Man and the Journalist*. Cambridge, Mass.: Harvard University Press, 1971.

Wortman, Richard. *The Crisis of Russian Populism*. Cambridge: Cambridge University Press, 1967.

———. "Koshelev, Samarin, and Cherkassky and the Fate of Liberal Slavophilism." *Slavic Review* 21 (1962): 247–61.

Yaney, George L. *The Systematization of Russian Government*. Urbana: University of Illinois Press, 1973.

———. *The Urge to Mobilize: Agrarian Reform in Russia 1861–1930*. Urbana: University of Illinois Press, 1982.

Zablotskii-Desiatovskii, A. P. *Graf P.D. Kiselev i ego vremia*. 4 vols. St. Petersburg: 1882.

Zaionchkovskii, P. A. *The Abolition of Serfdom in Russia*. Edited and translated by Susan Wobst. Gulf Breeze, Fla.: Academic International Press, 1978.

Zakharova, L. G. and John Bushnell. eds. *The Great Reforms in Russia*. Bloomington: Indiana University Press, 1994.

Ziber, N. I. *David Rikardo i Karl Marks v ikh obshchestvenno-ekonomicheskikh issledovaniiakh*. St. Petersburg: 1885.

Ziber, N. I. *Izbrannye ekonomicheskie proizvedeniia*. Moscow: 1959.

———. *Ocherki pervobytnoi ekonomicheskoi kultury*. Moscow: 1883.

———. "O Kollektivnom kharaktere pervonachal'noi nedvizhnoi sobstvennosti." In *Sobranie sochinenii*. St. Petersburg: 1900.

Zimmerman, Judith. "Russian Liberal Theory 1900–1917." *Canadian-American Slavic Studies* 14, no. 1 (1980): 1–20.

Zyrianov, P. N. *Krest'ianskaia obshchina evropeiskoi Rossii 1907–1914*. Moscow: 1992.

———. "Stolypin i sud'by russkoi derevni." *Obshchestvennye nauki i sovremennost'* 4 (1991): 117–25.

INDEX